Regions of the United States

HARPER & ROW SERIES IN GEOGRAPHY
Donald W. Meinig, Advisor

REGIONS OF THE UNITED STATES

JOHN FRASER HART, EDITOR
UNIVERSITY OF MINNESOTA

Harper & Row, Publishers
New York, Evanston, San Francisco, London

Cover photos, courtesy of American Airlines.

CONTENTS

INTRODUCTION

Regional geography, the skillful description of areas and places, is the highest form of the geographer's art. A good regional geography can bring an area to life and help us understand and appreciate what it is like, as well as how it came to be. Each region is distinctive and must be understood in its own terms, rather than according to some preconceived checklist. The regional geographer must know the land in all its moods and seasons and be sensitive to the values, aspirations, and talents of the people who live on it. The ability to write good regional geography does not come lightly or easily. Apart from literary skill, the evocation of a region demands a keen curiosity about it, along with a willingness to devote a lifetime to pondering and probing it, to reading about it and wandering through it, and to attempting to understand what makes it tick.

This volume is a collection of essays on the geography of various regions of the United States. The essays were first published in the June, 1972 issue of the *Annals of the Association of American Geographers*, which was distributed to all overseas registrants at the Twenty-Second International Geographical Congress in Montreal, in addition to its regular distribution to members of the Association and subscribers.

The authors are recognized as the leading authorities on the geography of the regions about which they have written. Each of these distinguished scholars was invited to present his latest thinking about the area he knows best, and he was encouraged to "think big" about it. The essays provide stimulating insights into the character and evolution of selected regions of the United States and should interest anyone desiring a better understanding of this fascinating nation.

Note Because it is a direct reprint of the June, 1972 issue of the *Annals of the Association of American Geographers*, the first page of this book is 155.

JOHN FRASER HART

Regions of the United States

ANNALS of the
Association of American Geographers

| Volume 62 | June, 1972 | Number 2 |

METAMORPHOSIS

J. B. JACKSON

THERE are landscapes in America, separated by hundreds of miles, which resemble one another in a striking degree, and many American towns, even many American cities, are all but indistinguishable as to layout, morphology, and architecture. The lack of variety in much of our man-made environment is recognized by anyone who has traveled widely in this country. Many deplore it, try to escape it, and because they cannot, suppose that America is altogether lacking the kind of landscape beauty characteristic of older parts of the world.

I have not found this to be the case. It is true that I cannot always remember the difference between one small town and another; both will have a main street flanked by solid buildings of brick, both will contain block after block of free-standing frame houses, each with a lawn; there will be a cluster of elegant white grain elevators near the railroad tracks in both of them, and a stretch of highway bordered by drive-ins; both are indeed much alike. But they are alike for a good reason: they consciously conform to what is a distinctive American style. Classical is the word for it, I think; and a rhythmic repetition (not to say occasional monotony) is a classical trait, the consequence of a singleminded devotion to clarity and order. But the style also possesses spaciousness and dignity; that is why I relish the similarity between the villages of New England, the similarity between wheatfields whether in Oklahoma or Oregon, or the stately

repetitiousness of North Dakota shelter belts: they illustrate on a vast and generous scale that "noble simplicity and quiet grandeur" which Winckelmann associated with classical works of art, and which, I believe, is more often met with in the landscape of the New World than in that of the Old. Much as the Roman traveler found reassurance in the identical grid layout, the almost identical forums of the new towns in the more remote provinces of the Empire, saw them as affirmations of Romanitas, the traveler in the United States finds evidence, wherever he goes, of a specifically national style of spatial organization. He may not care for it, he may prefer a greater variety, a romantic confusion; but he cannot fail to be impressed by it.

Since the classical American town is easy to understand, its interest is soon exhausted. There is little profit to be gained from walking the length of still another Maple Street, inspecting still another colonnaded courthouse, another bank with clock-thermometer and drive-in window. But I have found that overfamiliarity with a scene has compensations: it teaches sensitivity to change, a sharpened awareness of any deviation from the established style; and if the evidence I have garnered during many years of visiting small towns was of any value, it indicates that the American landscape, the manner, that is to say, in which we have organized our space, is undergoing a remarkable change.

Change in itself is not out of the ordinary; every cultural landscape has evolved, sometimes violently, more often slowly over the centuries. What differs here is that perhaps

Mr. Jackson, founder and former Editor of Landscape, *resides near Santa Fe, New Mexico.*

for the first time we are able to watch the transformation as it takes place; able to record it and even to understand some of its causes. Signs of abandoned or superseded spatial organizations surround us; every ruin, whether in Asia Minor or in the Southwest, reveals a fragment of a rural or urban landscape which became obsolete. But how? Obsolescence is a conveniently vague concept; in what stages was the place deserted? Which forms were first found wanting, which were maintained until the very end? Not all ruins mean sudden disaster, many represent a long series of decisions, choices between alternatives we have no inkling of. The decision was essentially this: can we go on living in the environment as it is now organized? Or shall we organize it in a different manner? Shall we move elsewhere? All cities, all landscapes sooner or later come to an end; that we know. What we do not always know is how or why.

There is something like a culture of environmental change, a pattern of day-by-day decisions worth exploring. It is here in America where we can, if we want to, begin; and it is easiest to begin with evidence that is commonplace and accessible.

Who has not noticed (to take an example) that in almost every American town the upper stories of the buildings flanking Main Street are gradually being deserted? Each year I see a few more windows dark and uncared for, even obliterated by commercial facades. Despite all the activity on the street floor, the second and third and fourth floors of the older brick buildings are no longer in demand. Not many years ago they accommodated the offices of lawyers and dentists and doctors; dance studios and certified public accountants. Now the gold lettering has vanished from the windows, and even the street door leading to the stairs is blocked. Sooner or later (we hardly have to be told) the buildings themselves will be torn down, to be replaced by one-story buildings or parking lots.

Such changes are so widespread that we rarely ask why they took place; we know the answer: the law firm needed more room, the doctor moved to be nearer the hospital, the dance studio required more modern wiring. Explanations vary, but they all indicate that the building had become obsolete. Obso-

lescence of a different kind accounts for the changes down along the tracks. Here the massive warehouses stand vacant, and the factory is closed; only on the ground floor, where a small firm makes handbags, is there activity. Ask why the factory has closed and the answer is simple: no one now buys castiron cookstoves; or the plant has moved to a better location on the highway. Either answer implies that these work spaces have ceased to serve their original purpose; given sufficient time and neglect and they will become ruins.

Two further examples of change drive home the same lesson. Away from the center of the classical American town there is a residential section of tree-lined streets with houses surrounded by wide verandas and still wider lawns. I knew it when it was lived in by prosperous families, when it was the most desirable part of town. What has happened? More than half the houses have been transformed into apartments. A school teacher lives on one floor, a retired couple on another, three students in the attic. The landlady occupies the rooms in the basement. Flanking the great front door of golden oak are four or five letter boxes. The lawn suffers from neglect. The original owners have either died or moved to a more spacious suburb.

One last typical change: the open country starts abruptly where the street becomes a road, and that is where a farmstead faces onto broad fields, with a large frame barn standing near it. Used until recently for storing feed, for sheltering some of the livestock, for many kinds of work, it has an air of being abandoned, of serving as a part-time garage. The two tall silos flanking it threaten to collapse. But back of the barn is a complex of brand new cement block buildings—long and low, with gleaming metal roofs.

We do not need to be told the significance of this melancholy change, nor do we need further instances of spatial reorganization brought about by obsolescence. But here is change of another sort: on the outskirts of the town, in the midst of fields, a housing development—what its promoters call a planned residential community—has recently come into being. A compact mass of some fifty all but identical dwellings, Meadowview Heights occupies a rigidly bounded portion of what a few years ago was a cornfield, entirely flat. The development is artfully laid out along a series of curving roads, leading to no particular destination. The houses, painted in bright colors, are still too new to have acquired individuality; they lack gardens and all but the slimmest of trees. Still, the development has a quality of its own: it is an orderly composition of clearcut, well defined forms, in no way blending into its natural environment. Meadowview Heights appears to me to be an authentic, latter-day expression of the classical American style: simple, easily understood, and not without something like elegance. It is easy to criticize its monotony, its unimaginative siting, its deliberate avoidance of picturesque variety; no one will deny its shortcomings. But groups of houses similar to this one have always proliferated in the United States; Plymouth in the seventeenth century was such a one; the frontier outpost, the railroad town, the company town were others. We produce them by instinct.

So the change which Meadowview Heights exemplified seems to be little more than a reaffirmation of American Classicism. Except for one characteristic: none of the houses is of more than one story. The traditional hierarchy of floors, honored in even the simplest of traditional American dwellings—cellar, ground-floor, attic—had been altogether done away with.

Thus the housing development is also part of the spatial transformation; but in what manner? How does Meadowview Heights, brand new and efficiently planned, explain—except by way of contrast—the struggle against spatial obsolescence so manifest in other parts of the town? The multistoried downtown "block" is abandoned; the multistoried factory is abandoned; the multistoried residence is converted in a series of one-story flats; the multistoried barn with its tall silos is abandoned in favor of the one-story cement-block structure; and the new houses in the development are of one story only. What explanation suffices for them all?

Clearly America is showing a preference for the horizontal over the vertical organization of space, and is changing the man-made environment accordingly.

It would be more precise to say that Americans prefer to *work* on a horizontal plane, for the technological reasons for the shift are the most conspicuous. An efficiently planned office is now seen as a system of information flow, most flexible, most effective, when horizontal. An industrial plant is likewise more efficient when its processes are horizontal, modern methods and equipment having largely eliminated gravity flow and difficulties of horizontal movement. This is no less true of the modern farm where mobile machinery and electric power have greatly encouraged a horizontal layout and the consequent abandonment of many vertical installations. And insofar as the contemporary dwelling is a highly mechanized structure, there too the horizontal flow, the horizontal organization of movement is preferred.

Everywhere the tendency to substitute the vertical is evident. What at first sight seems an important exception—the enormous increase in the number of highrise structures in our cities—is, I think, merely another and more complex form of horizontality. The modern multistoried office building differs from the earlier examples of the form in being essentially a stack of large, uninterrupted horizontal spaces: vastly improved construction methods have made this spaciousness possible. Exterior similarity between the old highrise and the new can be deceptive.

We have surely not reached the end of spatial transformation; and though it is in the city and in the industrial installation that horizontality produces its most sensational examples—strip mining being one of them—the small town contains its own share: the supermarket, the shopping center, the motel, the one-story consolidated high school, the one-story hospital, however commonplace they now may be, are still new and are still being built to replace the old vertical counterpart. The coming of the trench silo on the farm no doubt presages the development of the horizontal grain elevator; the landscape will be the poorer for the substitution.

I am by no means certain that the technological explanation for the change is the only one; that an esthetic explanation could not also be proposed. It is evident, I think, that Americans now perceive their environment in a new and as yet undefined manner. It is evident that increased mobility, and even more, an increased experience of uninterrupted speed—whether on the highway or the ski slope or on the surface of the water—bring with them a sharpened awareness of horizontal space, and the eventual transformation of many landscapes devoted to recreation.

It is changes such as these—fragmentary and pragmatic—that we should look for when we explore the American landscape. They are widespread and consequently inconspicuous; we shall soon see them wherever we go and learn to accept them as commonplace.

This means, I think, that the traditional uniformity, the Classical sameness of America will not be altered. Indeed it may be reinforced; horizontality will be incorporated into the national style, a universal American characteristic. The study and understanding of landscape metamorphosis can nowhere better be undertaken than here and now, in the contemporary United States, but it has to be undertaken in the proper frame of mind; and this, it seems to me, is largely a matter of recognizing and accepting our national landscape for what it is: something very different from the European.

AMERICAN WESTS: PREFACE TO A GEOGRAPHICAL INTERPRETATION

D. W. MEINIG

ABSTRACT. Geographers might make a very significant contribution to the interpretation of the American West and of the American nation by a systematic investigation of the West as a set of dynamic regions. The outline offered suggests a focus upon four categories of regional features (population, circulation, political areas, and culture) to be examined as complexes changing through four recognizable stages (nuclear, regional, regional-national, metropolitan-national) from initial European colonization to the present with projections into the future. KEY WORDS: *Circulation, Culture, National integration, Political areas, Population, Regions, Stages of development, West.*

THE four cardinal points—north, south, east, and west—are heavily charged with meaning in the American regional consciousness. Such terms do not denote simple grand quarters of the contiguous national territory but rather are used most commonly as pairs—North and South, East and West—referring to vaguely defined "halves" existing in some degree of contrast and tension. At times this set becomes a triad, in which a South and a West are seen as existing in some degree of subservience to a North/East long dominant in political, economic, and social power.

That such regional (or sectional, to use Turner's term) concepts are deeply imprinted in the American mind is attested to by everyday conversation and reporting as well as an enormous literature. That such concepts have received relatively little attention from American geographers, whose field most centrally embraces the intellectual concept of regionalism, may seem rather surprising. Yet this paradox is not really puzzling. For North, South, East, and West, however combined, form only the largest possible set of national regions, the crudest, most vaguely delimited areal frame of reference. It is really not very surprising that those who are especially trained to look intently at areal patterns are more impressed with the complexities lurking beneath such gross terms and therefore have concentrated most of their efforts at quite a different scale of regional investigation. Thus the American West, a world-famous area which has

fostered a huge volume of interpretive literature, has been of little concern as a region, as a single unit in a two- or threefold national set, to American geographers. In the main body of that literature this famous West is generally synonymous with the Frontier and thus is less a place than a process, the realm of a great influential recurring American experience. It is a powerful symbol within the national mythology, but as soon as we attempt to connect symbol with substance, to assess the relationships between the West as a place in the imagination and the West as a piece of the American continent, we are confronted with great variation from place to place. Thus geographers have said little about the West as *a* region, but a good deal about the West as a *set* of regions. The purpose of this paper is to suggest that they could yet say a great deal more, and do so in a way that might involve them much more effectively in the larger, persistent, and important task of national interpretation.

Given the marked variations within the American West, it is rather surprising that in all that interpretive literature there is no well-developed view of the West as a set of dynamic regions. The standard geographies offer several sets of regions, each set offering a consistent comprehensive coverage of the West. But most of these are grounded upon the framework of nature, within which certain patterns of population distribution, land use, and trafficways are apparent. The result is a useful view of the West as a set of regional environments and basic economies but with

Dr. Meinig is Professor of Geography at Syracuse University in Syracuse, New York.

little historical explication of how these human patterns came to be. On the other hand, the standard histories tend to be strongly Turnerian, recognizing specific regions (though usually but vaguely delimited) but concerned more with national impact than individual character. Thus these treatments are strongly episodic and do not offer anything approaching the continuous developmental history of each region as part of a larger developing West. There are of course more comprehensive histories of individual states and of regions at various scales but in total these prove a jumble of parts which cannot simply be fitted together to form a whole. Indeed historians of the West have been discussing extensively among themselves the lack of encompassing theories and the need to find new approaches and schemes in the search for more penetrating interpretations.[1]

It is important at the outset to distinguish between two possible views of the West as a set of dynamic regions. On the one hand is the West as the Frontier, shifting in specific area in conjunction with the sequential expansion of the nation. In this view the inland reaches of the seaboard colonies, Transappalachia, the Mississippi Valley, the Plains and Mountains, the Pacific Slope were each the "West" during a particular phase of American development. In such a usage "West" is a generic term referring to a specific *type* of area within a dynamic national context. On the other hand, there is the concept of the West as a specific "half" of the nation in apposition to the East, a huge area displaying some persisting basis of identity.

This paper is concerned only with this latter view. That means that we are dealing with the area which emerged as the "New West" or the "Far West" in the 1870s and 1880s. Such terms were coined to distinguish it from the older "West" which now increasingly became identified as the "Middle West." It was the area which lay westward of what were then considered the potential

limits of contiguous extension of typical American farm settlement, that is, country inaccessible to the direct expansion of Middle Western or Southern agricultures. Broadly, it remains the area which is most generally considered as the West yet today.

SCHEME

Some basic differences between East and West were readily apparent during the emergence of the West as a distinct realm: the marked contrasts in physical environments; the differences in peoples, the West being the country of Indians, Mexicans, Mormons, and of gold rush, cowboy, and other tumultuous frontier societies; and the differences in the overall settlement pattern, Western settlement having a clear insular character, each of the several main areas being isolated by great distances and inhospitable country from its nearest neighbors. These features were very generally perceived and emphasized even if only vaguely or confusedly understood at the time. Such characteristics offer clues for the formulation of a systematic comprehensive view of the West as a set of dynamic regions. Contrary to the popular emphasis of the time and to a later strong tradition in American geography, this proposed view emphasizes the insular pattern of colonizations more than the strong physical contrasts. For a retrospective look at the spatial character of American development does reveal a noticeable contrast in evolving patterns between East and West. Although folk colonization is always selective and uneven in area, in the East the general tide of settlement was relatively comprehensive and local nuclei and salients in the vanguard were soon engulfed and integrated into a generally contiguous pattern. Obviously such a description rests upon a particular scale of observation, but holding to the same scale, the pattern in the West is a marked contrast: several distinct major nuclei so widely separated from one another and so far removed from the advancing front of the East that each expands as a kind of discrete unit for several decades, only gradually becoming linked together and more closely integrated into the main functional systems of the nation. If we then add important dimensions of culture and environment to these nuclei we have

---

[1] See, for example, the report on the free-wheeling discussion at a recent meeting of the Western Historical Association: "Seminar on the Teaching of Western History," in John Alexander Carroll, editor, *Reflections of Western Historians* (Tucson, Arizona: University of Arizona Press, 1969), pp. 265–99.

the basis for a hypothetical scheme (Fig. 1), in which each Western area is viewed as passing through four general phases of development as expressed in four general categories: population (numbers and areal distribution), circulation (traffic patterns within and between regions), political areas (basic jurisdictional territories), and culture (selected features characteristic of the local society and its imprint upon the area).[2]

The remainder of this paper is a sketch of the principal specific features in the American West associated with this model of historical geographical change.

MAJOR NUCLEI (STAGES I AND II)

Hispano New Mexico

The first nucleus of European settlement in the American West was established by the Spanish in the upper Rio Grande Valley at the end of the sixteenth century. The process displayed a number of features common to many imperial movements: conquest of the richest and most densely populated areas, the founding of a new capital city, and the establishment of new towns alongside native settlements; the extraction of wealth from the labor of the native population, and the introduction of new technology and economic systems which greatly altered the resource potential; the emergence of a new "mixed" population, and the concomitant development of a class-structured plural society with chronic ethnic tensions; the abrupt imposition of new culture patterns upon the native population and the subsequent emergence of numerous cultural changes in the whole population arising from the imperial character of the society.

The Spanish superimposed themselves upon the entire Rio Grande Pueblo area of village agriculturists. Santa Fe was founded as a capital pivotal to important populations and security areas, and a number of other formal towns were laid out. The introduction of

[2] These four categories are considered to be central to any such analysis, but the scheme could readily be elaborated to bring others into similar focus. Perhaps the most obvious addition would be "economy," giving a more coherent place for topics herein included, if at all, under "circulation" and "culture."

sheep, cattle, horses, burros, and mules enlarged the resource possibilities of this semiarid region and provided the main basis for settlement expansion carried out by the mestizo population, which emerged as much the largest of the several peoples in the area. These "Hispanos" were a Spanish-speaking, Roman Catholic, peasant, and pastoral people living in close-knit communities structured on strong kinship and patronal relationships. The Pueblo Indians survived the heavy impact of this long imperial experience greatly reduced in numbers and area but basically intact as a general culture and as locally autonomous societies. Some of the peripheral Indian groups were significantly altered. The Navajo were transformed from a minor Apache band into a vigorous pastoral society with a strong sense of identity as a distinct people. Some other Apache bands were invigorated by the greatly enlarged social and economic returns from plundering the imperial frontiers.

For two and a half centuries New Mexico was one of the most isolated regions of European culture. Annual or less frequent caravans to Chihuahua long provided the only link with the civilized world. Under Mexican rule two new routes, the Santa Fe wagon road to Missouri and the droving trail from Los Angeles, somewhat mitigated the isolation but did not alter the insular character of the region. Such isolation over so long a time favored divergence from the mother culture, a feature most notably expressed in religion (i.e., the Penitentes).

American conquest initiated a new imperialism. The "Anglos" superimposed their polity and began to intrude into every important sector. Santa Fe was retained as the capital, but new Anglo facilities and at times whole new towns were established alongside those of the Hispanos. In the 1880s the railroads opened up greater economic possibilities and a considerably elaborated regional commercial system emerged, focused upon Las Vegas, Santa Fe, and Albuquerque and gathering from all but southernmost New Mexico. Wool and minerals were the principal regional exports exchanged for the manufactures ordered through the wholesale houses of Kansas City, St. Louis, and Chicago.

The strong outward extension of the Hispano

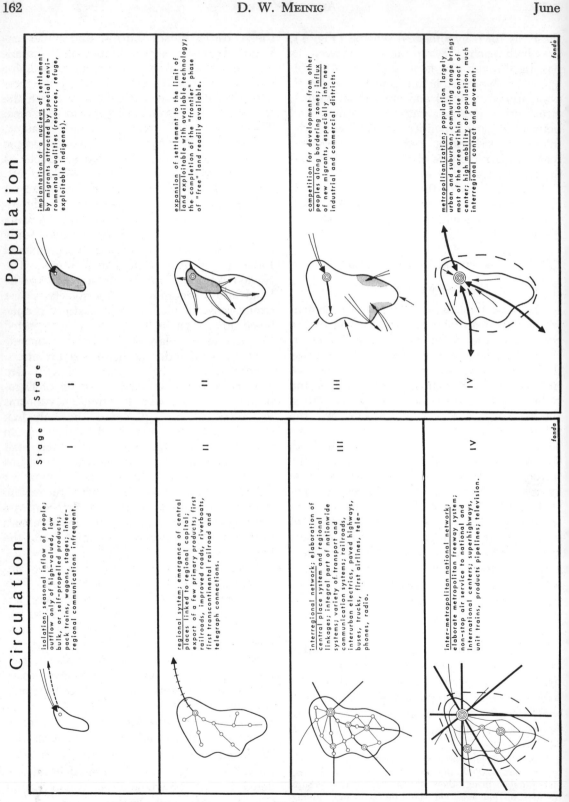

FIG. 1. Regional development within a national context through four stages; population and circulation.

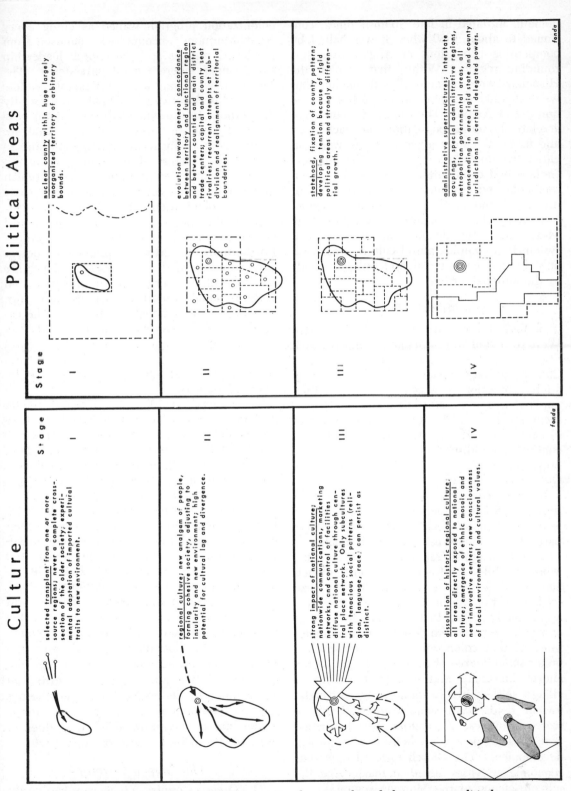

FIG. 1. Regional development within a national context through four stages; political areas and culture.

domain, initiated in late Spanish times, continued to about 1880 when it was halted by competitive expansions of Anglos from surrounding regions. Within that domain the Hispanos were numerically dominant, but were steadily declining in proportion to the number of Anglos. The Pueblo Indians were a relatively stable population and each town and its immediately adjacent lands were enclosed within federal reserves. The nomadic Indians had been ruthlessly reduced to small remnants and confined to large reserves of unwanted lands on the periphery of the region.

Thus by the late nineteenth century, New Mexico was a functionally coherent provincial system in a complex plural culture area, with only limited commercial and cultural bonds to the national system.

The Mormon Region

In 1847 the nucleus of a highly distinctive Western region was implanted in the Wasatch Oasis. The Mormons were a refugee population of unusual cohesion, originally formed by adult conversion to a common faith, unified under charismatic leadership, hardened by persecution, selected by the harsh experiences of expulsion and migration, sustained by the continuous addition of new converts, and powered by a strong faith in themselves as God's elected people.

Brigham Young, a powerful leader of great practical vision, undertook to create a vast Mormon commonwealth embracing a large part of the Far West. Although unable to sustain the original frame of this Deseret, the Mormons did spread north and south of their Salt Lake Valley nucleus until they had settled most of the habitable valleys from the upper Snake River to the Colorado and far east and west into the deserts and mountains. Most of that colonization was accomplished under some degree of formal direction by the church hierarchy and was in the form of village settlements surrounded by privately-owned fields with some communal use of scarce resources. Agriculture was by irrigation, to these people a wholly new, empirical development. The church fostered numerous economic activities aimed at maximizing the self-sufficiency of the Mormon region.

In the 1880s the momentum of that great colonization program waned as along every front Mormons encountered colonists from bordering regions and the church leadership came under severe federal harassment. The Mormons were long a suspect people, widely regarded in America as politically and socially dangerous. In the late 1850s the federal government sent an army to occupy Utah to quell a supposedly recalcitrant people and to protect the interest of the non-Mormon minority ("Gentiles" in Mormon parlance) which had entered Utah in the wake of the early Mormon colonization. The military posts overlooking the valley oases were thus typical landscape symbols of an imperial relationship. Furthermore, the Mormon practice of polygamy was regarded as a shocking departure from accepted American mores and produced wide popular support for its absolute suppression by the national government. The capitulation of the Mormon Church on that issue in 1890 after severe persecution by federal authorities was not untypical of the cultural conformity forced upon occupied peoples by imperial powers.

The mineral wealth in the Wasatch region and the strategic location of Salt Lake City and Ogden with reference to the whole Far West sustained a growing Gentile population, concentrated in these main commercial centers, the mining and smelting districts, and the railroad towns. The rural areas remained almost entirely Mormon. The two peoples were latently antagonistic, ever conscious of their differences, and thus a plural society developed which was peculiar to the region and little understood beyond. Salt Lake City, a focus of unusual power combining political, ecclesiastical, and commercial functions, was the main point of encounter and tension between the region and the nation. Although crossed by the thoroughfare to California, the Mormon dominated area retained a high degree of isolation and regional integrity, set apart more by its sociocultural peculiarities and the determined efforts of its theocratic leadership to minimize national influences than by its natural girdle of wastelands.

The Oregon Country

The Oregon Country, a huge chunk of northwestern America, was under joint claim by

Great Britain and the United States for several decades. Momentarily in the early 1840s competitive colonizations were juxtaposed in the lower Columbia district, with the British focus at Fort Vancouver, a major fur trade center with flourishing farms and mills, and American farmer-migrants settling in the lower Willamette Valley. But the British nucleus disintegrated after the compromise division of Oregon along the 49th Parallel and subsequent colonization was by a relatively homogeneous body of American migrants. Local Indian societies had already been virtually destroyed by disease and economic and social disruptions.

The Willamette nucleus was a long-distant transplant from the Missouri-Ohio Valley region with a strong reinfusion of Yankee influences. Migration in the 1840s and 1850s drew about equally from the Free States and from the Slave States of the Border South. The general settlement pattern, architecture, and agricultural system were similar to that broad source region, modified by the failure of corn and tobacco to thrive in the cooler, summer-dry environment. The New England influence was markedly apparent in church, school, and civic organizations, and in commercial and manufacturing activities.

Portland, below the falls on the Willamette and accessible to ocean vessels, became the principal focus with the upsurge of exports to California in the 1850s. In the 1860s it became the regional gateway and supply center for an array of new mining districts deep in the interior, competing for trade as far away as the Kootenay, western Montana, and southern Idaho. Walla Walla, the principal interior trade center, became the nucleus of an expanding ranching and farming region which was settled primarily from the Willamette and served by Portland firms. By the early 1880s Portland was the focus of an extensive system of waterways, roads, and railroads tapping much of the old Oregon Country. Puget Sound, directly accessible by sea with an economy based upon a scattering of large tidewater lumber mills, was in some degree separate. Its incipient geography was obscured by the nervous rivalries among aspiring ports and its first railroad line led south to the Columbia to tie in with the more substantial

Oregon nucleus. This Northwest system as a whole was bound into commercial networks focused on San Francisco. Californian capital was prominent in the lumbering and mining activities of the Northwest, and in the Willamette and especially in the drier Columbia Plain the grain farming system was strongly shaped by Californian innovations.

Thus Portland was the focus of a region which drew originally upon the mainstream of American western migration, but which was increasingly divergent from those antecedents because of environmental and locational differences. Even if it was nevertheless the most typically American of all Far Western regions, that in itself helped differentiate it from its neighbors.

Colorado

Although nearest to the main body of national population Colorado was the last of the major Western nuclei to be initiated, and that relative location and timing were important to the character of its beginnings. The discovery of gold along the base of the southern Rockies came a decade after similar electrifying news from California, and the nation responded eagerly to another possibility of such wealth, business opportunity, and adventure. By that time, 1858 1859, the edge of the Rockies was by comparison readily accessible. Tens of thousands of people had already crossed the Plains to other Western regions, railroads had almost reached the Missouri River, and settlers were spreading into Kansas and Nebraska. Thus in a matter of months prospectors were swarming over the Front Range, towns were laid out, businesses established, stage and freighting lines put in service, and ample Eastern capital was available to invest in anything that looked promising.

Early mineral discoveries could not sustain the full initial influx and there was considerable instability in population for many years. The first railroad connections to the East, made in 1870, encouraged more substantial and diversified developments. Eastern and European capital invested heavily in livestock ranching on the Colorado Piedmont. Irrigation agriculture was strongly promoted, and benefited from a few highly publicized and

successful colonies (e.g. Greeley and Long-
mont). Vigorous promotion of the scenic
wonders and health-restoring qualities of this
"American Switzerland" so conveniently accessible by railway car brought an ever greater
number of tourists, summer sojourners, health-
seekers, and those attracted by elegant towns
of social pretension (i.e., Colorado Springs).
Furthermore the mining industry itself underwent steady elaboration from placers to lode
mining, and from gold to silver and lead.
Location, timing, and special difficulties made
Colorado an innovative center of scientific
study, tools, and techniques in the American
mining industry. Major discoveries, such as
in the Leadville district, required far larger
machinery, mills, and smelters; coal, available
at several points along the Front Range, replaced charcoal. In 1880 a Bessemer iron and
steel plant using Colorado coke, ore, and
limestone was built at Pueblo to serve the
burgeoning demand for structural and railroad
iron.

Denver emerged successful from the town-
site rivalries at the first ephemeral diggings,
was well located to serve the first substantial
district (Central City area), and was thereafter never seriously rivaled as the commercial, financial, political, and social center of
Colorado. For thirty years its tributary region
was rapidly expanded and enriched by significant new mineral discoveries in the Southern
Rockies, each the basis for new railroads and
ancillary industries and the opening of new
ranching, farming, and resort districts.

Denver became the focus of a remarkable
railroad network which tapped every important mineral district. Much of it was narrow-
gauge, a special adaption to the formidable
terrain. No train service ran through Denver;
it was a true node, the point of interchange
between its tributary system and the trunk-
lines across the Plains. Pueblo provided gateway connections between lines from the East
and a route across the Rockies, but the actual
services were geared to the patterns of the
regional traffic focused upon Denver, and
Pueblo was not a significant commercial competitor.

Denver's domain was very nearly concor-
dant with the state along three sides. To the
north the Union Pacific provided the main

axis of Wyoming, the southerly reach of its
pull penetrating Colorado only in North Park.
On the west, the near-empty wasteland of the
Green River country effectively separated
Colorado from the main Mormon region. On
the south the Colorado line approximated the
Hispano-Anglo border zone, with the Colorado
railroad system penetrating slightly. On the
east, however, Denver served only the nar-
rowing ranching belt and the riverine irrigation strips between the mountains and the
advancing edge of dry farming grain agriculture created by the strong surge out of Kansas
and Nebraska in the 1880s.

This Colorado area had much clearer definition as a commercial region than as a culture
area. Its population was drawn very largely
but very broadly from the Northern states. The
development of an industrial labor class with
large numbers of foreign-born (and Hispanos
from New Mexico) was very like that of the
mining and industrial districts of the East but
quite unlike most regions in the West. What
set Colorado apart was its particular combination of important activities—mining, heavy
industry, ranching, irrigation agriculture, commerce, tourism, and recreation—which together
formed a rather concentrated, integrated complex sustaining a relatively diverse and cosmopolitan society. The strong focus on Denver
and a strong sense of regional identity
grounded upon the magnificent mountain
setting so boldly and abruptly set apart from
all lands to the east further combined to give
Colorado recognizable character as a special
part of the American West.

Northern California

On the eve of the Gold Rush Northern
California had only a few thousand mestizo
and white settlers. There was no clear and
substantial nucleus, only a scattering of points
and small districts (e. g., Monterey, the Santa
Clara, the Bay littoral, Sonoma, New Hel-
vetia). However, so great and creative was
the power of that event that a major urban
focus, a regional axis, and several distinctive
production districts were almost instantly apparent.

The general axis connected San Francisco
with the north-central Sierras, in detail a
water route bifurcating to the Valley centers

of Sacramento and Stockton from which wagon roads and pack trails fanned into the mountain mineral districts. The political capital of the new state was consciously placed on that axis. Carquinez Strait, the narrow passageway between the Bay and the Valley, was the preferred location (Vallejo 1851, Benicia 1853) although because of practical difficulties of accommodations it was soon shifted (by a very narrow vote) to the already-thriving Sacramento (1854). Readily made tributary to that axis was a series of rapidly developing subregions—the Sierra valleys, the Sacramento and San Joaquin, the Coastal valleys, and the Redwood and Monterey coasts —tapped by an ever expanding system of coastal vessels, river boats, railroads, wagon and stage roads.

Beyond this undisputed hinterland, San Francisco was the principal metropolitan center for the rest of California and all of Nevada, and reached out to compete for trade over the entire Pacific Slope from Interior British Columbia to Central Arizona. Indeed a good portion of the people and much of the money to develop this broad realm came from California. A critical feature in Western regionalism is the amount of locally-generated wealth concentrated in San Francisco which made it a financial center of considerable magnitude and independence rather than merely an outpost of Wall Street, as were most other cities in the nation. The building of the first transcontinental railroad, a feat of great practical and symbolic importance, is an effective illustration of this Californian autonomy, for the Central Pacific represented Californian capitalists reaching inland clear to the Great Salt Lake to meet on equal terms the Eastern-financed Union Pacific.

This emerging California was much more than a coherent and aggressive commercial system, it was world famous as a highly distinctive and attractive environment. This region of subtropical summer-dry climate, fertile soils, and beautiful landscapes of mountain, valley, and seacoast was unlike any other in the nation and it became firmly fixed in the national mind as a very special place, an American Eden, a Golden West symbolic of opportunity and dreams fulfilled. From very early in its modern history symbol and sub-

stance have been powerfully combined to make California a region of enormous attraction. The special character of its climate and its national location together with its history of sudden influx and continuous rapid growth thereafter has had some special effect upon every kind of economic activity. Speculation was endemic, innovation common, a larger scale and greater efficiency of operations notable.

So, too, there has long been general agreement among Californians and outsiders alike that California society is different, although commentators have not always found it easy to define the nature and basis of that difference. Part of that difficulty is inherent and is itself a feature of significance, for it relates to the dynamic, fluid, open character of a society never stabilized and hardened into fixed patterns. It is generally agreed that the Gold Rush initiated the elements: a great heterogeneous, restless, ambitious horde of relatively young people thrown together in a new kind of country detached from the stable patterns of home. Such people were drawn from all of America, most of Europe, parts of Asia and Latin America. Despite the imposition of caste (with regard to Asians) and some degree of stratification, it remained a relatively open society with widespread social and economic opportunity. Regional development was so dynamic as to make the geography of ethnic groups more a kaleidoscope than a mosaic. In sharp contrast with nearly all Western regions, this Californian population was as variegated and cosmopolitan as that of the East, but differed in specific elements and proportions, and the size and character of development fostered a much more open and broadly integrated society with generally less tension than was apparent among the large ethnic blocs in the urbanized and industrialized East. Most important was the strong self-consciousness of Californians as constituting a dynamic and creative new society, a closer realization of the American dream.

Southern California

The country lying south of San Luis Obispo and the Tehachapi Range was so remote from the Mother Lode as to escape the heavy impact of the Gold Rush. Many Anglos passed through the area and some stayed, especially in the Los Angeles Basin, but they had to share the region with the Californios, the Mexican population dominated by the big ranching families. Although the Anglos continually increased in numbers and power, for thirty years Southern California developed in considerable degree as a relatively balanced bi-cultural society. The extension of irrigation and subtropical crops provided a basis for growth, but the costs of development and difficulties of marketing impeded rapid expansion.

The great "Boom of the 80s" was Southern California's equivalent of the Gold Rush, a sudden transformation which set a new pattern and scale of development. The boom was generated by an enormous speculative real estate promotion campaign which followed hard upon the completion of competitive direct railroad lines to the East. Tens of thousands of people came in, lured by the widely-advertised virtues of life in America's subtropical paradise. Ranches were subdivided into thousands of suburban lots and scores of new towns. Although the fervor of the boom inevitably soon waned, the general character of regional development had been established. Southern California's foremost resource was its overall physical environment, its most persuasive symbol the family-size suburban lot amidst the orange groves between the sea and the mountains in a snowless land of sunshine.

Such a land proved a powerful attraction to persons of moderate capital resources in the Middle West, who could sell farm, home, small business, or professional practice and move to a land of greater comfort and interest. Thus the main body of population was a relatively mature, conservative, property-minded bourgeois, but yet a society loosened by migration, the lack of firm roots, the instability of local communities, and the attractive possibilities for changing styles of life in a new physical and social environment. Since the principal means of expanding wealth was through the sale of land to incoming migrants rather than from the product of the land itself, the dominant figures in the life of the region were not the great industrialists or mercantilists but the developers and pro-

moters and those who provided basic services to an ever-expanding population.

Los Angeles was from the first the main nucleus but it was the focus of a small region, hedged in by mountains and deserts. Irrigation projects provided an expanding agricultural base, but the main function of Los Angeles was to serve the ever-growing suburban population within its own immediate basin. By 1900 this last of the major Western nuclei to emerge was famous across the nation as a very distinctive place.

Summary

To class these six regions as the major ones apparent toward the end of the nineteenth century is not to suggest that together they encompass the whole of the American West (Fig. 2). Several cities and districts lay beyond the bounds of clear dominance by any one of these major centers, most notably El Paso and its riverine oases and mining hinterland, Central Arizona focused upon Phoenix, the Black Hills mining and ranching area, the Boise Basin and its extensive but thinly-populated surroundings, and the Montana mining and ranching complex around Butte and Helena. Each had some degree of regional autonomy because of distance from large western cities and location on a railroad with direct service to the East, but each was very considerably smaller in population and commercial significance than the average of the major regions.

Nor does this nomination of six regions as major within the West mean that they were equal in all basic features. San Francisco was at a higher level than any of the other cities, the regional metropolis of the entire Pacific Slope, analogous to the role shared by Kansas City, Chicago, and Minneapolis–St. Paul for the Rocky Mountain half of the Far West. Denver, Salt Lake City, and Los Angeles were unchallenged regional capitals; Portland also, but within a contracting region for the quick rise of Seattle near the end of the century firmly detached Puget Sound from any significant Portland influence and also threatened its dominance of the Columbia Interior. New Mexico was the chief variant among the six. Its total population was relatively small and it had no large city, but its special multi-

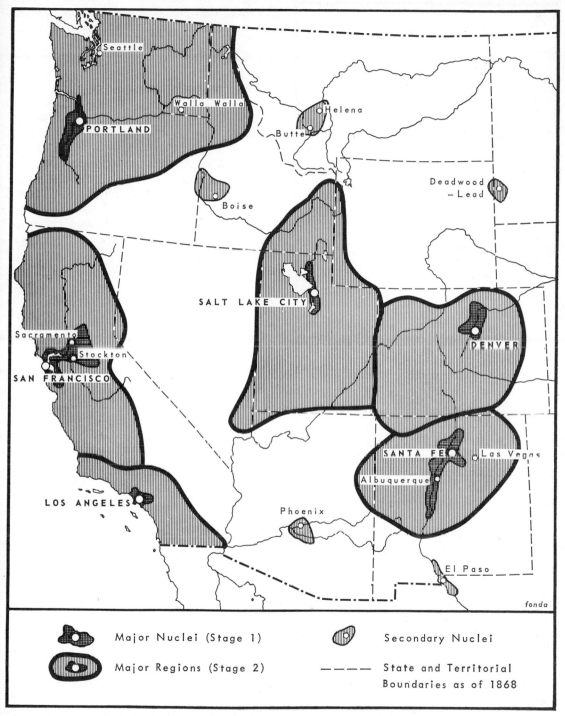

FIG. 2. Major nuclei and regions of the West in Stages I and II.

cultural, "imperial" character made it a very distinctive region wherein the relationships among its peoples had implications for a much broader Southwest. Santa Fe, though small in size and unable to dominate commercially even its own historic region, was nevertheless culturally a focal point of distinctly major significance.

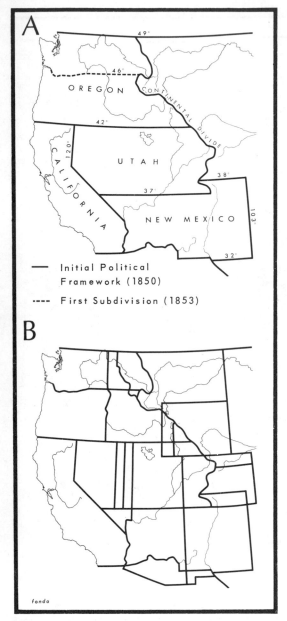

— Initial Political
  Framework (1850)

---- First Subdivision (1853)

fonda

FIG. 3. (A) The initial political framework. (B) Composite of boundaries used during evolution through the territorial stage.

POLITICAL AREAS (STAGES I AND II)

The creation of the state of California (1849) and the territories of Oregon (1848), New Mexico (1850), and Utah (1850) provided the first American political framework for the Far West (Fig. 3A). The eastern slope of the Rockies was as yet devoid of civilized settlement and remained unorganized Indian

Country until the creation of Nebraska and Kansas in 1854. This framework and its subsequent sequential modification to the states of today is illustrative of the general process of territorial evolution in the American political system.

Congress has the power to create political jurisdictions in newly-acquired national domain. Normally the first stage was the establishment of a *territory*, governed by officials appointed by the federal government; after further population growth and development a territory may seek admission as a *state*, equal in all legal respects with the other states. Congress has the power to change boundaries between territories. Boundaries between territories and states can only be changed by joint action of Congress and the states involved; boundaries between states may be changed only by agreement between the states with subsequent approval by Congress. Despite these prerogatives of Congress the intent of the system is to respond in large measure to local interests in their quest toward the American ideal of local control over their own affairs.

Because commerce, culture, and politics interact in myriad ways a concordance of their areas is generally desirable, but because commercial and culture areas. are inherently diffuse exact concordance is never attainable. Furthermore, although the system contains the legal means to adjust the size and shape of political areas in response to changes in other fundamental patterns, the cumulative complexities and vested interests make such boundary alterations increasingly difficult as the area develops.

The pattern of 1850 was characteristic of the first phase of this geopolitical evolution, each unit containing a settlement nucleus surrounded by a huge expanse of undomesticated country. The boundaries were simply convenient arbitrary lines dividing the total area into four roughly equal parts. Subsequent subdivision was generally in response to the requests from new settlement districts in some remote sector of the original territory. Thus Washington (1853) was a reflection of developments on Puget Sound, Colorado (1861) of the Denver-Central City nucleus, Nevada (1861) of the Comstock Lode district, Arizona

(1863) of the Anglo settlement along the southern routes to California, Idaho (1863) of Boise and a scattering of mineral districts, Montana (1864) of Helena and nearby mineral districts. Wyoming (1868) was more a residual area, a huge undeveloped block shifted among several jurisdictions, with at the time no more than an incipient coherence from the Union Pacific then under construction.

Most of these territories underwent further revisions after their initial formation and there have been many fruitless attempts to make additional modifications (Fig. 3B). In general, the whole process may be seen as an attempt to bring about a greater concordance of political areas with commercial and culture areas, although by the end of this phase (marked in general by statehood) numerous anomalies remained (Fig. 4A). Among the most important were: 1) the inclusion of two major regions within California, the result of California's direct admission as a state without passing through the more changeable territorial phase, and of the late development of Southern California; 2) the dominantly Mormon area of southeastern Idaho with much stronger cultural and commercial bonds to Salt Lake City than to Boise; 3) the failure to reshape political geography to the emerging regional coherence in the Columbia Interior, a pattern increasingly focused on Spokane, perpetuating a discordance which was the source of recurrent proposals for the creation of a new state or for at least the annexation of the Idaho Panhandle to Washington state; 4) the western promontory of Texas, putting El Paso and its main hinterland in separate political areas.

The issues involved in every one of these changes or proposals were complex and controversial, hinging upon a variety of local and national interests, but the resultant pattern in the American West suggests that Congressional decision-making in such matters was also influenced by some general sense of scale and symmetry. This is apparent from the very first. The 42nd Parallel was an obvious choice for the initial subdivision for it had long served as an international boundary between imperial claims, and was the boundary between the two separate acquisitions of Oregon and the Mexican Cession. But the fact that it was approximately midway between the new na-

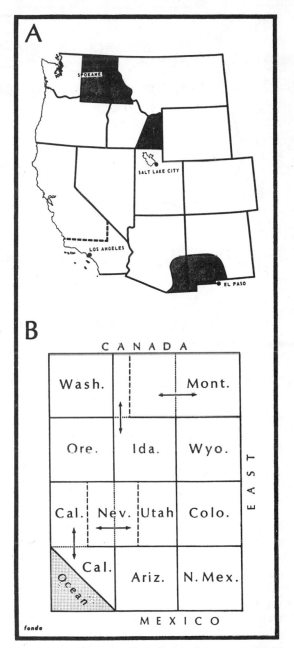

FIG. 4. (A) Major discordances between political and cultural or commercial areas. (B) Schematic representation of departures from theoretical symmetrical subdivision.

tional boundaries with British America and Mexico may have influenced the choice of the 37th and 46th parallels for a further halving (in part) of each of the original two segments, giving four latitudinal strips of approximately equal width (Fig. 3A). Sub-

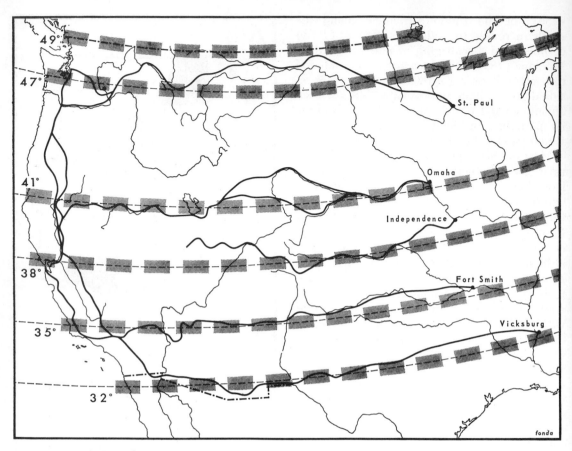

FIG. 5. United States government explorations for Pacific railroad routes, 1853–58. The routes were designated by reference to a particular parallel or parallels. The exploration of the 38th Parallel route ended when the leader of the exploration party was killed by Indians in Utah. All other routes were designated as practicable.

sequent longitudinal divisions suggest that a general pattern of three north-south strips was in keeping with the same sense of proportion. An utterly arbitrary geometry of the West based solely upon some such sense of form and size would result in twelve units (Fig. 4B). Fitting the actual eleven states to this arbitrary grid reveals only three major discordances: 1) the Idaho Panhandle, with anomalous elongations of Idaho (north-south) and of Montana (east-west); 2) Nevada as a fourth unit fitted into its tier at the expense (seemingly) of California and (actually) of Utah; 3) California elongated north-south to include two units (the angled eastern boundary of California was designed to be a simple geometric approximation of the trend of the coastline). Although unlike the anomalies cited in the previous paragraph, such depar-

tures from a theoretical pattern have no inherent significance, they do help us to visualize in fresh ways the regional character of the West.

CIRCULATION (STAGES I AND II)

Most of the famous Western trails were primarily emigrant roads, serving as a means of getting people across the wilderness to new areas of settlement but by the very nature of the vehicles inadequate for effective communication and profitable commerce spanning such distances. Even the relatively large systems of wagon freighting and scheduled stage and mail service of the late 1850s did not effectively alter the isolation of these Western nuclei. Much of the wagon freighting was in support of military posts and operations, heavily dependent upon government contracts. In the Oregon Country and California steamboats on the Columbia, Willamette, and Sacramento rivers aided the development of a commercial export agricultural economy, but elsewhere only goods of very high value, such as bullion or highly concentrated ores, or self-propelled, such as mules from New Mexico could meet the costs of shipment.

The construction of a railroad to the Pacific became a major national issue almost from the moment that the United States acquired its Pacific frontage. The selection of the route for such a line was widely understood to be a momentous geographical decision. Northern California was so much the most important of the several Western nuclei that San Francisco Bay was unquestioned as the Pacific terminus. But there were various possible routes for linking California with the East and it was generally assumed that the first railroad would become and long remain the principal transcontinental axis, the trunk line of the nation, with enormous consequences for subsequent patterns of development.

Because of the insular character of Western settlement within such a vast area it was also generally accepted that, contrary to the situation in the East, the Pacific railroad would require heavy federal subsidy. The decision as to the route rested with Congress and thus was enmeshed in sectional politics. To appease competing areas the initial feasibility study authorized reconnaissance of five general routes between the Mississippi and the Pacific: one northern, two central, and two southern (Fig. 5). The War Department agency which carried out these surveys reported four of these routes as possible for a railroad, but recommended the southernmost as the most advantageous. Sectional rivalries blocked any decision until after Southern secession, when Congress selected the central route which had been advocated by most Northern interests. The Overland Telegraph, another federally-subsidized service, was opened along the same general route in late 1861.

The central route was the shortest extending directly west from the most aggressive salients of the vigorously developing railroad system of the East. It had the added advantage of passing near Denver and Salt Lake City, thus

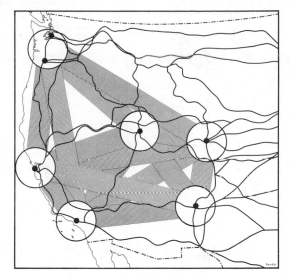

FIG. 6. Interregional railroad connections compared with a schematic pattern of direct links among all six regions of the West.

linking three of these Western regional systems with the nation. Land grant subsidies were later allocated to railroads building along all or major parts of the other five Pacific routes of the initial survey, and within twenty years after the first golden spike all of the Western regions were similarly linked by direct trunk lines to the East. That these several Western areas were more effectively linked to the East than to one another, except incidentally along transcontinental routes, was characteristic of this stage of development. Indeed the insular pattern was so marked and regional interdependence so limited among certain areas that a complete network of direct railroad connections among the six major nuclei was never completed (Fig. 6).

The railroad was a revolutionary instrument but it took a generation or more to work the revolution. The thirty years following the ceremony at Promontory was the culmination of Stage II and no more than a prelude to Stage III. During that time the other trunk lines to the East were completed, but the capacity and efficiency of these railroads was still very limited. As links between East and West they were more important in bringing people to the West than in carrying freight out. Meanwhile the regional railroad systems were being very extensively elaborated in

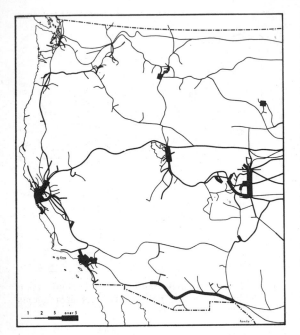

FIG. 7. Railroad passenger service at least six days per week near the beginning of Stage III. Source: *Official Guide of the Railway and Steam Navigation Lines in the United States, Canada, and Mexico,* September 1897.

support of rapid increases in the density of settlement and intensity of development within these several areas (Fig. 7).

POPULATION (STAGES III AND IV)

The end of the Turnerian frontier, when no large blocks of land suitable for traditional family farm colonization remained, marked the end of Stage II in the population pattern. Major expansions of agricultural colonization thereafter were dependent upon irrigation, and many of these were in large government projects such as in the Columbia Basin, the Snake River Plain, the San Joaquin, the Imperial Valley, and Central Arizona. Together with new mineral and forestry districts such developments altered Western settlement patterns in numerous details. The growth of a more complex industrial base in the West, something beyond the elemental processing of local primary products, was critically dependent on activities fostered by the federal government, chiefly during the several wars of the twentieth century: shipyards, aircraft, ordinance, steel, and aluminum plants, as well as military

installations. But migrants have also poured into certain areas for other reasons. "Westering" has continued to be a major feature of American life. In depressions as well as booms the image of the West as new country where one might embark upon a new life in more congenial circumstances has persisted as a powerful attraction. To a very considerable degree, industry has followed the population as well as lured it.

The total of such movements over a span of four or five decades did much to alter the shape and insularity of Western regions. Major nuclei persisted and the largest cities became very much larger, but many lesser centers in outlying districts grew notably (e.g., Bakersfield, Fresno, Klamath Falls, Richland, Yakima, Great Falls, Billings, Roswell), giving a more even incidence of urbanization and blurring the earlier regional border zones. Migration patterns became increasingly complex. Inflows from the East were predominantly channeled to the large urban areas, but affected every district. Two new immigrations of distinct peoples became significant: the northward influx of large numbers of Mexicans who spread widely though selectively over the West as an industrial and agricultural proletariat; and, more recently, the westward influx of blacks, chiefly from Texas, Arkansas, and Louisiana, especially into urban California. There was also much interregional movement within the West, primarily to California, Portland, and Puget Sound. Most of this migration is obscure, but some of the most important streams are readily identifiable, such as that of New Mexican Hispanos spreading into the industrial and farm-labor districts of Colorado, Mormons colonizing alongside other settlers in the new irrigation districts and moving in large numbers to Pacific Coast urban areas, and the influx early in the century of Japanese and the more recent upsurge in Chinese immigration to California.

In the 1970s the West seems to be entering a fourth stage characterized by the emergence of huge metropolitan clusters of population. The Los Angeles Basin, San Francisco Bay, and the eastern shore of Puget Sound now appear to be truly megalopolitan in character. The older metropolitan centers of Portland, Denver, Salt Lake City, and Spokane have been suddenly joined by San Diego, Phoenix, Tucson, Albuquerque, and Las Vegas, Nevada. The rapid growth of cities is a common feature of the West through several stages, but the scale, character, and impact of recent urbanization is quite unprecedented. The efficiencies of transportation and communication and the relative affluence of a growing number of people combine to spread persons who are an integral part of urban culture far beyond the obvious bounds of continuously built-up urban areas. The seemingly rural countrysides of many Western districts are actually dominated by essentially urban people scattered about in satellite towns, housing tracts, resorts, and homesteads, all in close functional and cultural connection with metropolitan areas by high-speed highways and individual or commuter air services.

CIRCULATION (STAGES III AND IV)

Stage III saw the development of a far more elaborate and efficient combination of transportation facilities than the early railroad-stage and wagon road-sporadic riverboat combination of Stage II. The electric interurban railroad was a temporary addition; paved highways, local air service, pipelines, and a barge system on the Columbia were successive additions to the earlier railroad network, which was itself completed and greatly increased in efficiency during this period.

There were important similarities in the developmental phases of these spatial networks. Electric railroads began as urban-suburban lines and were later extended to connect neighboring cities. In areas of relatively dense agricultural and urban settlement (such as the Los Angeles Basin, Sacramento Valley, Willamette Valley, and Puget Sound Lowlands) fairly extensive systems were built. The network of paved highways began in similar fashion but went much further: first radiating out from urban centers, then connecting adjacent cities, expanding into regional systems, gradually linking adjacent regions, and ultimately forming a complete interregional network of relatively uniform quality (Fig. 8). The superior efficiency of such government-financed trafficways soon drove the electric railroads out of business. Similarly, most of the local service airlines

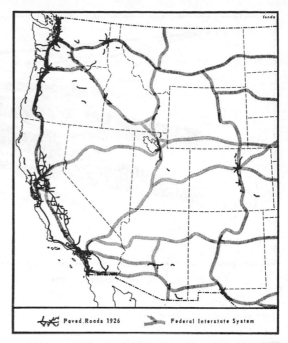

FIG. 8. Early stage of the highway network, 1926, and federal interstate highway system, 1971.

began as essentially regional companies connecting smaller cities with the regional metropolis. Next came links between adjacent regions, then the merger of companies to form comprehensive networks radiating from several metropolitan centers. So, too, by the 1930s telephone and radio broadcasting, each begun as local or regional operations, enveloped the nation in vast complexly interlocked networks.

By the 1950s every district was served by some form of modern efficient transportation, every region was served by an elaborate combination of communication services, and all of the Western regional networks were integral parts of a general national network which was itself a complex combination of overlapping regional systems.

The transition to Stage IV is marked most significantly by the initiation of transcontinental nonstop air service, which was rapidly extended during the early jet age of the 1960s. The critical differentiating feature is the very rapid uninterrupted direct connection between major Western urban centers and the national metropolises of New York and Washington and other cities in the national core, overflying intervening regions (Fig. 9). Such service

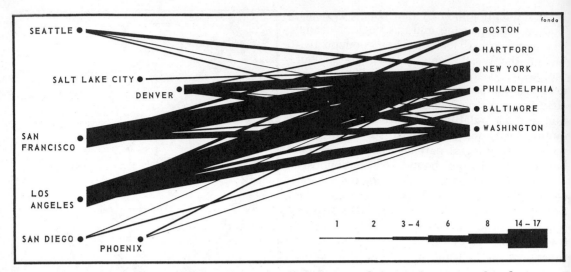

FIG. 9. Nonstop air service between cities of the West and the Northeastern Seaboard.

forms a national and international network of nodal links which obliterates surface regions. This network, like all others, has its own peculiar pattern of sequential development: first from the two largest Western metropolises, Los Angeles and San Francisco, to New York, then similar service from Seattle, then such service to other major Eastern cities, then service between lesser Western cities and the largest Eastern cities. Such a sequence could be projected to the point where every major city has direct nonstop air service with every other major city. An analogous sequence is also underway in international service, beginning with scheduled nonstop flights connecting San Francisco and Los Angeles with major European cities.

Meanwhile local feeder airlines continue to amalgamate to form ever-larger systems. Today one company (Air West) dominates the entire Pacific Slope and another (Frontier) the entire Rocky Mountain and High Plains country; the two systems interlock at Tucson, Phoenix, Salt Lake City, and Great Falls.

Complementing these developments are elaborate metropolitan freeway networks and the beginnings of a modern mass-transit system in the most congested megalopolis, and other forms of efficient long-distance transportation, such as pipelines, unit-trains, and the nationwide interstate superhighway system of uniform quality (Fig. 10). Such developments

point toward the emergence of a complex nationwide system of circulation which is fully and efficiently national in operation rather than a combination of interlocking regional systems with attendant inefficiencies of transfer points and separate managements. Direct-dial long-distance telephoning, intercity computer hookups, television and the prospect for a variety of specialized television networks are other major components.

POLITICAL AREAS (STAGES III AND IV)

The admission of New Mexico and Arizona in 1912 completed the statehood process in the West, an event delayed because of the special cultural character of New Mexico and the relatively small population of both. An effort to combine these two territories to form a single state was defeated largely on the grounds of their sharp cultural differences, a further illustration of the general concern to fit political areas to other basic areal patterns.

The territorial design of the eleven states completed in 1912 has remained unaltered. Discussion of a new state for the Columbia Interior was briefly revived in the 1930s. Much more significant is the growing agitation for the subdivision of California into two states, a chronic movement directly reflecting the existence of two major regions and megalopolitan clusters within a single political unit. Such discordance between state areas and

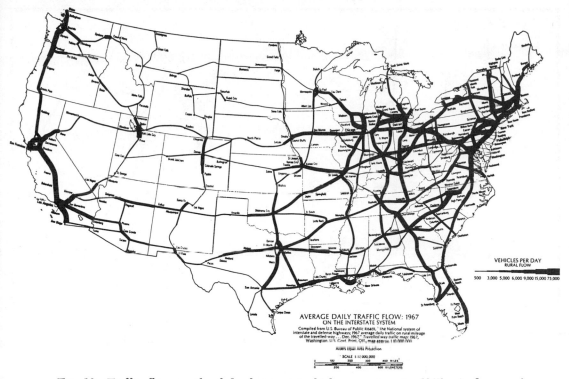

VEHICLES PER DAY
RURAL FLOW

500 3,000 5,000 6,000 9,000 15,000 75,000

AVERAGE DAILY TRAFFIC FLOW: 1967
ON THE INTERSTATE SYSTEM

Compiled from U.S. Bureau of Public Roads, "The National system of
interstate and defense highways; 1967 average daily traffic on rural mileage
of the travelled-way ... Dec. 1967." Travelled way traffic map: 1967,
Washington, U.S. Govt. Print. Off., map approx. 1:10,000,000

Albers Equal Area Projection

SCALE 1:12,000,000

FIG. 10. Traffic flow on the federal interstate highway system in 1967. A degree of separateness between East and West was still apparent. Source: *The National Atlas of the United States*, p. 227.

metropolitan areas, putting rival centers within a single state, influences nearly every aspect of political affairs in California and Washington. Oregon, Utah, and Colorado reflect a more singular metropolitan focus; Idaho, Montana, and, until recently, New Mexico, Arizona, and Nevada a more diffuse and non-metropolitan character.

The county pattern within each state was also completed early in the twentieth century. There has been neither subdivision nor amalgamation of any counties for more than half a century. That pattern is reflective of the settlement and transport conditions of Stage II, but it did not become at all inappropriate in areal scale until the very recent advent of intricate local networks of high-speed highways. Even today, the optimum size for counties is a moot point, depending as much upon philosophies of citizen-government relations as upon efficiencies of transportation.

The most significant geopolitical feature of Stage III was the discordances between a

changing population pattern and an unchanging political territorial pattern. As urban areas grew rapidly and most rural areas stabilized there was an ever-widening population differential among the counties of any particular state. To the degree that state governments operated on a basis of equal representation from and equal allocation of resources to counties very serious political tensions were created. Reapportionment of representation became a recurrent problem of major significance.

Because of the cumulative rigidities of autonomous political territories there is likely to be a long lag between generally recognized needs and any actual areal changes. Thus there are as yet no more than glimmers of a shift into a new stage in such geopolitical matters. The definition by the federal government and subsequent widespread use for a variety of public and private planning purposes of "standard metropolitan statistical areas," many of which are contiguous blocks

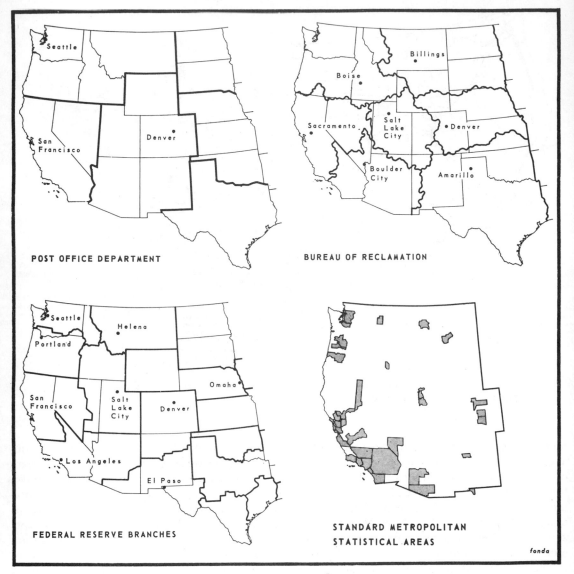

FIG. 11. Examples of current administrative areas.

of counties directly functioning as part of a metropolitan system, points up the problem. The creation of special metropolitan political agencies encompassing several incorporated municipalities and transcending county boundaries reflects the need for a new scale of political territory. At the state level, formation of interstate compacts, chiefly with reference to water and river basin development, and the fact that many federal agencies operate on the basis of larger-than-state regions, are further signs of similar needs (Fig. 11).

However, while further developments of this sort are almost inevitable, they are almost certainly going to be superstructures resting upon the existing county and state territorial grids. Before projecting the inevitable creation of giant metropolitan regions to bring form and function into accord and replace states as the prime units, it is well to remember that the United States is by definition a federal system of states and the significance, tenacity, and, perhaps, desirability, of the present state system can hardly be exaggerated.

CULTURE (STAGES III AND IV)

Stage III marks the end of insularity and a sharp increase in the power of forces working toward national cultural uniformity. Since most Westerners and Easterners have always shared a common basic "American" culture, it is important to define rather carefully the nature of this change.

The West was largely populated by migrants from the East who not only routinely brought their culture with them but sought to stay in touch with and to emulate the East in almost every way. Contrary to some of the more extreme and simple versions of the "frontier thesis," the West was always far more imitative than innovative. For example, in such basic social institutions as churches, fraternal organizations, political parties, and educational systems Westerners were mostly part of essentially national networks. Nevertheless, the insular conditions of Stage II allowed the preservation of conscious desired differences, as in the case of the Mormons and Hispanos; fostered divergences based upon isolation and environmental differences, as in diet, dialect, religious schism, and local economic and political issues; and caused a marked lag in the adoption of new features originating in the East because of the inefficiencies of diffusion processes.

Developments during the first half of the twentieth century continuously increased the intensity, rapidity, and comprehensiveness of the impact of national culture upon the regions. Mass-consumption journalism and radio poured out a relentless propaganda in support of standardized products, fashions, behavior, attitudes, and speech. The cinema had in some ways an even more powerful impact, not only as a mass-marketed entertainment that replaced nearly all local forms, but as displaying (at times quite unconsciously) powerfully persuasive examples of modern American life. Indeed, Hollywood put before all the world much the most effective definition of an "American standard of living," a standard which was for the most part not the level most common in America, but one to which most Americans aspired and felt was within possible reach.

The triumph of the national over the regional is perhaps most readily illustrated in commercial activity. In Stage II retailing was dominated by local firms. The rise of the great mail-order houses with the development of a nationwide railroad network provided the first direct link between the Western consumer and the Eastern distributor, but time, cost, and physical separation left it a tenuous relationship of low intensity which did not greatly modify the general insularity of Western regions. The development of national chain-stores and franchised service facilities, branch plants, and the acquisition of regional companies by national firms are the critical changes. Nationwide advertising combined with a nationwide network of distribution centers allowed new items to be introduced simultaneously into every region, and reduced the lag in adoption between center and periphery to relative insignificance.

Furthermore, "center" and "periphery" were no longer obvious characterizations for East and West. The national culture was being markedly influenced by Hollywood and other agencies which displayed a Southern Californian style of life as the most modern and glamorous and thus implicitly worthy of emulation. From the 1920s to the 1960s American patterns of living were profoundly shaped by innovations spreading out from this world-famed Western corner of the nation: the general style of informal, pleasure-centered living; the patio, barbecue, swimming pool, and stylish sports clothes; the architecture of houses and the design of interiors, as attested by the successive diffusion of the California "bungalow," "Spanish" stucco, "ranchhouse," and "contemporary" housetypes over all American suburbia. Above all, Southern California set the national style in the use of the automobile and in the design of automobile-centered facilities and environments—carports, freeways, strip-cities, shopping centers, motels, drive-ins of all kinds. Detroit manufactured the cars but California showed how to live with them, and this critical influential link between the historic core and a burgeoning Western region was a telling indication of a significant stage in national integration.

But the very fact that Southern California could play such a role was itself evidence that regionalism had not been completely eroded in the West. Both Californias, Southern especially, were areas of vigorous growth powered to an important degree by the continual influx of people consciously seeking a "California way of life" as something different and better than that to be found elsewhere in the nation. California's distinctiveness was more than locational and environmental, it was fundamentally cultural, a matter of attitudes and behavior which produce a new style of everyday living.

And despite the massive impact of national culture, other Western regions retained a considerable degree of identity during Stage III. Colorado, never an obvious, self-conscious culture area, continued as a nodal region encompassing a very distinctive physical environment and combination of economic activities. The Pacific Northwest was rather more complex, with its three major urban centers and sharply contrasting environments of coast and interior. Though it had little sense of cultural cohesion, a loose sense of regionalism was based upon economy and environment, location in a far corner, Alaskan and Oriental trade connections, and a feeling of being sharply separate from and very much overshadowed in the national mind by California.

The Mormons illustrate very well the combined national-regional character of Stage III. Although still vigorously nurturing a strong sense of cohesion and identity as a distinct religious society, Mormon leaders worked toward an amicable accommodation with the nation. Indeed one can detect a gradual shift in corporate self-image from a "peculiar people" to "model Americans," the latter not in the sense of typical, but of the ideal godly, familial, puritanical, industrious people prominent in our national mythology. And while a strong sense of Utah as hallowed historic ground remained, the continual influx of Gentiles into the Mormon coreland, and the continual exodus of Mormons into neighboring regions and especially into California metropolitan areas, inevitably modified the strength of such Mormon regionalism. The building of a Mormon temple in Los Angeles in the 1950s was an overt acknowledgment of an important change in regional character and consciousness.

So, too, even though the Hispano culture of New Mexico remained strongly resistant of many facets of national culture, the continual influx of Anglos, reducing the earlier people to a minority in their own homeland, and the dispersal of Hispanos into Colorado and elsewhere, tended to blur regional identities.

Thus, while national culture was clearly ascendant, the West continued to display marked variations in regional character based upon a somewhat different combination of factors in each region. It was still an immense land. The transcontinental traveler could hardly avoid being impressed with the differences in land and life from place to place, and the differences in each and all with those in the East.

Transition to the next stage seems clearly underway but far from complete. The characteristics of that stage are as yet more a projection than a reality but the direction of change seems so boldly evident to so many people and the pace of change so increasingly rapid that the future looms portentously. Briefly, current trends seem to suggest that the West will simply be the western half of a nation of many millions more people, of broadly uniform culture, living some form of urban life within a vast, intimately interconnected, nationwide, multi-metropolitan system. Such a population will be fluid, highly mobile in work, impermanent in residence, capable of almost instant dispersal in recreation; the great western mountain and desert landscapes will become mere parks, as accessible and intensely used as city parks of today.

Some of the instruments of this transition are notorious: television, the jet plane, and the all-terrain-vehicle; electronic communication and computational systems applied to nationwide management; the economic power of huge corporations and affluent individuals. And the evidence for such trends is readily apparent: the ever-increasing standardization of goods and services and efficiency of nationwide contacts, the continual westward migrations, the relentless expansion of metropolitan areas, the rapid emergence of large urban centers unsupported by the usual tributary areas (Las Vegas, Tucson, San Diego), the ever-expanding swarm of seasonal travelers over Western landscapes; above all, perhaps, the widespread feeling that all areas, no matter how hitherto remote, inaccessible, or undesirable, are wide open to penetration, immigration, investment, development, and control by "outside forces."

Even the common image of these "outside forces" has undergone change indicative of a shift from older patterns. The hold of "Eastern money" upon the West, the essentially "colonial" relationship between the old, rich, powerful, industrial workshop and the new, money-short, vulnerable, raw material producer was something long recognized and resented in the West. But this necessary dependence upon "Wall Street" which controlled railroads and mines, major industries and financial institutions, was on the surface a scarcely visible link which did not seem to shape directly daily lives and local landscapes (though in fact it did in myriad ways). But in the 1960s the magnitude, comprehensiveness, and mobility of economic speculation and development had so increased and was so different in character as to cause widespread concern. Interestingly, in many parts of the West, the greatest resentment is not directed against "Easterners," but against Californians or Texans. In neither case is this feeling based primarily upon a strong sense of obvious cultural differences (although there is often some tinge of such feeling with regard to Texans); rather it is a fear of an aggressive entrepreneurship backed by great wealth and vigorously growing and restless populations. Residents of neighboring regions see a kind of insidious relentless imperialism, the one spreading over the entire Pacific Slope, the other north and west over Colorado and New Mexico, expressed in a wave of activities: speculators buying farm and ranch lands, choice urban sites, huge suburban tracts, entire recreational districts; financiers investing in retail chains, banks, newspapers, and broadcasting stations; people pouring in as vacationers, hunters, seasonal sojourners, and students. How extensive such movements really are, and the degree to which they can be appropriately identified as Texan or Californian, is not at all clear, but they are common topics of conversation and commonly regarded as threatening whatever remains of local regional autonomy and character.

Despite such developments, the historic regionalism in the West is by no means wholly dissolved, and these common projections are not necessarily immutable. While the West has grown rapidly during the last thirty years it (the eleven westernmost states) still contains only sixteen percent of the nation's population in thirty-eight percent of the area of the coterminous forty-eight. Large areas of the West are growing very slowly if at all; Montana and Wyoming were stagnant during the last decade, and Idaho and New Mexico grew by less than five percent, as did large sections of several other states. However, much the most remarkable demographic statistic is that net migration into California was only 26,000 in 1970 and may be transformed into a net exodus in 1971. Among the most remarkable recent events was the bold pronouncement by the Governor of Oregon that his state had enough people and he would be pleased if no more moved in. Such things reflect something far more profound than temporary economic problems. They express some basic changes in attitude which could have major impact upon the evolving geography of America. For it is now widely appreciated that California is in grave danger of foundering on its own growth. Simple projections of the most obvious trends will define the complete despoliation of the American Eden. If the California dream becomes the California nightmare, and California begins to lose more people than it attracts over a considerable period of time, it would surely mark an important shift in the tide of American affairs. An end to westering would seem at least as important a change as was the end of the Turnerian frontier.

Such a shift can hardly be predicted with confidence at this point. Migrational changes are unlikely to be abrupt or uniform in effect, many other Western areas are still relatively uncrowded and attractive, and the emergence of new attitudes about "growth" and "progress" and "development" will be slow and complex. But the very fact that trends of the recent past do loom in the minds of many Westerners as a threat to their own future may have in itself halted the decline in regional consciousness. A heightened environmental awareness cannot but reinforce in some degree an appreciation of physical and cultural variations from place to place.

These very changes in attitudes have a geography of origin and diffusion, the outlines of which are recognizable in general if inscrutable in detail. Just as Southern California exerted a massive impact upon American society in Stage III, so Northern California seems destined to do so in Stage IV. Here seems to be the most concentrated awareness of many national problems and concern for solutions or alternatives. From here has come the main impetus of the new environmental consciousness, as epitomized by the Sierra Club. Here, certainly, is the major hearth of the "counter-culture" which has mounted a comprehensive critique of American society and markedly influenced national patterns of fashion, behavior, and attitudes. Berkeley, San Francisco, Oakland, and Big Sur have replaced Hollywood in offering images of new ways of life, and although much that is now in vogue will prove as superficial and transient as that of the earlier era, it does appear that vastly deeper philosophical matters are overtly involved. Although national in scope, the impact of such movements is regionally varied, and their prominence and power in Northern California serves to set that region, or at least its diverse metropolitan area, apart from other Western regions, reinforcing earlier cultural distinctions.

Furthermore, some long-standing cultural differences within the West have lately been reinforced and seem certain to become even more prominent. Through all the decades, while national culture was eroding regional differences, a few resistant peaks remained above the broadening plain. A recent series of upheavals makes them loom much larger, and continuing tremors suggest more changes are incipient. American Indians, New Mexican Hispanos, Mexican Americans, and Black Americans, never accorded full social integration and long resistant to cultural assimilation, now demand full rights and recognition as Americans even while they accentuate their own distinct culture patterns. Thereby many areas take on a new significance in the social landscape of America: areas such as the Central Valley, the Mexican border country, and the Indian reservations in various states. No one of these constitutes a new region on the scale and with the kind of functional integrity of the old. They are subregions of special distinction, and together with Hutterite colonies on the High Plains, conservative Mormon back valleys, the Hispano stronghold in the mountains, and, perhaps eventually, districts of Basques, Portuguese, Italians, Finnish, and other white groups of heightened ethnic consciousness, they form pieces in a complex American mosaic. That mosaic, which is becoming ever more visible, and which represents another reversal of long-projected trends, would seem to be a particularly important pattern for the future.

Thus, while the historic regions have markedly faded as discrete entities, the West is far from even an incipient uniform or united area. And the real test lies beyond academic evidence in what daily life is really like in the actual communities of the West. To any sensitive soul, surely, it does make a difference whether one lives in Provo, Pueblo, Pasadena, Pendleton, or Puyallup; such differences are rooted in historical legacies as well as environmental settings, in what kinds of people came and in what they have created and experienced in particular places.

CONCLUSION

This is a sketch of an approach which would seem to offer good possibilities for breaking new ground in the study of the American West and in the interpretation of the American nation. It combines a number of advantageous qualities.

It is comprehensive as to time and area. Time is divided into periods and although both the peak of each stage and the transitions between stages are of special interest, the entire course of events (since the entry of Europeans) is a logical and necessary part of the scheme. So too, the area of the West is divided into parts and although special attention is directed to the cores and peripheries of major regions, full application of the scheme requires that the entire area be examined at every stage. Thus every locality at every point in time has an identifiable place within the scheme.

Secondly, it is developmental. It focuses attention upon a set of interrelated processes which appear to be producing a sequence of recognizable eras, each characterized by a certain general magnitude, intensity, and quality in regional, interregional, and national relationships. In an important sense there is an equal concern for past, present, and future;

for although inherently historical in emphasis, this approach offers a perspective which would seem essential for an understanding of the present and for prediction of the future. Indeed, any characterization of Stage IV necessarily is in part a projection of trends and a speculation about new possibilities.

Thirdly, it is synthetic. It requires that a great diversity of elements and processes— environmental, cultural, social, political, economic—be examined in search of structural and historical interrelationships. This will require a great deal of new analysis of detail, but with the aim of contributing toward a richer synthesis, a better knowledge of the parts in order to have a better understanding and appreciation of the whole. It is an approach therefore which invites the attention of anthropologists, sociologists, economists, and political scientists as well as geographers and historians.

Finally, it is a generic scheme. Although shaped specially to fit the general contours of development in the American West, it is a model with wider applications. Clearly it would seem applicable with little adjustment to some other roughly contemporary colonizations in the Neo-European World, in Canada, Australia, Argentina, Brazil, and Siberia. Furthermore, it can be fitted logically into a somewhat more comprehensive model of nation-building, and it bears some important similarities to models of "modernization" now being worked out for the study of the transformation of the long-settled but "underdeveloped world."

As a new perspective it requires a shift in focus from things long studied to things little known. The unsatisfying exposition of many matters in this paper is not alone due to limitations of space and an incomplete knowledge of that which may have already been done by other students of the West, but also to the undoubted fact that little has been done on many topics which now loom as important. There are many inherent difficulties in this approach: how, for example, to define regional cultures, how to measure interregional linkages, how to identify historical changes, how to trace important diffusions. But we are not complete novices in the study of such things. The application of present skills to such questions could quickly yield important results. In recent American geography, especially, the development of techniques seems to have outstripped the formulation of a significant set of problems worthy of their application. For example, this scheme could provide a productive focus for numerous analyses of spatial diffusion, giving a coherence and sense of purpose to an area of interest which currently seems far too fragmentary and eclectic, too much a trying out of techniques rather than an investigation of major topics.

There are of course many inherent limitations as well. No single approach can hope to yield equally significant answers to all possible major questions. Explicitly regional in focus and scale, it is clearly not the most efficient tool for the examination of those features which are narrowly local or broadly national. But it finds a special justification in the fact that it is precisely this intermediate, regional, scale which in many ways seems most weakly developed in the literature extant.

An approach which focuses upon the American West can be no more than a partial view of American development, yet this regional scheme has significance for national interpretation in two ways. First, as presented in this paper, in each topic at every stage the West is explicitly linked with the East, and the series of stages describes a cycle of divergence and convergence as between Western regions and the national core and culture. Secondly, if this is indeed a useful generic model for the study of colonization and nation-building, the entire scheme could well be applied to the entire nation. For example, the initial European footholds on the American Atlantic shore as clearly fit the characteristics of Stage I as do the nuclear areas of the Far West. Carried forward, it would help define the regional complexities which existed underneath the broad sectional concepts of North, South, and West. With certain modifications the scheme could accommodate the emergence and unique position of a national core to which all other areas have been in some degree subordinate. Although profiting from the rich lode of Turnerian studies, the results would be very different from the old sectional interpretation.

But whether applied to the West or to the nation, such an approach invites American geographers to address themselves directly to a task that they have never seriously undertaken as a field: a really comprehensive look at the full course of their nation's development with the object of contributing to a general assessment of its character. If it is true, as a leading historian has stated, that in the wake of disillusion with a sequence of once widely-espoused and now discredited theories, American historians now recognize Alexis de Tocqueville's *Democracy in America* as "the most respected of all interpretations of the United States," it would seem an especially opportune time for the geographers to join in the common quest for significant generalizations.[3] For Tocqueville's interpretation rests

[3] John Higham, *History, The Development of Historical Studies in the United States* (Princeton: Princeton University Press, 1965) pp. 221–22. All of the words and phrases in quotations in this paragraph are taken directly from Higham.

upon a view of the United States as an "organic whole" with a recognizable "national character" which encompasses, under great tension, "oppressive conformity" and "kaleidoscopic variety," unmistakable "continuity" and "endless flux," regional diversity held together by multitudinous bonds of heritage and advantage. A penetrating systematic study of the United States as a varying set of regional parts developing through a recognizable sequence of interrelationships would seem to be essential to the explication of such an interpretation or any modern variant therefrom. Thus those American geographers who still see their own field in its historic wholeness, enriched by an equal concern for past and present, regional and topical, the particular and the general, ought to have something fresh and valuable to contribute.

CALIFORNIA AND THE SEARCH FOR THE IDEAL

JAMES E. VANCE, JR.

ABSTRACT. Throughout American history city men have looked upon the countryside as a place for a specialized form of urban settlement. Initially interest centered on the physically therapeutic qualities of the countryside, followed, in turn, by the mental recruitment to be experienced there. At the end of the last century this outward migration focussed into two attitudes, the Hudsonian search for the primitive and socially pristine and the Concordian seeking of urban pastorialism. The Concordian led to the shaping of a new settlement form, located largely in Megalopolis, which can be called exurbia, whereas the Hudsonian search encouraged the migration to California as the heartland of "the geography of the ideal" expressed in social detachment and the cult of the wilderness. There arcadia became the settlement form. In the years since the Second World War the social and intellectual thought of the California arcadia has gained worldwide attention suggesting the importance of an analysis of the urban form in a frame of "three cities" resolution—the special social districts of the core city, the nativist culture of the suburbs, and the geography of the ideal in arcadia and exurbia.
KEY WORDS: *American ideal, Arcadia, California, Exurbia, Suburbia, Urban ideal.*

SOON after the Civil War the American city began its rapid expansion, in area as well as population. That spread made obvious a condition previously somewhat masked by the relatively small size of settlements in the United States; that the New World was adopting new geographical forms for urban living. Areal specialization of function and search for the pristine environment for new growth contributed mightily to shaping a new morphology. In the nineteenth century the "city in a garden" was devised with housing scattered widely over the urban setting, creating the clear-cut detached single-family house pattern that has persisted as distinctly North American ever since, however much it has been castigated by American planners and European critics as wasteful and tasteless. Americans nonetheless have argued the better life afforded by free-standing residence, and, through its construction, have made a new kind of city. Because it was obvious that morphological innovation had to be backstayed by transportation innovation, most urban transport innovation was initiated in the United States.

The "city in a garden" was America's first fundamental contribution to urban form, so much so that the most original-minded of nineteenth century cities, Chicago, adopted the phrase as its official motto. It is hard to establish without question that Ebenezer Howard first conceived of the Garden City from the example of the Windy City, but he resided there during the several years when the urban fabric was being rebuilt on an open pattern following the fire of 1871, and what Howard reproduced in Letchworth a generation later was strikingly like the New World's city in a garden. Sir Ebenezer, in acknowledging his conceptual debt both to Edward Bellamy and to Henry George, gave evidence of the first repayment to Europe of America's earlier borrowing of urban forms and institutions.[1]

The single-family house standing detached on its own lot, either cramped or expansive, became the basic element of American housing; it proved a short step from the Chicago residential streets of the seventies to the massive housing tracts that shape all our cities a century later. The scalar expansion was accomplished through the evolution of a cheap and widespread urban transportation, begun by the electric trolley in the eighties and made more spatially competent by the automobile in this century.

Dr. Vance is Professor of Geography at the University of California in Berkeley.

---

[1] Walter L. Creese, *The Search for Environment: The Garden City Before and After* (New Haven: Yale University Press, 1966), Chapter Six.

If the city in a garden was the initial New World urban innovation, the discrete suburb came next. Although London had grown over the inner parts of the Home Counties in late Victorian times, that expansion had come pretty much as well-contained growth rings feeding on the countryside but not making great isolated thrusts into its body. American residential expansion showed more force if less pattern. The result was the shaping of lines of discrete suburbs, strung like beads on the strings of iron rails radiating from central cities. The forceful impact on the inner band of countryside quickly spread the zone of anticipation of urbanization outward; actual development along the rail lines, but mere increase in demand prices for land in the interstices. When the trolley car and the automobile made suburban residence more democratic, the fingers of urban anticipation came to be filled both by less affluent migrants from the old central city and by new higher-income housing built by a later generation of suburban dwellers.

This search for the new suburban environment expressed what seems to have been an ever-present element in our increasingly urban culture, the use of changing morphology of residence to create or enhance new ideas as to the desirable life-style. The middle class after the Civil War turned to the house in a garden, often from having lived previously in boarding houses, to accomplish their desire for a simple and orderly social environment. The suburb was not so much a place of economic class as it was one of native culture, contrasted with the ethnic groupings that took over central-city areas. In a sense the suburb grew out of the desire to reject a plural society and maintain the distinctive American culture that had emerged in the years between the War of Independence and the onset of the great immigrations of the 1840s. The older Americans sought such preservation by moving out of the city and the newer Americans sought acculturation thereto by following in their wake in the second generation.

Once having established this equation between residential location within the city and cultural practice, each rising generation tended to find it necessary to recreate the pristine conditions its parents had looked for in residence. So long as the economic support of the group was tied to the city, notably to its center, the growth of the city could be peripheral but was unlikely to be discontinuous. Expanding suburbs resulted and the inner parts of the city came to be abandoned to those ethnic groupings migrating into the city from the countryside or from overseas. Sociologists have thought of this process as one of invasion and succession, but in truth it was one of abandonment and retrieval. The economically most advantaged sought generational-shift in residence, into new developments, so that the newest style of life could be enjoyed uncluttered by survivals from past generations. Filtering down of housing from the rich to the less well-to-do came because society's leaders wished to recreate a simple socially-integrated area rather than as the direct working of economic forces alone, as Alonso has argued.[2] The attempts to find in economic terms the cause of peripheral shift in the housing of the prosperous has always proved difficult, and to many unconvincing. If, however, we examine the hypothesis of the search for identity of life-style and viewpoint, and its defense against cosmopolitanism in a sequestered residential area, the explanation is both more organic and more convincing. To test that hypothesis of the social basis of residential choice we need to consider two extra-urban settlement forms, both as to causation and as to location. The first of these, "exurbia," is an adjunct of East Coast settlement whereas the second, "arcadia," ties more directly to the West Coast and California settlement.

URBAN SETTLEMENT BEYOND THE CITY

Because the European pattern of settlement evolved under conditions that required cities, almost as their first concern, to look to their defense, the edge of the city tended to become and remain a boundary between two cultures, the bourgeois, economically-structured life of the town and the aristocratic, socially-structured existence of the countryside. Townsmen gained independence and

[2] William Alonso, *Location and Land Use: Toward a General Theory of Land Rent* (Cambridge: Harvard University Press, 1965).

power by staying within the walls, while the lord of the manor lost his power when he passed through the city gate. Two discrete systems arose, and only in the site of the court, with its aristocratic attendance, were they intermixed. But in America the dichotomy was never well developed. In the northern colonies the towns dominated and the countryside stood as an economic workroom to support urban dominance.[3] As Jean Gottmann has wisely noted in his *Megalopolis*, rural residence conferred no status, so ownership of land was not sought for other than economic purposes. In the southern colonies, on the other hand, land itself was the basis of social and economic organization. The mercantile structure was replaced by a central-place one, hierarchically organized and definitely aristocratic in nature. Boston and Charleston stand as archetypes of the two systems. The northern townsman had little reason for country living so he made, at most, only necessary business journeys outside the urban bounds. In the South, where the town grew out of the countryside, in contrast, those places had a social function in a periodic "season" for the planters, and it was mainly that southern aristocracy which had both country and town houses. So long as the North remained mercantile, it showed little interest in the reverse pattern of periodic residence in the country. There was no economic necessity for country houses, and thrift and self-discipline discouraged them.

The Bucolic Search For Health

The North's first interest in the rural areas, other than for the staples of trade they produced and consumed, came in the search for health in an era when the nature of disease was actually unknown. Before the germ theory of disease was advanced coincidental relationships could be cited as cures, and palliatives were earnestly sought. Bathing in various waters and their internal consumption had been advocated since classical times so,

in a culture steeped in classical learning and attitudes, the watering place had the support both of ancient authority and present-day utility. With such backing the Puritan merchant could justify traveling outside the town to some likely spring to take the waters. As Carl Bridenbaugh tells us the water cures were at first sought within the town:[4]

> Seventeenth-century colonists being English were nearly as prone as those who stayed at home to seek out and try the efficacy of mineral springs. In this they were aided by the Indians whose faith in the recuperative powers of mineral waters was of long standing. . . . Bostonians patronized Lynn Red Spring as early as 1669, and William Penn, to his surprise, discovered that 'there are mineral springs . . . that are not two miles from Philadelphia.'

The efficacy of urban mineral springs proved slight, and their corruption easy. "All Philadelphia was agog in the spring of 1773 with the news of the discovery of a mineral well on a vacant lot . . . just across from the State House . . . [the analysis of whose waters by] the apothecary of the Hospital and Medical School . . . yielded the conclusion that the waters, with their 'slight faetid smell' exceeded any spring in the province in strength of chalybeate properties." But Vice Provost Allison told that "The water lost its virtue within a few months after investigation owing to the contents of a neighboring necessary. The well being exhausted on account of the quantity drunk, it was found the well communicated with the necessary which gave the smell and sediment."[5]

After such experiences the turn to country springs is easily understood. Cleveland Amory has argued that Stafford Springs [Connecticut] was the first American resort, having been visited by the Plymouth Pilgrims in their search for health.[6] The combination of pas-

---

[3] This argument for the initiation of a settlement pattern in North America along lines of long-distance trade, and in mercantile cities, is presented in my *The Merchant's World: The Geography of Wholesaling* (Englewood Cliffs, New Jersey: Prentice-Hall, Inc., 1970). Its specification will be omitted here.

[4] Carl Bridenbaugh, "Baths and Watering Places of Colonial America," *The William and Mary Quarterly*, Third Series, Volume III (1946), p. 152.

[5] Bridenbaugh, op. cit., footnote 4, pp. 172–73.

[6] Cleveland Amory, *The Last Resorts* (New York: Harper and Brothers, 1952), p. 17. Amory shapes his book as the history of socially elevated American resorts reaching in time between the first such place, Stafford Springs, ca. 1650, and the last resort, Palm Springs, made fashionable in the 1930s. Social neutrality was always important; Stafford Springs grew up on a site where the antagonistic Podunks and Nipmucks had met in peace for centuries.

toral cleanliness and social neutrality after 1770 popularized the springs at Bristol in Bucks County [Pennsylvania]. As Bridenbaugh said of the Virginia springs, "The result was something less than Arcadian, but on the whole it was exceedingly human and very American" because the colonial gentry mingled with the "sturdy yeomanry" of the area and its "coonskin democrats."[7]

Whether such places succeeded to the arcadian state or not they certainly widely sought its suggestion of rude good health. The growth of the American republic was accompanied by the discovery of numerous mineral waters, and the active "booming" of such springs became widespread after 1829 when "hydropathic" medicine was formulated in Germany. Any flow of underground water had a sufficiently arcane origin to suggest its possible therapeutic use. Perhaps the most striking example is furnished by Poland Spring [Maine] where a cold, pleasant tasting drinking-water spring yielded "not mineral water, but the least mineral of waters; [such that] therein, and in certain unknown but irresistible potencies, its mysterious power consists." That power came in "reviving dormant or dying organs."[8] Several generations of traveling Americans looked upon Poland Water as a panacea, taking such precautions in European travel as demanding its use at table, or even for the hotel bath. As late as the 1920s a Palm Beach swimming pool was filled with this Maine water.[9] America's first ambassador to the Soviet Union went to Moscow in the mid-thirties well stocked with this water of "irresistible potencies."

The spa had two purposes for nineteenth century Americans. One was health-seeking and social gathering for the prosperous. The other, the chance of developing a spa, gave to landowners some hope of increasing the value of rural land through bestowing on a particular site such qualities of attraction as to encourage the conflux of visitors. Under our economic system of land rent, such collecting of people enhanced the value of the land and allowed the owner to profit either

from operating accommodations for visitors or by selling land at a value much elevated over his initial cost.

Both Walter Christaller and Edwin von Böventer have commented upon such conflux on non-central places as a basis of town formation, calling upon scholars to investigate the process and formulate its model.[10] No doubt there is an economic measure of such forces, but here the argumentation is cultural and societal, and the formulation of an economic surrogate is left to others. Let it suffice to note that there was an economic motivation for developers of watering places and other components of an American arcadia. We should not confuse processes at work. The developer may seek an economic return but the city man turning toward arcadia does not. Such a gravitation, though measurable in money terms, cannot even in its rudiments be appraised in strictly economic abstractions. As Etienne Gilson noted, "if a man is completely dominated by his emotions and impressions, it is possible to influence his behavior only through those forms and objects which surround him and more or less obscurely touch his sensibility."[11] The fact that it costs the man seeking the countryside money to journey and reside there may have a dominant role in setting the limits of his pastoral existence, but it does not explain his reason for leaving the city or the road he will take out of town.

Because the appeal of the countryside to the city dweller is considerably "dominated by his emotions and impressions," our search for the forces drawing men away from the seat of commerce and the national ecumene must center on a concept of cultural satisfaction to be gained at a distance.

The Romantic-Climatic Countryside

Given our problem—of assessing the calls that take men outside their home city and determine the place to which they will resort

---

[7] Bridenbaugh, op. cit., footnote 4, p. 161.

[8] Entry in *King's Handbook of the United States* (Buffalo: Mathews-Northrup Co., 1891).

[9] Amory, op. cit., footnote 6, p. 384.

[10] Walter Christaller, "How I Came to Think of Central Place Theory," Translated by Gisela Heathcote for School of Social Sciences, The Flinders University of South Australia from original in *Geographische Zeitschrift*, Volume 56 (1968), pp. 88–102.

[11] Quoted in paraphrase by André Chastel, "The Moralizing Architecture of John-Jacques Lequeu," in *Art News Annual*, Volume 32 (1966) p. 71.

for psychological and physical satisfaction—a formulation of the processes at work allows succinct and integrated analysis. In the early republican years it seems that the main force for periodic shift was the search for health, perhaps somewhat artificially induced in the north where the excuse of healthful leisure was used to salve the Puritan conscience, but in the south in earnest, because malaria and other fevers were endemic to the countryside as well as the coastal towns. "In the familiar guise of taking the waters at a summer resort, genteel valetudinarians sought that prized conjunction—restoration of health and relief from *ennui*."[12] This pairing goes far toward explaining the location of such places. The deterioration of health as a consequence of the seaboard's highly continental summer climate led men to seek relief in higher and more airy places. The spring-towns in the folded Appalachians of western Virginia and Pennsylvania, the country around the base of the Adirondacks, and the uplands of central New England all began to be considered a proper siting of a summer resort. To begin with, these places were endowed with arcadian virtue and rectitude, as noted by Edward Kimball on visiting Stafford Springs in 1808, when he tells us "evenings at the Springs were generally spent by the young women in singing hymns."[13] Not so Saratoga, where almost from the beginning the local conduct was much more on the model of Dionysius than Cincinnatus. And it was not long before the general practice grew up for those with the money to go off to the country in the summer.

What went on at the "Springs" may not bear too detailed an investigation, but the plausible reason for going to them was obvious. Yet by the middle of the last century a more geographically encompassing and less mundane pull to the country than hydropathy could be perceived. That attraction was for the pastoral scene itself, fully divorced from the therapy of clean air and unpleasant-tasting waters. It seems that earlier in American social experience nature as such was viewed as brutal, unkempt, frightening, and tending to induce morose and uncivil conduct. Health could draw men away from the plantation

and the counting house, but not to the American wilderness. The change came with the wide acceptance of romanticism in the early nineteenth century, after several centuries of more restricted approval among the *cognoscenti*. "The paradise of the mediaeval and sixteenth-century scenic descriptions [had been] viewed as an ideal, arcadian, landscape."[14] That landscape was composed to portray the dual virtues of "picturesqueness" and "sublimity," which must obtain for romantic satisfaction.

It was difficult indeed to make America picturesque, for that required "associations" of a literary and dynastic sort, which were absent in the New World. Only when sublimity was sought could Jonathan compete, and then mainly under the philosophy that wildness showed most clearly the hand of God. In the wildwood two reactions predominated; one was emotional, and a bit turgid, whereas the other was ethical, and a bit heavily ratiocinative. Out of the first grew the Hudson River School of painting and nature appreciation whereas from the other came what Roland Van Zandt has called the "Concordian sense of the word" romantic, in reference to the Massachusetts sages.[15] Along the shores of the Hudson "the Catskills, a by-passed bastion of wild beauty close by the most civilized centers of the Eastern coast, became symbol of the whole and a leading motif of the American romantic movement."[16] There Irving and Cooper had established a prototype of a primitive and unspoiled America which Henry James even in this century saw as taking its "place in the geography of the ideal." That place was conferred by "a shimmer of association that still more refuses to be reduced to terms; some sense of legend, of aboriginal mystery, with a still earlier past for its dim background . . . as above all romantic for its warrant."[17] The primitivism

[14] Christopher Hussey, *The Picturesque: Studies in a Point of View* (London: G. P. Putnam's Sons, 1927), p. 103.
[15] Roland Van Zandt, *The Catskill Mountain House* (New Brunswick: Rutgers University Press, 1966), p. 157.
[16] Van Zandt, op. cit., footnote 15, p. 153.
[17] Henry James, "New York and the Hudson: A Spring Impression," *North American Review*, Vol. 181 (1905), p. 828; subsequently reissued as part of *The American Scene*.

[12] Bridenbaugh, op. cit., footnote 4, p. 152.
[13] Quoted in Amory, op. cit., footnote 6, p. 18.

of Natty Bumppo typified this Hudson River romanticism and explains the sensitivity it showed toward increasing numbers. Van Zandt tells us that "in 1870 it was estimated that 'not over two thousand persons' went into the [Catskill] mountains; during the 1880's this figure had risen to sixty or seventy thousand visitors annually," and by 1907 to 300,000.[18] The coming of the railroad signalled the end of the Catskills as a force in American romanticism for nearly a hundred years, in fact until the emotional uprising at the Woodstock Festival in 1969.

A much more placid form of romanticism, perhaps rather a pastoralism, came expectedly from Concord. The discovery of the New England countryside was the outcome of a search for the picturesque. Raw nature seemed depraved to the grandsons of the Puritans, and the combination of an order furnished by man's works, growing out of the elevating struggle for improvement, and the sublimity of nature's wildness was thought to produce the most noble landscapes. Thomas Starr King first sought "to direct attention to the noble landscapes that lie along the routes by which the White Mountains are now approached by tourists" and "to associate with the principal scenes poetic passages" which through imported association served to humanize brute nature.[19] It should not be lost on us that Thoreau's meadows had been mown for nearly two hundred years, and that before he built his sylvan cabin Emerson had bought land at Walden on which to erect a summer cottage.[20] This was a human landscape in which Henry settled near the shack of Irish track layers, on a pond that yielded ice for export to Calcutta, and so located that the winter sunset glinted briefly on the iron rails of the Fitchburg Railroad. Much as Thoreau wandered and observed and wrote about various expressions of an encompassing nature, he did not turn his back on man. Rather he argued for a heightened attention to the complexity that existed in a single spot, an atten-

tion that would be less distracted by social complexity beyond the edge of the city but not impoverished of human association, as it might be in the wilderness. Van Wyck Brooks sums up Thoreau's low regard for the romantic's flight from the human landscape by asking:[21]

> Were not all the essentials of life to be found in Concord, ten times found if one properly valued them? — which a man could only do if he stood his ground. Henry had something to say to the men in the covered wagons, who were running away from something besides the rocks. If the men in the covered wagons had no ears for Henry, he would be glad to wait a few generations. The great-great-grandsons of the covered wagons would be ready to listen to him.

The Shaping of Exurbia

The close of the Civil War left the United States a very different nation from that which surrounded the romantics and pastoralists of the fifties. The economy burgeoned in cities and factory towns and the railroads served to contract space. The prosperity that came from economic takeoff was accompanied by grim costs. Health in cities declined, both from their enlargement and from their attraction of ships and immigrants which brought cholera, yellow fever, and other epidemic diseases. And the chill and heat of factories and shops often taxed health in the slower deterioration of consumption and "nervous disorders." No wonder there seemed to be a persistent craving that affected city dwellers, which made them long for yet another taste of the countryside they had so recently left.

The railroad destroyed the romantic primitivism of the Catskills and other eastern wildlands, but it spread urban-pastoralism widely, in fact so widely that a new settlement form emerged on the northeastern coast of the United States. There, in what Jean Gottmann christened Megalopolis, a strikingly original urban morphology was shaped, not distinctive, as Gottmann would have it, for the alignment of cities, but rather exceptional for the use made of the space between those metropolises.

To understand the meaning of that megalopolitan countryside we may reconsider briefly the meaning of the countryside to earlier generations of Americans. To the

---

[18] Van Zandt, op. cit., footnote 15, p. 223.
[19] Thomas Starr King, *The White Hills: Their Legends, Landscape, and Poetry* (Boston: Crosby and Nichols, 1862), p. vii.
[20] Van Wyck Brooks, *The Flowering of New England* (New York: The Modern Library, n.d.), p. 360.

[21] Brooks, op. cit., footnote 20, p. 369.

colonial the rural frame in which either his trading town or his plantation stood had little but economic interest. Only when the search for health drew him to the Springs did he make a different, and at first timid, use of the country. The romantic movement of the early nineteenth century endowed the area not merely with putative healing qualities but also with grandeur and sublimity, with a mental recruitment to join the physical. In the Catskills and their environs grew the Hudsonian approach to landscape which,[22]

carried the eye over scenes of wild grandeur peculiar to our country, over our ariel [sic] mountaintops with their mighty growth of forest never touched by the axe, along the banks of streams never deformed by culture, and into the depth of skies bright with the hues of our own climate.

When the merchant's culture began to spread along rail lines toward the wilderness and his numbers caused human voices to ring through the forest, at least in summer, the obsession with the primitive and primeval that drew men up the Hudson in times past now turned their course westward.

But for the Concordian approach to landscape the course was indeed different. With man an accepted factor in the rural frame, the Concordian was not dismayed by the increase of access and numbers that came to the countryside in the latter half of the last century. For those with this view pastoralism was the fit state and, particularly in New England, it was man's "highest use." Henry James noted this fact of New England land when he held,[23]

It is perhaps absurd to have to hasten to add that doing what you would with it, in these irresponsible senses, simply left out of account, for the country in general, the proved, the notorious fact that nothing useful, nothing profitable, nothing directly economic, *could* be done at all.

The failure of New England to prosper, in any long-term manner, from the production of rural commodities, if you will its signal inability to shape a living central-place system,

meant that there the urge toward urban-pastoralism could become dominant.[24]

The appeal was thus not only from the rude absence of the company [of active farmers] that had gone, and the still ruder presence of the company left, the scattered families, of poor spirit and loose habits, who had feared the risk of change; it was to a listening ear, directly—that of the "summer people," to whom, in general, one soon began to figure so much of the country, in New England, as looking for its future; . . . for this vision of the relation so established, the disinherited, the impracticable land throwing itself, as for a finer argument, on the non-rural, the intensely urban class, and the class in question throwing itself upon the land for reasons of its own.

Still there were those who could find little to commend in the countryside surrounding the cities of Megalopolis. James himself faulted the structureless landscape, as he thought it, and[25]

went on counting up all the blessings we [in Europe] had, too unthankfully, elsewhere owed to [that remnant of feudalism, the squire]; we lost ourselves in the intensity of the truth that to compare a simplified social order with a social order in which feudalism had once struck deep was the right way to measure the penetration of feudalism.

And "in the New Hampshire hills" the "absence made such a hole." What bothered the European-minded most was the absence of order, "What the squire and the parson do, between them, for appearances . . . in scenes . . . subject to their sway." Today we might be more straightforward in our analysis and say that what the urban pastoralist seemed to want was the countryside without the rustics, or at least to have those natives in a subservient position. James's call for feudalism was the call for a picturesque environment, socially trained, defined by a non-economic occupation structure, and bucolic but not brutish. Such a rural environment was not in existence at the turn of the century in America, save in the recently slave-holding South, which was too distant from the centers of wealth and activity to be of much use. Instead, men in Megalopolis envisaged and produced a new settlement form, that home of urban pastoralism that in the last decade has come to be called exurbia.

---

[22] Louis L. Noble, *The Course of Empire, Voyage of Life and Other Pictures by Thomas Cole, N.A.*, quoted in Howard Mumford Jones, *O Strange New Land* (New York: The Viking Press, 1964), p. 361.

[23] Henry James, "New England: An Autumn Impression," *North American Review*, Vol. 180 (1905), p. 496; also reissued in *The American Scene*.

[24] James, op. cit., footnote 23, p. 497.

[25] James, op. cit., footnote 23, p. 499.

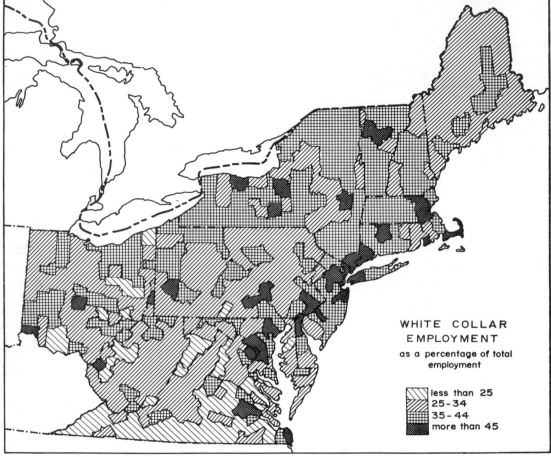

WHITE COLLAR
EMPLOYMENT
as a percentage of total
employment

less than 25
25 - 34
35 - 44
more than 45

FIGURE 1

What then is exurbia?

As it developed the large cities in the Northeast came, with the advent of cars, to dominate the seemingly rural land 'round about themselves. The automobile was a necessary element because it allowed an urban middle class to turn its collective back on city life without having to become a serious day-in and day-out farmer. To live in the country before the car meant either commanding enough money to have a farm run for you, or else doing the job yourself. Being reduced to plodding dusty roads was not what the tired bourgeoisie had in mind for a pastoral existence. In the middle of the last century the wealthy had turned to the rural penumbra of the city, and such areas as Westchester County outside New York, The North Shore adjacent to Boston, and The Peninsula

south of San Francisco grew up as rural housing areas for rich city people. At first, as Gertrude Atherton tells us about San Francisco, the rich families maintained a city house and a country cottage, but as time progressed the precedence turned about and the country villa became the family hearth whereas in town there might be little more than a suite at a fashionable hotel. San Francisco's famous and massively ostentatious Palace Hotel came to house the town life of such economic titans, while their wives, children, and numerous neo-feudal retainers lived on the country estate. Because those estates could provide a painless form of bucolic existence for the very rich, they came into being before the car. The middle-income people had, however, to wait.

With the use of automobiles the fields could

become mainly decorative, the stable a part of the human accommodation, and pastoral life a seeming pleasure to the middle class. Unlike the titans, they had more regular hours in the city center, and they became commuters, but commuters of a very particular sort, as Spectorsky perceived nearly a generation ago.[26]

> So, let us, right now, give this group [of commuters] and its milieus a name. The name of the subspecies, then is Exurbanite; its habitat, the Exurbs. The exurb is generally further from New York than the suburb on the same railway line. Its houses are more widely spaced and generally more expensive. The town center tends to quaintness and class, rather than modernity and glass, and the further one lives from the [exurban] station the better.

As Spectorsky conceived the exurbanite, he was tied to a job in the communications trade in New York City, but we may borrow his terms and refine them a bit for use in a discussion of the morphology of the urban countryside. The critical point of his argument is that some families reside at such a distance from the city that the working father has a very long distance to commute each day, a distance so great, in fact, that it seems the place of residence is in a region not normally thought within the city's extended limits. In the environs of large Northeastern cities this may mean a daily journey to work of one to two hours even with reasonably efficient and fast transportation. Such a radial journey from the city encloses a very large total area, and only a part of it could or would fall within this commuting exurbia. In the interstices between those prongs of the city-life there would be a variant form, of periodic exurbia, where people lived who must get to town only periodically, and for whom a still greater journey would be acceptable. In this class would fall writers, painters, and others in increasing numbers who work largely "at home" and need only reasonable periodic ties with the central cities.

Under such a system all of rural Megalopolis can be included in a periodic exurbia whose attitudes and designs have shaped a very distinctive rural landscape, an urban pastoralism, which has given Megalopolis its unique quality. Unlike the environs of most European cities, the Northeastern countryside had no pre-urban social structure that survived intact and no "forms" that dominated the landscape. Henry James thought urban migrants, "so far as they should be capable or worthy of it, by contact with the consoling background, so full of charming [rural] secrets, and the forces thus conjoined for the production and the imposition of forms," would shape a rural life rich in forms and possessed of physical beauty.[27] In the three-quarters of a century since he observed rural Megalopolis that transformation has begun and been considerably accomplished. In fact that most seemingly urbane and form-conscious of American periodicals, The New Yorker, may begin with the talk of New York City, but it stands in truth as the voice of exurbia. When it recently reprinted with vast approval sections of Charles Reich's fantasy-filled The Greening of America, The New Yorker revealed its departure from the realism of city life into the xenophilic detachment of exurbia. It held up for approval the contrived forms of a new leisure class residing in exurbia or arcadia. Reich's utopia owes far more to the imagined persecutions enjoyed in the Berkeley coffee houses than the yearnings of the poor and brutalized blacks of New York City.[28]

CALIFORNIA AND THE GEOGRAPHY OF THE IDEAL

By the time that most of the countryside of Megalopolis could be encompassed in a periodic exurbia, or else in parks visited by masses in the summer, the search for the beneficent landscape had to look elsewhere. In the early nineteenth century aspirations for utopia, for restored health, for other contributions of the physical environment to life-style could be entertained in the East, as the Shaker villages, the various springs, and the emerging summer resorts show us. But the railroad began a foreclosure which the automobile completed, leaving the East beyond the limits of a "geography of the ideal." It is the purpose of the remainder of this paper to analyze the

---

[26] A. C. Spectorsky, The Exurbanites (Philadelphia: J. P. Lippincott Co., 1955), p. 4.

[27] James, op. cit., footnote 23, p. 501.

[28] Charles Reich, The Greening of America (New York: Random House, 1970; paperback Bantam, 1971). On the general worth of this book and its adequacy as a picture of America's and man's future, see the pleasantly rational review by Henry Fairlie, "The Practice of Puffers," in Encounter, August, 1971, pp. 3–13.

notion of the geography of the ideal and to apply that concept in a search for understanding of the settlement of California.

It might be argued that most fundamentally the historical geography of North America is a study of the forces that cause men to move, starting with the transatlantic migration itself and carrying on through the wanderings over the continent the migrants reached. Little question remains in our minds as to the economic forces that induced these migrations, and the most central social forces have been studied. We have traditionally thought in terms of the search for freedom and liberty and the pull toward economic opportunity. These attractions, however, do not completely duplicate all of the allurements of another objective, the search for the image of the good life, not the second best or the compromise, but the ideal in the mind of the searcher.

It seems that the reactions to the New World by literary European visitors and migrants in the last century were cast in molds of congratulation or castigation mainly based on the comparison of the observer's notion of the ideal with the reality of America. Snobs such as Basil Hall and Mrs. Trollope, and later Henry James, could never forgive America the jarring inconsistencies that grow out of the honest effort toward democracy, whereas the more humble or exalted could be more indulgent, probably because manners did not greatly concern them. The contrast lay in the notion of the "ideal" each group held. If distinctively American culture was rejected by James, or later by Charles Reich and his disciples, then the realm of the ideal lay as far from the native as geography and custom allowed.

The concept of the ideal is deliberately relative because in that way we reach a level of generalization amenable to recording various expressions of a single process, in this case residential shift. For some men, perhaps most of us, the ideal of a good life is an ordered existence wherein we derive satisfaction from constructive employment and participation in an extended and complex social grouping, what Reich calls "meritocracy" or "consciousness II." Yet for others, perhaps a majority of the proponents of radical ecology and existentialism, the ideal is the contraction of human associations to a small biologically-involved community and the concentration of attention upon the interests and standards of individuals, the shaping of a "consciousness III." This contrast in ideals goes far toward explaining the location of residence that meets the image of the good life.

The concept of ideal is related to regional and national cultures, and migrations can be induced or retarded by the degree to which the regional or national culture approaches satisfaction for the individual or group. The exodus from New England in the nineteenth century was not totally an economic phenomenon; considerable numbers left because they were tired of traditional life and puritanism (Reich's "consciousness I"). In the same way, many Americans at the end of World War II were tired of traditional small-city American living, and chose urban California as the probable habitat of a New Life. Today, however, the have-it-both-ways thought of the new "consciousness," with its cry of "repressive tolerance" (Herbert Marcuse), leads seekers of the ideal into the countryside of California, a logical objective for proponents of asocial thought and total self-concern. Fully in the tradition of American loners and social dissenters, the self-styled "freaks" have turned to rural life and, uplifting the vague "nervous disorders" of the last century to the central component of health, that of the mind, have become a new valetudinarian generation seeking escape into arcadia. Again, the image is the pull.

Early Migration to California

Internal migration, which has always been more a norm in America than elsewhere, has fed upon images. The first of these, historically and in weight, was the image of better land or more congenial agriculture in the land beyond. That mental conception emptied the New England countryside in the process of populating the Middle West, and subsequently drew the latter region's rentier and retired groups onward to California. Because so much of the accomplished work of American historical geography centers on the images and migrations of agriculturalists, that subject will be disregarded for the most part here.

Instead the main emphasis will fall on the images of urban people and the migrations they construct to seek the satisfaction of the ideal. Already we have seen the limited ideal of urban-pastoralism and its role in making exurbia. What now remains is to look at the more vivid image creation that helped to shape California.

We could plausibly argue that the beginning of California, and its pubescence, were both creations of idealization rather than organic life. The name California was coined to represent, in 1510, an imaginary island "to the right of the Indies, very near the quarter of the terrestrial paradise" which, oddly for such paradisiacal environs, was ruled by black amazons.[29] The image of the favored land continued with the Gold Rush of 1849, which drew the first large group of Europeans to California, yet the successors to the traders of a generation earlier, the Boston men, collected the real wealth. Hyperbole and etherealization continued California's history, even in the hands of H. H. Bancroft, who first made history-writing a manufacturing process. He called the state "a winterless earth's end perpetually refreshed by ocean, a land surpassed neither by the island grotto of Calypso, the Elysian fields of Homer, nor the island Valley of Avalon seen by King Arthur in his dying thought."[30] Remarkably Henry James found California,[31]

> ever so amiably strong: which came from the art with which she makes the stoutnesses . . . of natural beauty stand you in temporary stead of the leannesses of everything else (everything that might be of an order equally interesting). This she is . . . able to do thanks to her belonging so completely to the 'handsome' side of the continent, of which she is the finest expression. The aspect of natural objects, up and down the Pacific coast, is as 'aristocratic' as the comprehensive American condition permits anything to be: it indeed appears to the ingenious mind to represent an instinct on the part of nature, a sort of shuddering bristling need, to brace herself in advance against the assault of a society so much less marked with distinction than herself.

---

[29] Entry for history of California in *Encyclopaedia Britannica*, Eleventh Edition, 1910.
[30] Quoted in Franklin Walker, *A Literary History of Southern California* (Berkeley: University of California Press, 1950), p. 2.
[31] Henry James, *The American Scene* (London: Chapman and Hall, Ltd., 1907), p. 412.

Once the Gold Rush was over, which it was almost completely by the mid-fifties, California found herself overdeveloped and undersupported. Her population had grown from twenty-seventh of twenty-nine states in 1850 to twenty-sixth of thirty-four in 1860, and the Golden State had outdistanced the rapid expansion typical of the West, increasing her part of the area's population from fifty-one percent in 1850 to sixty-one percent a decade later. Such considerable population growth took place rather in an economic vacuum. The decline in prospecting for gold left the state dissatisfied with a return to her former "cow country" support, but without a real substitute. The discovery of silver in the Comstock Lode of Nevada reinvigorated San Francisco in 1859, and another bonanza was found temporarily in the raising of wheat on the virgin lands of the Central Valley. Irrigation agriculture had not yet been developed in a fully commercial fashion. In 1871 the average irrigation project watered only ten acres, and there were no more than ninety thousand acres under the ditch in the entire state. Hittell as late as 1879 could state authoritatively "California is [only] now about to enter the era of irrigation."[32]

At this time of rather indefinite support for an emptied bonanza the American search for the beneficent landscape turned to California. The romantic movement and the lust for improvement, both of which gripped the United States in the last century, caused men to turn away from the no-longer arcadian East and toward an area where distance and a strange nature held hope for a rediscovery of the ideal. The push might come from those disenchanted with the East, but the Californians put in hard work to make their home seem the place to realize most of the images that beckoned men to make long journeys. California became the core area of the geography of the ideal precisely because there men were led to expect the "transcendent entity that is a real pattern of which existing things are imperfect representations." And as Agatha Christie has told us "So the author has produced the ideas, and the characters [of a

---

[32] John S. Hittell, *The Resources of California*, seventh edition (San Francisco: A. L. Bancroft & Co.), pp. 268–69.

you what?

transcendent entity]—but now comes the third necessity—the setting. The first two come from inside sources, but the third is outside—it must be there—waiting—in existence already. You don't invent that—it's there —it's real."[33] Real, that is, in the acromegalic way that California is real.

The truth is that, with the decline of the Gold Rush, California needed some other economic base, yet none was ready to hand. The Comstock boom of the early sixties helped, as did the short-lived wheat bonanza, but neither provided a continuing support nor one useful in all parts of the state. Gold and silver and wheat all favored the Bay Area, leaving southern California a backwater. The Los Angeles merchants plumped for a mining boom in the Panamints, but even there the shortest road ultimately led to San Francisco. Partly in desperation, those hapless traders began trying to make manifest the images that were an unexpectedly real part of nineteenth century American social thinking, and to localize them in California. Northern California at first disdained the effort, and never fully recognized the try, perhaps in the hope that the land north of the Tehachapis would be looked upon outside as the legitimate continuation of the East, distinguished only by an enlarged Nature. It is ironical indeed that as things now stand the heartland of the image has moved poleward, leaving Los Angeles more national in its mien than the Bay Area city.

The Health Seekers

Colonial Americans looked upon a trip to the Springs as a way of improving health, but their day-to-day trials were somewhat less than those that beset settlers in the Mississippi Valley, where miasmas and fevers were rife. In 1850 Dr. Daniel Drake, "the most important medical figure of his age in America," called for "Journeys of Health on the Great Plains," which he viewed as reaching to the Pacific.[34] In the same year he published his monumental *Diseases of the Interior Valley of North America*, which remains the primary

medical geography of aboriginal North America. Drake, in its preparation, traveled over the settled part of the continent from the villages of the Seminoles to the northern frontiers of Canada.[35] He called for travel for therapeutic purposes that abounded in the exactions of the simple frontier life. "Take them away," he held, "and the journey over the desert to the Rocky Mountains [and California] would be scarcely more efficacious than the fashionable voyage to Europe."[36]

Soon Drake's call was amplified by the establishment of what was termed "medical climatology," an effort to relate the cure or remission of disease to conditions of climate. In the 1860s his prescription of therapeutic travel was widely adopted, but the best geographical objective was in doubt. Specifically the question arose with respect to pulmonary and rheumatic diseases, and the contestants for favor were the high dry areas of Colorado and New Mexico, the low desert of Arizona, and southern California. Perhaps the most influential book ever to consider California, Charles Nordhoff's *California*, published in 1873, placed health first in its subtitle, ahead of pleasure and residence.[37] This *vade mecum* not only encouraged interest in the Golden State, but dealt with it in a reasonably balanced fashion, so the emphasis is significant.

In 1867 the cattle ranching industry in the southern part of the state was toppled by drought and then floods, which bankrupt most of the ranchers. These disasters, for the first time, cracked the aristocratic social and economic organization, "brought about the subdivision of many of the large ranchos into farms and homesteads, and led to concerted efforts to stimulate immigration and attract settlers."[38] All the conditions existed for the re-

[33] Agatha Christie, *Passenger to Frankfurt, An Extravaganza* (New York: Dodd, Mead & Co., 1970), p. vi.

[34] Billy M. Jones, *Health-Seekers in the Southwest, 1817–1900* (Norman: University of Oklahoma Press, 1967), pp. 39–40.

[35] For an extensive discussion of the preparation and significance of this medical geography, see Emmet Field Horine, M.D., "Daniel Drake and His Medical Classic," *Journal of the Kentucky State Medical Association*, Vol. L (1952), pp. 68–79, and "Early Medicine in Kentucky and the Mississippi Valley: A Tribute to Daniel Drake, M.D.," in *Journal of the History of Medicine*, Volume III (1948), pp. 263–78.

[36] Quoted in Jones, op. cit., footnote 34, p. 42.

[37] Charles Nordhoff, *California: For Health, Pleasure, and Residence, A Book for Travellers and Settlers* (New York: Harper & Brothers, 1873).

[38] Robert Glass Cleland, *The Cattle on a Thousand Hills*, second edition (San Marino, California: The Huntington Library, 1951), p. 212.

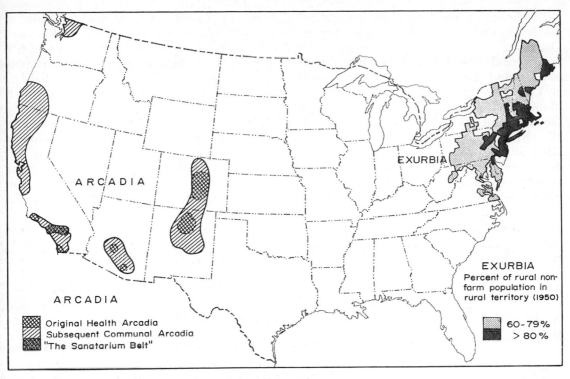

EXURBIA

EXURBIA
Percent of rural non-
farm population in
rural territory (1950)

60-79%
> 80%

ARCADIA

ARCADIA
Original Health Arcadia
Subsequent Communal Arcadia
"The Sanatarium Belt"

FIGURE 2

ception of settlers, but they did not come. The truth emerged that California was too distant and too unknown and, despite the local efforts at a boom, "there was little in Southern California in the way of tangible assets, to justify this boom. The agricultural resources of the region were virtually untapped and undeveloped. Little irrigation was practiced and suitable methods of soil cultivation had yet to be evolved."[39] A straightforward economic pull could not suffice; what was needed was the spatially independent attraction of the geographical image.

The image, which was at least partially fabricated, was that of California as the land of restorative climate. Good health was widespread in the state, not least because the median age of population was so very young, and there was little doubt that the most environmentally-responsive diseases were benefited by the dry, warm climate, even if they might respond better still to the medical cli

matology of Colorado or New Mexico. Nordhoff touted the healthful climate at exactly the right moment. As John E. Baur analyzed the southern California health rush of the seventies, "this increasingly large migration for health could not have occurred at any earlier date. ... Before this period, the American standard of living had not been high enough for such a mass movement of invalids across the continent . . . ."[40] Thus, in Los Angeles "probably there were still only a few score of health seekers in town by 1869," but within a decade of the opening of the transcontinental railroad the southern California center became the metropolis of a sanatarium belt.[41] Stretching from Riverside and San Bernardino in the east along the southern fans of the San Gabriel Mountains as far west as Pasadena and Los Angeles, this belt had notable valetudinarian towns at Pasadena— "for Pasadena's founders asthma chose the spot"—Sierra Madre, Monrovia, and Pomona.

[39] Carey McWilliams, *Southern California Country, An Island on the Land* (New York: Duell, Sloan & Pearce, 1946), p. 114.

[40] John E. Baur, *Health Seekers of Southern California, 1870–1900* (San Marino, California: The Huntington Library, 1959), p. 44.
[41] Baur, op. cit., footnote 40, p. 33.

The image of health was also a major economic support in Santa Barbara and San Diego, in each of which an important hotel was erected—the Arlington at Santa Barbara in 1876 and the still-standing Del Coronado at Coronado in 1888. These, like the Del Monte Hotel opened at Monterey in 1880 and the Raymond completed at Pasadena in 1886, allowed the more prosperous invalids to visit California for the winter but without the rigor that Daniel Drake a generation before thought essential to a cure. At least for a time primitivism receded into the memory. Also these hotels encouraged relatives and friends of the sickly to undertake a western winter tour in comfort. This generally affluent and educated group of health seekers, and their friends and relatives, proved of great economic value even though they had originally been induced to wander by ideals, not profit. The Great Boom of the Eighties collapsed strikingly in 1888 and[42]

> although the speculators may have fled, most health seekers, who had not been foremost in producing the illogical boom, remained in the region. While tens of thousands of speculators and climate seekers left Los Angeles, the center, brain, and purse of the land boom, the health migration continued into the next decade.

The practice of medical climatology was encouraged by the founding of the American Climatological Association in Washington in 1884 for "the study of climatology and the diseases of the respiratory organs."[43] The wide dissemination of climatological data may have been aimed at consumptives, but it could not fail to catch the attention of others, healthy in body but desirous of a New Life in a natural setting important for its difference from the American norm.

The morphological expression of health seeking was rather complex and class-stratified. The sanatarium belt and its outliers in Santa Barbara and San Diego housed the seasonal or permanent visitors of independent income, creating for the first time a substantial middle class in the formerly nearly feudal "cow country." The poorer invalids tended to cluster in the cities, giving support to very modest boarding houses and hotels, and creating what

today we would call a welfare problem, or at least an occupation problem. It has been argued that Los Angeles's non-union tradition grows at least in part out of the oversupply of skilled workers who came there in the late nineteenth century in search of health.[44] Certainly the health seekers filled the ranks of a white-collar class, which set Los Angeles apart from most other cities, giving it a slightly straight-laced quality despite its patent eccentricities. And finally the geography of the ideal of health opened up a wide spread of mineral springs, then used only periodically, but ultimately forming the base for a California exurbia in the Napa and Sonoma and Santa Clara valleys, at Palm Springs, and in the country around Monterey.

The image of health in California has not disappeared, but advances in medicine have changed it. Climate is seldom today treated as a cure, and the interest in the Golden State comes more from the life-style it induces than from outright therapy. Psychology and nutrition have taken the place of simple medicine. The Battle Creek methods of food reform and outdoor living took hold in southern California before 1910, notably in the Seventh Day Adventist settlements at the east end of the sanatarium belt, at Loma Linda. A similar center of such activity, again backed by the Adventists, came into being at St. Helena and Angwin in the shadow of Mt. St. Helena, where Robert Louis Stevenson had sought health in 1880. What remains of the health rush is mainly that hardy California perennial the back-to-nature movement, and the exaggeration of food reform into "health-food fadism."

The Search for an Agricultural Arcadia

It is an axiom of American social thinking, which is only now under question, that the rural life is the natural state of man, and thereby an ideal to seek in any general improvement of his lot. The Homestead Act of 1862 lent the support of national policy to this agriculturalism, seeking to allay unrest among eastern industrial workers by offering them free land. But homesteading could never become a universal panacea, given the physical and psychological attributes of a number of

---

[42] Baur, op. cit., footnote 40, p. 46.
[43] Jones, op. cit., footnote 34, p. 133.

[44] Baur, op. cit., footnote 40, pp. 49–51.

the potential agriculturalists. For many California rather than Kansas furnished the image, a fact that has become increasingly true even for those who first struggled with Kansas. When the collapse of the cattle economy opened the feudal holdings to division among the humble settlers, it was possible for boomers to portray many parts of California as a rural arcadia where ten acres, or even a single acre, in a fine social environment could support a family in good democratic comfort, if not aristocratic luxury. To provide this ideal rural environment free of the loneliness of the isolated farmstead, the crushing toil of the Great Plains pioneer's plot, and the withering worry of rain-farming in the marginal areas that were often the site of Homestead lands, the irrigation colonies of California seemed providential. And serving well as a device to introduce urban men to rural life, the colonies were very appropriate to the needs of settlers in the Golden State of the 1880s.

Probably the first agricultural colony was at Anaheim on the southern side of the Los Angeles Basin where, in 1857, a group of settlers from the German artisan community of San Francisco bought land and laid out a cooperative agricultural community, which came ultimately to be divided into twenty acre plots.[45] In this smallholding tenure the Germans were similar to the Mormons who had settled in San Bernardino in 1851, only to be called back to Salt Lake City in the year the Anaheim settlement was founded. A Tennessee group, the Southern California Colony Association, began the similar development of the Riverside site in 1870, and there three years later came the beginnings of the California seedless-orange industry, which proved the sturdiest support of colony settlement, and one that appealed in a romantic fashion as much to the dirt farmers of Kansas as the potential smallholders of Chicago. The expected return from a few acres of orange trees was thought adequate to support a family. Great numbers of ten acre smallholdings were laid out on the alluvial fans, supplied with irrigation water, and sold perhaps most often to city men gripped with the image of life in a California agricultural arcadia. Because so many knew little of farming, yet much of the glorious future, there was a great tendency to seek reassurance of its attainment by banding together with other believers.

It seems that California's distance beyond the settlement frontier had always encouraged this banding together of travelers. The tourists of the 1870s had customarily traveled in organized groups, in what Charles Fletcher Loomis called a "Reasoned Migration" that contrasted sharply with the Forty-niner's "Sheer Adventure," and the colony settlers of the eighties continued communal pioneering.[46] When the tourists came as winter and then year-round residents they set up in towns of like-mindedness, to the point that parts of the Basin "out-Easted the East," thereby creating an exaggeration of Boston's gentility and making of Harrison Gray Otis's *Los Angeles Times* the great fossil of nineteenth century thought it remained until quite recently. In part this group settlement effort was assured by the social class of the early settlers. This was a Pullman-car migration, causing it in Loomis's words to be "the least heroic migration in history, but the most judicious; the least impulsive but the most reasonable." The tourists had come in parties in the late seventies and early eighties, ridden in Pullmans, put up in good hotels, and been intrigued. Seeking a new ideal, they became aware of the horticultural experiments at Riverside, and, as McWilliams said of the contrast between argonauts of '49 and '86, "Gold lured the one group; oranges and climate the other."[47] The prosperous tourist became the agricultural settler when oranges provided romance in the fields, but he was not in the least seeking the rude equality of the frontier. His success in attaining something else was observed by Robert E. Park, who found in southern California a population which "lives in more or less complete cultural independence of the world about them."[48] The original social and morphological organization may have come from the needs of irrigation agriculture but, as Winston Churchill knew, "we shape our dwellings and afterwards

[45] W. Lindley and J. P. Widney, *California of the South: Its Physical Geography, Climate, Resources, Routes of Travel, and Health-Resorts* (New York: D. Appleton and Co.), pp. 173–76.

[46] Quoted in McWilliams, op. cit., footnote 39, p. 150.
[47] McWilliams, op. cit., footnote 39, p. 150.
[48] McWilliams, op. cit., footnote 39, p. 314.

our dwellings shape us." The small, rural-seeming community became the ideal, and ultimately it shaped the strangely parochial social thought of California, which caused the state to lead the nation in the formation of utopias during its American period.

Before looking at those utopias it is well to recall the peculiar quality of California migration, which McWilliams does succinctly:[49]

> Generally speaking, the first wave of American migration to the region [of southern California] was made up of the well-to-do (1870–90), the second of people in medium circumstances (1900–1920), the third of lower middle-class elements (1920–1930), and the fourth of working-class people (1930–1945). Reversing the process of western settlement, each successive wave of migrants to Southern California has been made up, in the main, of people less important economically and socially than the one which preceeded it. And the basic explanation of this curious reversal of the pattern of migration is that people have always been attracted to Southern California for other reasons than to better their economic position.

Since these words were written, in 1946, southern Califorina has largely lost its image as the land of the ideal, and subsequent migration thence has come to reflect a more normative pull, that of money, whereas the geography of the more illusive image has shifted successively poleward, first to the Bay Area (1945–1960), then to rural northern California (1960–1970), and, it seems now, northward to Oregon, Washington, and British Columbia (1970–   ). This pull of the ideal has been felt most directly and continuously by men both well provided for and living in an urban state. Perhaps the peculiar quality of the California migration was its origin in the nation's cities for two generations before the countrymen started to move.

Colony formation of a much more specialized form came in the utopias, which blossomed all over California during most of the last one hundred years, though most importantly in the periods of upper- and then middle-income in-migration. It is difficult to separate the normally cooperative agricultural colonies, with their social cohesion and economic attitudes, from the more self-consciously utopian communities. Each sought an ideal existence and each tended to base it on rural residence. The basically agricultural colonies did not deliberately seek geographical isolation, merely social immurement. Each might be parochial, but none sought to be a direct accusation of imperfection of the existing social geography. The utopias, on the other hand, were often dogmatically detached, frequently uneconomically located to the point of being quixotic.[50] "From 1850 to 1950 California witnessed the formation of a larger number of utopian colonies than any other state in the Union," with some seventeen groups in contrast to the three each in the nearest competitors—New York, Wisconsin, and Washington.[51] Eleven of California's communities were secular, confirming the idealistic as opposed to religious quality of the movement. There is no accurate estimate of less-than-utopian colonies established in California, though they certainly numbered several score. Each of these communities had a rather specific search for an ideal normally expressed in strongly environmental terms. Before 1850 there were numerous utopian settlements—Shaker, Fourierist, Owenite, and other—in the eastern United States, more in New York or Massachusetts than in the country as a whole since 1850. After 1850 the focus shifted heavily to California, and utopianism declined notably elsewhere. Such communities were not made impossible outside California by the growth of population elsewhere; the Shaker villages, for example, from the beginning were integrated into a fairly dense general rural settlement. Rather it seems that the realm of social experimentation had become somewhat conterminous with that of romantic primitivism, and thereby domesticated in California.

More than chance tied primitivism and utopianism; they were united by the notion of the ideal, which cannot avoid being a relative concept. Men might be rejecting the pastoralism and "development" of the East, or they might be turning away from the characteristics of American society, yet the geographical effect would be the same, to turn their steps to the West. Early utopians

---

[49] McWilliams, op. cit., footnote 39, pp. 150–51.

[50] Robert V. Hine, *California Utopian Communities* (New Haven: Yale University Press, 1966).
[51] Hine, op. cit., footnote 50, pp. 6–7.

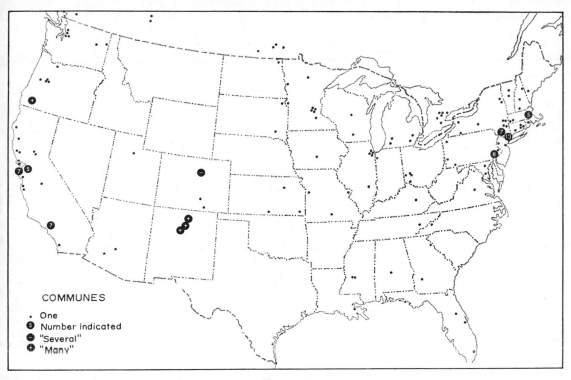

FIGURE 3

managed to live as neighbors of their contemporary pragmatic world, whose residents Howells named "egotists," but latter day communitarians and improvers found isolation, or at least rural living, essential.[52] Hine tells us, "many a man joined a colony with the idea of exchanging city life for an escape into the country. The propaganda pamphlets for Altruria [and other utopian communities] . . . persistently painted the beauties and healthfulness of their rural environs."[53] They followed Howells' model exactly, as his Altruria was pastoral and the *Traveller from Altruria*,

Mr. Homos, found great pleasure in helping in the haying at the White Mountain hotel where he first described his utopian homeland to Americans.

Both the romantic primitivists and the utopians refused to accept standard American life, and their turn to California represented moving on to a new natural and social setting where a New Life could be attempted. We find in this turn westward a strong parallel with Frederick Jackson Turner's observations. Although there should be no attempt to deny the material attractions of California, it would be foolish indeed to think that Horatio Alger was the symbol of most Golden State migrants. They were not all romantics and utopians, but they were not as uncomfortable in such company as Eastern residents had been. Over the years fleeing from American life has probably become more important for the members of the incoming group, at least in northern California, where an autonomous enclave distinct from normative American culture seems to have inspired much that has happened since 1945.

[52] William Dean Howells, *The Altrurian Romances* (Bloomington: Indiana University Press, for the Howells Edition Center, 1968). Howells contrasts his vision of a new utopia, Altruria, and the conduct of its citizens, as witnessed by the traveler, Mr. Homos, with that of the American hosts, whom he terms "egotists." Anti-utopianism seems to have gained a vastly firmer hold in the present period of self-discovery through "consciousness III." The only Altrurian community was established in Sonoma County, California, where a group of Berkeley Unitarians sought to substitute altruism for egotism. Their experiment was short-lived.

[53] Hine, op. cit., footnote 50, p. 168.

TABLE 1.—STATES IN ORDER OF NUMBER OF IN-MIGRANTS, BY DECADE, 1870–1960

Thousands of in-migrants			
Total		Native white	
1870 to 1879			
Kansas	366.8	Kansas	290.1
Texas	308.5	Texas	233.9
Nebraska	204.4	Nebraska	139.2
Michigan	161.4	Colorado	86.7
Minnesota	156.2	California	56.0
Massachusetts	140.2	Arkansas	53.0
California	129.6	Dakota Ter.	43.5
Colorado	119.1	Minnesota	38.2
Dakota Ter.	86.8	Michigan	25.8
Iowa	65.1	Oregon	25.7
1880 to 1889			
New York	395.4	Nebraska	244.3
Nebraska	362.5	Washington	133.2
Massachusetts	295.7	Dakota Ter.	126.0
Pennsylvania	285.1	California	109.6
Minnesota	264.1	Kansas	106.3
Dakota Ter.	243.4	Colorado	101.1
California	214.2	Texas	90.9
Washington	205.4	Oregon	57.4
Michigan	172.3	Montana	39.8
Illinois	170.3	Oklahoma	39.6
1890 to 1899			
New York	604.8	Oklahoma	404.3
Oklahoma	501.3	California	96.3
Illinois	340.0	Texas	95.5
Massachusetts	334.9	Washington	54.0
Pennsylvania	262.0	Massachusetts	46.9
New Jersey	218.3	New Jersey	46.3
California	172.7	Illinois	44.0
Minnesota	148.4	Montana	37.1
Texas	147.7	Colorado	33.1
Connecticut	90.8	Idaho	31.0
1900 to 1909			
New York	1,061.0	California	425.2
California	694.1	Oklahoma	414.2
Oklahoma	491.5	Washington	311.4
Washington	464.7	Oregon	132.0
Pennsylvania	444.6	Colorado	108.8
New Jersey	376.1	Idaho	81.9
Massachusetts	307.3	North Dakota	81.8
Illinois	223.0	New Jersey	71.4
Ohio	207.7	Texas	60.5
Oregon	189.9	South Dakota	59.6
1910 to 1919			
California	804.1	California	537.7
Ohio	499.4	Ohio	233.4
New York	467.4	Michigan	181.5
Michigan	465.2	Florida	84.5
New Jersey	278.2	Montana	75.4
Illinois	255.6	New Jersey	72.0
Massachusetts	192.2	D. C.	69.3
Connecticut	122.1	Oklahoma	54.5
Texas	114.2	Washington	51.9
Florida	101.6	Arizona	39.9

TABLE 1.—CONTINUED

Thousands of in-migrants			
Total		Native white	
1920 to 1929			
California	1,695.2	California	1,244.5
New York	1,062.1	Michigan	239.9
Michigan	549.6	Florida	221.1
New Jersey	442.3	Texas	197.5
Illinois	414.0	New Jersey	179.3
Florida	297.6	New York	138.1
Ohio	214.7	Illinois	80.3
Oregon	96.5	Oregon	74.3
Washington	81.6	Ohio	58.1
Connecticut	64.1	Washington	42.2
1930 to 1939			
California	974.6	California	899.5
New York	396.3	Florida	208.4
Florida	280.3	New York	140.3
D. C.	157.8	D. C.	101.2
Washington	109.2	Washington	100.3
Oregon	94.1	Oregon	90.4
Maryland	87.0	Maryland	72.2
Connecticut	39.2	Virginia	33.7
Minnesota	36.0	Connecticut	30.2
Idaho	20.5	Minnesota	27.1
1940 to 1949			
California	2,399.1	California	1,874.7
Florida	510.9	Florida	438.4
Washington	351.3	Washington	303.9
Michigan	251.4	Oregon	222.9
Oregon	244.0	Virginia	169.1
Maryland	213.3	Maryland	167.6
New Jersey	200.7	Texas	134.4
Virginia	152.0	Arizona	97.6
Ohio	151.6	New Jersey	88.6
Texas	132.9	Michigan	51.7
1950 to 1959			
California	3,145.0	California	2,791.0
Florida	1,617.0	Florida	1,516.0
New Jersey	577.0	New Jersey	465.0
Ohio	409.0	Arizona	340.0
Arizona	330.0	Maryland	284.0
Maryland	320.0	Ohio	276.0
Connecticut	234.0	Connecticut	195.0
New York	215.0	Colorado	149.0
Colorado	164.0	Texas	141.0
Michigan	157.0	Virginia	84.0

Migrants to Arcadia

The basic argument of this paper, that California was settled in large measure by those searching for the desirable life-style and seeking the heartland of the geography of the ideal, is difficult to prove other than through literature, social comment, and the propaganda of boomers. Some rough evidence, however, is provided by census data on net in-migration (Table 1). The state of California took the lead in net native white in-migration only in the first decade of this century, and in net total in-migration only in the second, suggesting that the more prosperous natives first formulated a life-style image that might be fulfilled in California, and the total population began to be caught up in the image only during the decade of World War I. As McWilliams observed, California met a nativist and a middle-class ideal for fifty years. In the first decade (1870–1880) the nation's native white population was still most gripped by the appeal of available farmlands, maybe even in California, but the total population with its immigrant component was more attracted by the industrial states. In the eighties industrial attraction continued strongest for the population as a whole, and land the main pull on the native whites, with only the role of California seeming to stand in doubt. This was the decade of the first great boom in southern California, and most of the net in-migration was to that area. If health and small-holding were the greatest attractions there, then perhaps we can first perceive the working of the image of the better life-style. Colorado was then the tough rival of California for the health trade, and it stands high in appeal among the in-migrant states for native whites.

The traditional migration attractions—the free farmlands and the industrial cities of the East and Middle West—should be joined by a third, the search for life-style. Showing up first in the appeal of California for native whites as early as the seventies, *genre de vie* seems to have lifted Colorado to a high place in the next three decades, and Florida into the running for native whites as early as World War I. By 1910 the search for farmland dropped way behind as an inducement for migration and industrial and urban migration formed the main adjunct of image seeking. By the time of World War II the search for life-style dominated movement to the arcadian existence of California, Florida, Arizona, and Colorado and to the exurban existence of New Jersey, Connecticut, Maryland, and Virginia. Geographers should give increasing attention to these New Life Morphologies.

California and the New Life

In a sense the Golden State was never part of the American norm; its history, though scanty, was Latin and Catholic in a fundamentally Anglo-Saxon and Protestant country. The state's adherence to the national union itself was unique, depending upon the acceptance by the national government of a *fait accompli*, California's election of senators before it was created a state. And certainly its long-term reliance on images to induce settlement and support has been unmatched. Thus, to talk about a New Life as a support for California could be deceptive; there may never have been anything else. "Here is our Mediterranean! Here is our Italy! It is a Mediterranean without marshes and without malaria. . . . It is a Mediterranean with a more equable climate, warmer winters and cooler summers."[54]

There may never have been an old life; it would be hard to find a place with a less organic history. The popular conception of California's past is considerably fiction, glorifying the Franciscan missions, which practiced slavery among the local Indians, and making the distinctly parvenu Mexican ranchers Castilian, cultured, and kind-hearted toward the Indians, none of which was even vaguely true. McWilliams blames this legendary history on a Boston tea party where Helen Hunt Jackson met two Ponca Indians and took up the romanticized cause of improving the lot of the southern Californian Indians.[55] In 1884 she published an attack on American policies in an idealization of the past, the novel *Ramona*. She, and most of California's converts during the last ninety years, have blamed the Yankees for destroying what they imagine to have been a grand adjustment of the Mexican settler to nature and native population. If Amherst's Helen Hunt Jackson in *Ramona* tars the Americans, Boston's Richard Henry Dana lent balance, as well as considerably more authentic observation, when he visited California in 1835 and

[54] Charles Dudley Warner, *Our Italy. The Complete Writings of Charles Dudley Warner* (Hartford: The American Publishing Company, 1904) Vol. IX, pp. 269–71.

[55] McWilliams, op. cit., footnote 39, Chapter IV, "The Growth of a Legend."

found "that hated coast" was only "half-civilized" and the Mexicans "a people on whom the curse had fallen, and stripped them of everything but their pride, their manners, and their voices" leaving them "idle, thriftless people."[56] But the migrant to California was principally drawn by Mrs. Jackson's romance, not Dana's puritan critique, and the guilty "gringo" has long been a component of California's social geography. His role as the local villain joins the giantism of the Golden State's Nature in encouraging the idea of successfully moving away from the American values through migration to California.

The early rush to California was a phenomenon of prosperity easily dampened by economic recession, as in 1873 and again in the nineties. But the growth of the image of California as the exception also changed migration in times of economic stress. In the depression of the 1930s the trek from the South Central States to California actually increased, based on the romantic notion that the exceptional state would be protected from economic down-cycles. Perhaps no stronger proof could be presented of the popular notion of California the charmed exception to the American norm.

The years since 1945 have witnessed the greatest of all California booms. The state's population has trebled in three decades. As an industrial "power" California probably ranks after Britain, and as a social hearth perhaps ahead of it. For good or ill, much of the shape of the postwar world has come from the culture which California has fostered and launched, far more successfully in the last decade than it ever did during the shining hours of Hollywood glamour in the 1930s. This assault of the California culture on the rest of the world has not been accepted quietly; the B.B.C. was calm but disapproving when it told the world that California contains the disquieting features of 1984, or perhaps even the year 2000, and European intelligentsia find justification for a haughty anti-Americanism in the state's cultural exports. The paradox of haughtiness is complete when cultural innovators within California bend their efforts to making the local culture as

distinct from the rest of the country as possible. The current actions differ little from those of the past, when Californians endlessly enlarged their crotchets to gain distinction from the American norm. Economic questioning of the supposedly American capitalist formula that so grips the radical establishment is neither new nor very thoughtful when expressed in the bombast and bombs of the Students for a Democratic Society. The Golden State nurtured Henry George and his single tax a century ago, and in the 1930s witnessed the campaign of Democratic gubernatorial candidate Upton Sinclair with EPIC [End Poverty in California] and that archetypal welfare state of Dr. Townsend and "Ham and Eggs." Similarly California has over the years been disproportionately fond of expatriation and xenophilia. Bret Harte, Isadora Duncan, and Gertrude Stein may exemplify the former and the emotional attachment of Helen Jackson and William Randolph Hearst to papist, feudal, and aristocratic ideas the latter.

California as Foreign Country

The most consistent migration pull exercised by the Golden State throughout its history within the Union has been its externality, socially as well as physically, which has allowed California to seem foreign to the American type and tradition, if that was the newcomer's wish. Charles Dudley Warner called the state "Our Italy," the Okies had it an economic Eden, most other Americans still think it a bit of a never-never land, and those whose adolescent rigidity and impatience are angered by socially essential accommodation think California the home of a saving radicalism and "a new consciousness." For all, however, California does stand out for its departure from the American norm. Geographers have tended to over-analyze Iowa, for its assumed representativeness; alongside it we should place California, for its role as the standard of detachment. We should examine its recent history and social geography in seeking to discover not the economically-oriented normative geography, for which Iowa serves well, but rather the cultural dynamics which will foretell the social geography that may well await us all in the near

---

[56] Quotations from Walker, op. cit., footnote 30, pp. 22–32.

future. For many persons change is a doctrine, and there is value in trying to discern its probable face.

Tolerance of social peculiarity has long been a measure of the Golden State's departure from the norm, with anomalous groups more common in the south and eccentric individuals in the north. Robert Louis Stevenson, in reference to "Emperor" Norton, asked about San Francisco, "in what other city would a harmless madman who supposed himself emperor of the two Americas have been fostered and encouraged? Where else would even the people of the streets have respected the poor soul's illusions?" Perhaps as unexpected was the 1968 decision of a most proper bank to issue checkblanks with pictures on them, and having done so to have made Emperor Norton one of those first portrayed.[57]

Stevenson was merely one of the earlier Europeans to say of San Francisco, "it is the only city which interests me in the whole United States. . . . California to me is a grand combination of natural beauties," thus juxtaposing the city acceptable to the foreigner, often a critic of things American, with the wonderous nature of California.[58] Henry James followed the pattern two decades later, and over the years quite a literature has condemned America by exaltation of its least typical city and landscape. Pretty consistently the criticism has revealed the critics as being uncomfortable in a mass culture and calling for the leadership of a traditional hierarchy of status, wealth, or today, "consciousness." This élite has frequently expressed its dissatisfaction with the necessary vastness of housing areas in the fairly egalitarian society of American suburbs, and with the absence of an ordered [feudal] countryside. In San Francisco it found a city of so complex a mixture of cultures—Chinese who came to the mines, Frenchmen fleeing the collapse of the Revolution of 1848, Chileans, Kanakas, and convicts from Australia—that it was not believably American, and therefore open to high regard

without conferring approval on the nation itself. And in the California landscape these social critics found a Nature in which feudalism seemed neither necessary nor relevant. Both the European visiting the United States and the native coming from the East could agree that this was the home of xenogenesis, of cosmopolitanism.

Before World War II this land outside the American norm might aspire to leadership but little did it enjoy it, seemingly because of its placement in a backwater. The War brought the West Coast, and the Bay Area in particular, into the realm of central interest. Many men passed through on the way to the Pacific and the founding of the United Nations in the San Francisco Opera House in 1945 may well have symbolized the integration of California into the heartland of ideas and actions more than an accommodation among nations.

In a more national frame the increasing influence of the Bay Area on American life seems strongly related to the intellectual force that has brought about a mass exodus from central cities in the East to the enclosing suburbia, and from suburbia to exurbia. We are witnessing the birth of a new complex urbanism in which the specialized social districts have begun to replace a synoptic pattern (of land rent) in shaping the morphology of settlement. In such a context normative geography is not so enlightening as dynamic geography and, in a fascinating cultural-geographical isostasy, the Bay Area, California, and the West Coast have risen in their impact on American settlement structure as New York and Megalopolis have sunk.

These specialized social districts are both more cultural in origin and more separation-seeking than our location theory for residence has previously envisioned. The fundamental residential location theory of Homer Hoyt has argued that the urge to associate with higher economic groups motivates the choice of housing, and that general peripheral movement of city people is triggered largely by a family's increasing affluence. Yet today detachment is a more discernible force than attraction, and migration toward the edge of the city is largely unrelated to income. Spectorsky may furnish the key when he calls

[57] Robert Louis Stevenson with Lloyd Osborne, *The Wreaker* (New York: Charles Scribner's Sons, 1906), p. 132. The bank is Wells Fargo, which originated the picture check.

[58] Anne Roller Issler, *Happier for His Presence, San Francisco and Robert Louis Stevenson* (Stanford: Stanford University Press, 1949), pp. 69–70.

exurbanites "short-haul expatriates;" outward
shift is for separation and for the molding of
a distinctive life-style that makes no bones
about increasingly catering to the psychological demands of individuals.[59] It has become
accepted that "individual rights" of self-actualization may be asserted largely in disregard of
social concerns. This Fourierist concentration
on self rather than society unites the slick
culture of Madison Avenue in the East's exurbia with the youth obsession of "Consciousness III" in California's arcadia. California
has become characterized by "long-haul expatriates," with the emphasis on expatriation,
to the extent that the Golden State is rather
foreign country within the national boundary;
the flocking there, during the postwar years,
of the intellectual and social expatriates is more
readily understood.

When the local literary critic of the Bay
Area, Kenneth Rexroth, was asked to appraise
the region's postwar experience he, not without
significance, saw the time as a "Renaissance
by the Bay" and likened it to the transformation of France since 1945.[60] In each area there
had been a decline of provincialism leading
to an increased, but a somewhat disrupting,
international importance. The generally accepted beginning of the Bay Area renaissance
came with the region's discovery by many
wartime visitors and the spreading of the
knowledge of its sybaritic and cosmopolitan
attractions. Thus, in the years since 1945 San
Francisco has offered an ever-present life-
style alternative to a man's past or the nation's
present, a pull of detachment charged much
more with intellectual than economic force.

The intellectual life of the Bay Area has
been active ever since the 1860s when Bret
Harte, Mark Twain, and lesser lights created
a local literary movement, but in the past it
tended toward transience as the successful
practitioners often sought expatriation in
Europe (Bret Harte and Gertrude Stein were
examples).[61] Only during World War II did
the movement turn inward, with the visits of
conscientious objectors on leave from their

camp at Waldport, Oregon, where the objectors from the "creative arts" had been isolated from other C.O.s because of their more
common radicalism.[62]

> Out of Waldport came a surprising number of the
> leading cultural institutions of post-war San Fran-
> cisco. . . . On leave, the people from the camps
> . . . made contact with a slightly older generation
> which preserved, all during the war and for several
> years thereafter, what was probably the largest
> anarchist circle ever to exist in the United States,
> the Randolph Bourne Council.

The conscientious objectors had widespread
connections, which the Bay Area anarchists
did not, and the wartime conjunction served to
make known northern California as a potential
homeland for outsiders, if such thinkers can
be said to have a homeland.

In 1945 knowledge of the qualities of northern California was widespread both among
the traditionally footloose American youth who
had passed through in uniform and the literary
community awakened by the C.O.s. For the
literary it was a critical time of change; they
were just emerging from the Depression,
with its emphasis upon saving and recon-
structing society, into a postwar state of mind
which came to reject national goals, concern
external to the individual, and the Puritanism
so characteristic of the 1930s in favor of
anational attitudes, expatriation, introversion,
sensuality, "soul," and a mix of sensate experiences in place of social objectives.

For this generation, displaying increasing
attachment to mental images rather than economic attainments, the growth of the Bay
Area literary community was important. In
the fifties the community was small and
closely-knit, a Beat Generation living mostly
in San Francisco's North Beach quarter. But
as the Beats' writings were published, an ever
increasing intellectual migration brought large
numbers of the young, and their older followers, to the Bay Area. Jack Kerouac served
as the symbol, as well as the most fertile
imagination of the movement, for "he was
the first articulate member of a postwar breed,
the Beat Transcontinental American . . . Ab-
sorbing the life for his work by scattering
around the country . . . . And Transcontinental though Kerouac was, the West Coast, and

[59] Spectorsky, op. cit., footnote 26, p. 6.
[60] Kenneth Rexroth, "Renaissance by the Bay,"
Saturday Review, September 23, 1967. p. 35.
[61] Franklin Walker, *San Francisco's Literary Frontier* (New York: Alfred A. Knopf, 1939).

[62] Rexroth, op. cit., footnote 60, p. 36.

the Frisco [sic] area in particular, were to prove culturally more ready for him than the East."[63] Kerouac unified surprising numbers of underground Americans and set them migrating to the Bay Area. These followers, the "Beatniks," began by 1960 to make a visible impression on the Bay Area to match that made the decade before by the grey flannel suits of the more traditional in-migrating young people. The Beatniks sought the lifestyle of the Beats, even if their creative faculties were far more modest. What they proposed was after a fashion new-Fourierism, and like the classic form, social and moral conflict with society at large was engendered to such a degree that they also had to seek a place of sequestration from a unsympathetic society. The Beat philosophy initially favored city life, and their followers the Beatniks sought a special social district within the city where they might operate their sensual and non-rational lives. Such a "turf" was hacked out of the Haight Asbury district of San Francisco and occupied until it became befouled by crime in the late 1960s. Then the group shifted across the Bay to Berkeley's South Side, where a new turf and a transformed life-style were formed. The earlier rather simple drug-culture took on a politically radical persuasion and an eroticism that would have totally scandalized the activists of the New Deal years.

But this is preface to the more central concern of geography, the physical expression of social thinking on the California landscape. In the state an arcadia was shaped which joined the other components of a very complex urbanism—the core city, suburbia, commuting exurbia, and its more periodic exurban realm. Arcadia inherits from the long history of American social geography: concern for images, the search for utopianism and primitivism, and the sheltering in an hygienic countryside. In the last case modern urban escapists maintain the sort of fears that affected Adna Weber in 1899, when he questioned the biological survival of man in the

city.[64] Such fear led the Edwardians to depart for the suburbs whereas today's fearful, the mental valetudinarians, seek to hide in the deeper countryside of arcadia.

We may draw many insights from the Beat Generation as the original lectors of the cult of wandering. "There is in all of them an innate fidget . . . the last thing they know how to do is sit still."[65] Sensualism requires sensate progression and "environmentalism" seems to require a voracious devouring of unspoiled landscapes. The fidget merely expands the geographical impact of culture change, leaving the active agents, rather than inert "ideas," to do the moving. At first the new consciousness and "soul" required residence in an ethnic quarter, as such areas were thought unspoiled by the materialist and mass culture of America. But soon Jane Jacobs and the Beat found that you don't have to speak English to hold traditional American ideas, and the wandering began again.

When Jack Kerouac spent a summer as a firewatcher in the Cascades east of Bellingham, Washington, he wrote a curious pastoral about this "rucksack revolution," of "going up to the hills to meditate and ignore society." In the end, however, he cried, "Enough, enough of rocks and trees and yalloping y-birds. I wanta go where there's lamps and telephones and rumpled couches with women on them, where there's rich thick rugs for toes, where the drama rages all unthinking . . . ."[66] As late as the 1950s the piper's call was to the panting reality of the city slum, and there remained compassion for the urban poor. Seeking to share in their "honesty," the hip community occupied an enclave, a turf, within the city's minority housing until the Beatniks became so introverted as to destroy any organic ties to normal urban groupings. Introversion reached the point that detachment was almost complete, all they could share was their unquestioned youth. With this came the geographical shift out of the ghetto, at least

---

[63] From the introduction by Seymour Krim to Kerouac's *Desolation Angels* (New York: Coward-McCann, Inc., 1965), pp. xvi–xvii.

[64] Adna Ferrin Weber, *The Growth of Cities in the Nineteenth Century* (Ithaca: Cornell University Press, 1962; original edition by Columbia University Press, 1899). Note particularly Weber's extolling the virtues of suburbs, pp. 458–59.

[65] John Ciardi, *Saturday Review*, February 6, 1960.

[66] Kerouac, op. cit., footnote 63, pp. 62–63.

into the student quarters of Berkeley, Madison, or Toronto, or more fundamentally into social adolescence in Big Sur and other rural areas of escape from social responsibility. Although the minds of the wanderers may not consciously have sought the detachment and unreality of an endlessly youthful community, the hedonism that was their objective could hardly be found anywhere else. Suburbs were overrun with what Charles Reich has castigated as "meritocracy." The outcome has been the establishment of a new leisure and age class, with its specialized social districts as distinct as the economically established "country club" districts of the past. The main distinction comes in the probable term of occupancy. Economic-class districts provide housing so long as the money lasts or increases, but in the specialized "district of youth" time cannot help but create a group of misfits because the aging of individuals cannot be arrested.

In this way the seekers of self-actualization, drawn mainly from the youth of the white middle class, ultimately took up the California countryside and there shaped small units of community based on age and life-style. The Big Sur country was followed by the Mendocino Coast, the Coast Ranges of the state's northwest, the foothills of the Sierra, and other areas of pleasant climate and scenery, until, by 1971, much of the more attractive country of the West Coast had been occupied by those practicing a new consciousness, individual and hedonistic.

For the black and other ethnic groups physical detachment from the city was never so practicable. Instead the youth of minority groups had to attempt to shape areas of detachment within the city where they might stand less socially exposed and economically imperilled. The Black Panther Party was formed in Oakland in 1966, to be followed soon after by the Spanish language *La Raza* movement. Separatism and autonomy, rather than integration, was the objective of these groups, and the means of accomplishment foreseen was that of force and fairly naked exercise of power. The specialized social district of a particular sort, the extra-legal clan area with vendettas and other trappings of medieval Italian urban life, has been attempted. The

relentless attack of the Black Panthers on the police and the resulting police surveillance reminds us of Genoa at its worst. In 1970 the Panthers joined with groupings of drug users and political radicals in Berkeley to try for a dismemberment of the city's police force into what they termed "community control" areas. These would have institutionalized distinctive life-styles, even those clearly illegal at present and would have confirmed by city-charter amendment the concept of social detachment. The initiative petition was lost and the Panthers shifted to extortionate picketing to force black merchants in west Oakland to make money contributions, on a weekly basis, to the Party for its own unaccounted use. This effort succeeded in early 1972, so one of the prime requisites of a functional political corporation, the "right to tax," has been given to the Panther Party, creating a clan area without legislative authorization. Given this climate in the urban East Bay, it is not surprising that the politically radical, even anarchistic, monumentally misnamed group, Students for a Democratic Society, has taken up residence in an urban commune, the "Red Family," on Berkeley's South Side.

Consideration of urban communes may seem anomalous in a study of arcadia, but in truth such social districts are nurtured by the same dynamic that produces arcadia itself, the group's detachment from geographically extensive society in favor of the localized intentional community. However, in the city the absence of open space encourages the clustering of a number of communes as a defense for their distinctive life-style. It has been argued that "what Wall Street in Manhattan is to the world of finance, Parker Street in Berkeley is to the world of urban communes," with a concentration of some hundreds of intentional communities.[67] The specific siting of such a special social district appears to result from the transformation of an area formerly given over to small student apartments and rooming houses. Such a shift requires a very free interpretation of zoning ordinances and laws relating to morality, and often an indulgence in the enforcement of

---

[67] *Berkeley Gazette*, August 30, 1971. The paper's investigation suggests that there may be as many as eight hundred communes in Berkeley.

drug laws. Cities have tended to look upon such communal areas in much the way they once viewed brothels; these institutions were difficult to suppress, and they were tolerated, but as public nuisances they were restricted to a special district of the city jointly occupied by the like-minded. Such clustering does not come only from a real suppression. The communalists themselves seem to desire a turf where there is a reduction of conflict with the mass of society and where their numbers give power.

The search for power by residents of the communal turf of Berkeley was evident in the effort to shape "community control" of police and to gain a clan district. Its failure seems to have discouraged the more radical elements, or at least turned them to other areas. The communalists have become more interested in arcadia. The increasing numbers of more highly political black college students now on the scene have shaken the geographical thinking of the Panthers, encouraging Huey Newton, their chief strategist, to suggest a removal of party headquarters from Oakland to Atlanta. Such a move would be in keeping with the apparently increasing interest of "activists" of the new life-styles in seeking a concrete expression of geographical detachment best found in the countryside. For the Panthers this may well appear as a campaign for an autonomous "Republic of New Africa" at some indeterminate spot in the American South.

In the countryside the commune has taken on a strong back-to-nature quality which is to a remarkable degree a reproduction, telescoped in time, of the search for images that has drawn men to California for over a century. The romantic confrontation of nature, the search for utopia, the quest for health, both physical and mental, and the turning away from the American norm all emerge in the descriptions of individual and communal objectives.[68] The result is a definite geographical pattern of detachment. Although Jack

Kerouac had "enough" of the "rucksack revolution" east of Bellingham, that Washington city has currently become a central place in the geography of the ideal of detachment. The reasons would not exactly pair it with the Iowa examples:[69]

Why do people come to Whatcom and Skagit Counties? In addition to the desire to shun the plastic life of the cities for the natural life-style of the country, many say they came because they had heard that Bellingham had a cool dope scene— few busts and good relations with the local cops—a minimal amount of urban-type problems, easy-to-obtain food stamps, and a laid-back but sophisticated cultural scene. But, above all, for the geography: what it is and what it stands for. Northwest Washington is open space and tall trees and rugged mountains and clear rivers and (though it rains almost continuously from November to February) relatively easy winters—in short, all the benefits of physical and psychological 'elbow room' and untrammeled beauty at the same time.

Little question exists that arcadia shares most of the fears and forces that shape suburbia, but suburbia was tarred with "togetherness" in the 1950s and must therefore be shunned by those seeking a new image.

The pattern of American social geography has, over the years, reflected a great range of images reaching in time from Plymouth to the present. The search for the ideal has been historically consistent but geographically shifting, showing a progressive transformation of the morphology of settlement. During the last one hundred years California has served in many ways as the ideal, mainly as an arcadia detached from the American norm. In this role it has shared, with exurbia in the East, the function of furnishing "a city in nature." It is easy today to fear that this peaceful role will be abandoned in Charles Reich's "Coming American Revolution," but hope may return when Manuel reminds us that,[70]

If contemporary Fourierists evoke new states of consciousness (Charles Reich's Consciousness III is the most recent serial number), their derivative quality is patent, and they lack the freshness of new discovery. Why hearken to the gospels of the

---

[68] It is hard to secure comparative data on communes but the peripatetic journal *The Modern Utopian*, first published in Medford, Massachusetts, then in Berkeley, and, at the moment, in Sebastopol, California, gives a directory of sorts, which has been used in preparing the map of "intentional communities."

[69] Bernard Weiner, "Laid Back to the Earth in Bellingham," *Clear Creek*, August, 1971, pp. 12–14.
[70] Frank Manuel, *Design for Utopia: Selected Writings of Charles Fourier* (New York: Schocken Books, 1971), p. 8.

two Reichs, Marcuse, or Norman Brown when the grandest Pied Piper of them all, Fourier, has stood before us for a century and three-quarters?

Somehow the blueprint of a revolution that has lain revealed for 175 years does not frighten so readily as does a more recent fabrication, and its morphological impact should be tolerable. Despite the wild talk of the current emigrants to arcadia, we may still hope that society will survive when those wanderers come to realize that their objectives call neither for an unknown life-style nor a true revolution in a nation that has consistently shown the elasticity of real social compromise and accommodation. Arcadia has long been part of the American geographical norm, even in its isolation from the social norm, furnishing a pattern that allows a tradition of social diversity. The locale of arcadia has had to shift but its fundamental role has persisted, remaining, for at least a time-span equal to that of Fourierist "solutions," an important force in shaping American urban settlement. In more recent decades California has stood the anchor, if not the total range, of arcadian settlement.

American urban fabric has been made up of three basic elements, all rooted firmly in our history. The most central, the heart of the metropolis, continues to be a reception area for rural and foreign in-migrants to the city, who today are heavily non-Caucasian. The reception area "culture" has become black or Spanish-American, in sharp contrast to the more homogenous "culture" of the suburbs.

A contrast between core and suburb is traditional. Without historical perspective, it appears that the present division is racially engendered, but accession to the nativist urban culture has always led adherents outward. Departure itself should not be condemned, even if social confinement of the nonwhite population and restriction of financial responsibility for its well-being to the central city should be soundly castigated. The second element of the urban fabric, the suburb, has been both most internally and temporally consistent and most geographically extensive, forming a wide ring surrounding the core and its more diverse social districts. Beyond the edge of the suburbs lies the realm of urban pastoralists and primitivists—exurbia and arcadia—that forms the subject of this essay. It is as integral a part of American urbanism as the core and suburbia. The size of the prosperous and relatively leisured population of the United States is such that exurbia and arcadia have become the site of a number of exterior special social districts of a purpose similar to those that make up the core of the city. Only by perceiving the morphology of these three "cities" and their history is it possible to understand America in 1972, and perhaps cities in the whole developed world in years to come. Having in the past set the model of the city-in-a-garden, may we not now have set in motion the shaping of the city-in-the-countryside, perhaps to spread over as wide a geographical sweep?

THE COLORADO PLATEAU

ROBERT DURRENBERGER

ABSTRACT. The Colorado Plateau was one of the last areas in the United States to be developed economically. Before the 1880s it was virtually empty except for Indians. Today the vast scenic and energy resources of the area are under development, and projections for future development are frightening. Problems of land use management are directly related to the fragmented nature of landholdings. Present methods of consolidation are inadequate, and new approaches to the organization of space must be devised if further degradation of the environment is to be prevented. KEY WORDS: *Colorado Plateau, Colorado River, Energy, Indians, Land use, Settlement, Southwestern United States.*

IN the United States increasing affluence, growing population, and dependence on advanced technology have placed new and increased demands on our resource base. The attempts of decision-makers to satisfy new and increased demands for water, energy, lumber, and land for open space and for recreation are confronted by vocal advocates of preservation. Perhaps no other part of the nation has greater pressures for change than the Colorado Plateau country of Utah, Colorado, New Mexico, and Arizona, and perhaps nowhere else is there more interest in preserving the natural landscape.

It was only little over a century ago that this area was the home of primitive Indian groups living in mud and stone villages or leading a nomadic life based on herding or hunting and gathering. On maps of the 1860s much of the territory was shown as unknown and unexplored, and much of it had not been seen by a white man. This was one of the areas which George Perkins Marsh had in mind in 1864 when he said:[1]

> There is still, an immense extent of North American soil where the industry and folly of man have as yet produced little appreciable change. Here too, with the present increased facilities for scientific observation, the future effects, direct and contingent, of man's labors, can be measured, and such precautions taken in these rural processes we call improvements, as to mitigate evils, perhaps, in some degree, inseparable from every attempt to control the action of natural laws.

As if in answer to Marsh's suggestions, government survey teams took to the field to gather data needed to comprehend the nature of the territory newly acquired from Mexico. The federal geographical and geological surveys of the 1860s and 1870s grew out of the need to know more about the lands and peoples of these areas.[2] Three of the surveys were concerned with portions of the Colorado Plateau, and voluminous reports provided decision-makers of that time with sufficient information to develop sound resource-management policies. One of the survey leaders, John Wesley Powell, spent the next thirty years in and out of the halls of Congress attempting to convince the government that new approaches were needed in the management of the arid lands of the West. Most of his recommendations were ignored; the public domain was surveyed and disposed of in traditional units and traditional ways except for minor modifications which permitted disposal in units up to 640 acres in size.[3]

Federal and state agencies have recently completed comprehensive inventories of the land and water resources of this nation, and we stand on the threshold of a new era when sophisticated data-gathering techniques will permit constant monitoring of environmental

Dr. Durrenberger is Professor of Geography at Arizona State University in Tempe.

[1] G. P. Marsh, *Man and Nature* (Cambridge: Harvard University Press, 1965), p. 52.

[2] These surveys are discussed at length in R. A. Bartlett, *Great Surveys of the American West* (Norman: University of Oklahoma Press, 1962).

[3] M. C. Rabbitt, "John Wesley Powell: Pioneer Statesman of Federal Science," in *The Colorado River Region and John Wesley Powell*, Geological Survey Professional Paper 669 (Washington: Government Printing Office 1969), p. 16.

change.[4] We now have abundant information on which to develop rational plans for the utilization of our land and its resources. However, alternative courses of action are not clearly understood, and decisions have already been made which will have long-term effects on future development. Moreover, debate over the National Land Use Act has indicated the lack of any sense of urgency in utilizing this information.[5]

Meanwhile, pressure to develop land and water resources on the Colorado Plateau has led to confrontations between conservationists and developers, and long-range plans for the utilization of the area are needed. The resolution of these controversies requires a better understanding of problems of local and regional development than we now possess. In this paper I will examine some of the factors responsible for current dilemmas, and suggest a course of action which could be pursued.

PHYSICAL FEATURES

The Colorado Plateau is not a homogeneous surface, nor has it had a simple geologic history.[6] The Plateau covers over 150,000

square miles in northern Arizona, southeastern Utah, southwestern Colorado, and northwestern New Mexico. Most of the area is drained by the Colorado River. The Plateau contains over one-half of the total drainage basin of the river (Fig. 1).

The "Plateau Province" is a great crustal block. To the west and southwest it breaks off in escarpments that overlook the more diversified and broken country of the Basin and Range Province. The northern and eastern edges are bounded by the ranges of the Rocky Mountains. This is a land of plateaus, canyons, and escarpments, with volcanic forms in certain sections. The sedimentary rock layers have been gently warped by a series of broad uplifts with intervening basins. Wide areas of nearly horizontal beds may be separated by abrupt folds or monoclinal bends.

The Datil Section on the southeastern side of the Plateau is deeply covered with volcanic material. The eastern edge of this section is not clearly marked, for it is bounded by other volcanic forms and the underlying structures are masked by lava. Only in the area east of Mount Taylor do the fault zones associated with the Rio Grande depression form a distinct break between the adjoining areas.

The Grand Canyon Section is similar to the Datil Section but is higher and more easily differentiated from the sections around it.[7] Much of the area is a broad basin sloping upward to the Mogollon Rim on the south and to the Kaibab upwarp and the fault blocks west and north of the Grand Canyon. With the exception of the Colorado River few streams have cut into the surface of the Plateau in this section.

The High Plateau Section reflects topographic control by faulting. Most of the land forms are linear. North-south plateaus ranging from 9,000 to 11,000 feet in elevation are separated by tributaries of the Sevier River which lie in fault zones.

The Uinta Basin Section on the northern edge is structurally the lowest part of the Plateau,

[4] Reports covering the four drainage basins of the American Southwest were prepared by the Pacific Southwest Inter-Agency Committee. All state and federal agencies with interests in land and water resources participated. The pertinent reports for the Colorado River Basin are: *Upper Colorado Region Comprehensive Framework Study* (Salt Lake City: Pacific Southwest Inter-Agency Committee, 1971); *Lower Colorado Region Comprehensive Framework Study* (Boulder City, Nevada: Pacific Southwest Inter-Agency Committee, 1971). The National Land Law Review Commission has completed its studies and published a series of reports. Its recommendations are summarized in *One Third of the Nation's Land* (Washington: Government Printing Office, 1970)

[5] *A Bill to Establish a National Land Use Policy*, undated draft statement from Secretary of the Interior, Rogers C. B. Morton, to Spiro T. Agnew, President of the Senate, and the Honorable Carl B. Albert, Speaker of the House.

[6] Charles B. Hunt, *Cenozoic Geology of the Colorado Plateau*, U. S. Geological Survey, Professional Paper 279 (Washington: Government Printing Office, 1956); N. M. Fenneman, *Physiography of Western United States* (New York: McGraw-Hill, 1931); Chapter VII; C. B. Hunt, *Physiography of the United States* (San Francisco: Freeman, 1967), Chapter 14; and W. D. Thornbury, *Regional Geomorphology of the United States* (New York: Wiley, 1965), Chapter 22.

[7] References to the Grand Canyon may be found in F. P. Farquhar, *The Books of the Grand Canyon: A Descriptive Bibliography* (Los Angeles: Dawson, 1953).

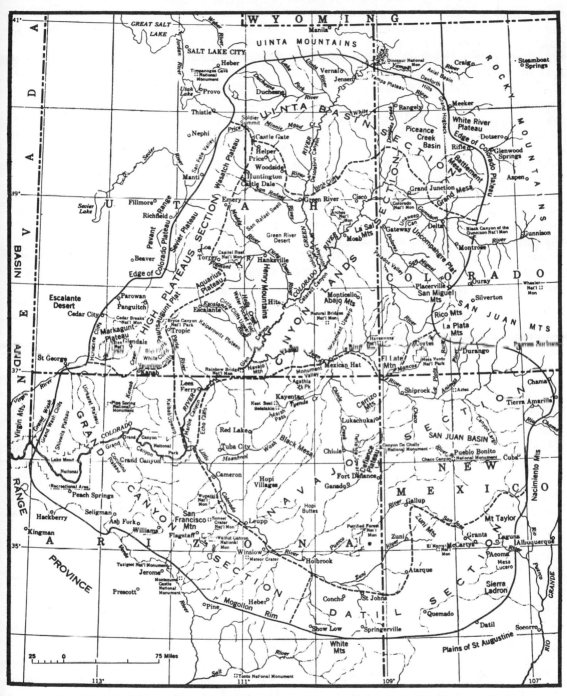

FIG. 1. The Colorado Plateau Region. Source: *Cenozoic Geology of the Colorado Plateau,* op. cit., footnote 6, p. 3.

and has retained a fairly thick portion of Tertiary rocks. The central part lies about 6,000 feet above sea level. Surface elevations increase both to the north and to the south.

On the north, hogbacks lying at the foot of the Uinta Mountains mark the edge of the Plateau. The Book Cliffs overlook the Canyonlands Section to the south.

The Canyonlands Section contains some of the more unusual geologic features and scenic attractions, including the Henry Mountains, formed by giant laccoliths, and the natural bridges, arches, and unusual spires of Monument Valley. This whole section has been upwarped, with several folds. Drainage has been deeply incised and created canyons. Little Tertiary or Quaternary rock material remains.

The Navajo Section is almost as high as the Canyonlands Section, but is much less dissected. It consists mainly of mesas separated by broad open valleys. Black Mesa and San Juan Basin contain many layers of rock of Tertiary age, including valuable coal and uranium deposits. Scattered about the surface are volcanic necks, dikes, and remnants of volcanic cones and lava flows.

Climate and Water

In the summer months relatively long days, nearly vertical noontime solar rays, clear dry air, and high elevation result in extremely large amounts of radiant energy being received at ground level.[8] The greatest amounts of radiant energy at the time of the summer solstice are received in the vicinity of the thirty-seventh parallel, which virtually bisects the Plateau. Summer temperatures even at these elevations are high, and individuals in the sun feel the effects of the intense solar radiation.[9]

Winters are cold. Relatively short days, clear dry air, and high elevations permit rapid

[8] Climatic data were derived from the National Weather Services publications, *Climates of the States* for *Arizona, Colorado, New Mexico,* and *Utah* (Washington: Government Printing Office, various dates); C. R. Green and W. D. Sellers, *Arizona Climate* (Tucson: University of Arizona Press, 1968); and Yi-Fu Tuan, C. E. Everard, and J. G. Widdison, *The Climate of New Mexico* (Santa Fe: State Planning Office, 1969). A good discussion of climate and climatic change on the Plateau is in C. W. Thornthwaite, C. F. S. Sharpe, and E. F. Dosch, *Climate and Accelerated Erosion in the Arid and Semi-Arid Southwest with Special Reference to the Polacca Wash Drainage Basin, Arizona,* Technical Bulletin No. 808 (Washington: U. S. Department of Agriculture, 1942).

[9] I. Bennett, "Climatology of Insolation in the Intermontane Basins and Plateaus of the Western United States," unpublished doctoral dissertation, Boston University, 1962.

loss of terrestrial energy, but persons in the sun around noon feel warm. Shade and night temperatures, however, remain low. At times in the winter a high pressure area may stagnate over the Plateau, and temperatures will drop below normal in the river valleys and basins where most of the people live. Atmospheric pollution can become a problem where there are large emission sources or concentrations of human activity.

The average growing season is only 90 to 180 days, and freezing weather may be experienced in almost any season over much of the Plateau. The dry atmosphere contributes to great radiational exchanges between earth and sky, and great diurnal temperature fluctuations result. The short growing season severely limits the crops that can be produced, and influences the yield of those grown.

Most of the Plateau receives less than fifteen inches of rainfall, and moisture deficiencies are compounded in other ways (Fig. 2). A relatively large portion of the precipitation (particularly in the south) falls from thunderstorms which occur mainly in July and August when rates of evapotranspiration are highest. High-intensity showers produce rapid runoff and little recharge of groundwater basins. In some parts of the Plateau, porous volcanic soils permit the quick percolation of water through the surface zones so that it is not available for plant growth. Thus, most of the usable moisture is derived from winter snow storms. Moisture from the melting snow is released slowly into the subsoil and provides much of the water stored in the reservoirs which dot the southern and western edges of the Plateau.

On the eastern and northern margins the Colorado and its tributaries (the San Juan, Gunnison, and Green) provide water for limited agricultural development, but over much of the Plateau these streams are so deeply entrenched that use of their waters is difficult. The small tributaries present other kinds of difficulties. Many are intermittent, and all have highly variable flows. Most are subject to flood. Drought and flood are constant companions along the streams of the Plateau Country. Dams are wrecked and

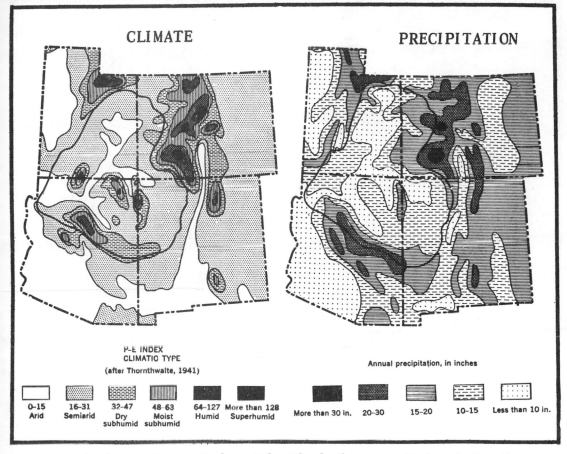

FIG. 2. Source: *Cenozoic Geology of the Colorado Plateau*, op. cit., footnote 6, p. 7.

roads and railroads are frequently washed out by summer flash floods.[10]

Soils and Vegetation

Soils and vegetation reflect the harsh climatic conditions.[11] Northern desert shrub species predominate over much of the Plateau.

---

[10] References to floods and their effects on life in this region may be found in abundance in the daily and weekly newspapers of the Plateau communities. For a discussion of excessive precipitation in the Southwest see Thornthwaite, op. cit., footnote 8, pp. 22–27 and pp. 112–19. Many floods on the Plateau go unnoticed by newspaper editors if there is no loss of life or property damage. Some floods on the Indian reservations have been noted in the annual reports of the Indian agents.

[11] The best overall references are: *The Atlas of American Agriculture* (Washington: U.S. Department of Agriculture, 1936); and the Yearbooks of the Department of Agriculture, *Trees* (Washington: U. S. Department of Agriculture, 1949) and *Soils*

The higher, more mesic areas are wooded; pinyon and juniper on lower slopes give way to spruce, pine, and fir above. Extensive sections of the region in Arizona and New Mexico were originally covered by a luxuriant growth of short grasses which formed the basis for the livestock industry, but the original grassland cover has been appreciably altered by overgrazing and erosion (Fig. 3).

(Washington: U. S. Department of Agriculture, 1938). For maps and a discussion of natural vegetation in each state see the publications of the Intermountain Forest and Range Experiment Station in Ogden, Utah entitled: *Arizona's Forests, New Mexico's Forest Resources, The Forest Resource of Colorado*, and *Forests in Utah*. For detailed descriptions of soils and vegetation see the individual soil surveys; e.g., U. S. Department of Agriculture, Forest Service, and Soil Conservation Service, *Soil Survey of Beaver Creek Area, Arizona* (Washington: Government Printing Office, 1967).

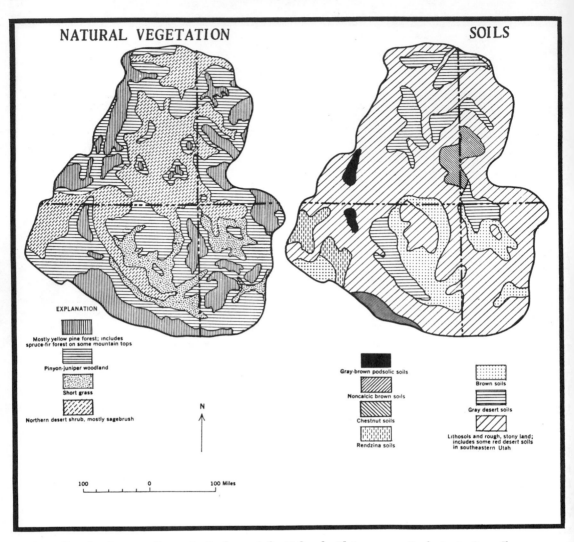

FIG. 3. Source: *Cenozoic Geology of the Colorado Plateau*, op. cit., footnote 6, p. 7.

Recent gray or brown desert soils prevail over much of the Plateau, with small areas of recent alluvial soils along the valleys, and rather extensive lithosols in areas of rapid erosion. In general, the soils below 7,000 to 8,000 feet in the wooded or non-forested zones have a basic reaction; those at higher elevations, acid. An extensive area of chestnut-brown soil along the Colorado-Utah border is derived from Pleistocene loess and alluvium. Over much of the area soils vary appreciably within short distances, depending on the nature of the parent material. Because of the sparse natural vegetation and periodic drought accelerated erosion is a major problem.

EXPLORATION AND SETTLEMENT

Man has been eking out an existence on the Colorado Plateau for a long time.[12] The struggle for survival has been difficult, as can be seen by the many abandoned settlements scattered about the Plateau and Rim country. "Ghost towns," a featured attraction of the region today, represent almost all periods of occupance.

---

[12] Much of the material in this section has been derived from publications of the National Park Service and from J. C. McGregor, *Southwestern Archaeology* (Champaign: University of Illinois Press, 1965)

Indians

Some of the primitive men who crossed over from Asia filtered through the mountains and the basins of the West to occupy small pockets of better-watered land on the Plateau and along its rim. They grew maize and other vegetable crops, and occupied permanent abodes near sources of water. A group known today as the Anasazi (Navajo for "the ancient ones") occupied much of the southern part of the Colorado Plateau and its rim.[13] About 200 B. C. they lived in cave and brush shelters, and subsisted principally by hunting and gathering, augmented by production of maize and squash. About 700 A. D. they began to build twenty-to-thirty room pueblos which had considerable regional variation in size and character; the Chaco Canyon settlements were largest and most spectacular. The development of deep-rooted, drought-resistant maize, squash, and beans enabled them to produce food under extremely difficult conditions. Cotton was introduced, and cloth was produced. Various arts and crafts developed, and a number of tools and implements were manufactured.

Around 1100 A. D. the location and structure of the pueblos began to change markedly.[14] Larger and more compact villages replaced the older ones, and pueblo sites with good farm land were abandoned. There was also a certain amount of movement to shallow cave and cliff dwellings near dependable water sources, such as springs. The total population of the area began to decline as the people migrated southward off the Plateau. By 1300 A. D. most settlements had been abandoned.[15] Precisely why they left their pueblos is not known, but a number of factors probably were involved.[16] Perhaps nomadic predatory groups became more numerous, and their raids

made life unbearable for the sedentary villagers. This period coincides with colder and stormier weather in Europe; late spring and early fall frosts could have so shortened the growing season that crops failed and food stores were consumed. Tree-ring analysis indicates that a great drought between 1276 and 1298 A. D. could have been a contributing factor.[17] Perhaps the Rio Grande valley offered superior amenities to the rather harsh climatic zones of the high plateau. In the last analysis, the decision to move was still a human one.

At the time of Spanish entry into the American Southwest pueblo dwellers were in only four areas, the Acoma, Hopi, and Zuni settlements, and the Pueblo villages of the Rio Grande. The Navajo had taken over much of the Plateau north and east of the Zuni villages. To the south their cousins, the Apache, roamed freely across central and southern Arizona and New Mexico, and the northern provinces of Mexico.[18] To the north the Utes and their various subgroups and relatives, the Shoshone, Paiute, Washo, and Shivwits, occupied the mountain and plateau country of Nevada, Utah, and Colorado.

The Navajo and Apache are fairly recent migrants to the Southwest. They apparently arrived on this continent from Asia about 3,000 years ago, and migrated southward along the Rocky Mountain Front into the Rio Grande drainage basin before moving westward (Fig. 4). Hogan sites of the fifteenth century have been identified in the Dinetaa or old Navajo Country in northwestern New Mexico and southwestern Colorado. Soon after their first contact with the Spanish the Navajo acquired horses and sheep and began to spread westward, but it was well into the nineteenth century before they began to utilize much of the area in which they now live.[19] Both the

[13] Pertinent publications include H. S. Gladwin, A History of the Ancient Southwest (Portland, Maine: Bond Wheelwright Co., 1957); W. H. Haas, "The Cliff Dweller and His Habitat," Annals, Association of American Geographers, Vol. 16 (1926), pp. 167–216; and K. Bryan, "Pre-Columbian Agriculture in the Southwest, as Conditioned by Periods of Alluviation," Annals, Association of American Geographers, Vol. 31 (1941), pp. 219–42.

[14] McGregor, op. cit., footnote 12, pp. 278–320.
[15] McGregor, op. cit., footnote 12, pp. 401–04.
[16] Bryan, op. cit., footnote 13, pp. 237–40; and H. S. Colton, "The Rise and Fall of the Prehistoric

Population of Northern Arizona," Science, Vol. 84 (1936), pp. 337–43.
[17] A. E. Douglass, "Dating Pueblo Bonito and Other Ruins of the Southwest," Pueblo Bonito Series, National Geographic Society, no. 1 (1935), pp. 36–39 and 49.
[18] E. H. Spicer, Cycles of Conquest (Tucson: The University of Arizona Press, 1962), pp. 229–30.
[19] J. Hester, Early Navajo Migrations and Acculturation in the Southwest, Papers in Anthropology, No. 6 (Santa Fe: Museum of New Mexico Press, 1963).

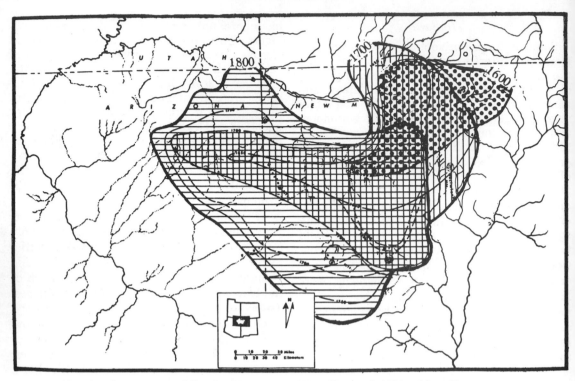

FIG. 4.   Areas occupied by the Navajo in 1600, 1700, and 1800. After Hester, op. cit., footnote 19, figure 25.

Apache and the Navajo had originally lived by hunting and gathering. With the acquisition of sheep the Navajo also became herdsmen. Both groups also acquired food and other forms of material wealth by raiding. At first their forays were against other Indian groups but later the Spanish, Mexicans, and Americans suffered at their hands.

When the Mexican territory was transferred to the United States in 1848 there were probably fewer than 40,000 Indians on the Plateau.[20] Some progress in the pacification of these groups had been made before the Civil War. On November 22, 1846, a group of Navajo signed a treaty of peace with Colonel Doniphan of the Army of the West. Six more treaties were signed in the next fifteen years without producing peace. Individual bands of Indians continued to live by raiding established settlements. It was not until 1864 that about half of the Navajo were captured and

placed on a reservation, and not until 1886 that Geronimo surrendered and was transported to a Florida reservation.[21] The Indians posed greater difficulties than severe environmental conditions for Americans seeking to pass through the area or to settle in it.

The Spanish

Initial European knowledge of the Plateau came from the vague reports of Cabeza de Vaca, who probably never reached it.[22] However, his tales of the Seven Golden Cities soon drew other men. In 1539 Fray de Marcos and the black slave, Esteban, set out on a journey which ended with Esteban dead in the Zuni villages and Fray Marcos scurrying back to the safety of Mexico City.[23] Factual accounts

---

[20] E. E. Dale, The Indians of the Southwest (Norman: The University of Oklahoma Press, 1949), pp. 12–24.

[21] Dale, op. cit., footnote 20, pp. 109–11.
[22] Cabeza de Vaca, "Narrative," in F. W. Hodge and T. H. Lewis, eds., Spanish Explorers in the Southern United States, 1528–1593 (New York: Charles Scribner, 1907), pp. 1–123.
[23] Marcos de Niza, The Journey of Fray Marcos de Niza, translated by Cleve Hallenbeck (Dallas: University Press, 1949).

of the Plateau and its inhabitants did not become available to the outside world until after 1540, and these contained little on the nature of the natural environment, despite the fact that members of Coronado's parties ranged for some time among the Zuni and Hopi villages and penetrated as far as the Grand Canyon.[24] Spanish interests were further titillated in 1582 when a merchant, Espejo, visited the pueblos of the Zuni and Hopi and traveled west across the Plateau to near modern-day Prescott to prospect for silver and gold.[25] From the newly-founded capital of New Mexico additional parties were sent out in 1598 to visit the Pueblo Indians and to search for wealth. They retraced Espejo's path.

Additional expeditions led to the founding of five missions among the Hopi by the Franciscans beginning in 1629. These missions were destroyed in the Pueblo Indian revolts of 1680, and no further attempts were made to establish settlements on the Plateau, although Spanish soldiers and priests visited the area from time to time.[26] Although they added little knowledge and left little evidence of having been there, the Spanish must be credited with courageous efforts to explore and settle in a hostile area.

Early American Interest

Perhaps the first American to reach the Colorado Plateau was James O. Pattie, whose description of "the horrid mountains which cage" the Colorado River "as to deprive all human beings of the ability to descend its banks and make use of its waters" was not calculated to inspire others to follow in his footsteps.[27] For Pattie and others like him, mountain men, the Colorado Plateau must

have been especially unattractive. Beaver could be found only where perennial streams drained its margins. Taos, north of Santa Fe, had become the center of the fur trade in the Southwest after 1820, and trappers ranged throughout the West, many as far as California, from their Taos homes.[28] Most traveled the southern route along the Gila River to Yuma, but a few went over the Plateau along the route found by the Spaniard, Escalante, in 1776. The trade between Santa Fe and Southern California exchanged manufactured goods and slaves for mules and horses.[29] With a decline in animal numbers and changes in styles the fur trade ceased to be profitable, and by the 1840s the mountain men had settled down to lead more prosaic lives. The trade between Los Angeles and Santa Fe continued on an intermittent basis, and an occasional missionary or party of explorers crossed the margins of the Plateau, but few white men penetrated the region.[30]

Road and Railroad Surveys

The migration of Mormons to Utah and the discovery of gold in California brought change. Most of the overland movement was north and south of the Plateau, but an occasional party took off along the Old Spanish Trail to southern California. The greatest activity was generated by official attempts to discover the best routes for wagon roads and railroads.[31]

---

[24] P. de Castenada, "The Narrative of the Expedition of Coronado," in Hodge and Lewis, op. cit., footnote 22, pp. 275–387; Coronado's route is also discussed in C. O. Sauer, "The Road to Cibola," *Ibero–Americana*, Vol. 3 (1932), pp. 1–58.
[25] "The Espejo Expedition, 1582–1583," in H. E. Bolton, *Spanish Exploration in the Southwest, 1542–1706* (New York: Barnes & Noble, 1952).
[26] H. H. Bancroft, *History of Arizona and New Mexico* (San Francisco: The History Co., 1889), pp. 261–62 and 394–96.
[27] J. H. Pattie, *The Personal Narrative of James O. Pattie of Kentucky*, 1831 edition (Philadelphia and New York: Lippincott, 1962), p. 89.

[28] H. M. Chittenden, *The American Fur Trade of the Far West* (New York: Scribners, 1902); and R. G. Cleland, *This Reckless Breed of Men: The Trappers and Fur Traders of the Southwest* (New York: Knopf, 1950).
[29] L. Hafen, *Old Spanish Trail: Santa Fe to Los Angeles* (Glendale, California: The Arthur Clark Company, 1954).
[30] Fremont traversed the northern margins of the Plateau on several of his journeys in the 1840s, but did not contribute greatly to knowledge of the region; E. W. Gilbert, *The Exploration of Western America, 1800–1850* (Cambridge: The University Press, 1933), pp. 177–91.
[31] The publications of these agencies are listed in *Federal Exploration of the American West before 1880*, Publication 64–6 (Washington: U. S. National Archives, 1963); military exploration is discussed in W. H. Goetzmann, *Army Exploration in the American West, 1803–1863* (New Haven: Yale University Press, 1959); and a short summary of the government documents may be found in G. S. Albright, *Official Explorations for Pacific Railroads, 1853–1855* (Berkeley: University of California Press, 1921).

It was recognized that both would have to be built. In general, wagon roads would precede the railroads, although even after the railroads were completed, wagon roads would still be needed.[32]

The earliest army exploration of the Plateau was by officers of the Corps of Topographical Engineers attached to punitive expeditions against the Navajo. Expeditions in 1846, 1849, and 1851 added to knowledge about the Plateau. The 1851 expedition under Captain Lorenzo Sitgreaves made the first reconnaissance survey to determine the best wagon route from Santa Fe west to California. He followed the well-worn route to the Zuni villages, down the Zuni River to the Little Colorado, and thence almost due west to the Colorado River north of Needles.[33] It is paralleled by modern routes across much of the Plateau.

In 1853, Congress authorized four surveys to determine the best route for a railroad to the Pacific.[34] Two additional private surveys were organized by Senator Thomas Benton and St. Louis business interests and led by Fremont and Beale. These surveys did not generate any great enthusiasm for the 38th parallel route across the Colorado Plateau. In fact, the federal survey ended in disaster when its leader, Gunnison, and seven members of his party were killed by Ute Indians in the Sevier River Valley after having crossed the very difficult terrain of western Colorado and eastern Utah.[35]

The southern passage along the 35th parallel met with greater success. Led by Lt. Amiel Whipple it left Fort Smith, Arkansas in July, 1853, for Albuquerque and the familiar route to the Zuni pueblos. In general, his route ran south of that of Sitgreaves and reached the Colorado River near its confluence with the Bill Williams River. Whipple was impressed, and wrote that "in climate, as well as in soil, this country far surpasses that of Kansas."[36] There was a final survey along the 32nd and 35th parallels.[37] The railroad surveys showed that several routes were feasible for the Pacific Railroad, and added immeasurably to knowledge of the West.

The Thirty-fourth Congress had authorized construction of the Pacific Wagon Road.[38] On June 25, 1857, Edward Beale, accompanied by a wagon train and seventy-six camels, left San Antonio, Texas, for Albuquerque to begin the task. Beale and his men completed major sections of his road from the Zuni villages to the Colorado River, but in 1860 funds to complete it were not authorized by Congress. Like Whipple's, his description of the territory was extravagant:[39]

> Without intending to draw invidious comparisons between the various routes from our western border to the Pacific Ocean in favor of that by the 35th parallel, I think I can, with safety, say that none other offers the same facilities for either wagon or railroad.
> It is the shortest, the best timbered, the best grassed, the best watered, and certainly in point of grade, better than any other line between the two oceans with which I am acquainted.

National considerations emanating from the Civil War made political factors dominant, and the Pacific Railroad was built along the forty-first parallel, bypassing the Colorado Plateau and thus delaying its development.

The Mormon Settlements

The Mormons had established their base at the foot of the Wasatch in 1847, and shortly

---

[32] W. T. Jackson, Wagon Roads West: A Study of Federal Road Surveys and Construction in the Trans-Mississippi West, 1846–1869 (Berkeley: University of California Press, 1952), pp. 319–328.

[33] U. S. Congress, Senate, Report of an Expedition Down the Zuni and Colorado Rivers, 32nd Cong., 2nd sess., 1853, Exec. Doc. 59.

[34] For accounts of these surveys see U. S. Secretary of War, Pacific Railroad Reports, (Washington: Government Printing Office, 1855–1861); E. F. Beale and G. F. Heap, A Central Route to the Pacific . . . (Philadelphia: 1852); and S. N. Carvalho, Incidents of Travel and Adventure in the Far West with Colonel Fremont's Last Expedition (New York: Derby and Jackson, 1857).

[35] Goetzman, op. cit., footnote 31, pp. 285–89.

[36] Secretary of War, op. cit., footnote 34, Vol. 3, pp. 124.

[37] General W. J. Palmer, Report of Surveys Across the Continent on the Thirty-Fifth and Thirty-Second Parallels for a Route Extending the Kansas Pacific Railway to the Pacific Ocean at San Francisco and San Diego (Philadelphia: W. B. Selheimer, 1869).

[38] U. S. Congress, House, Wagon Road from Fort Defiance to the Colorado River, 35th Cong., 1st sess., 1857–1858, Exec. Doc. 124; U. S. Congress, House, Wagon Road—Fort Smith to Colorado River, 36th Cong., 1st. sess., 1859–1860, Exec. Doc. 42.

[39] U. S. Congress, House, op. cit., footnote 38, p. 7.

thereafter began their penetration of the valleys leading into the Colorado Plateau, damming and diverting the waters to irrigate their fields.[40] The Virgin and Sevier valleys were settled in the 1850s and early 1860s but most of the area was evacuated during the Blackhawk War of the late 1860s. Resettlement of the western margins of the Plateau and attempts to penetrate farther into the interior began again after the treaty with the Utes in 1868. A crossing of the Colorado River near the mouth of the Paria River at Lee's Ferry was discovered by Jacob Hamblin in 1864, and a wagon road was constructed from Lee's Ferry across the Plateau to the Little Colorado River by way of Moencopi.[41]

By 1873 the road was in use and Mormon settlers who had assembled at Kanab began the movement onto the Little Colorado Plateau in numbers.[42] The initial attempt at settlement was a failure. The settlers were so discouraged by its water resources that they returned to the better lands along the margins. One member of the group left the following vivid appraisal[43]

> From the first we struck the little Collorado op 150 miles, it is the seam thing all they way, no plase fit for a human being to dwell upon. In case of hie water the bottoms are all floded. [There is] no please for a dam for if we could get plenty of water it would back up about 6 or 8 miles op the Rivver and the Cottonwood is so scrubby and crukked so it would only be fit for fierr wood. No rock for bilding, no pine timber within 50 or 75 miles of her. Wher ever you may luck the country is all broken op. The moste desert lukking plase that I ever saw, Amen.

Permanent settlement of the Little Colorado Plateau country dates from 1876, but even then

the settlers met with death, disappointment, and frustration. At Joseph City dams built to store and divert the waters of the Little Colorado River were washed away or damaged annually. By 1894 the settlers had built eight dams, had expended innumerable hours of energy, and had spent $50,000. Many of the small agricultural settlements lasted only a few years.[44] There were continuing troubles with the Indians. The Mormons not only had their livestock stolen, but they found themselves dispossessed as the Navajo Reservation was expanded westward. In 1900 Moencopi Ward had a population of about 150 persons squatting on Indian land. The federal government paid them $45,000 for their investments, and they left the Tuba City area in 1903.[45]

The Colorado Plateau settlements of the Mormons were made in the face of drought, short growing season, unreliable stream flow, and a hostile federal government.[46] Nevertheless, some Mormons were able to establish themselves wherever small pieces of land could be irrigated. Eventually, however, like the Anasazi before them, many abandoned their homes in favor of lands lying south of the Plateau where their settlements were more successful. Today, most of the Mormon villages on the Plateau are declining in population as family sizes are decreasing and the younger members of the families pursue their life goals in other places.

The Great Surveys

The end of the Civil War released a number of restless, energetic men and made available government funds to pursue the exploration of the western territories. The Wheeler, King, Hayden, and Powell surveys grew out of the need for knowledge about the lands so recently acquired (Fig. 5).[47] Three of these surveys

---

[40] J. E. Ricks, *Forms and Methods of Early Mormon Settlements in Utah and the Surrounding Regions, 1847 to 1877* (Logan: Utah State University Press, 1964); D. W. Meinig, "The Mormon Culture Region," *Annals,* Association of American Geographers, Vol. 55 (1965), pp. 91–120; and J. E. Spencer, "The Development of Agricultural Villages in Southern Utah," *Agricultural History,* Vol. 14 (1940), pp. 181–90.

[41] J. H. McClintock, *Mormon Settlement in Arizona* (Phoenix: The Author, 1921) pp. 82–84.

[42] C. S. Peterson, "Settlement on the Little Colorado, 1873–1900: A Study of the Processes and Institutions of Mormon Expansion," unpublished doctoral dissertation, University of Utah, 1967.

[43] A. Amundsen, quoted in Peterson, op. cit., footnote 42, p. 29.

[44] McClintock, op. cit., footnote 41, pp. 182–83.

[45] McClintock, op. cit., footnote 41, pp. 160–61.

[46] The hardships encountered in settling the San Juan Country at about the same time were apparently even greater; C. A. Perkins, M. G. Nielson, and L. B. Jones, *Saga of the San Juan* (N. P.: San Juan Daughters of Utah Pioneers, 1968).

[47] Publications resulting from the surveys are indexed in L. F. Schmeckebier, *Catalogue and Index of the Hayden, King, Powell and Wheeler Surveys,* U. S. Geological Survey Bulletin 222 (Washington: Government Printing Office, 1904); documents on file

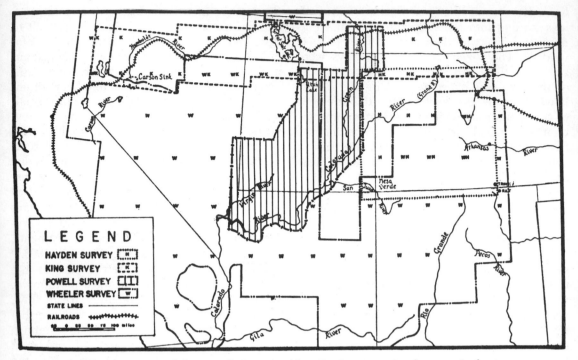

FIG. 5.   Area covered by Powell Survey.   After Bartlett, op. cit., footnote 2, front map.

were devoted, at least in part, to the Colorado Plateau Country. Wheeler and Powell mapped parts of the Plateau in Utah and northern Arizona at the time that Hayden was investigating northeastern Arizona and western Colorado. Powell's survey had the greatest long-range significance for an understanding of the Plateau Country, but all contributed to making the area better known.[48]

In the late 1860s the West was still wrapped in a veil of mystery. The Central Pacific and Union Pacific had not yet met at Promontory, Utah, and there were still streams and mountains that had not been searched for gold and silver. On the maps of one of the last of the railroad surveys along the thirty-fifth parallel, the cartographer had left much of the heart of

the Plateau blank, with only the general outline of the Colorado River and some of its tributaries sketched in to fill the space.[49] It was to fill the voids on the maps and in the minds of men that geographical and geological survey parties scrambled across the rugged terrain of the West in the period from 1867 until 1879, when the U. S. Geological Survey took over their duties. With the exception of a few spectacular feats, such as the exploration of the Colorado by Powell, the comprehensive compilations of data in the survey reports have not received the attention they deserve.[50] These data provide a base for examining environmental change on the Colorado Plateau. For the financiers and developers of the latter part of the nineteenth century the reports indicated places for mineral exploration and for railroad and municipal development. On the heels of the surveyors and the soldiers came others who would benefit from their efforts.

in the National Archives are listed in *Geographical Exploration and Topographic Mapping by the United States Government*, Publication 53–2 (Washington: U. S. National Archives, 1952).

[48] J. W. Powell, *Report on the Lands of the Arid Region of the United States*, U. S. Geographical and Geological Survey of the Rocky Mountain Region (Washington: Government Printing Office, 1879); and W. Stegner, *Beyond the Hundredth Meridian, John Wesley Powell and the Second Opening of the West* (Boston: Houghton-Mifflin Co., 1954).

[49] Palmer, op. cit., footnote 37, end map.
[50] U. S. Congress, House, *Exploration of the Colorado River of the West and Its Tributaries*, 43rd Cong., 1st sess., 1875, Misc. Doc. 300.

Soldiers, Agents, Traders, and Missionaries

Four groups participated in the conquest of the Indians. American policy toward them was not markedly different from that of the Spanish. Soldiers were needed for conquest; representatives of the government (often military men) signed the treaties and administered the territories; traders exchanged the material culture of the conquerors for the handicrafts and agricultural products of the natives; and missionaries came to convert the Indians and modify their non-material culture.[51]

In the American period forts were established at strategic locations to control the Indians. Some continued as government centers after reservations were created, and others became the nuclei for small towns which developed as the territory outside the reservations was settled. Government agents sometimes traveled with the military, but at other times they disassociated themselves in order to gain the confidence of the Indians. As the Bureau of Indian Affairs expanded its influence and the number of its employees, each Indian Agency became a small Anglo enclave on the reservation, with separate schools and a social life separate from that of the Indians.

Following closely on the heels of the military and the government agents were the traders and the missionaries, groups whose paths had crossed many times in the West. Fur traders of the pre-reservation era were essentially nomads who went out from fixed bases, such as Taos or Bent's Fort, to meet the Indians on their home grounds and exchange manufactured goods for pelts. Many of them worked for corporations, such as the Rocky Mountain Fur Company. Some unscrupulous traders exchanged liquor, arms, and ammunition with the Indians for booty captured in border raids.[52]

The Indian Intercourse Act of 1834 specified that no one could trade with the Indians without a license from the Superintendent of Indian Affairs or one of his agents.[53] Later Acts specified conditions under which trading

might be done, and the Indian Trader became institutionalized rather early. A pattern had been set by the time reservations were established in the Southwest. The Indian trade was in the hands of a relatively large number of small businessmen. By 1885 there were 123 firms operating 146 posts in the United States. On the Plateau fourteen firms were operating twenty-one posts on Indian reservations.[54] The pattern of the off-reservation post was also developing. Trading posts came into existence on the edge of the reservation as settlement grew. In 1890, for example, it has been estimated that there were nine posts on the Navajo Reservation and thirty on its borders.[55] On most of the smaller reservations in the United States the Indian Trading Post began to lose out early in the twentieth century, but on the Navajo Reservation it continued to thrive. In recent years many Indians have acquired light trucks, and with improved roads they can go to the neighboring towns to take advantage of lower prices, but there are still over one hundred trading posts on the Navajo Reservation.[56]

Missionary groups have had varying impacts on the Indians of the Plateau. Spanish attempts to Christianize the Plateau Indians failed. The Mormons were equally unsuccessful in proselytizing the Hopi, among whom they concentrated their efforts. Virtually all religious groups have established missions on the reservations; none has had notable success. Perhaps the attitudes reported by doctors working among the Navajo illustrate how difficult it is to change traditional views. The Navajo feels that white doctors are all right for bodily ailments, but for illnesses of the mind and soul their own medicine men are the only ones qualified to treat them.[57] Traditional beliefs still dominate among the older people but as a greater proportion of the

[51] Spicer, op. cit., footnote 18, pp. 343–67.

[52] R. M. Utley, *Hubbell Trading Post*, Special Report of the National Survey of Historic Sites and Buildings (Santa Fe: National Park Service, 1959), p. 3.

[53] Utley, op. cit., footnote 52, p. 5.

[54] U. S. Congress, Senate, "Indian Traderships," in *Senate Report*, 50th Cong., 2nd sess., 1888–1889, Exec. Doc. 2707, pp. 172–175.

[55] Utley, op. cit., footnote 52, p. 50.

[56] *Something about Trading Posts* (Window Rock, Arizona: The Navajo Tribe, 1968); and E. E. McIntire, "Central Places on the Navajo Reservation, A Special Case," *Yearbook*, Association of Pacific Coast Geographers, Vol. 29 (1967), pp. 91–96.

[57] "Wise Navajo Outlook," editorial, *Phoenix Gazette*, November 4, 1971.

Indians complete high school and college, the old concepts are being replaced by new.[58]

The influence of other groups has lessened considerably as Indians have taken over the management of their own affairs. Indians are now the government agents, and cooperative Indian trading posts dispense handicrafts to the tourists. Some vestiges of the past hang on, but the Indian is fast achieving his own identity at the same time that he is achieving a higher standard of living and acquiring more of the world's goods.

The Railroad

In the West there was perhaps no more effective agent for change than the railroad.[59] It opened the way for the development of mineral and forest resources, and enabled farmers and ranchers to ship their produce to market. This was particularly true on the Colorado Plateau, which had only a few crude wagon roads at the time of the building of the railroads. Most of these roads had been built by Mormons or by the Army. Although the advantages of the 35th parallel for railroad construction had been identified many times,

a railroad was not completed across the southern part of the Plateau until the early 1880s. At about the same time, Denver capitalists began sending narrow-gauge lines into the mountain and plateau country of western Colorado and eastern Utah, and short narrow-gauge lines began to tap the mineral wealth south and east of Salt Lake City.

In 1880 the Santa Fe Railroad, in partnership with the Atlantic and Pacific Railroad, obtained the right of way along the 35th parallel route, and by 1884 it had laid its rails as far as the Colorado River.[60] At the same time, the Denver & Rio Grande had commenced building its narrow-gauge line into the interior of Colorado, reaching south from Denver to Pueblo, and thence up the Arkansas drainage to Leadville, which it reached in May, 1880. By 1882 the Denver & Rio Grande had reached the eastern edge of the Plateau, with lines to Durango and Montrose. It had also purchased a number of short lines along the western edge in Utah. By March, 1883, a line connecting Denver and Salt Lake City had been completed across the Plateau.[61]

The Santa Fe had entered the Plateau Country as a transcontinental carrier, but soon sent out spur lines to tap the adjacent forested and mineralized areas. In 1887 a line between Seligman and Prescott was completed, and in 1890 thirty-five miles of logging railroad line reached out of Flagstaff to tap the forests of the Rim Country. The road from Ash Fork to Phoenix was completed in 1895.[62] The Denver & Rio Grande, which had been incorporated in 1870 by General William Palmer to follow the valley of the Rio Grande to El Paso and thence to Mexico City with a branch line from Salida to Salt Lake City, ended up serving the many mining and agricultural districts of Colorado and Utah. It eventually became part of a transcontinental route when the Western Pacific Route was built to California.

Both roads helped open large sections of the Plateau for settlement, and helped estab-

---

[58] The Navajo now have their own two-year college at Many Farms, Arizona, and are encouraging industries to locate on or near their reservation. The Hopi, Apache, and Ute Indians are all developing tourist facilities which include motels, camping sites, and ski resorts. Each group is encouraging its young to attend colleges and universities, and is providing scholarships for them. The standard works are C. Kluckhohn and D. Leighton, *The Navaho* (Cambridge: Harvard University Press, 1946); and R. D. Simpson, "The Hopi Indians," *Southwest Museum Leaflets*, No. 25 (1953), pp. 1–91. Two works which treat changing conditions are J. M. Christian, "The Navajo, A People in Transition," *Southwestern Studies*, Vol. 2 (1964), pp. 1–35 and 39–69; and E. G. McIntire, "The Hopi Villages of Arizona: A Case Study in Changing Patterns," *Proceedings*, Association of American Geographers, Vol. I(1969), pp. 95–99.

[59] R. G. Athearn, *Rebel of the Rockies* (New Haven: Yale University Press, 1964); T. D. Best, "The Role of the Atchison, Topeka, and Santa Fe Railway System in the Economic Development of Southwestern United States, 1859–1952," unpublished doctoral dissertation, Northwestern University, 1958; W. S. Greever, *Arid Domain: The Santa Fe Railway and Its Western Land Grant* (Stanford: Stanford University Press, 1954); and F. H. Thomas, "The Denver and Rio Grande Western Railroad: A Geographic Analysis," unpublished doctoral dissertation, Northwestern University, 1960.

[60] W. S. Greever, "Railway Development in the Southwest," *New Mexico Historical Review*, Vol. 32 (1957), p. 165.

[61] Athearn, op. cit., footnote 59, p. 122.

[62] Greever, op. cit., footnote 60, pp. 171–172.

lish town sites and patterns of land ownership and utilization which persist today. Communities such as Winslow, Holbrook, and Flagstaff on the Santa Fe and Durango, Gunnison, and Montrose on the Denver & Rio Grande owe their importance, if not their origin, to location on the railroad. Communities which came into existence as railheads continued as shipping points for the cattle ranches and farms which developed on public domain or land which the railroads had been given by the government.

The construction of the Santa Fe had a particular impact on the settlement patterns of the southern margins of the Plateau. Its partner, the Atlantic and Pacific Railroad, had been given an enormous grant of over thirteen million acres of land, alternate odd-numbered sections in a belt forty miles wide on either side of the track. In addition, it was given a right of way one hundred feet wide with additional space for stations or shops. Because some of its lands had been preempted by early settlers and by Indian reservations, the railroad was entitled to choose "in lieu" lands from additional strips ten miles wide on each side of its belt.[63] Some of this land quickly passed into the hands of private individuals. In 1885 over a million acres was sold to the Aztec Land and Cattle Company of New York, which introduced 50,000 head of Texas longhorns.[64] Much of the railroad land was leased or used by ranchers without payment for a considerable period of time, however, because the 1880s and 1890s were not an ideal time to try to sell marginal land; the Desert Land Act and other homestead acts permitted settlers to acquire up to 640 acres for virtually nothing.[65] The railroad was not able to dispose of its property until well into the twentieth century.

The railhead towns brought saloons, bawdy houses, and disreputable characters to areas

of conservative Mormon settlement.[66] The Santa Fe drove a wedge through the heart of their Little Colorado settlements, and the Denver & Rio Grande did the same in east central Utah. But most of the effects of railroad construction were positive. It opened up the rangelands to greater numbers of sheep and beef cattle, and aided the development of irrigated agriculture along the tributaries of the Colorado River. Demand for coal to fuel the locomotives and stoke the smelters in the adjacent metalliferous districts initiated a thriving business in northwestern New Mexico and central Utah. Lumber was needed for ties and for the buildings of the villages which developed along the right-of-way. Tourism became significant with the completion of branch lines to the Grand Canyon (1901) and other scenic points.[67]

Roads

Travel across the Plateau by any means other than the railroad remained a difficult undertaking for many years. Beale's wagon road from Albuquerque to southern California was never completed. Hamblin's road from Lee's Ferry to the Little Colorado settlements was impassible whenever heavy rainstorms occurred. Parts of the Army road along the Mogollon Rim connecting Fort Apache with Camp Verde were used until the 1930s.[68] Many of the roads connecting settlements on the Plateau to the railroads evolved from the tracks left by horse-drawn wagons which traveled between the Indian trading posts and the nearest railroad depot. The old military routes continued to be used as the civilian settlements which developed around them grew in size. Discovery of mineral deposits in the adjacent areas stimulated discussion and

---

[63] Greever, op. cit., footnote 59, pp. 20–21.

[64] G. T. Tinker, *Northern Arizona and Flagstaff in 1887: The People and Resources* (Glendale, Calif.: Arthur Clark, 1969), pp. 24–28.

[65] J. T. Ganoe, "The Desert Land Act in Operation, 1877–1891," *Agricultural History*, Vol. 11 (1937), pp. 142–57; J. T. Ganoe, "The Desert Land Act Since 1891," *Agricultural History*, Vol. 11 (1937), pp. 266–77; and Greever, op. cit., footnote 60, pp. 164–66.

[66] Fish, in his history of the Eastern Arizona Stake of the Mormon Church, reported over fifty violent killings in the vicinity of Holbrook in the decade following the completion of the railroad; Peterson, op. cit., footnote 42, p. 406. Not all of the violence was directly attributable to the railroad and the towns; some involved competition for grazing rights and the kinds of activities so vividly portrayed in western movies; see E. R. Forrest, *Arizona's Dark and Bloody Ground* (Caldwell, Idaho: The Caxton Printers, 1936).

[67] Greever, op. cit., footnote 60, p. 172.

[68] J. E. Cook, "The General's Shortcut," *Arizona*, July 25, 1971, pp. 20–30.

plans for a better road system. Some of these plans materialized; some of them did not. Most of the roads were nothing more than ruts, and were perhaps at their best in the winter when the ground was frozen. In the spring they became muddy and slippery from melting snow, and in summer they often became impassable when storms washed out roads and bridges.[69]

The first automobiles appeared in the Southwest at the beginning of the twentieth century, but did not become important on the Plateau until the 1920s.[70] Roads were improved to permit the hauling of ore, timber, and farm produce to processing plants, and to permit tourists to reach scenic attractions. Wagon roads which had been built from Flagstaff and Williams to the Grand Canyon in the 1890s were gradually improved for automobile use.[71] In the 1920s, when major thoroughfares were being completed in many parts of the Plateau, there was even serious consideration of a bridge across the Grand Canyon to connect Utah and Arizona, but the site eventually selected for the crossing of the Colorado was near that used by the Mormon pioneers at Lee's Ferry.[72] Many of the roads then in use on the Plateau were not much more than dusty trails.

The automobile extended the range of individuals intent on developing the resources of the Plateau. Numerous scenic and historical sites could now be reached by the average family in its touring car. More of the natural wonders of the Plateau became accessible and more roads were built. The demand for energy sources led to exploration and development of oil and gas fields, uranium ores, and coal deposits, all of which entailed a tighter road net. Greater affluence among the Indians led to a demand for hard-surfaced roads on their lands. Where new centers of activity were generated by the needs of tourists or by the discovery of mineral resources, new roads came into being.

CURRENT CONTROVERSIES

Patterns established in the past create problems today. Powell, in his comprehensive analysis of the arid lands of the Colorado Plateau in 1879, argued the need for classification of lands in terms of their highest use, and suggested that society needed a better system for the disposal of the public domain than then existed. He also pointed out the difficulties of using a rectangular survey system in a mountainous region. His recommendations for communal management of water and grazing resources were unacceptable to politicians of that time, who rejected them.[73] Today, we readily accept the notion of public management of recreational, forest, and grazing areas, and have developed land-use planning for our communities, but outside our government preserves and our cities most Americans will still not accept the idea of social responsibility in the use of privately-held rural land. Nationwide land-use planning is anathema to most citizens. Current controversies on the Colorado Plateau accentuate this point.

Energy

Growing population in the metropolitan areas of California, Utah, Colorado, New Mexico, and Arizona has had a marked impact on the Plateau. Increasing numbers of people with an increasing number and variety of electrical equipment have created an insatiable demand for energy. As one example, it is estimated that California will require twenty to twenty-five times as much electricity in 2020 as it did in 1965.[74] Population growth

[69] "Road Conditions," *St. John's Herald*, January 8, 1891, p. 1.
[70] The first automobile on the Plateau arrived by train from Southern California in 1902. It was steam-propelled and ran out of fuel on its first long run to the Grand Canyon. Four horses pulled it to Grand Canyon where it was repaired and refueled before returning to Flagstaff; "First Automobile to Grand Canyon," *The Sun*, January 21, 1916.
[71] The National Old Trails Highway (later U. S. Highway 66) was built originally of volcanic cinder; paving commenced in 1928. The principal traffic was to the Grand Canyon from either Williams or Flagstaff. A paved road to the Grand Canyon was completed in 1930 from a point near Williams. J. R. Fuchs, *A History of Williams, Arizona*, Social Science Bulletin No. 23 (Tucson: University of Arizona Press, 1953), pp. 124–26.
[72] R. A. Hoffman, "Grand Canyon Bridge Opens New Route across Greatest of all Natural Barriers," in *Official Program of the Dedication of the Grand Canyon Bridge, Arizona, June 14, 15, 1929* (Flagstaff: Coconino Sun, n. d.).

[73] Rabbitt, op. cit., footnote 3, pp. 16–18.

has also been accompanied by pollution, and in reaction, people in cities have vociferously opposed the construction of additional sources of pollution in their local areas. In 1969 public pressure halted plans to build a large steam electric plant on the coast near Los Angeles.[75] The proposed construction of a nuclear power and desalting plant on a man-made island off Orange County has been postponed.[76] Decisions to tap the energy resources of the Colorado Plateau, made years ago, involved large dams on the Colorado and steam plants in the Four Corners area.[77] Conservationists defeated the proposals to build additional dams on the Colorado but were unable to prevent the construction of the coal-fueled electric plants. The enormity of the new construction required by the burgeoning population of the American Southwest has brought reaction from citizens across the land.[78]

The controversy involves three principal facets: 1) the topographic and environmental upheaval associated with strip-mining of coal; 2) the pollution of the atmosphere resulting from burning large quantities of coal in power plants; and 3) the use of large quantities of water in conjunction with the production of power.

Over much of the Intermountain West a feverish search for buried wealth is reminiscent of mineral rushes of former years, only now the search is not for metal but for energy sources. Most of the areas containing coal, oil shales, and sands have been well identified,

TABLE 1.—SULPHUR CONTENT OF STRIPPABLE COAL RESERVES

	Millions of tons by sulphur content			
	Low	Medium	High	Total
Wyoming	13,377	65	529	13,971
Montana	6,133	764	0	6,897
New Mexico	2,474	0	0	2,474
North Dakota	1,678	397	0	2,075
West Virginia	1,138	669	311	2,118
Texas	625	684'	0	1,309
Kentucky (East)	532	189	60	781
Colorado	476	24	0	500
Arizona	387	0	0	387
South Dakota	160	0	0	160
Virginia	154	99	6	258
Washington	135	0	0	135
Alabama	33	74	27	134
Arkansas	28	118	28	174
California	25	0	0	25
Oklahoma	10	44	57	111
Utah	6	136	8	150

Source: *New York Times*, August 22, 1971.

but the search for additional deposits of uranium, oil, and gas continues. Many of these deposits are on government or Indian land and pose difficult questions of public policy. Many leases have been granted to private industry with only small return to the Indians or to the governments.[79]

Although coal has been one of the major sources of particulate matter and of sulphur dioxide in our atmosphere, it will probably be the major source of energy utilized in the production of electricity for the next three decades. With increased demand for electricity will come increased demands for coal, and the cheapest and most easily mined coal is strip-mined coal. The greatest deposits of low-sulphur coal lying near the surface are in the Western States, and much of this coal is on the Colorado Plateau relatively near the growth centers of Southern California, Phoenix, and Salt Lake City (Table 1).

In 1971 the coal-burning electric plants of the Four Corners area were creating the greatest amount of discussion and causing the

[74] *Main Report, Comprehensive Framework Study, California Region* (Sacramento: Pacific Southwest Inter-Agency Committee, Water Resources Council, 1971), p. 58.
[75] "City Bows to Smog Board and Suspends Work on Power Plant," *Los Angeles Times*, Part 1, December 10, 1969, pp. 1 and 26.
[76] *Letter*, Metropolitan Water District, Public Relations Office, dated November 27, 1971.
[77] The proposed Hualapai (formerly Bridge Canyon) and Marble Canyon dams on the Colorado were designed primarily to produce hydroelectric power, some of which would have been used to pump water into the Central Arizona Project. The Sierra Club marshalled its forces to defeat legislation authorizing them. "Southwest Gropes for New Ways to End Water Shortage," *U. S. News and World Report*, December 12, 1966, pp. 59–61.
[78] The *Sierra Club, Friends of the Earth, Nature Conservancy,* and *Native American Rights Fund* have all involved themselves in the controversy.

[79] Public Land Law Review Commission, *One Third of the Nation's Land* (Washington: Government Printing Office, 1970), pp. 128–29. The Hopi and Navajo Indians are receiving a royalty of twenty-five cents a ton from Peabody Coal Company for the coal mined at Black Mesa; *Mining Coal on Black Mesa* (St. Louis: Peabody Coal Company, 1970), p. 3.

greatest amount of anguish. The Black Mesa coal mine and the Mojave and Navajo electric plants were particularly in the spotlight. In 1970 the Peabody Coal Company began supplying coal through an underground pipeline to the Mojave Power Plant near Bullhead City, Nevada. The mine will be expanded to supply coal to the Navajo Plant near Page, Arizona. This coal will be moved by train over tracks which were being laid in 1971. Controversy over this, and the other plants now operating and scheduled to begin operating in the future, revolves around the reclamation of the strip-mined areas, the use and pollution of water, and the degradation of the air resource in one of our last wild recreational areas.

The fact that this is just the beginning of the invasion of the Colorado Plateau by outside forces seeking to capitalize on the stores of energy locked in her layers of sedimentary rocks is what frightens those who wish to save portions of this continent for posterity. In 1869 the President of the American Association for the Advancement of Science, in commenting on one of the characteristics of our national character, said that we assign "an exaggerated value to immediate utility and a low estimate to what real utility is. It cannot be denied that the attainment of riches is becoming more and more the chief aim of existence."[80]

Deposits of oil, gas, uranium, coal, and oil shales and sands are widely distributed over the Plateau. All of these, except for the oil shales and sands, have been mined for some time, but in quantities which were small in comparison with future requirements. In addition to use in thermal electric plants, it is anticipated that tremendous quantities of coal will be required by gasification plants which will be located in areas with large coal deposits. Of the 176 site locations studied by the American Gas Association, 156 are reported to be in the West.[81] With the anticipated development and acceptance of atomic-fueled electric generating plants, the demands for

ores of uranium will increase greatly. Already, prospectors and speculators are active in their search for additional sources for such ores on the Colorado Plateau.[82]

Eventual depletion of our known reserves of gas and oil is anticipated. Although the supplies from the San Juan Basin in the Four Corners region will last for some time, it is essential that other energy resources be developed. The oil shales and sands of the Uintah and Piceance basins of Utah and Colorado appear to be the Cinderellas of the energy field, awaiting a fairy godmother to transform them into glittering princesses. Technology does not as yet permit their widespread conversion on a commercial basis, but forecast shortages of gas and oil from conventional sources could change that picture drastically. Again, the question of how to supply energy needs without environmental disruption is a difficult one. Meanwhile, pilot plants in northwestern Colorado are seeking ways to produce fuel at a lower cost.[83]

Water Resources

Flood and drought were major problems of the Anasazi; they remain significant problems for the people of the Plateau today. Variability of precipitation and uncertainty about groundwater reserves pose additional questions for those seeking to develop the lands and resources of the Arid West. Is there sufficient water to maintain a viable flow in the Colorado River, its tributaries, and the many streams that flow off the edge of the Plateau? Is there enough water to develop additional agricultural land on the Plateau and adjacent lowland areas? Or is there even enough water to sustain irrigated agriculture in the areas now being farmed? Is the generation of electricity a higher use and, hence, does it have greater priorities for water on the Colorado Plateau? And what effect will the return of heated water have on the groundwater reservoirs and on the streams into which it is injected? These are but a few of the

[80] B. A. Gould, "Address of the Ex-President," in *Proceedings*, American Association for the Advancement of Sciences (Salem: 1869), p. 28–30.

[81] B. A. Franklin, "Coal Rush is On As Strip Mining Spreads into West," *New York Times*, August 22, 1971, pp. 1 and 49.

[82] Personal communication, Willis H. Ellis, College of Law, The University of New Mexico, December 13, 1971.

[83] *A Summary of Mineral Industry Activities in Colorado, 1970* (Denver: Colorado Bureau of Mines, 1971), p. 22.

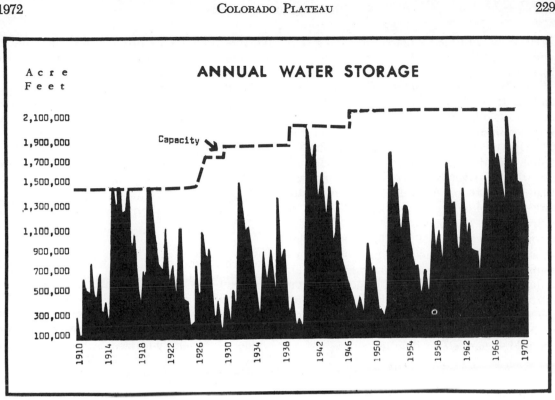

FIG. 6. Variation of annual water storage in the six reservoirs of the Salt River Project. Source: Salt River Water Users Association.

difficult questions being posed by citizens concerned with environmental problems.

Flood and drought continue to plague residents of the Colorado Plateau today as they have in the past, but larger areas and greater numbers of people are involved. Periodically, drought has seared the rangelands of the southern part of the Plateau. Light snowfall in the winter of 1970–71 and virtually no spring rains produced crisis conditions among the Navajo, Apache, and Anglo ranchers. For the first time on record cloud-seeding was attempted. The Bureau of Reclamation program was pronounced a success, as somewhat heavier than normal rainfall occurred from the summer thunderstorms.[84] Only a few months later floods were occurring along the Little Colorado River, and surplus waters were pouring off the Plateau into the reservoirs of the Salt River Project and the Colorado River.

Population growth on the Plateau has created serious water shortages. The Navajo are constantly hauling water for their livestock. Flagstaff, which procures most of its water from drainage into a reservoir, Lake Mary, is facing a certain shortage. Cloudseeding has been recommended as a temporary expedient.[85] The construction of another large reservoir thirty miles south of Winslow on a tributary of the Little Colorado River is being considered.[86]

Erection of large power facilities on the Plateau will accentuate these water shortages. Water for the Black Mesa coal mining operation will come from deep wells tapping an aquifer at about the 3,000 foot level.[87] Water for the Navajo, Mohave, and Kaiparowitz plants will be taken from the Colorado River.

---

[84] Personal communication, Clement C. Todd, Assistant Chief, Atmospheric Water Branch, U. S. Bureau of Reclamation, Denver, Colorado, December 7, 1971.

[85] Vincent J. Schaefer, personal communication.

[86] U. S. Bureau of Reclamation, "Summary Sheets, Mogollon Mesa Project," preliminary, unpublished draft (Phoenix: District Office, U. S. Bureau of Reclamation, c. 1971).

[87] *Mining Coal on Black Mesa*, op. cit., footnote 79, pp. 8–10.

Return water to the Colorado drainage system will be highly saline and have higher temperatures than that taken from the stream.[88]

Variability of flow in the Colorado River and in the Salt-Gila system have generated questions over further development of the water resources of the Colorado Basin (Fig. 6). Opponents of the Central Arizona Project, which will draw its water from Lake Havasu, say that the river is overcommitted now, and that its development will only benefit the large landholders to whom the water will be delivered.[89] Proponents say that this is a resource of value to all of the people of Arizona.[90] At fifty dollars an acre-foot it represents an annual income of over fifty million dollars a year. If the project is not built, the citizens of California will benefit at the expense of the citizens of Arizona. The project is in its initial stages of development and should be completed within ten years.

Recreation

Much of the pressure to preserve our nation's heritage of clear skies and open vistas comes from the affluent citizens of our urban centers, who have the time and money to escape from the dreary urban environments which many of them have helped to create. The conservation movement has been essentially an upper and middle income phenomenon. Many of these individuals are among the decision-makers in our society, which has particular significance in the conflict on the Plateau.

A large proportion of the visitors to the National Monuments and Parks in the Four Corners region come from the metropolitan areas of the Southwest. The number of visitors is increasing at alarming rates.[91] The National

Park Service is currently considering ways to manage their holdings in light of projections of increased visitations in the years ahead.[92] California entrepreneurs have developed ski resorts in the area, and skiers from Southern California dominate the slopes at Alta, Utah, and at other ski resorts on the Plateau. Along the Rim Country of the Plateau well-to-do citizens from metropolitan Phoenix are establishing second homes among the pines to escape the searing summer heat of the Salt River lowland.[93] In the Indian Reservations tourism is being encouraged. Motels and travel trailer facilities are being built, rivers are being dammed to form lakes, and ski runs and lifts are being developed.[94]

The group with the greatest stake in preserving open space for themselves and for posterity is destroying a resource of priceless value. A federally-funded agency, the Four Corners Commission, is seeking new ways to

cation from Gary K. Howe, Plans and Programs Specialist, Grand Canyon National Park, December 3, 1971.

[92] "Canyon Plan a Balancing Act," *Arizona Republic*, November 18, 1971.

[93] The most serious problems are the remote subdivisions on former railroad sections of the Rim Country. In most areas easily reached by road from Phoenix real estate developers are selling recreational lots in developments with euphonious names: Kachina Village, Pinetop Lakes, and White Mountain Country Club Estates. Personal interview with L. A. Lindquist, Forester, Sitgreaves National Forest, Arizona, November 15, 1971.

[94] Studies of the tourist resources and potential of the region include U. S. National Park Service, *Survey of the Recreational Resources of the Colorado River Basin* (Washington: Government Printing Office, 1950); J. R. Gale, *Tourist Potential on the Navajo Indian Reservation* (Stanford: Stanford Research Institute, 1955); J. G. Morey, *A Survey of Tourist Potential and Adequacy of Water Supply on the Hopi Indian Reservation* (Chicago: Armour Research Foundation, 1963); *Development Possibilities along Navajo Highway 1* (Albuquerque: Chambers and Campbell, Inc., 1963); S. C. Jett, *Tourism in the Navajo Country: Resources and Planning* (Window Rock, Arizona: The Navajo Nation, 1967); and *Recreation, Tourism, and Retirement Study* (Los Angeles: Development Research Associates, 1971). Reports on the present state of development of recreational facilities on each reservation may be obtained by writing directly to each agency. For an example of the kinds of development now in progress, see J. E. Cook, "You ought to see What the Apaches are doing," *The New York Times*, August 1, 1971, p. 3.

[88] Bechtel Corporation, *Status Report: Environmental Planning for the Navajo Generating Station* (N.P.: 1970), pp. 36–53.

[89] D. Yetman, *A Need for the Central Arizona Project?* (Tucson: Committee for a Sane Water Policy, n.d.); *The Nation's Most Fantastic Project* (Los Angeles: Colorado River Association, 1950).

[90] *Central Arizona Project Facts* (Phoenix: Central Arizona Project Association, 1971).

[91] Attendance at Grand Canyon National Park in the year of its creation as a national park (1919) was 44,170 people; at the end of World War II it had reached about half a million people; in 1970 it was 2,258,195 people, and restrictions had been placed on utilization of the park; personal communi-

TABLE 2.—LAND OWNERSHIP IN THE FOUR CORNERS STATES (ACRES—IN THOUSANDS)

State	Federal Land		Indian Trust Lands		State-Local Lands		Private Land	
	Acreage	Percentage	Acreage	Percentage	Acreage	Percentage	Acreage	Percentage
Arizona	32,500	44.7	19,700	27.0	9,200	12.7	11,300	15.6
Colorado	23,500	35.3	700	1.1	3,400	5.0	39,100	58.6
New Mexico	26,700	34.0	7,300	9.0	9,700	13.0	34,000	44.0
Utah	34,600	65.5	2,000	4.0	3,600	7.0	12,500	23.5

Source: 1969 Arizona, Colorado, New Mexico and Utah State Investment Plans.

develop the area.[95] Federal money dispensed through state agencies is being used to promote industrialization and commercialization of the whole region on the premise that it will improve the lives of the people; to a certain extent it will. But along with greater income will come greater numbers of people, greyer skies, and a degraded landscape. At times, now, one can only dimly perceive the details of landforms on the opposite side of the Grand Canyon. In alleviating the problem of pollution in our cities we are contributing to the degradation of some of the finest scenic resources of our nation. We urgently need solutions to our energy problems so that some parts of our nation may be retained for those who seek solitude in nature away from man and his urban complex.

Land-Use Management

Basic to most of the man-environment dilemmas on the Plateau are questions relating to the way in which the land is used and managed. Most result from changing perceptions of the value of the land to individuals and to society. John Wesley Powell had foreseen that many of the current problems might develop unless new institutions and new methods were utilized in developing the Plateau lands. In commenting upon what he thought might happen if traditional methods prevailed, Powell said:[96]

> If divisional surveys were extended over the pasturage lands, favorable sites at springs and along small streams would be rapidly taken under the homestead and preemption privileges for the nuclei of pasturage farms.
>
> Unentered lands contiguous to such pasturage farms could be controlled to a greater or less extent by those holding the water, and in this manner the pasturage of the country would be rendered practicable. But the great body of land would remain in the possession of the Government; the farmers owning the favorable spots could not obtain possession of the adjacent lands by homestead or preemption methods, and if such adjacent lands were offered for sale, they could not afford to pay the Government price.

To prevent this, Powell had recommended that cooperative irrigation and pasturage districts be organized. Each pasturage district should be composed of nine or more units, each of which should have at least 2,560 acres and include some irrigable land. The boundaries of the units and the districts should be controlled by topographic features.[97] As the record shows, traditional methods of survey and disposal were used, and Powell's predictions were realized. Today, the Colorado Plateau is a crazy-quilt of private, Indian, state, and federal holdings, with each individual and each agency having management philosophies, policies, and practices at variance with those of adjacent landholders (Table 2).

The federal government is by far the largest

---

[95] The Four Corners Regional Commission is a state-federal partnership created in 1966 to develop the resources of the ninety-two counties of the designated area in Utah, Colorado, New Mexico, and Arizona. It is one of a number of large regional economic development programs of the United States Department of Commerce aimed at stimulating the economies of "depressed areas" in the United States. The programs stress the role of planning and economic aid in promoting the welfare of the people residing in each region. Matching funds are provided by the federal government for projects initiated by local and state groups. Funds have been provided for such things as the promotion of tourism and the building of roads, sewage systems, hospitals, and schools. For a discussion of the regional commissions see M. R. Levin, "The Big Regions," Journal, American Institute of Planners, Vol. 34 (1968), pp. 66–79; for the activities of the Four Corners Regional Commission consult their Annual Report (Farmington, New Mexico: Four Corners Regional Commission, various years).

[96] Powell, op. cit., footnote 48, p. 28.
[97] Powell, op. cit., footnote 48, pp. 38–39.

landholding body in the Four Corner states, but different agencies manage the land in different ways. Indian lands represent the second largest class of holdings in some states. By virtue of the treaties which created them, Indian reservations have been accorded special status. They are literally "nations within a nation," and are not subject to the laws of the states in which they lie. Each of the Plateau states received generous grants of federal land upon achieving statehood, but no good management practices have been developed by the states to manage these lands. The principal difficulty associated with the management of the public lands is their fragmented nature. The Plateau was settled at a time when the frontier and the frontier spirit were coming to an end. The better lands of this nation had been occupied, and the basic settlement patterns had fairly well evolved. The new wave of conservation and preservation was just beginning. It was a time of changing attitudes, policies, and practices. The consequence of conflicting federal land policies was to create a fragmented, fractured pattern attributable to land disposal practices developed in a different era and a different environment.

Private landholdings dot the Plateau surface but are most numerous around the margins. In Utah small Mormon villages cluster around alluvial plains; other communities have developed around mineral supplies and tourist attractions. Areas of rich alluvial soils and abundant water led to extensive settlement of western Colorado. In Arizona and New Mexico early Mormon settlers competed with the railroad and livestock ranchers for land, but much of the Plateau had little value or was already occupied by Indians. The largest landholder was the Atlantic and Pacific Railroad, which had received a grant of alternate, odd-numbered sections totaling 13,413,212 acres, and only even-numbered sections of land were available over much of Arizona and New Mexico.

As a further complication, the federal government began its program of withdrawing land to create forest preserves before the railroad had developed a land disposal policy and even before it had completed the process of selecting its "in lieu" lands. The Indian reser-

vations had also expanded to include both railroad and private holdings, thus necessitating the granting of additional acreage in other areas as compensation for the lost land. The difficulties created by these policies might have been solved had it not been for yet another set of policies adopted by the federal government. The states had been given sections 2, 16, 32, and 36 of every township for school purposes, and were given authority to select several million more acres for other purposes. Because of the late date at which they achieved statehood, Arizona and New Mexico have had a difficult time finding enough land from which to make their selections, and in 1971 they had not completed their task. Both states adopted policies which have tended to keep these lands in state ownership, leasing rather than selling the land.[98] Conflicts were inevitable when individuals, corporations, government agencies, and Indian tribes were all acquiring land at virtually the same time, and some still have not been settled.[99]

Abuse of the land has been associated with fragmented landholdings and uncertain titles. Nowhere else on the continent have there been more rapid rates of soil and vegetative change, and perhaps nowhere else is the relative importance of man and of nature in promoting change more difficult to assess.[100] Accelerated erosion and arroyo cutting were

---

[98] *Ownership and Administration of Public Lands in Arizona* (Phoenix: State Department of Economic Planning and Development, 1971); *Agricultural Land and Water In New Mexico* (Santa Fe, New Mexico: State Planning Office, 1966); and S. A. Mosk, "Land Policy and Stock Raising in the Western States," *Agricultural History*, Vol. 17 (1943), pp. 14–30.

[99] A band of eighty Yavapai (Tonto) Apaches are currently fighting to have the land on which they are living declared an Indian reservation. The land was incorporated into Tonto National Forest in 1905 even though the Indians and their ancestors had made it their home for centuries. "Yavapai-Apaches Refuse Government Offer in Reservation Squabble," *The Arizona Republic*, October 29, 1971, p. 35.

[100] This problem has been studied by scholars from a wide range of academic disciplines for a long time. One of the most recent and most complete discussions is Yi-Fu Tuan, "New Mexico Gullies: A Critical Review and Some Recent Observations," *Annals*, Association of American Geographers, Vol. 56 (1966), pp. 573–97; others include Thornthwaite et al., op. cit., footnote 8; and J. W. Hoover, "Navajo Land Problems," *Economic Geography*, 13(1937), 281–300.

first noted in the 1880s shortly after large herds of cattle and sheep had commenced grazing on the pasture lands of the Plateau.[101] In the years that followed stream channels cut ever more deeply into floodplains and lowered the water table, with consequent changes in the vegetative cover.[102] Additional erosional action by the wind has created dunes where rich grasses once grew. Grazing lands which once carried hundreds of head of cattle and sheep now provide forage for only a few.[103]

At first the experts were prone to place full blame on overgrazing.[104] There were attempts to control the number of sheep and cattle permitted on the land.[105] These practices somewhat ameliorated the effects of sudden downpours of rain on arid land, but erosion remains a significant land management problem on the Plateau. The discovery of ancient gullies attests to the fact that overgrazing is not entirely responsible for accelerated rates of erosion, because these fossil gullies were created before there were any herds of domesticated animals in the Southwest. It has been suggested that gullying is associated with periods of prolonged drought and consequent desiccation of the vegetative cover.[106] Much modern channel widening, however, appears to be associated with floods caused by the melting of heavy winter snowpacks or with unusually heavy spring and summer storms.[107]

The highest sediment yield is derived from the drainage basin of the Little Colorado River, and it is here that erosion poses the greatest problem.[108] In this area the rangeland represents one of the most important natural resources available to man, but little attention has been given to its proper management. Heavy winter and spring grazing has caused a significant decrease in desirable grasses, forbs, and shrubs. These plants have been replaced by such undesirable plants as loco weed, sagebrush, snakewood, and rabbitbrush. Pinyon and juniper have invaded many areas formerly in grass. Much of the area is unfenced, and the movement of livestock is uncontrolled. The nomadic grazing practices of the Navajo result in severe overgrazing near sources of water and near the hogans, with little or no grazing in areas away from these points. Hopefully, the creation of a resource conservation and development district in the area will help alleviate some of these problems.

Better management will also become possible through further consolidation of private and public landholdings. This is generally accomplished by direct exchange between agencies, but it may be done by intermediaries who act as middlemen in purchasing private landholdings for federal agencies.[109] Purchased land is generally exchanged for federal holdings in other areas. However, the problem of checkerboard development remains as the most serious management problem for vast areas of the Colorado Plateau. Increased pressure on land and water resources brought on by population growth, increased affluence, and greater leisure time has intensified this problem.

THE FUTURE

As one moves from the open-pit mine at Black Mesa to the edge of the Grand Canyon one is impressed with the great power of the

[101] J. T. Duce, "The Effect of Cattle on the Erosion of Canyon Bottoms," *Science,* Vol. 47(1918), pp. 450–52; and J. L. Rich, "Recent Stream Trenching in the Semi-arid Portion of Southwestern New Mexico, a Result of Removal of Vegetation Cover," *American Journal of Science,* Vol. 32 (1911), pp. 237–45.

[102] K. Bryan, "Change in Plant Associations by Change in Groundwater Level," *Ecology,* Vol. 9 (1928), pp. 474–78.

[103] Thornthwaite et al., op. cit., footnote 8, p. 3.

[104] R. Bailey, "Epicycles of Erosion in the Valleys of the Colorado Plateau Province," *Journal of Geology,* Vol. 43 (1935), pp. 337–55; and A. B. Reagan, "Recent Changes in the Plateau Region," *Science,* Vol. 60 (1924), pp. 283–85.

[105] Some of the problems of controlling the numbers of sheep on the Navajo Reservation have been examined by L. S. Fonaroff, "Conservation and Stock Reduction on the Navajo Tribal Range," *Geographical Review,* Vol. 53 (1963), pp. 200–23; and idem, "The Trouble with the Navaho," *The Johns Hopkins Magazine,* December, 1961, pp. 14–18 and 30–31.

[106] Bryan, op. cit., footnote 13, pp. 240–42.

[107] Tuan, op. cit., footnote 100, pp. 593–95.

[108] *Little Colorado River Plateau Resource Conservation and Development Project Plan* (Holbrook, Arizona: U. S. Soil Conservation Service, 1971), pp. 45–46.

[109] Land brokers have operated in the West for a long time, serving as agents for the railroads, the states, and the federal government in attempts to consolidate their landholdings. Some of them evolved out of large ranching operations which later became land sales corporations.

natural forces which have created the strange and beautiful landscapes of the Plateau. If the visit coincides with a low-level inversion, one will also be impressed with the ability of man to make significant environmental changes. And, as one reflects on the natural and human events that have helped shape the Plateau, one is struck by the impermanence of both the human and natural structures which presently exist. J. B. Jackson has said:[110]

> Speaking as a tourist who has merely traveled there many times and over many years, I have always thought of it as a landscape where almost everyone else was, like myself, in transit; where no one really put down roots and was forever on the move. I have thought of it as a landscape where a special relationship—tenuous and fleeting but nonetheless real—prevailed between the enormous emptiness and the people who passed through it. There were reasons for my feeling this. The geographical characteristics of the Colorado Plateau (which is by way of being the core area)—its profusion of canyons and mesas and buttes, its altitude and its extremely dry climate—discourage permanent settlement throughout most of the area. The Navaho, who have been here more than six hundred years, have never really stopped moving; neither townsmen nor farmers, they wander from one valley and plain to another, following their sheep and goats. Spanish explorers passed through, but all that they left was a scattering of place-names. Only the Hopis, isolated on their extraordinary mesas to the south, have taken root as farming people do. In the course of centuries they have created their own miniature landscape in the midst of the much larger one; yet even Hopi farms have a disconcerting way of shifting location.

The passage of time has brought great fluctuations in the numbers of people who have been supported by the resources of the Plateau. Mild, humid periods permitted primitive man to expand his ecumene; drought and flood, famine and pestilence, reduced his numbers and induced migration. Modern man, though less affected by natural disasters, must still cope with them. Construction of dams may ameliorate the effects of summer thunderstorms, but floods still occur. Seeding may slightly increase the amount of water that falls from clouds over the Plateau, but modern rainmakers can do little that Indian rain dancers could not accomplish when clouds do not form.

Changing technology and changing eco-nomic policies have had a greater impact on the white man than have environmental hazards. The construction of railroads and roads established centers where the needs of individuals in transit across the Plateau might be cared for. Construction and maintenance crews contributed to the population and income of the Plateau. Construction of Glen Canyon Dam created an instant federal city at Page. Discovery of oil, uranium, and coal has stimulated the growth of many Plateau communities.

Technological advances and economic development have both aided and hurt the Indian. They have permitted rapid population growth, but this has contributed to mass unemployment, inadequate housing, and inadequate water and waste disposal systems; these contribute to lower life expectancies among Indian groups. Although the infusion of new ideas and new industries has aided some, the transition from a primitive, dependent society to one that is self-sufficient is difficult. Not everyone benefits from the program of economic development currently underway in the Four Corners region, but change is essential and will continue. Not everyone has been satisfied with the direction that change has taken. Almost from the first, those who have settled on the Plateau or who have studied it have recognized the need for new policies, practices, and institutions to cope with its peculiar environmental conditions. Fortunately, federal land policies were being changed at about the time the Plateau was being occupied. The creation of forest preserves around the turn of the century represented one effort to conserve and manage some of the remaining portions of the public domain. The Taylor Grazing Act of 1934 set aside most of the remaining public domain and established management practices for it. In the 1930s the National Resources Board pointed out the necessity for state, regional, and national planning.[111] Federal agencies surveyed our needs and problems and made their recommendations known. World War II

---

[110] J. B. Jackson, "The Four Corners Country," *Landscape*, Vol. 10 (1960), pp. 20–26.

[111] National Resources Board, *A Report on National Planning and Public Works in Relation to Natural Resources and Including Land Use and Water Resources*, (Washington: Government Printing Office, 1934), pp. 8–25.

intervened, and until recently the attention of the nation has been directed outward toward the solution of problems of foreign policy.

With the realization that domestic environmental degradation had reached crisis levels, our government has again directed its attention to the management of its land, air, and water resources. It has passed a number of laws governing the use of these resources. It has also completed significant studies of our land and water resources which contain recommendations for future development.[112] All suggest that there is a great need for long-range comprehensive land-use plans for each state or region and a heed to relate such plans not only to internal agency programs but also to land-use plans and management programs of other agencies.

A bill before Congress would require each state to evolve a plan for the use of private lands within it, and many states are at work establishing the machinery to accomplish this task. None of these recommendations, however, goes far enough in a region such as the Colorado Plateau. In 1925 J. Russell Smith wrote:[113]

Most of the Colorado Plateau must continue as now, either as the Indian's or the white man's ranch —a ranch of low productivity . . . . The first impression is that this land, so nearly devoid of minerals, should be left for national forests, parks and Indians. But it has resources also for gigantic enterprises of the age of scientific engineering.

Smith perceived some of the questions facing decision-makers of today. The issues now being debated involve questions of immediate versus long-term benefits, and of the rights of the individual and the corporation versus the rights of society. Can the values to be gained from strip-mining and the production of energy compensate society for the degradation of the environment associated with such activities? Or do the long-term values associated with the preservation of clean air and an undisturbed natural environment outweigh the immediate gains and needs of society?

Can the people of the West (long the bastion of free enterprise) accept the idea that future generations also have rights? If they do, can they accept the notion that it is necessary to adopt comprehensive, long range planning and zoning even in rural and wilderness areas?

The answers to the above questions are, of course, difficult if not impossible to ascertain. But, is it not time to consider radical solutions to persistent problems? Perhaps we should consider the creation of a new national district encompassing the public and Indian lands of the Colorado Plateau in which a uniform set of management policies and procedures might be applied to the whole area by a single agency. And, shouldn't the principal question which governs the policies and procedures adopted be, "How can we manage the land in a manner to provide maximum long-term benefits to all of society?"

This may sound like a radical solution to a persistent problem, but not if a new Department of Natural Resources is created. This agency could consolidate public landholdings on the Plateau and represent the federal government in its negotiations with the Indians. It could also supervise the activities of private entrepreneurs, and devise methods of preserving scenic areas. This or some similar solution is needed if the aesthetic values of the area are to be preserved for posterity.

In looking ahead to the kinds of environmental changes which appear inevitable if projected programs for development of energy resources materialize, one can share the fears of the traditional Indian groups who have expressed opposition to strip-mining operations on the Plateau. Should the values which the traditional Hopi attach to the Colorado Plateau be respected, or should society accept and adopt benefits and values associated with the development of the material resources of the Plateau? Perhaps we should at least pause and consider these words of the Hopi leaders:[114]

Hopi land is held in trust in a spiritual way for the Great Spirit, Massau's. Sacred Hopi ruins are planted all over the Four Corners area, including

---

[112] *Upper Colorado Region Comprehensive Framework Study*, op. cit., footnote 4; *Lower Colorado Region Comprehensive Framework Study*, op. cit., footnote 4; and *One Third of the Nation's Land*, op. cit., footnote 4.

[113] J. R. Smith, *North America* (New York: Harcourt, Brace and Company, 1925), p. 481.

[114] Statement filed as basis for a suit on behalf of Traditional Hopis against the Secretary of the Interior and the Peabody Coal Company by the Native American Rights Fund, May 14, 1971.

Black Mesa. This land is like the sacred inner chamber of a church—our Jerusalem.

The area we call "Tukunavi" (which includes Black Mesa) is part of the heart of our Mother Earth. Within this heart, the Hopi has left his seal by leaving religious items and clan markings and plantings and ancient burial grounds as his landmarks and shrines and as his directions to others that the land is his. The ruins are the Hopi's landmark. Only the Hopi will know what is here for him to identify—others will not know.

This land was granted to the Hopi by a power greater than man can explain. Title is invested in the whole makeup of Hopi life. Everything is dependent on it. The land is sacred and if the land is abused, the sacredness of Hopi life will disappear and all other life as well.

The Great Spirit has told the Hopi leaders that the great wealth and resources beneath the lands at Black Mesa must not be disturbed or taken out until after purification when mankind will know how to live in harmony among themselves and with nature. The Hopi were given special guidance in caring for our sacred lands so as not to disrupt the fragile harmony that holds things together.

·   ·   ·

If these places are disturbed or destroyed, our prayers and ceremonies will lose their force and a great calamity will befall not only the Hopi, but all of mankind.

Hopi are the caretakers for all the world, for all mankind. Hopi lands extend all over the con-tinent, from sea to sea. But the lands at the sacred center are the key to life. By caring for these lands in the Hopi way, in accordance with instructions from the Great Spirit, we keep the rest of the world in balance . . . .

·   ·   ·

We, the Hopi religious leaders, have watched as the white man has destroyed his lands, his water and his air. The white man has made it harder for us to maintain our traditional ways and religious life. Now—for the first time—we have decided to intervene actively in the white man's courts to prevent the final devastation. We should not have had to go this far. Our words have not been heeded. This might be our last chance. We can no longer watch as our sacred lands are wrest from our control, as our spiritual center disintegrates. We cannot allow our control over our spiritual homelands to be taken from us. The hour is already very late.

In this conflict, who is to say which set of values and beliefs shall prevail? Can we not arrive at some other solution to this dilemma? With the knowledge that we have gained since the time of Marsh and Powell is it not possible to supply our material needs without further degradation of the environment of the few remaining areas of wild lands left in this nation?

THE AMERICAN GREAT PLAINS*

E. COTTON MATHER

ABSTRACT. Despite the economic and physical diversity of the Great Plains region, certain cultural traits have persisted since early white settlement and are prominent throughout the region. The romantic aura of the cowboy has had both regional and national ramifications, and the regional fancy has been captivated by big ventures and much movement. KEY WORDS: *Cowboy complex, Great Plains, Megalophilia, Transit region.*

THE American Great Plains is a physiographic region which exhibits great physical and economic variety, yet the region possesses traits which give it coherence, such as its cowboy complex, its character as a transit region, and its cultural megalophilia. Despite its varied landscapes, its remarkable productivity, and its record of rapid transformation, the region commonly has been viewed as a broad stretch of monotony. Numerous scholars have lamented this fact, and Fenneman remarked about it in the first paragraph of his famous *Physiography of Western United States.*[1] The popular viewpoint is readily comprehended when one bears in mind the American predilection for equating size and substance, and the general experience of Americans traversing the Great Plains with the regional grain rather than across it. For example, the three most heavily travelled highway routes over the Great Plains are Interstate Highways 20, 40, and 80. The first two cross the Staked Plains, one of the world's flattest regions, and the other follows the broad Platte Valley. These routes afford the traveller no high mountains or spectacular grades, just a repetitive array of highway service establishments and gaudy, blinking, neon signs.

* Acknowledgment is made to Arnold Alanen, William F. Forbes, Mark Heitlinger, Myongsup Shin, Terry Simmons, and R. W. Vockrodt, who generously shared observations with me on the 1971 University of Minnesota graduate field seminar in geography.

Dr. Mather is Professor of Geography at the University of Minnesota in Minneapolis.

[1] Nevin M. Fenneman, *Physiography of Western United States* (New York: McGraw-Hill Book Company, Inc., 1931), p. 1.

REGIONAL DELIMITATION

In the vernacular language, the Great Plains as a region remains unarticulated. Sectionalism rather than regionalism appears to have dominated the layman's framework for subdividing the land into large blocks. A recent study of American vernacular regionalization indicated no category which approximated the Great Plains in either name or area, but instead, such national subdivisions as the Pacific Northwest, the Rocky Mountain States, and the Southwest.[2] Many local names, such as Black Hills, Edwards Plateau, Trans-Pecos, High Plains, Platte Valley, and Gypsum Hills, revealed a predilection for geographic location and expression (Fig. 1). Such regional names as Big Country and Triangle Area were less inspired than Permian Basin. Panhandle, which occurred three times, might have appeared even more often but for cartographic limitations.

Scholars in various disciplines recognize the Great Plains as a region, although the term "Great Plains" is of relatively recent origin. The area was once considered merely part of "The Great American Desert." Zebulon Pike fostered this idea in his report on explorations in 1806. Many subsequent reports lent authenticity to this notion, and Jefferson Davis urged Congress to import camels. The sum of $30,000 was appropriated for the two loads of camels that were imported to Indianola, Texas, in the 1850s.

Great Plains was used as a regional designation during the early part of the twentieth century, but it gained rapid and widespread

[2] Ruth F. Hale, "A Map of Vernacular Regions in America," unpublished doctoral dissertation, University of Minnesota, 1971.

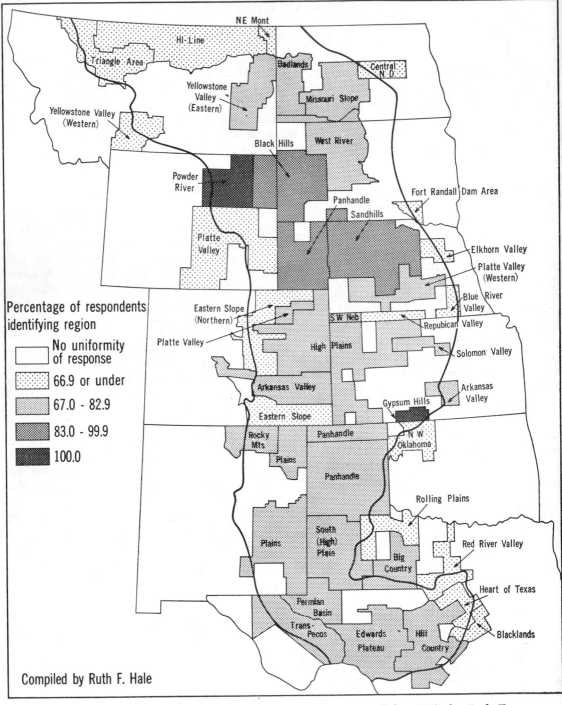

FIG. 1. Vernacular regionalization of the Great Plains. Compiled in 1970 by Ruth Feser Hale.

acceptance in the scholarly world only after 1931, when two extraordinarily important volumes appeared: *Physiography of Western United States*, by Nevin M. Fenneman, and *The Great Plains*, by Walter Prescott Webb.[3] Fenneman defined the region, and Webb explained it in terms of a special cultural confrontation. Subsequently many specialists have added to the spate of regional literature on the Great Plains. Climatological, sociological, vegetational, meridional, and other criteria have been used in the delimitation of the region.[4] The result has been a motley assortment of regional boundaries.

Although the layman's regionalization has been quite deficient on the national scale, it has expressed elements of place and areal character on the local scale. The scholar's map, on the other hand, embraced the essential area but has quibbled about the margins. The stark fact, however, is that the words "great" and "plains" simply denote that the region is physiographic and of vast extent.

REGIONAL VARIETY

Man's occupance of the Great Plains mirrors both the nature of the region and the nature of man. The Indian used the area as a hunting ground and the white man later used it as livestock range. Eventually, possibilities of cropping, mining, forestry, tourism, and urban development were explored. These probes outlined natural resources but they also reflected man's perception of those resources. Both man and natural resources have been dynamic elements and their interaction has progressively refined the regional patterns and compounded the rate of change.

Fenneman subdivided the Great Plains into sections. The significance of those physiographic subdivisions persists, but the regional complex involves numerous other geographic components.

The Glaciated Missouri Plateau Section differs markedly in landforms and drainage

from the Unglaciated Missouri Plateau (Fig. 2, Secs. I and II). The former section is now the most heavily cropped part of the northern Great Plains. Cash cropping of wheat is the main agricultural enterprise, and no other part of America has so much strip cropping (Fig. 3). In contrast, the Unglaciated Missouri Plateau is mostly short grass country used for ranching. Two extensive badlands are along the Little Missouri in western North Dakota, and the White and Cheyenne rivers east of the Black Hills (Fig. 4). The most sparsely populated parts of the northern or central Great Plains are in the Unglaciated Missouri Plateau between the Missouri and Yellowstone rivers and in the Powder River Country of Wyoming.

The Black Hills Section stands out as a geographic island of the Great Plains (Fig. 2, Sec. III). It is a mountainous area of about 6,000 square miles (15,500 km^2) that rises 4,000 feet (1,200 m) above the encircling plains. The Black Hills are forested with western yellow pine and Douglas fir in contrast to the surrounding land of short grass. Gold mining, lumbering, and tourism are important (Fig. 5). Although not as widely heralded as the Wall Drug Store, the impressive defacement of Mt. Rushmore has been memorialized as a national monument.

The Sand Hills Section is the most extensive area of dunes in North America (Fig. 2, Sec. IV). The Sand Hills represent the major eastern extension of the western range and the westernmost projection of prairie grassland. No other section of the Great Plains is used by man so overwhelmingly for a single purpose (cattle production), yet only seven decades ago the Sand Hills were wildly homesteaded by croppers (Fig. 6). Although the land use does not vary, the dunes are diverse in form and in geographic distribution (Fig. 7). This section of remarkably stable stream and lake levels has a great water resource which only in recent years has been exported as irrigation water.

The Central High Plains Section extends from the Canadian River in the Texas Panhandle to the Missouri Plateau and the Sand Hills Section (Fig. 2, Sec. V). Most of the Central High Plains is relatively smooth topographically and was short grass country prior to cultivation. Now a larger proportion of its

---

[3] Fenneman, op. cit., footnote 1, and Walter Prescott Webb, *The Great Plains* (New York: Ginn and Company, 1931).

[4] Three delineations often referred to were made by Fenneman, op. cit., footnote 1, Plate 1; Webb, op. cit., footnote 3, pp. 4–5; and Carl Frederick Kraenzel, *The Great Plains in Transition* (Norman, Oklahoma: University of Oklahoma Press, 1955).

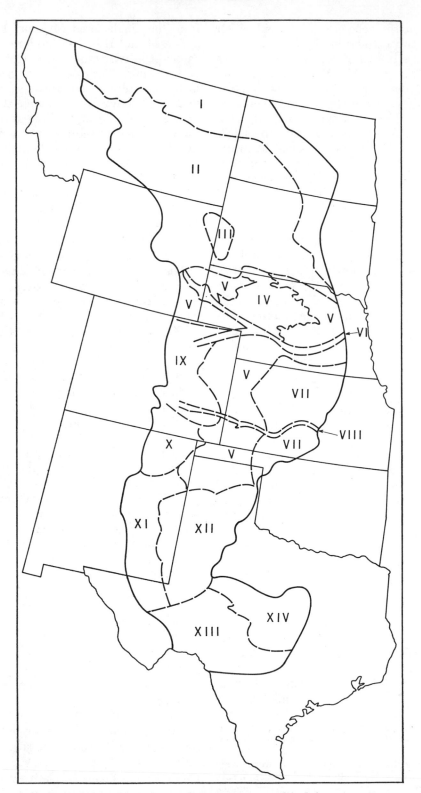

Fig. 2. Sections of the Great Plains Region. Modified from Fenneman.

FIG. 3. Strips of fallow land alternating with winter wheat southwest of Havre, Montana.

FIG. 5. Highway billboards near Mt. Rushmore in the Black Hills.

total area is under the plow than even the Glaciated Missouri Plateau Section. Winter wheat is grazed and later harvested for grain on both the central and southern Great Plains. Though winter and spring wheat are grown north to the Canadian Border, they are not both grazed and combined north of the Platte Valley.

The two striking breaks across the Central High Plains are the Platte and Arkansas Valleys (Fig. 2, Secs. VI and VIII). Both are major transport thoroughfares, both have long strips of intensive irrigated cropland, both are major population alignments, and both are ribbons of land incised below the general level of topography. Most important is the Platte-North Platte ribbon from Guernsey, Wyoming, to Kearney, Nebraska (Fig. 8). This 330-mile (530 km) stretch of intensive agriculture is the longest continuous irrigation strip on the Great Plains. The Platte Valley has been the most

important line across the Great Plains since the days of the Oregon and Mormon Trails. It has been used by the pony express, the overland stagecoach lines, the Union Pacific Railroad, the Lincoln Highway, and Interstate Highway 80. Along this thoroughfare has developed the major line of towns on the Great Plains.

Strong contrasts have developed within the Colorado Piedmont (Fig. 2, Sec. IX). The northern subdivision, drained by the South Platte River, has more irrigation, much dryland cropping, and only a modest amount of rangeland. This northern subdivision has numerous small towns and cities, and the large interregional center of Denver. All counties in the irrigated zone of the northern subdivision gained population in the last decade. In contrast, the southern subdivision, drained by the Arkansas River, is mostly steppe grassland used for grazing by sheep and beef cattle.

FIG. 4. The "Big Badlands" near the White River, South Dakota.

FIG. 6. Headquarters of Monahan ranch east of Hyannis, Nebraska.

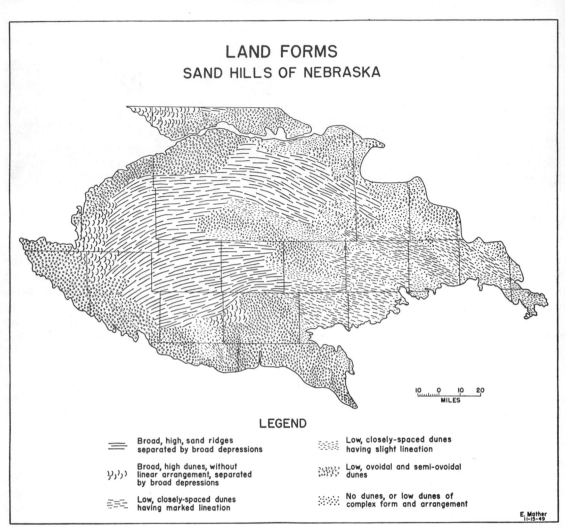

FIGURE 7.

No large interregional center exists. The two major urban developments are Pueblo, an iron and steel center, and Colorado Springs, renowned for its tourist industry and the nearby Air Force Academy. All counties in the irrigated zone of the southern subdivision lost population in the last decade.

The Southern High Plains is comprised of two distinctive areas, the Edwards Plateau and the Staked Plains (Fig. 2, Secs. XII and XIII). The former is hard limestone country (a stripped plain) with shallow and discontinuous soil cover; the Staked Plains (a depositional plain) has soft fluviatile materials. On the Edwards Plateau, relief is low in the north and west and increases markedly toward the

southeast (Fig. 9). The Staked Plains is so flat that stakes and piles of bones were used to mark the early trails.

The Staked Plains remained short grass rangeland until the advent of the irrigation well. Over three billion gallons of water are now pumped daily; no other section of the Great Plains has such heavy withdrawal. More and deeper wells in the Staked Plains have been drilled in recent years; the deepest ones yield vast quantities of oil. Perhaps this inspired the cartoon of the frustrated rancher surrounded by wells while his cattle were clamoring for just one drink of water. The Staked Plains are subtropical and can produce cotton. Rich soils, level land, and huge irriga-

FIG. 8. Irrigated North Platte Valley northwest of Scottsbluff, Nebraska.

FIG. 9. Dissected southeastern part of Edwards Plateau.

tion wells make a great farming combination for vast acreages of cotton, grain sorghum, alfalfa, and truck crops. Multiple cropping is practiced; winter wheat fields may be used in summer for grain sorghum or truck crops. Winter wheat generally yields more grain if it is grazed.

The Edwards Plateau is overwhelmingly ranch country. In Indian days, grass was widespread. Since the white man arrived, the pressure of livestock grazing has reduced grass growth. Old photographs substantiate old ranchers' recollections that mesquite and other woody growth have supplanted extensive areas of grass.[5] Cattle prefer the taller, more mature,

---

[5] Old ranchers also recollect cultural changes that range from guns and women to education. Some of the reminiscences are difficult to corroborate, and would be even harder to publish in a professional journal. Even those that would meet editorial standards of decorum are of dubious reliability. Nevertheless, I will attempt to slip this footnote past the editor's scrutiny in an effort to suggest how the cultural milieu and its portrayal has been altered with the passage of time. Professor J. B. Bird's *Second Annual Catalogue*, Rocksprings High School, Rocksprings, Texas, 1902, pp. 4 and 6, states that "our people have entirely outgrown the rusticity of frontier days, and we have not acquired the evils of city life. The people are highly cultured in every respect . . . . While we are not running any reformatory, if you have any bad boys or girls that have not been controlled heretofore, send them to us on trial. We guarantee satisfaction." Should these illuminating remarks be eliminated, I will preserve scholarly footnote respectability by stating simply that most of America's Angora goats are on the Edwards Plateau, and that over half of the nation's mohair production is exported to the United Kingdom. (Ed. Note: —Prof. Mather has a teratological perception of editorial standards of decorum.)

grasses. Sheep relish the shorter grasses and eat forbs. Goats, however, thrive on grass and forbs but prefer browse. The Edwards Plateau has all three of these livestock classes, all were brought by white man, and all graze the same land at the same time. This section is unique on the Great Plains in that cattle, sheep, and goats are raised on the same ranch, and in that this ranching region did not go through a homesteading dry farming cycle. Although dude ranching is scattered and rather unimportant almost everywhere on the Great Plains, the dissected Edwards Plateau near San Antonio is becoming a focus for the dude rancher as well as for corporate rural residential subdivisions.[6]

The Raton Section has extensive lava-capped plateaux and high mesas, deep canyons, and volcanic mountains (Fig. 2, Sec. X). The main economic activities are coal mining near Raton and Trinidad, and serving the streams of people who course along Interstate Highway 25, whose location approximates the old Santa Fe Trail. Coal is shipped about 100 miles (160 km) northward to Pueblo's steel mill.

The Pecos Valley is an elongated lowland bounded by steep slopes (Fig. 2, Sec. XI). The central part of the valley (the Roswell Basin) is over 100 miles (160 km) long and has thick alluvial fill. At the south end is the alluvial surface of the Toyah Basin. Both alluvial areas have considerable irrigated cotton and alfalfa. These are the most subtropical

---

[6] The Edwards Plateau is far-famed for its deer and wild turkey. Large corporations lease hunting rights on ranches for this game.

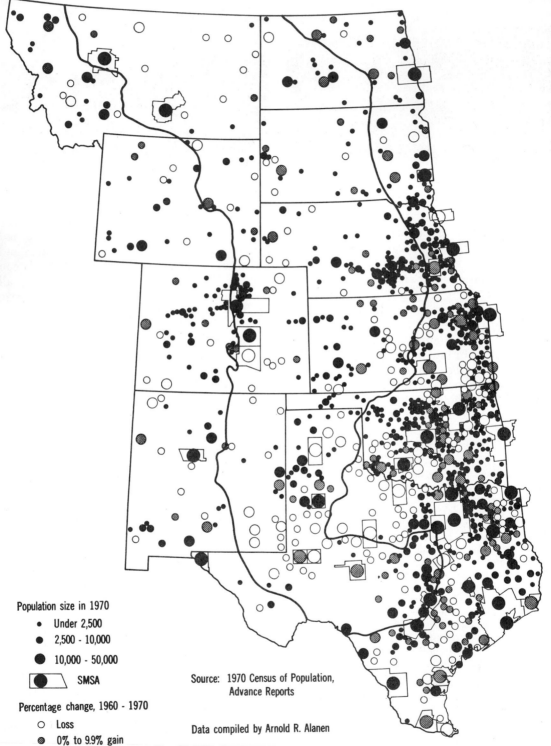

Population size in 1970

- Under 2,500
- 2,500 - 10,000
- 10,000 - 50,000
- SMSA

Percentage change, 1960 - 1970

- ○ Loss
- ◉ 0% to 9.9% gain
- ● 10% or more gain

Source: 1970 Census of Population, Advance Reports

Data compiled by Arnold R. Alanen

FIG. 10. Cities in and near the Great Plains. Places excluded were under 2,500 inhabitants with less than ten percent gain in population from 1960 to 1970.

agricultural areas of the Great Plains. Five cuttings of alfalfa per year in the Pecos Valley contrast with two cuttings annually on the northern Great Plains.

The Central Texas Section has strong relief, moderate elevation, and complex topography (Fig. 2, Sec. XIV). Agricultural operations are diverse, but the emphasis is upon mixed crop (grain sorghum, cotton, peanuts, corn, and small grains) and livestock (sheep and cattle) operations. This section is culturally the most "Southern" part of the Great Plains. No other section of the Great Plains has so many part-time and part-retirement farms, so many blacks, and so many families with exceedingly low income; these characteristics are particularly evident in the eastern part of the section near the large urban centers of Austin, Waco, and Fort Worth, and along the interstate highway which links them.

The Plains Border Section is a dissected cuestaform area east of the Central High Plains (Fig. 2, Sec. VII). This is one of the most extensively cropped areas of the Great Plains. Winter wheat is raised mainly for cash sale, and grain sorghum for livestock feed. Some suitcase farming and relatively high farm tenancy both are indicative of the area's outstanding productivity.

The human activities of the Great Plains focus on the large interregional cities. Kansas City, Omaha, Dallas, El Paso, San Antonio, and Denver are major interregional cities serving the Great Plains, and all are located near the periphery of the region (Fig. 10). The northern plains are served by Minneapolis-St. Paul, 400 miles (650 km) east of the Great Plains. No third order center exists between Seattle and Minneapolis-St. Paul. Generally, the growth of regional centers on the Great Plains has been modest, whereas interregional centers have had pronounced expansion. Dallas is functionally an interregional city, but Fort Worth is basically a Great Plains city. Most of the urban growth near the region has been along the east-central and east-southern margin. Several major lines of towns are along trunk transportation routes, such as Interstate Highways 94 and 70. The major line, however, follows the Platte Valley.

These geographic patterns portray great regional contrasts: mountains, plateaux, hills, and plains; forest, prairie, steppe, and desert shrub; hardy wheat and barley to subtropical cotton and peanuts; and population varying from enormous empty stretches to dense rural population and lines of towns. Despite this diversity, however, several psychic or cultural forces have transcended the region and have persisted since early white settlement.

A TRANSIT REGION

Vast volumes of people, livestock, and inanimate commodities move across the Great Plains. To a large degree the area is simply a transit region. This was true when the plains were the domain of the nomadic Indian. It was so later, especially from 1867 to 1881, when drovers moved millions of beeves northward from Texas to the cowtowns of Ogalalla, Abilene, Ellsworth, Dodge City, and Caldwell. Then there were the epic migrations in covered wagons across the region via the Mormon, Oregon, Santa Fe, and Southern Trails. The building of great trunk railways such as the Northern Pacific, Great Northern, Union Pacific, and Santa Fe furthered the flow of freight and people. Today the movement has been broadened along the interstate highways.

This movement is especially significant for the Great Plains because of:

1) the historic steadfastness of mass transportation as a major regional aspect;
2) the high proportion of transit through rather than to the region;
3) the singular types of transit;
4) the effect of transit on settlement forms, especially urban development;
5) the pronounced seasonality of movement; and
6) the pervasive effect that this has had on the Great Plains temperament.

Nomadism is a fundamental feature of the Great Plains culture.[7] Since it has always been characteristic, it is accepted casually. The Staked Plains farmer may pull his boat 300 miles (480 km) round trip on Sunday to have

---

[7] No attempt is made here to explore the many facets of Great Plains culture and economic development, nor has any effort been made to review the substantive contributions of such eminent scholars of the Great Plains as Walter Kollmorgen, Leslie Hewes, E. S. Osgood, Carl Frederick Kraenzel, Addison E. Sheldon, E. E. Dale, John R. Borchert, and Walter Prescott Webb. Most geographers who have studied

FIG. 11. Summer swarm of tourists in Black Hills.

FIG. 13. Trailer homes in the oil boomtown of Gillette, Wyoming.

a bit of recreational activity on water. The small town resident of the Platte Valley views out-of-state cars with the same nonchalance as an Easterner notes county license numbers on cars from his own state. The Great Plainsman considers periodicity of movement as natural as the change of seasons. Summer tourists clog his highways and holiday havens (Fig. 11). Suitcase farmers go from one wheat

area to another. Sheep shearers work northward from the Edwards Plateau to Wyoming and Montana. Mexican and Spanish-American "stoop labor" roves northward each summer. Each year about 45,000 custom combines traverse state lines on the Great Plains. They start in June in Texas and Oklahoma; some keep moving until they finish in September along the Canadian line (Fig. 12). Cattle from

---

the Great Plains have either ignored their culture or have succumbed to the "melting pot" myth; this explains the dearth of geographical studies on Great Plains culture. One extraordinarily commendable exception is D. W. Meinig, *Imperial Texas* (Austin: University of Texas Press, 1969), which exemplifies the type of geographical exploration that could be made in other parts of the region. Our awareness of the Great Plains would be enhanced if we freed ourselves from the fetters of market psychology, from statistical limitations, and from our dependence on ocular perception. Then we might hear the creaks and squeaks of windmills, the blaring radios in tractor cabs, the whine of snowmobiles at night wending their way to country bars, the shrill vibrations of

the cicada, the coo of mourning doves, the rustle of the breeze in cottonwood trees, the clatter of freight trains along the Union Pacific tracks, and the incessant roar of diesel engines along interstate highways. These and countless other sounds characterize the "silent countryside." Perhaps, too, our ecological consciousness would be sharpened if we could recognize the smell of prairie hay curing in the windrow, the feedlot stench at Dodge City, the chemical odors of cotton-field insecticides, the fragrance of wild flowers along the stream valleys, the distinctive smell of sugar beet refineries, and the pungent aroma of alfalfa pelletizing mills. All of these pertain to the nature of the environment, but they are mostly beyond our ken.

FIG. 12. Oklahoma custom combines in South Dakota.

FIG. 14. New land for prospective irrigation agriculturists on the Staked Plains.

FIG. 15. Transcontinental truck driver asleep on New Mexico roadside table.

FIG. 17. Empty farmstead north of Cimarron, Kansas. A product of rural depopulation.

southwestern Texas are moved onto the winter wheat pastures of northern Texas, Oklahoma, and Kansas. Even the antelope migrate over the plains.

Non-seasonal movement results from the changing fortunes of oil, and towns rise and fall accordingly (Fig. 13). New irrigation developments generate movement (Fig. 14). Transportation on the Great Plains is a major activity, and keeps many workers shifting (Fig. 15). Bigger machinery and bigger farms shift rural residents cityward, and the rural population declines (Fig. 16).

Small or empty places dot the Great Plains (Figs. 17–21).[8] Bill, Wyoming, is the only "town" in the 112 miles (180 km) between

---

[8] I once spent two hours trying to find a "town" in the Sand Hills of Nebraska. The difficulty was that the town's only edifice had been moved seven miles and was then empty. No inhabitants there could speak of the changed location.

Douglas and Gillette. Bill has a population of two, Dean Munkres and his dog, Charlie (Fig. 22). Munkres dominates the local political scene. He is mayor, fireman, policeman, and postmaster. Forty people from a radius of thirty-five miles (60 km) call for mail at Bill. Based on volume, however, the main urban functions are the retailing of gasoline and beer. Munkres says that "gasoline gets you across the wide open spaces and beer makes you forget them." Dull Center, twenty-five miles (40 km) northeast of Bill, has twice the population, but simply is not a trade competitor because of its off-highway location.

Its transit nature gives the typical Great Plains town a special character and form. Billboards, gas stations, motels, truck stops, hamburger joints, and other highway phenomena stretch endlessly. Official signs designate "combine routes" as well as "truck routes" through town, and occasionally other official

FIG. 16. New apartment buildings in Denver to accommodate cityward population shift.

FIG. 18. Closed section-line road near McCook, Nebraska. A product of rural depopulation.

FIG. 19. Streetside speculation at Utopia, Texas. The season for this type of specialization is longer on the southern Great Plains.

FIG. 21. Main street of Oberlin, Kansas. A county seat, on an east-west federal highway, with over 2,000 people. Arcaded sidewalks are common only on the central and southern Great Plains.

signs give employment directions in Spanish to migrant field laborers. Most major highways in the region trend east-west, and the typical urban center is attenuated in that direction. The main exception is along the base of the Rockies where the elongation is north-south (Fig. 23). The principal business streets follow these axes, and the chief residential avenues are at right angles to the commercial thoroughfares. The trunk railroads, like the highways, are also mostly east-west. Livestock yards, grain elevators, and warehouses are strung out along the railroads and accentuate the elongated urban form. This form emphasizes the dominant east-west regional movement which has prevailed throughout the past 125 years.

The base of nomadism is tenuous and far removed from the oldest cultural centers. This is true in the New World as in the Old World.

Although the nomad is restless, he yearns for the symbols of high culture and distinguished achievement. Moving a London Bridge across an ocean to a desert is less surprising than moving it a like distance in the same type of environment.

Space is an obvious attribute of the Great Plains, yet areas of newfound affluence project their symbolic centers more pronouncedly skyward. The state capitol buildings of Nebraska and North Dakota emphasize the Great Plains psyche (Fig. 24). The downtown skylines of Dallas, Kansas City, and Denver follow the same pattern (Fig. 25). The Price Tower in Bartlesville, Oklahoma, not only accentuates the vertical component, but it fairly reeks of culture in the regional mind, since it was designed by Frank Lloyd Wright. Wright understood this aspect of the Great Plains mind just as surely as he comprehended the

FIG. 20. Main street of Gove, Kansas. A county seat, on a north-south state highway, with about 150 people.

FIG. 22. Heart of the central business district in Bill, Wyoming.

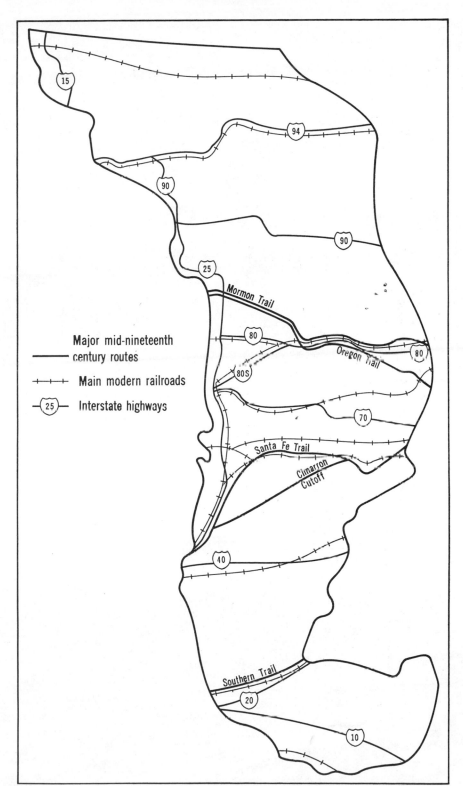

FIG. 23. Trunk routes on the Great Plains for over a century have been oriented mainly east-west.

FIG. 24. State Capitol at Bismarck, North Dakota.

FIG. 25. Skyline of downtown Dallas, Texas.

desert environment when he laid out the basic design for the auditorium at Arizona State University.

The northern plains have no nearby large interregional center. Minneapolis-St. Paul, although it is 400 miles (650 km) east of the regional boundary, serves almost the entire northern plains. Of this the "Twin Cities" are highly conscious, with their historic flour milling industry, their great transcontinental railway linkages westward, and their huge inflow of Great Plains migrants. Small wonder that that metropolitan area in 1972 had the tallest building between the Mississippi and the Pacific Coast, an overblown university, a state capitol with the "largest unsupported marble dome in the world," the internationally famed Tyrone Guthrie Theater, big league baseball, football, and hockey teams, and other assumed accoutrements of urbanity. Such remarkable societal inputs make the regional and interregional centers somewhat astounding unless the psychological factor is borne in mind. This same factor makes a Nieman–Marcus type of department store appropriate to Dallas, and makes possible the type of urban development, unique in America, that one finds along the river in San Antonio.

THE COWBOY COMPLEX

The heroic figure on the Great Plains is the cowboy (Figs. 26 and 27). This figure has been romanticized and embellished since the days of epic cattle drives from Texas northward along such routes as the Chisholm Trail (Fig. 28). The Western novel, the Western movie, and the Western television show have brought the tale to reader and non-reader alike. Chapters in the legend include the westward building railroads, the rise of the cowtowns of Abilene, Dodge City, and Ogalalla, the supplying of meat contracts to Indian agencies, the stocking of the ranges on the northern plains, the buffalo hunts, and the conflicts between cattleman and sheepman and between rancher and sodbuster. Eventually the Wild West show and Buffalo Bill were added to the theme, and the rodeo as a cowboy tournament spread across the nation (Fig. 29). Today the local business magnate places a set of Longhorns over his fireplace, hangs a reproduction of a Charles M. Russell or Frederic Remington painting in his den, and dons a cowboy hat as a proud regional insignia that is nationally recognized. When a Great Plainsman taps a rich oil deposit or otherwise strikes it rich, he purchases a ranch or suburban ranchette, builds a ranch style home, obtains a "string" of horses, attends the famous Denver livestock show in winter, and takes his family in summer to Cheyenne's "Frontier Days" (Figs. 30 and 31). Though the college football fields of the Midwest have Wolverines, Gophers, and Badgers, Great Plains gridirons are overrun by Longhorns, Bison, Buffaloes, and Cowboys. Even staid business journals feature articles on big "cattle spreads."

The cowboy complex, that was cradled on the Great Plains and the Texas Coastal Plain, now has national ramifications. For example, the horse is presently enjoying a popularity that has stunned conventional agriculturalists. Although the horse as a work animal on the plains has been largely displaced by the pickup truck, the region's horse population is booming. The 1970 tax rolls, for example, indicated the presence of 1,268 horses in Edwards County, Texas. But Texan tax conservatism was manifested when far more than 1,268 were rushed forward for inoculation as a dread equine disease spread across the state. The national horse population is also expanding. It soared from about three million head in 1959 to over eight million in 1971. Sales for feeding and outfitting them approximately tripled in the same period. Now many fashionable colleges have a "horsey" set of students who sponsor a college rodeo, wear Western garb, and drive "ranch wagons" adorned with brand insignia. In addition, courses of study have been added in horseshoeing and horse husbandry. The average horse of five decades ago was a work animal in a rural environment used by a person of modest education. Today the typical horse is a pleasure animal living in or adjacent to an urban area, and is a status symbol of the educated and affluent class. This transformation of the horse on the social scene is the reason that the Denver metropolitan area now has the greatest density of horses on the Great Plains.

Cows and cowboys are not just legendary

FIG. 26. Youngsters at 4-H livestock show at Faith, South Dakota. Cowboy garb is common.

FIG. 29. Livestock auctions, an important community element in the cowboy complex, are social events enjoyed by men and women.

FIG. 27. The 1971 American Angora Goat Breeders' Association show in Rocksprings, Texas. Even goat breeders favor cowboy attire.

FIG. 30. Cheyenne's "Frontier Days," America's most popular cowboy celebration.

FIG. 28. Billboard at Kenna, New Mexico, the home of the World's Champion Steer Roper in 1964 and 1966.

FIG. 31. A revered symbol of the cowboy complex is the log house. This one at Vandalia, Montana, was built in 1901 from cottonwood logs.

figures from the past or symbolic expressions of the present. Huge modern cattle feedlots have developed mostly since 1954. Up to that time range livestock on the Great Plains were mostly cattle (Fig. 32). Even the famous

sheep country of northwestern South Dakota and southeastern Montana was dominated by cattle. The only part of the Great Plains where cattle comprised less than fifty percent of the total livestock units was on the Edwards

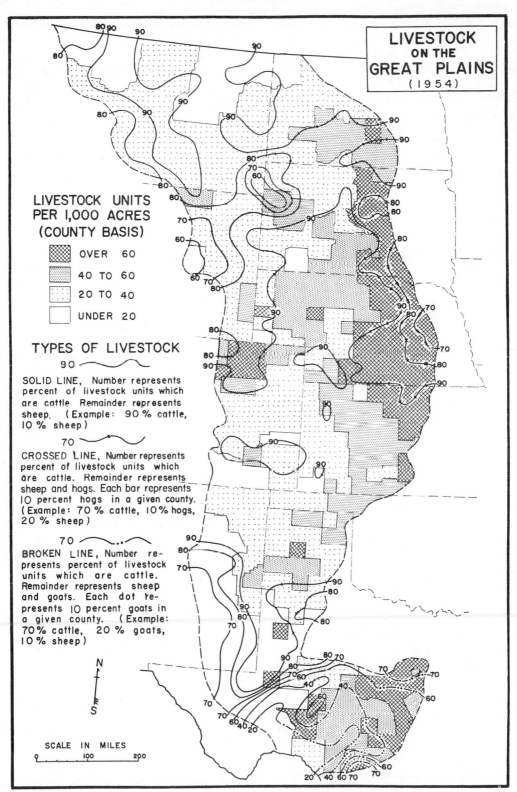

FIG. 32. Compilation by Jameson C. H. Lin, National Taiwan Normal University, Taipei, Taiwan, and cartography by Randall D. Sale, University of Wisconsin, Madison.

Plateau. Yet even there sheep and goat ranchers wore cowboy hats and also had herds of cattle. The nostalgic dream of the South may be of the Ante-Bellum plantation and the mint julep, but the Great Plainsman views his cowboy as a transcendent figure. This idol is a complex of past and present, and of the biologic, economic, and symbolic realms.

MEGALOPHILIA

No large region in the United States was so rapidly encompassed by the white man as the Great Plains. Huge cattle drives swept shortly from Texas northward across the entire grassland to the Canadian border. Wyoming, for example, had only slight stocking of its land by 1868. In 1871, according to a report of the Surveyor General of Wyoming Territory, forty stock-raising enterprises had a total of 86,000 cattle south of the North Platte and Sweetwater Rivers. Five years later Wyoming had an estimated 1,250,000 head, or approximately eighty-five percent of the 1970 total.

The ingress of farmers was similarly spectacular and resulted in dramatic population surges. Kansas had more than a ninefold increase in population between 1860 and 1880. Nebraska's population expanded fifteenfold during the same period.

Big holdings were established at the outset. The American Cattle Company of Scotland, one of the first big "outfits" in Nebraska, purchased their range of about one million acres along the Niobrara River in 1881. Purchased with the range were 23,000 head of cattle. One large Wyoming cattle company had over 200,000 head. The John Chisum ranch, in southeastern New Mexico, extended 200 miles along the Pecos River and in 1878 had over 100,000 cattle.

Big developments on the Great Plains were not restricted to the good old days (Figs. 33–38). They have continued to the present time. Even homestead laws were unable to restrain the cultural predilection for innovation and large scale operations. Various maneuvers were employed by homesteaders to circumvent the intent of the law. Legislators pushed through bills which permitted enlarged homestead acquisitions. The Sand Hills of Nebraska was the last large prairie area to be invaded by settlers; the Kincaid Act, enacted in 1904,

enabled a homesteader to acquire 640 acres (260 ha) without ruse, yet within a few years, huge ranch operations had been reestablished (Fig. 39). By 1945, one of the Nebraska Sand Hill ranches had 80,000 acres (32,000 ha) and another exceeded 100,000 acres (40,000 ha). The latter had a "cow-calf" pasture of thirty square miles in which a cowboy on horseback got lost!

Who were these people who were successful in amassing large acreages of recently homesteaded lands? In many cases they were the same families who had operated large ranches during the open range period. "Cream always rises to the top" is a phrase not unknown to the beef ranching areas of the Great Plains. Many Americans assert that the large landholdings have resulted from farm mechanization. In this region, however, large landholdings preceded mechanization; the latter simply accelerated the process.

Farm mechanization on the Great Plains is now on an unparalleled scale. The agricultural service man, with ten custom combines in his fleet and the necessary complement of trucks, is a nomad with about a third of a million dollars of capital investment. He harvests wheat all the way from the Staked Plains of Texas to the Saskatchewan boundary, a crow-flight distance of 1,200 miles (1,900 km). The wheat farmer in Montana, who "duckfoots" or chisel plows with a machine that takes a strip 100 feet (30 m) wide, will cover fifty acres (20 ha) per hour. A quarter century ago the Peterson Brothers of Garden County, Nebraska, were harvesting 20,000 acres (8,100 ha) of hay annually on their ranch with a crew of thirty-seven people, including the cook's wife.

National opinion holds that absolutely nothing approximates the bounds of a Texas joke.[9] Although the nation laughs at the supposed humor, Texans make reality loom ever larger. Texans want the biggest cattle ranch, the largest drive-in theater, the most immense enclosed athletic arena, and the tallest windmill in the world. Texans either have these things now, or they are under construction.

---

[9] Humor is a mirror both of culture and of the age of settlement. The main basis of Anglo humor in the older settled areas is pithy understatement; in newer areas its basis is flamboyant overstatement.

FIG. 33. Huge steam engine used in agriculture at Chinook, Montana in about 1900.

FIG. 36. Sheep on 20,000 acre ranch near Buffalo, South Dakota.

FIG. 34. A Sand Hills extended-family ranch with over 1,400 cattle.

FIG. 37. A 640 acre irrigated cotton field northwest of Lubbock, Texas.

FIG. 35. Texas combines at Carter, Montana, in August. In October they will be in soybean fields on the Yazoo Delta.

FIG. 38. Part of the Monfort feedlots at Greeley, Colorado, in which 600,000 animals are fattened annually.

Those who doubt this should visit Littlefield, Texas.

Texans are the leading promulgators of the Great Plains culture. Nowhere else is the transit character of the Great Plains exemplified so vividly, nowhere else is the cowboy so deified, and in no other area are so many innovations executed on such a grand scale.[10]

---

[10] Foreign observers often indicate that these propensities are American, and are not limited to the Great Plains, but the Great Plains represents these features in exaggerated form.

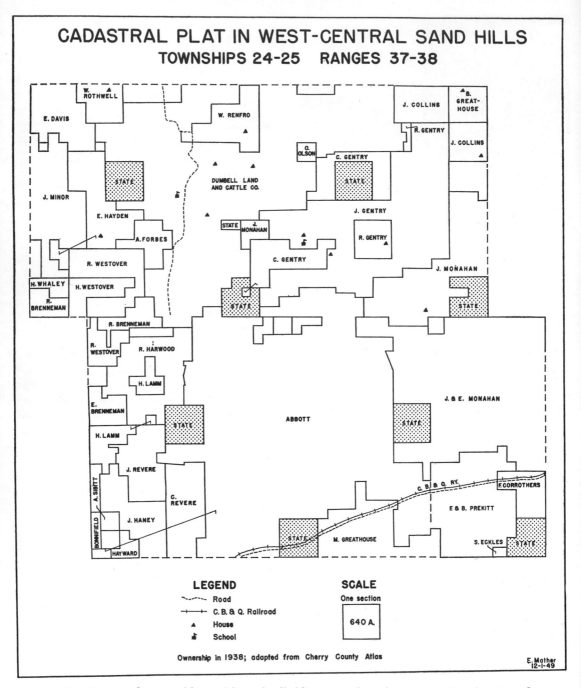

FIG. 39. Rapid reassemblage of large landholdings just thirty-four years after the Kincaid Act of 1904.

The religious map of the Great Plains reveals that the northern plains are dominated by Lutherans, the central plains by Methodists, and the southern plains by Baptists. Some observers maintain that the latter, who are mostly Texans, are narrow-minded and lazy. Such an interpretation, however, may be a consequence of taking liquor laws seriously, accepting the Protestant "work ethic" as gospel, and subscribing to social equality. Be that as it may, it was Texans who initiated most of the great cattle drives a century ago to the northern railheads, it was Texans who pioneered the introduction of Brahma cattle in the United States, and it was Texans who were responsible for developing the first officially recognized American breed of beef cattle, the Santa Gertrudis.[11] Texans opened most of the oil fields on the southern, central, and northern Great Plains. They initiated suitcase farming, they own and operate most of the migratory custom combines, they instituted the planting of winter wheat in the "spring wheat belt," and they have done the most to lower ground water tables on the Great Plains by well irrigation.

The cultural preoccupation with grand scale is exemplified by the development of large cattle feedlots. One hundred feedlots now supply sixteen percent of all the nation's fed cattle. Most of these are on the Great Plains or in the Southwest. The pioneer prototype of these mechanized operations was started by Warren Monfort near Greeley, Colorado (Fig. 38). During World War II he was feeding 3,400 head at a time. Experts were

---

[11] Colonel Charles Goodnight, who established the first large ranch in the Texas Panhandle, produced "cattaloes" in the 1880s by crossbreeding buffaloes and cattle.

impressed by the scale of operation. Now 200,000 head are fed simultaneously or 600,000 head annually. Two million gallons of drinking water are required daily. About 400,000 tons of manure are produced each year and sold to Colorado farmers. Keeping this feedlot in operation requires a total land area of approximately 25,000,000 acres to support 700,000 brood cows and bulls, to raise 600,000 yearlings to feedlot stage, and to produce 250,000 tons of silage, 365,000 tons of green chopped alfalfa, 25,000,000 bushels of corn, and minor feed ingredients. Monfort does not own all this land, but he is the entrepreneur who has organized and integrated the resources for the 800 acres of feedlots which he operates. Today he owns grain storage facilities with a 3,500,000 bushel capacity and purchases corn as far east as Iowa. Some of the meat is marketed through a national restaurant chain. The grain-fed beef produced by Monfort's feedlots is sufficient to supply all of the beef requirements for every man, woman, and child in the states of North Dakota, South Dakota, Wyoming, Montana, and Idaho. This type of enterprise evokes strong regional pride and challenges the Great Plainsman in his next step as a megalophile. That step will be taken in a non-monotonous environment, with an unencumbered past, and no doubt by a cowboy on a horse named "Trigger."

THE MIDDLE WEST

JOHN FRASER HART

ABSTRACT. Most of the Middle West was settled before the passage of the Homestead Act in 1863 by people of northern and western European ancestry who relied heavily upon water transport. Their commercial agriculture was based upon a standard rotation of corn, small grains, and hay, and most of the crops were fed to hogs or cattle. A century of rural stability produced a pecuniary value system associated with the family farm ideology. Part-owner operation has facilitated recent increases in farm size. Manufacturing in the west remains agriculturally-oriented, but the automobile industry has become more important in the east. The metropolitan Democratic vote is balanced by a Republican tradition in rural areas. The traits of the Middle West have strongly influenced the geographic profession in the United States. KEY WORDS: *Agriculture, Family farm, Farm size, Homesteads, Middle West, Prairies, Tenure of land, United States, Value systems, Voting patterns.*

THE Middle West is flát. Some parts, to be sure, have slopes so steep as to preclude cultivation, but such slopes are short, and the surface of the land is choppy rather than rough; the giant swells of Appalachia and the Ozarks fade out along the eastern and southern margins, and to the west a thousand miles of plainsland separate the Middle West from the mighty whitecaps of the Rocky Mountains. A few hilly sections lie within the region, but are not part of it. The average Midwesterner is more familiar with lakes and ponds than with hills and downs; the cultivator has greater problems with sand and swale than with steepness of slope.

In theory, perhaps, this level land, so bountifully endowed by Nature, might have served as an ideal laboratory for cultural geography, an essentially homogeneous area in which the cultural eccentricities of different human groups might have flowered to the fullest without environmental let or hindrance. In fact, it became the domain of *Homo economicus,* the altar upon which Babbitt sacrificed Clio to Mammon.

THE FIRST STAGE

The first human occupants of the Middle West were Indian hunters and a handful of Frenchmen. Like Kilroy, the Indians and the French were here, but they have left little evidence of the fact other than their names. Dedicated and diligent scholars can pick out

Indian trails which were used by French fur traders and later became routes of major highways; focal points on the trails became trading posts, and some developed into modern cities; and the treaty lines of Indian land cessions, or the long lots of French settlers, still appear on topographic maps.[1] A few Indian reservations are tucked away in odd and unwanted corners, but contemporary Midwesterners seldom stop to think that the Chicago and the Iowa were tribes of Indians, or that St. Louis was the King of France from 1226 to 1270.

Perhaps the most significant onomastic legacy of the French is the name they gave to the vast natural grasslands and open parklands, the "prairies," which were strange to Frenchman, Englishman, and American alike. The English language has no good and appropriate general word for grassland, only such special terms as "barren," "glade," "meadow," "green," "lawn," and "lea," each properly descriptive of a quite different and distinctive type.[2] The lack of such a name was of no import in the wooded areas east of

Dr. Hart is Professor of Geography at the University of Minnesota in Minneapolis.

[1] Sam B. Hilliard, "Indian Land Cessions," Map Supplement Number Sixteen, *Annals,* Association of American Geographers, Vol. 62 (1972); John Fraser Hart, "Field Patterns in Indiana," *Geographical Review,* Vol. 58 (1968), pp. 450–71; and topographic maps of such places as Detroit, Michigan; Green Bay, Wisconsin; and Vincennes, Indiana.

[2] Carl Ortwin Sauer, *Geography of the Pennyroyal: A Study of the Influence of Geology and Physiography upon the Industry, Commerce and Life of the People,* Series VI, Vol. 25 (Frankfort: Kentucky

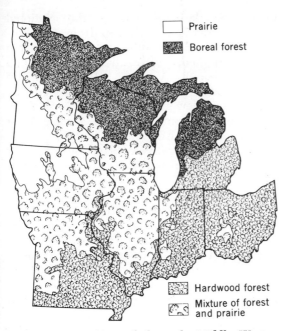

FIG. 1. Vegetation of the eight Middle Western states, generalized from the map by A. W. Küchler on pp. 90–91 of *The National Atlas of the United States of America.*

FIG. 2. Early routeways into the Middle West.

the Appalachians, but it began to matter in the Ohio valley, and became critical farther west as the eastern hardwood forest shaded through parkland into river bottom woodland and treeless grassland. None of the available English names was really appropriate for the strange form of vegetation, and the English-speaking pioneers were only too happy to adopt the alien name.

The eastern Middle West had forests of oak, hickory, beech, maple, and other deciduous hardwoods (Fig. 1). These trees were familiar to anyone of European stock; the details of their distribution told the intending settler much about the quality of the land. The bottomland forests farther west had similar species, but in drier climes these gradually gave way to elm, ash, and cottonwood. Narrow strips of valley woodland interfingered in enormously complex fashion with narrow prairie areas on the interstream uplands, and as far west as central Iowa most prairie areas were within a few miles of

woodland.[3] The treeless "barren" prairie lay in northwestern Iowa and southwestern Minnesota. To the north was the boreal forest, a mixture of conifers (pine, spruce, and fir) and northern hardwoods (maple and beech in the south, birch and aspen northwards).

The French *coureurs de bois* were primarily fur people, and they preferred the boreal forest to areas farther south, because the best pelts were in the north. Although the Middle West was of only marginal interest to them, they did explore and establish trading posts along the remarkably useful set of waterways which connects the Great Lakes with the Mississippi and Ohio rivers (Fig. 2).[4] The Wisconsin and Fox rivers, the Illinois River, and the Wabash and Maumee rivers occupy glacial spillways, relics of the time when ice sheets dammed the northward outlets of the Great Lakes and forced their waters to back up until they could overflow to the south. Rivers and streams, the trails of the French, became the avenues of American settlement.

THE SPREAD OF SETTLEMENT

For nearly three centuries the tangled uplands of Appalachia discouraged westward

Geological Survey, 1927), pp. 123–34. I remember talking with an oldtimer in Iowa who happened to mention that he had been born on the "barren" (by which he meant "treeless") prairie.

[3] Leslie Hewes, "Some Features of Early Woodland and Prairie Settlement in a Central Iowa County," *Annals,* Association of American Geographers, Vol. 50 (1960), pp. 40–57.

[4] Harlan H. Barrows, *Lectures on the Historical Geography of the United States as given in 1933,* edited by William A. Koelsch, Research Paper No. 17 (Chicago: University of Chicago Department of Geography, 1962), pp. 39–58.

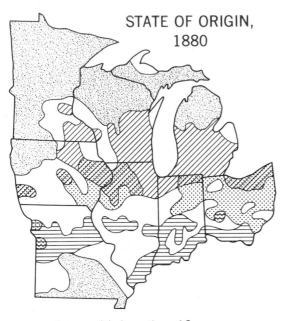

STATE OF ORIGIN,
1880

  Areas with less than 18 persons per
square mile

Two or more persons per square mile who
were born in

New York

Pennsylvania

Kentucky

FIG. 3. State of origin in 1880, compiled from
maps in Volume 1 of the 1880 *Census of Population*
which show the distribution of natives of Kentucky
(p. 416), New York (p. 480), Pennsylvania (p.
528), and a few other states.

movement from the eastern seaboard of the
United States. American settlers used three
principal entryways through Appalachia when
they finally did begin to flood into the Middle
West. Scotch-Irish frontiersmen, such as
Daniel Boone and Davy Crockett, from the
Watauga country of northeastern Tennessee
crossed over Cumberland Gap to the headwaters of the Kentucky and Cumberland
rivers, which drain into the Ohio (Fig. 2).
Men from the mid-Atlantic states crossed
Pennsylvania to the Forks of the Ohio, a
river which begins full-blown where the
Allegheny meets the Monongahela at Pittsburgh's Golden Triangle. This route was most
direct, but also the most difficult, and early
on it was supplemented by the Cumberland

Road (popularly known as the National
Road), a macadamized strip from Cumberland, Maryland, to Wheeling on the Ohio
River, and thence across the states of Ohio
and Indiana to Vandalia, Illinois, in an
abortive effort to reach St. Louis on the
Mississippi. New Englanders and New Yorkers made their entry into the Middle West
by way of the Erie Canal and the Great
Lakes, a comparatively easy water level
passage which became the principal route of
commerce.

Each entryway served a migration stream
from a distinctive source region, and these
streams remained remarkably separate as they
continued westward across the Middle West.
The *1880 Census of Population* contains a
scatter of maps which show the distribution,
by county, of persons born in selected states.
In 1880 natives of Kentucky were concentrated in the hilly southern fringe of the
Middle West, most natives of Pennsylvania
were in the middle just north of the National
Road, and natives of New York were concentrated in the north, to the west of Lakes
Erie and Michigan (Fig. 3). The northern
entryway also influenced streams of migration
which came directly from Europe. Many
Germans and Scandinavians who landed at
New York City, the principal nineteenth
century port of immigration, were channeled
westward into Wisconsin and Minnesota,
respectively, rather than into more southerly
areas.

The major river valleys and ports on the
Great Lakes strongly influenced the spread
of settlement within the Middle West (Fig.
4).[5] The settled area in 1820 focused on the

———————

[5] I mapped the spread of settlement in the Middle
West by superimposing the isopleths for eighteen
persons per square mile from each census between
1820 and 1900 (Fig. 4). With all due respect to
Frederick Jackson Turner, but considerably less to
others who have slavishly followed his lead in using
a density of only two persons per square mile to
mark the frontier, I feel compelled to agree with the
Introduction to the *1880 Census of Population*, which
stated quite categorically that agricultural settlement
could only be considered successful where the population density exceeded eighteen persons, or approximately four families, per square mile; John Fraser
Hart, "The Westward Movement of the Frontier,
1820–1860," in *The Kniffen Festschrift* (Baton
Rouge: Louisiana State University Press, forthcoming).

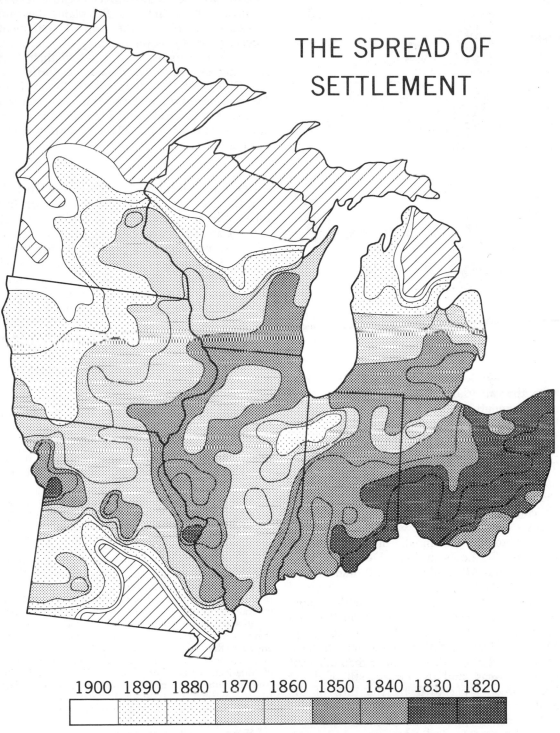

THE SPREAD OF
SETTLEMENT

1900   1890   1880   1870   1860   1850   1840   1830   1820

FIG. 4. The spread of settlement in the Middle West, as indicated by the isopleths for eighteen persons per square mile at each census between 1820 and 1900.

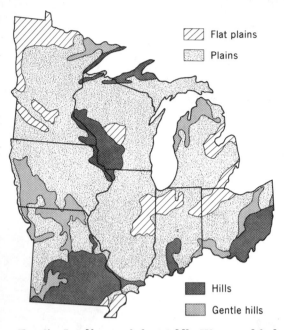

Flat plains

Plains

Hills

Gentle hills

FIG. 5. Landforms of the Middle West, modified from the map by Edwin H. Hammond on pp. 62–63 of *The National Atlas of the United States of America*.

Ohio valley between Cincinnati and Louisville, the valleys of the two Miami rivers north of Cincinnati, and the National Road. In successive decades it expanded into the valleys of the Wabash, the Mississippi, the Missouri, the Illinois, and the Des Moines. Tentacles reaching up the river valleys met and coalesced with movement inland from the Great Lake ports, especially Detroit, Chicago, and Milwaukee. The leading metropolitan centers of today were the initial foci of settlement: Cincinnati in 1820, Kansas City and St. Louis in 1830, Detroit in 1840, Chicago and Milwaukee in 1850, and Minneapolis-St. Paul in 1860.

The interstream areas were settled more slowly, some because they were too flat, and some because they were not flat enough (Fig. 5). The hills of southern Ohio and Indiana were settled a decade or so later than adjacent lowland areas, and the Ozarks still had not been effectively settled by the turn of the century (Fig. 4). The first generation of settlers also bypassed the bogs, bottomlands, and other poorly drained areas, which were used, if at all, only as a kind of unregulated common grazing or meadow land. Flat land, which today seems quite attractive, was

avoided by the early settlers because it was so difficult to drain.[6] The flat plains show up almost as clearly on the map of settlement spread (Fig. 4) as on the map of landforms (Fig. 5), and many have acquired their own local names: the Black Swamp in northwestern Ohio, the Kankakee Marsh in northern Indiana, the Grand Prairie in east central Illinois, the Central Sand Plain in Wisconsin, and the Mankato Till Plain in southwestern Minnesota.

The Prairies

Contrary to a fairly widespread belief, prairie areas appear to have had remarkably little influence on the spread of settlement (Figs. 1 and 4). Extensive prairies should have come as no very great shock to the early settlers, because they had already encountered smaller versions in Kentucky, Ohio, and Indiana (Fig. 1). Of course they needed timber for firewood, and to a lesser extent for fencing and buildings; if given a choice, they selected land at the edge of the woods rather than on the prairie, but even on the open prairie most farms were no more than a few miles from a valley woodlot.[7] The larger prairies were bypassed because they were inaccessible, poorly drained, or both, but not because they were treeless.[8] Early routes followed the stream valleys, and settlement followed the routes; prairie land was taken up wherever road construction made it ac-

[6] With a few exceptions, geographers have almost completely ignored the enormous amount of artificial drainage which has been necessary in the Middle West before the land could be cultivated; Leslie Hewes, "The Northern Wet Prairie of the United States: Nature, Sources of Information, and Extent," *Annals,* Association of American Geographers, Vol. 41 (1951), pp. 307–23. Perhaps the explanation lies in the fact that a casual observer sees little evidence of drainage works, and their end product is similarity to adjacent areas, rather than distinctiveness from them; Leslie Hewes and Philip E. Frandson, "Occupying the Wet Prairie: The Role of Artificial Drainage in Story County, Iowa," *Annals,* Association of American Geographers, Vol. 42 (1952), pp. 24–50. Another notable exception is Martin R. Kaatz, "The Black Swamp: A Study in Historical Geography," *Annals,* Association of American Geographers, Vol. 45 (1955), pp. 1–35.

[7] Hewes, op. cit., footnote 3.

[8] Douglas R. McManis, *The Initial Evaluation and Utilization of the Illinois Prairies, 1815–1840,* Research Paper No. 94 (Chicago: University of Chicago Department of Geography, 1964).

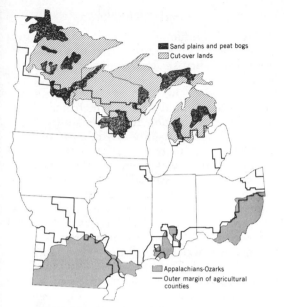

FIG. 6. The outer margin of the agricultural counties of the Middle West in 1964 (from Hart, op. cit., footnote 25) superimposed on a map of major land types after C. P. Barnes and F. J. Marschner, "Natural Land-Use Areas of the United States," 1:4,000,000 (Washington: U. S. Department of Agriculture, Bureau of Agricultural Economics, 1933); the unshaded areas (Mid-continent land type) contain "little land the best use of which is problematical."

TABLE 1.—THOUSANDS OF ACRES HOMESTEADED, BY STATE, 1868–1961

	Thousands of acres	Percentage of total area
Minnesota	10,389,606	20.4
Missouri	3,644,306	8.3
Wisconsin	3,110,990	8.5
Michigan	2,321,937	6.6
Iowa	903,164	2.5
Ohio	7,707	0.03
Illinois	5,667	0.016
Indiana	1,785	0.008
MIDDLE WEST	20,386,162	7.1

Source: Bureau of Land Management, *Homesteads* (Washington: U. S. Department of the Interior, Bureau of Land Management, 1962), p. 2.

cessible, although the settlement of some of the larger prairie areas had to await the coming of the railroads.[9]

Why have geographers and historians been so preoccupied with the prairie? Perhaps we have been bemused by the fine romantic notion that pioneers from the wooded areas were surprised and baffled when they burst forth onto the prairie. It certainly gives our egos a boost to think that those tough old-timers, hardy lot though they were, could not match us in intelligence. Whatever the explanation, this preoccupation with the prairie has diverted our attention from another vegetational boundary where the frontier really did stall, and where it has remained stalled for a century. The westward flow of settlement was not seriously hindered by the prairie, but its northward flow was halted rather abruptly when it encountered the boreal forest, and it

[9] Charles E. Dingman, "Land Alienation in Houston County, Minnesota: Preferences in Land Selection," *Geographical Bulletin*, in press.

has remained halted ever since (Fig. 6). The prairies have been farmed for more than half a century, but the boreal forest to the north and the hills to the south remain essentially negative areas as far as agriculture is concerned.

Homesteads and Immigrants

The settlement isochrones for 1860 and 1890 are especially important, because they more or less coincide with two major events in American history (Fig. 4). In 1863, when the Homestead Act was passed, most of the better land in the Middle West had already been purchased from the General Land Office, and precious little remained free for the taking in farms of 160 acres. Minnesota was the only state in the Middle West in which any significant amount of good farm land was homesteaded, although seekers after free land did pick over the carcass in the boreal forest to the north and the Ozarks to the south (Table 1). The common notion that the Middle West is a checkerboard of 160-acre homesteaded farms divided into four square 40-acre fields has little basis in fact.

The isochrone for 1890 more or less coincides with a major shift in the country of birth of the foreign-born population (Fig. 7). Earlier immigrants had come from western and northern Europe (Germany, the British Isles, and Scandinavia); by and large they spoke the same languages, practiced the same religions, and shared the same social and political traditions as those who were already on the ground. By 1890 the original settlers

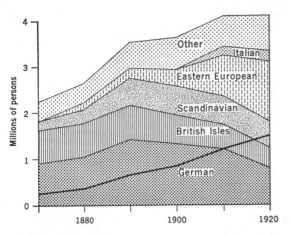

FIG. 7. The foreign-born population of the eight Middle Western states, 1870–1920, by area of birth. The heavy line across the base of the graph indicates the total foreign-born population of three counties: Cook (Chicago), Illinois; Cuyahoga (Cleveland), Ohio; and Wayne (Detroit), Michigan.

had begun to die off, but their native-born children and grandchildren were taking over their farms. Little land was left for the immigrants flooding in from eastern and southern Europe (Bohemia, Poland, Russia, Italy, and the Balkans), who were different in nearly every way imaginable: they were Catholic rather than Protestant, spoke Romance or Slavic rather than Germanic languages, and were accustomed to communal rather than individual societies and to feudal and authoritarian rather than to democratic political systems.

The new immigrants sought opportunity in the cities rather than in the countryside. Three cities (Chicago, Detroit, and Cleveland) increased their share of the total foreign-born population of the eight Middle Western states from 12.5 percent in 1890 to 36.4 percent in 1920 (Fig. 7); in both years they contained roughly half of those born in southern and eastern Europe. The new immigrants were hard-working and thrifty, but culturally insecure. They faced great pressures to conform, to demonstrate their love for their adopted country, and to become more American than the Americans themselves; their sons have been members of the welcoming committees of "hard hats" which have greeted later immigrants from the South, whether poor blacks from cotton country or poor whites from Appalachia.

Land Alienation

Virginia militiamen led by George Rogers Clark liberated the eastern part of the Middle West from British forces during the Revolutionary War. In 1784 the Commonwealth of Virginia ceded this territory, the Old Northwest, to the United States, which had to develop a technique for alienating it to individual citizens. The Ordinance of 1785 established a rectangular system of land survey (variously known as the township-and-range, congressional, and General Land Office system) which is discussed in considerable detail in most introductory geography textbooks. The land was surveyed before it was alienated, to forestall some of the malpractices and abuses which had developed in the East, and then it was sold at public auction for a minimum price and in minimal acreages.

I suspect that the size of farms in the Middle West continues to be significantly influenced by the minimal acreage of land that had to be purchased. The limited evidence available indicates that the size and boundaries of farm ownership units remained remarkably stable from the date of alienation until around the start of World War II.[10] The minimal price of $1.25 an acre might seem pathetically low to a contemporary Middle Westerner, but it probably was quite a large obstacle to many purchasers in the early days, and one must assume that many settlers, perhaps the majority, bought no more land than the law required. The minimal purchase unit was set at 160 acres in 1804, 80 acres in 1820, and 40 acres in 1832, which could have permitted the settlement of most of the Middle West in farms no larger than forty acres. The reduction in size of minimal purchase unit in 1832 implies that some body of opinion must have considered forty acres either an adequate size for a farm, or the most land that a poor settler ought to be required to buy.

[10] Norman J. W. Thrower, *Original Survey and Land Subdivision*, Association of American Geographers Monograph Series, Number Four (Chicago: Rand McNally, 1966), pp. 60–71; Wayne E. Kiefer, *Rush County, Indiana: A Study in Rural Settlement Geography*, Geographic Monograph Series, Vol. 2 (Bloomington: Indiana University Department of Geography, 1969), pp. 27–37; and Pierce County Geographical Society, *Upper Coulee Country* (Prescott, Wisconsin: Trimbelle Press, forthcoming).

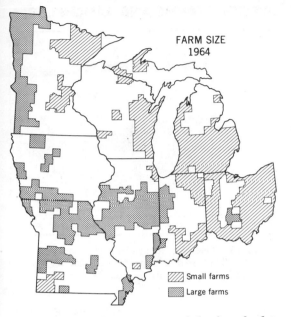

FARM SIZE
1964

Small farms

Large farms

FIG. 8. More than a quarter of the farm land in the "small farm" areas was in farms smaller than 140 acres in 1964, and more than three quarters of the farm land in the "large farm" areas was in farms larger than 220 acres.

The date of settlement (Fig. 4) has a broad similarity to the pattern of farm size in 1964 (Fig. 8). The older areas in Ohio, Indiana, and even eastern Wisconsin had smaller farms than the newer areas in central Illinois, northern Missouri, and western Minnesota. The suggestion that farms are smaller where woodland had to be cleared, and larger on the prairie, seems somewhat glib and overly simplistic; the patterns on the map of farm size (Fig. 8) have no greater congruence with the patterns on the vegetation map (Fig. 1) than with those on the map of settlement spread (Fig. 4).[11]

---

[11] Ethnic factors might also have influenced the initial size of farms, although at present this is little more than a hunch that requires considerable investigation. Swain and Mather suggest that many Norwegian farmers who settled in western Wisconsin under the provisions of the Homestead Act appear to have claimed less than the 160 acres to which they were entitled. The new settlers, aware that eighty acres, or even forty, would have been a veritable estate back in the old country, saw no point in taking more land even when it was free; Harry Swain and Cotton Mather, *St. Croix Border Country* (Prescott, Wisconsin: Trimbelle Press, 1968), p. 64.

Why did settlers farther west purchase larger acreages? Perhaps the declining value of the dollar played a significant role, because the minimum price of $1.25 an acre remained unchanged from 1820 until the Homestead Act was passed in 1863, and this figure probably did not loom nearly so large after the passage of three or four decades. Vastly improved farm machinery must also have been extremely important, because it enabled a family to handle a larger acreage. Cyrus McCormick invented the reaper in 1831, John Deere introduced the steel plow in 1837, and between 1847 and 1864 major improvements were made in revolving disc harrows, binders, balers, and checkrow corn planters. By 1840 the cast-iron plow had replaced the wooden moldboard plow, and in turn it was superseded by the steel plow.

FARMING SYSTEMS

The men who took up farm land in the Middle West were materialists, not escapists. They did not flee to the wilderness to get away from society, they came to the frontier to secure the blessings of the good life for themselves and for their posterity. They were ready and willing to work hard, and all they needed was a commercial product, something they could send back to the older settled areas to pay for the goods they desired. They sought land and a farming system which would deliver such a product. The early settlers in the Middle West, with surprising quickness, developed a farming system which was economically successful and ecologically sound, and an efficient infrastructure evolved to serve it. Later arrivals were not compelled to adopt a system which was already working, paying handsome rewards to its practitioners, and served by an efficient infrastructure, but most of them did so, and most of the rest lived to regret their failure to conform.

The only crop that offered any appreciable cash return in the early days was wheat, which moved westward with the frontier, especially in the north, where the Yankees and Yorkers who came to roost in Michigan, Wisconsin, and Minnesota could remember the glory days of wheat in the Genessee country. They shipped their wheat eastward by way of the Great Lakes and the Erie Canal, but wheat is a bulky commodity, and

DAIRY FARMS, 1964

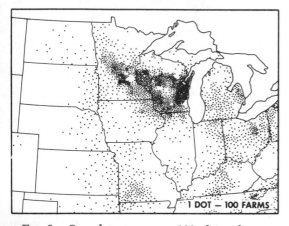

FIG. 9. One dot represents 100 dairy farms in 1964. This map is reproduced from an original provided by the U. S. Bureau of the Census.

LIVESTOCK FARMS AND RANCHES, 1964

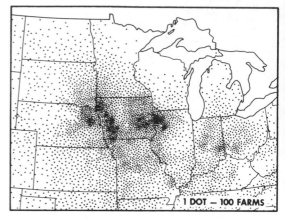

FIG. 10. One dot represents 100 livestock farms in 1964. This map is reproduced from an original provided by the U. S. Bureau of the Census.

expensive to transport. Furthermore, the first few crops of wheat reaped the accumulated fertility of the soil, and an alternative farm product soon became mandatory.

Many farmers in Wisconsin and Minnesota turned to livestock when wheat ceased to be profitable. They could not produce good feed crops for fattening hogs and beef cattle, but they had abundant roughage, which was well suited to the sustenance of dairy cattle (Fig. 9). The Yankees and Yorkers who settled the dairy country had brought with them the regular work habits and frugality for which New England is notorious, and these have been reinforced by later infusion of immigrants from Germany and Scandinavia.

Farther south, in the Ohio valley, the men who had come from Pennsylvania and the middle states were more inclined to walk their crops to market in the form of fat hogs or fat cattle, and their principal crop, corn, was ideal for fattening livestock. They found a ready market for salt pork down the Mississippi River. Corn-hog farming had become established in the Miami valleys of southwestern Ohio by 1820, and Cincinnati had earned its nickname of "Porkopolis." The mixed crop and livestock farming system which developed in southwestern Ohio has become the basic farming system of the Corn Belt (Fig. 10).

The major gaps between concentrations of livestock farms in the Corn Belt are pre-

dominantly the large level areas of poorly drained land that were bypassed by the first generation of settlers (Figs. 4, 5, and 11). The Grand Prairie of east central Illinois is a good example.[12] Drainage on the required scale demanded more capital than individual farmers could muster, and the job was eventually accomplished by entrepreneurs who attempted to recoup their investments as quickly as possible by selling the land in large blocks (Fig. 8). These blocks of land were so large that the men who farmed them had no time to spare for livestock, and the Grand Prairie has produced an exportable surplus of corn from the very beginning; favorable freight rates and marketing facilities have developed in response to this surplus. Much of the land was bought by investors who rented it to tenants, and farm tenancy became an accepted fact of farm life in the area.

The Rotation of Crops

For more than a hundred years farmers in the Middle West have practiced a standard three-year crop rotation (corn, small grains, and hay), and they have fed most of their crops to hogs and cattle. The basic crop rotation is a modified form of a southeastern

---

[12] I am deeply indebted to Arlin Fentem for sharing with me his intimate knowledge of the agricultural evolution of the Grand Prairie in Illinois; Kaatz, op. cit., footnote 6, pp. 32–34, implied that the Black Swamp has a similar history.

CASH-GRAIN FARMS, 1964

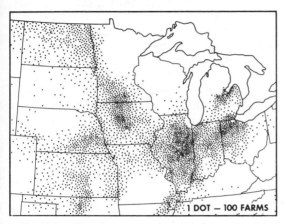

1 DOT — 100 FARMS

FIG. 11. One dot represents 100 cash grain farms in 1964. This map is reproduced from an original provided by the U. S. Bureau of the Census.

Pennsylvania rotation system, which in turn was a modification of a rotation system used fairly widely on the better lands of western Europe.[13] The standard Middle Western crop rotation had been developed in southwestern Ohio by 1820, probably by settlers from southeastern Pennsylvania, and it remained unchanged, except in detail, for well over a century.

[13] The medieval three-field rotation was food grain, feed grain, and fallow (wheat, barley, and fallow on the better soils; rye, oats, and fallow on the poorer ones). In the Agricultural Revolution this rotation was replaced by a four-year rotation of food grain, fodder root row crop, feed grain, and hay (wheat, turnips, barley, and clover on the better soils). In the New World corn replaced both turnips (fodder row crop) and barley (feed grain), and it took first place in a new three-year rotation of corn, small grains, and hay. Winter wheat was the customary small grain in the southern part of the Middle West, and oats in the northern part; alfalfa has replaced clover as the leading hay crop since World War I. Between the two world wars farmers in some areas replaced small grains and hay with a cash crop, soybeans, and developed a two-year rotation of corn and soybeans. Although these four rotations are the basic models, any farmer might modify any one of them on any field by extending one year of the rotation to two or more. European rotations are discussed briefly in John Fraser Hart, "The Turnip and the Agricultural Revolution in England," *Geographical Review*, Vol. 60 (1970), pp. 568–69, and at much greater length in H. G. Sanders, *Rotations*, Bulletin No. 85 of the Ministry of Agriculture and Fisheries (London: Her Majesty's Stationery Office, 1944); the rotations of southeastern Pennsylvania are discussed

The traditional rotation makes good sense both ecologically and economically. Corn, the linchpin, is an almost ideal crop for the deep fertile soils and abominable climate of the Middle West.[14] The grain is the world's best feed, as witness the high esteem of "corn-fed" when applied to certain forms of livestock.[15] In the northern parts of the Middle West, where early frost might ambush the crop before the grain has had a chance to ripen, the entire plant can be cut green, chopped, and stored in silos for winter feed.

in Walter M. Kollmorgen, *Culture of a Contemporary Rural Community: The Old Order Amish of Lancaster County, Pennsylvania,* Rural Life Studies 4 (Washington: U. S. Department of Agriculture, Bureau of Agricultural Economics, 1942), p. 15; rotations in the Corn Belt are discussed in Clyde E. Leighty, "Crop Rotation," pp. 406–30 of *Soils and Men,* Yearbook of Agriculture, 1938 (Washington: U. S. Department of Agriculture, 1938); and the rationale for the Corn Belt rotation is discussed in Karl H. W. Klages, *Ecological Crop Geography* (New York: Macmillan, 1942), pp. 379–80.

[14] Geographers have long extolled the virtues of the Middle West for growing corn, as well they should have, but for anyone whose aesthetic requirements transcend those of a cornstalk the climate is pretty darned miserable, winter or summer. Winter snow, sleet, and ice regularly convert highways into skating rinks, and entire regions are tied up when the fierce driving winds of the dreaded blizzard pile deep drifts of snow to the lee of any obstacle; John F. Rooney, Jr., "The Urban Snow Hazard in the United States: An Appraisal of Disruption," *Geographical Review*, Vol. 57 (1967), pp. 538–59. Summers are disagreeably muggy, hot, and humid, but many people, including their elected representatives, still consider air-conditioning slightly sinful, because you can survive a summer without it. True enough, but given the chance, few Middle Westerners will pass up the chance to escape to an air-conditioned building, or even to an air-conditioned car, at every possible opportunity during the long, hot, summer months. Thundershowers may be great for the crops, but they don't help people very much, because windows have to be closed to keep out the driving rain, and the humidity rises inside even though the air outside might have been "freshened." It's a great climate for making a living, but it's no place to have to live, unless you consider making a living the principal purpose of living.

[15] In 1949 five of every ten ears of corn were fed to hogs, three to cattle, and one to other forms of livestock; the tenth ear provided the raw material for more than six hundred industrial products, including corn starch, which people used to make their shirt collars stiff, and a popular national beverage, which had the same effect upon the people themselves.

The standard small grain crop was either winter wheat or oats. Winter wheat was dominant in the south, but gave way to oats in northerly areas where the growing season was too short to permit a farmer to seed winter wheat in a field after he had removed the corn crop from it. Wheat was sold as a cash crop; most of the oats was fed on the farm where it was produced, mainly to breeding stock or young animals.

The relatively limited economic return from the small grain crop was augmented by its ecological value, because it was a "nurse crop" for the soil-building hay crop which followed it in the rotation. The seeds of a leguminous hay crop (alfalfa or clover) were planted with the small grain seed, and the faster-growing small grain gave some protection against sun and rain while the young forage plants were becoming established.

The basic rotation was modified in many ways. On fertile, level land, for example, a farmer might take two crops of corn from a field before planting small grain. The hay crop might be left a second year and used as rotation pasture, especially on steep land subject to erosion. A major modification resulted from the introduction of soybeans between the two world wars.[16] Soybeans replaced small grains and hay in the second and third years of the standard rotation, and led to a two-year cash crop rotation of corn and soybeans.

Toward the peripheries of the Middle West the standard three-year rotation of corn, small grains, and hay was modified in response to

increasing environmental stress.[17] In the drier areas to the west, for example, corn and hay were low production or even risky crops, and farmers concentrated their efforts on the small grain, wheat. Farmers in the hilly areas to the south and east practiced the standard rotation on level areas, but much of the land was too steep for any use but pasture or woodland. Steepness of slope was also a problem in recently glaciated areas to the north, where good soil management required that more of the land should be used for pasture, and more of the rotation should be devoted to hay. The shorter and cooler growing season to the north encouraged an emphasis on corn for silage rather than corn for grain, and oats replaced winter wheat as the dominant small grain. Summers on the fringes of the boreal forest were too cool for any crop but hay, and even hay was a risky crop in the northern reaches of the Middle West.

The Choice of Livestock

Any attempt to understand the nature of farming in an area must be based on an understanding of functional relationships, such as crop rotations and livestock feeding systems, which influence the decisions made by individual farmers.[18] The crop rotation, which must be in nice ecological balance, produces an assemblage of crops which the farmer can consume (subsistence farming), feed to livestock (mixed farming), or sell (cash crop farming). The kinds of crops he produces, and the kinds of feed he has available, will have an important influence on the farmer's decisions as to the nature of the livestock

[16] The high-protein soybean must be considered something of a miracle crop, and it certainly is a relatively new one to the Middle West, because data on soybeans were not even published in the U. S. Census of Agriculture until 1929. The crop is a leguminous soil-enricher if it is grazed, cut for hay, or plowed under for green manure, but much of its nitrogen is transferred from its root nodules to its beans if the beans are allowed to ripen. Oil crushed from the beans is an ingredient of shortening, margarine, and other food products, and it has numerous industrial uses; the residual meal is an excellent concentrated feed for livestock. Before World War II the crop was used primarily for soil improvement, but the switch to a cash grain oil crop has resulted from a steadily increasing demand. The soybean is one of the few crops that has not managed to glut the market in the last few decades, and the demand is international; approximately forty percent of each year's crop is exported.

[17] Apart from soybeans, and perhaps grain sorghums on the drier western margins, new crops have not made much of a dent in the standard rotation, but tinkering by plant breeders has greatly modified the climatic range of grain corn, silage corn, winter wheat, oats, and hay, and government acreage restrictions on certain crops have played havoc with their traditional distribution patterns.

[18] John Fraser Hart, "Geographic Covariants of Types of Farming Areas," pp. 7–9 of E. S. Simpson, ed., Agricultural Geography, I. G. U. Symposium, Research Paper No. 3 (Liverpool: University of Liverpool Department of Geography, 1965). Conversely, the computation of mere mathematical relationships between crop acreages or livestock numbers can be a blind alley leading only to neat and tidy maps of combinations which are essentially meaningless because they are not based on any functional relationship.

operation in which he will engage, but other factors will also influence his thinking.

Consider, for example, the question of hogs versus cattle. Cattle are more prestigious and demand less work; many hog farmers dream of the day when they can "trade up" from hogs to cattle. Hogs have shorter intestines, and are better than cattle at converting corn and other concentrated feeds into meat, but cattle are more efficient converters of roughages, such as silage, hay, and pasture. One might think that a farmer with lots of hay and pasture land might lean toward a cattle operation, which is indeed usually the case, but a farmer who produces quantities of concentrated feeds does not necessarily turn to hogs. Hogs and corn compete for the same labor, and the size of the hog operation tends to decrease as the amount of corn produced on the farm increases. A hog farmer breeds his own animals, because hogs eat like hogs, gain better than a pound a day, and are fat and ready for market at an age of six months; the farmer must tend to his hogs at the same time that he is busy with his crops. The beef farmer can afford to pay a rancher to put bone and hide on the lean feeder calves (six months old) and yearlings (eighteen months old) which he buys in the fall after he has harvested the crops he will use to fatten them in his feedlot.[19]

As a general rule, the farmer with a small corn acreage can afford the time to fatten hogs, the intermediate farmer fattens cattle, and the farmer with a large acreage of corn does not have enough time to fiddle around with livestock. Within the Corn Belt, therefore, the small farms of Ohio and Indiana tend to concentrate on hogs, the large farms of central Illinois tend to sell their grain rather than feeding it to livestock, and the medium-sized farms of Iowa tend to concentrate on the fattening of beef cattle which have been shipped in from ranch areas to the west (Figs. 10 and 11). A concentration on dairy farming

in Wisconsin and Minnesota can be related to the abundance of roughages, such as corn silage, hay, and pasture on farms in the cooler lands north of the Corn Belt (Fig. 9).

The Look of the Land

Areas of agricultural specialization within the Middle West are manifest by differences in their farmsteads, in the size and fencing of their fields, and in the distinctive establishments of their small rural service centers. Some of these differences may be detected by careful study of topographic maps, but others require observant travel.[20]

The corn-hog farming areas of the eastern Middle West have small farms and simple farmsteads. The township containing the topographic map excerpt has six to eight farmsteads per square mile, which can be translated into an average farm size of eighty to a hundred acres (Fig. 12). Most farmsteads have only one large general purpose barn, although many also have a corn crib, farrowing sheds, and other buildings too small to be shown on the topographic map. Fields of ten to twenty acres are securely fenced with hog-tight woven wire; most are interchangeable squares, because every field is used for pasture at some time in the crop rotation. The rectangular woodlots at the backs of many farms are relics of the mixed hardwood forest which covered the area before it was settled (Fig. 1). The villages of the area have few establishments which are distinctively related to the agricultural economy, because fat hogs, the principal product, are trucked to central stockyards for sale.

The corn-cattle-hog farming areas of the western Middle West have the largest number of buildings per farmstead (Fig. 10). The township which contains the topographic map excerpt has four farmsteads per square mile, or 160-acre farms (Fig. 13). Each farmstead is a complex of well-maintained buildings which provide shelter and storage space for corn, oats, hay, cattle, hogs, and farm machinery. Most farmsteads include an old horse barn which is now used for general storage, a steer barn which opens onto a

---

[19] The model described here, like any model, is a gross over-simplification of reality. For example, the farmer who fattens beef animals on corn is well aware that "the sow hangs on the cow's tail;" much concentrated feed passes straight through a beef animal and drops to the ground behind it, where it is eagerly devoured by hogs. The usual "cow-sow ratio" in a Middle Western feedlot is two hogs behind each steer or heifer.

[20] The following discussion is indebted, in large measure, to a longtime fascination with the two maps on pp. 234–35 of Preston E. James, *An Outline of Geography* (Boston: Ginn, 1935).

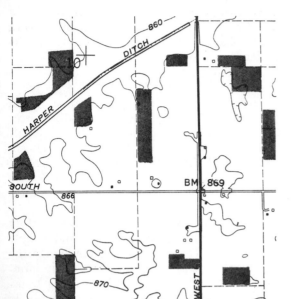

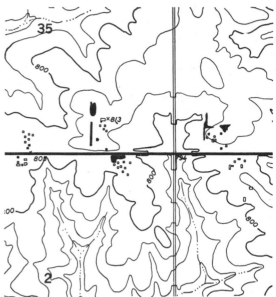

FIG. 12. A corn-hog farming area, as illustrated by part of the Point Isabel, Ind., 1:24,000 topographic sheet, which was published in 1960. The township had seven or eight farmsteads per square mile, indicating a mean farm size of eighty to ninety acres. If the population of the township at each census is divided by the number of houses in 1960, the mean number of persons per household has ranged from 5.8 in 1880 to 2.9 in 1960 and 3.0 in 1970. The woodlots are relicts of the mixed forest which formerly covered the area. A drainage ditch crosses the upper left corner.

FIG. 13. A corn-cattle-hog farming area, as illustrated by part of the Tipton East, Iowa, 1:24,000 topographic sheet, which was published in 1953. The township had slightly more than four farmsteads per square mile, indicating a mean farm size of 160 acres. If the population of the township at each census is divided by the number of houses in 1953, the mean number of persons per household has ranged from 5.9 in 1870 to 3.5 in 1970. Small windbreaks have been planted to the north and west of several farmsteads.

stoutly fenced feedlot, a large corn crib and granary, a machine shed and repair shop, and a variety of other buildings. Many farmsteads have windbreaks to shelter them from fierce north and west winds. Interchangeable, square, forty-acre fields are fenced with woven wire. Many small towns have holding pens beside the railroad tracks for lean feeder cattle shipped in from western ranches; the feeders normally arrive in October, and have been fattened for sale by mid-February.

The cash grain farming areas have the largest farms and the smallest and simplest farmsteads in the Middle West (Fig. 11). The township which contains the topographic map excerpt has 3.3 farmsteads per square mile, and farms which average 200 acres or more (Fig. 14). Each farmstead has a corn crib/granary for storing corn and soybeans, but only a few have a machine shed/repair shop, and the old horse barn is long gone. Farm-

stead windbreaks are common. Eighty-acre fields are elongated to reduce the turnaround time of large farm machines at the ends of rows. Many fields are unfenced, and existing fences are being removed, because corn and soybean plants are not likely to dash out onto the highway and get run over by a truck. Impressive batteries of grain elevators line the railroad tracks in the small rural service centers, and storage bins for government-owned surplus grain are scattered across the countryside.

Imposing barns and silos are the dominant features of farmsteads in the dairy farming areas of the Middle West (Fig. 9). The township which contains the topographic map excerpt had five or six farmsteads per square mile of cleared and drained land, or a mean farm size of around 120 acres (Fig. 15). The massive dairy barns have large lofts for hay storage and sturdy masonry ground floors

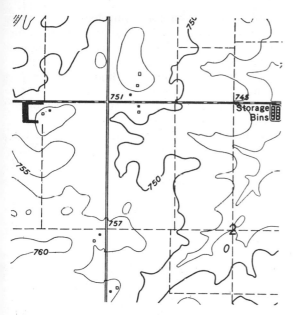

FIG. 14. A cash grain farming area, as illustrated by part of the Mount Gilboa, Ind., 1:24,000 topographic sheet, which was published in 1962. The township had three and one-third farmsteads per square mile, indicating a mean farm size of 200 acres. If the population of the township at each census is divided by the number of houses in 1962, the mean number of persons per household has ranged from 7.7 in 1880 to 3.0 in 1970. A windbreak has been planted to the west of one farmstead. The storage bins are for surplus corn which has been purchased by the government as part of the farm price support program.

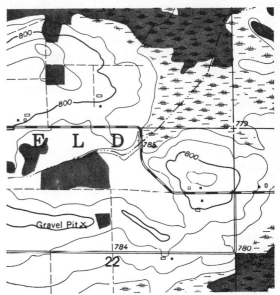

FIG. 15. A dairy farming area, as illustrated by part of the Poy Sippi, Wisc., 1:24,000 topographic sheet, which was published in 1961. The township had five or six farmsteads per square mile of cleared and drained land, indicating a mean farm size of around 120 acres. If the population of the township at each census is divided by the number of houses in 1961, the mean number of persons per household has ranged from 5.7 in 1880 to 2.9 in 1960 and 3.0 in 1970. Steep slopes, gravel pits, marshes, swamps, and uncleared woodland are not uncommon in areas of recent glaciation.

with numerous windows to admit light and air. Cattle are tied to stanchions on the ground floor for milking, and they are fed from the cylindrical silo which towers at one end of the barn. Most dairy farmsteads have no other buildings large enough to be shown on the topographic map. Fields of ten to twenty acres are securely fenced, many with barbed wire, which is adequate for cattle but not for hogs. Numerous areas of forest, swamp, and marsh still await clearance and drainage. Cheese factories and creameries, many now defunct, are common in the small rural service centers.

THE FAMILY FARM

The overwhelming majority of farms in the Middle West are family farms. A family farm may be defined quite simply as a father and son operation, with a hired man while the son is approaching maturity, and when the father is too old to be of much help. The concept has become so value-laden, however, and so encrusted with emotionalism and partisan politics, that most discussions of the family farm have about as much relationship to the realities of farming as discussions of God, motherhood, and apple pie. Few people have any clear understanding of what a family farm really is, but everyone seems agreed that it is a Good Thing which should be maintained and preserved.

The ideology of the family farm appears to be founded on four basic sentiments:

1) each farmer should own the land he farms;

2) each farm should be large enough to provide a decent living;

3) the farmer and his family should do most of the work; and

4) they should receive a fair price for their products.

These sentiments, in turn, assume the fol-lowing values:

1) hard work is a virtue;
2) anyone who works hard can make good;
3) anyone who fails to make good is lazy;
4) a man's true worth can be determined by his income;
5) a self-made man is better than one to the manor born;
6) a family is responsible for its own eco-nomic security; and
7) the best government is the least govern-ment.

The family farm ideology took root and flourished in the Middle West. National policies dictated that the land should be alienated in small, standardized, interchange-able units. The land was good. Successful corn-livestock farming demanded hard work all year round, and ceaseless, relentless, driv-ing physical effort during the peak labor seasons, but such work paid off handsomely.[21] Commercial agriculture was established very quickly. It was well adjusted to the environ-ment, an efficient infrastructure was de-veloped to support it, and most major devi-ations proved unsuccessful. Newcomers were rewarded economically if they conformed, but they also faced strong social pressures to do so: "a farmer who does not practice the well-established rotation system is believed to be neither intelligent nor moral."[22]

The Value System

The rapidity with which commercial agri-culture was established, its stability, and its continued prosperity have engendered among Middle Western farmers an attitude of con-fidence that often borders on arrogance. They are convinced that they are better than most people; they are harder workers, better man-agers, more intelligent citizens, more moral persons, and they have the cash income to back up their convictions. They believe in individual independence, and are suspicious of "the courthouse gang" and the higher echelons of government generally. The gov-ernment belongs to and is run by strangers,

people who do no hard physical labor, and therefore must be bad. The tax collector, the census taker, the draft board, all are inter-connected in some vast mysterious plot to take advantage of the poor honest farmer.

Change is equated with progress, old is bad, new is good, "if you don't grow, you're dead," and death is the ultimate obscenity. "Any farmer who uses anything less than the most modern machinery is considered both incompetent and backward."[23] Science and knowledge are good, because they represent progress, but scientists and scholars are as suspect as anyone else who does no physical labor. The great state universities of the Middle West are encouraged to emphasize the practical and applied side of knowledge ("It's got to help me make money, or it's no good") rather than its liberalizing function, and mere training often usurps education ("Don't try to explain how it works, just teach me how to use it.").[24]

A deep anti-intellectualism lies just beneath the surface, yet nowhere else is there such an abiding faith in technology, and properly so. The ofttold tale of hybrid corn is but one of many success stories of the wonders worked by plant breeders in developing new, better, higher-yielding, and more resistant crop strains. The modern Middle Western farmer relies on a veritable laboratory of chemicals to fertilize his soil and to eradicate weed and insect pests. A successful farmer must have at least two tractors, plus an impressive array of other farm machinery. The efficient oper-ation of new and larger machines demands larger fields and larger farms.

The increasingly complex technology and scale of farming in the Middle West require new and higher levels of management. Many farmers have begun to concentrate all their efforts on the most efficient and profitable aspect of the farm operation, and to eliminate all others. A generation ago most farmers

[21] Carl C. Taylor, "The Corn Belt," pp. 360–82 of Carl C. Taylor, et al., *Rural Life in the United States* (New York: Alfred A. Knopf, 1955).

[22] Taylor, op. cit., footnote 21, p. 378.

[23] Taylor, op. cit., footnote 21, p. 378.

[24] The Middle Western state universities have pro-grams in a wide range of practical subjects, such as engineering, mortuary science, home economics, and agriculture, and they expend massive sums of money on the demonstration and testing of existing knowl-edge (experimentation) as well as on the creation of new knowledge (research); by and large, the aptly named Agricultural Experiment Stations are not agricultural research stations.

raised the crops they fed to their livestock, but today the specialized crop producer and the specialized livestock man have become increasingly common, even in dairy farming areas.

The successful family farm of the past required hard work and willingness to accept changes, but most changes were gradual and only matters of detail. The changes which have occurred since World War II seem more basic and fundamental, and the pace of change seems to be accelerating. Hard work is no longer enough; hard-working, clean-living, completely decent people who have lived by all the rules have been badly hurt by changes which are beyond their control and even their comprehension. Such an ego-shattering experience has been especially galling for complacent, self-confident, Middle Western farmers, and it has generated anger, frustration, and luddism. Perhaps these changes are only magnified by proximity, but agriculture today seems to be undergoing an experience quite similar to that which wracked manufacturing activities during the Industrial Revolution. No one can predict the eventual result of the impact of new machines, new management skills, and new forms of organization, but this is a fascinating time to be a student of farming in the United States.

The Changing Size of Farms

Changes in farm size provide an especially vivid illustration of the changes that are occurring in the organization of agricultural production in the Middle West. The figures on average size of farm which have been published regularly in the various Censuses of Agriculture must be suspect, because the census definition of a farm is quite unrealistic.[25] A better estimate can be based upon changes in the acreage of farm land which is in specific size categories. Such a procedure eliminates the statistical "noise" generated by the myriads of small farms which clutter up the census data.

The acreage of farm land in various size

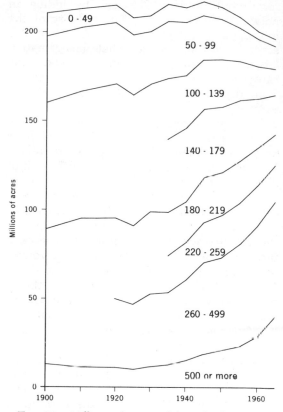

FIG. 16. Millions of acres of farm land in specified size categories in the eight Middle Western states, 1900–1964.

categories in the eight Middle Western states remained remarkably stable between 1900 and 1935 (Fig. 16).[26] Since 1935 the principal change has been an increase in the amount of land in farms of 50 to 179 acres and an increase in the amount of land in farms larger than 259 acres. In 1935 roughly half the land was in 50–179 acre farms and a quarter was in farms larger than 259 acres; in 1964 these proportions were almost exactly reversed.

The size of a farm could be increased either by amalgamation with another whole farm unit (e.g., two 160-acre farms would make one 320-acre farm), or by accretion of smaller parcels to an existing farm (e.g., a 160-acre

[25] John Fraser Hart, "A Map of the Agricultural Implosion," *Proceedings,* Association of American Geographers, Vol. 2 (1970), pp. 68–71. A stroke of a bureaucratic pen in Washington, D. C., can do more to change the average size of farm in the United States than anything that happens at the grass roots.

[26] Only a great deal of patient investigation can prove or disprove my hunch that this pre-1935 stability has persisted ever since the land was first alienated and settled. I have briefly discussed some of the kinds of evidence which might be useful in Pierce County Geographical Society, op. cit., footnote 10.

farm would grow to 200 acres by adding an adjacent 40-acre field). The stability of the intermediate category, farms of 180 to 259 acres, seems to indicate that amalgamation has been more important than accretion; the category of 260–499 acre farms has grown primarily at the expense of the 140–179 acre category.

If present trends persist, by 1984 the total farm acreage in the Middle West will have dropped to around 170 million acres from a 1964 total of 197 million (and a 1945 peak of 219 million), and all of the land will be in farms of 220 acres or more. To extrapolate a bit farther, these trends indicate that a 260-acre farm in the Middle West at the end of the century will seem as small as a 40-acre farm in 1964. Even today, however, throughout much of the region the old traditional homestead of 160 acres has the same throbbing vitality as the dodo. In 1969 Van Arsdall and Elder estimated that the optimal size was 1,641 acres for a two-man cash grain farm in eastern Illinois, and 770 acres for a two-man hog farm in the western part of the state.[27] They also estimated that the necessary capital investment in land, buildings, and equipment was $901,336 for the cash grain farm and $359,626 for the hog farm.

The young man who has not been fortunate enough to inherit a farm, or to marry one, faces a difficult problem if he tries to put together a farm of adequate size. Few young men can command the kind of capital necessary; many of those who can are unwilling to invest it in farm land; the risk-taking entrepreneurs are vying with each other for a scarce and finite commodity; and owners often are reluctant to part with an asset which has been in the family a long time and whose value has been steadily appreciating in

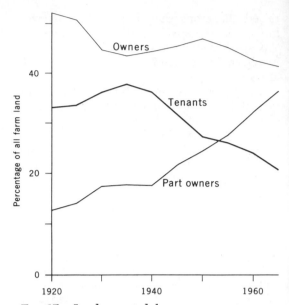

FIG. 17.   Land operated by owners, part-owners, and tenants as a percentage of all farm land in the eight Middle Western states, 1920–1964.

recent decades.[28] Many a farmer who has wished to expand the size of his operation has been forced to rent land because he has been unable to buy it, and some have gone quite remarkable distances to find land which could be rented.[29]

The man who owns part of the land he farms, and rents the rest, is classified by the census as a part-owner farmer (Fig. 17). The proportion of the farm land in the Middle West which was operated by part-owners rose from 12.8 percent in 1920 to 17.6 percent in 1940, and then jumped to 36.6 percent in 1964, whereas the proportion of the land farmed by owners was declining slowly, and the proportion farmed by tenants was dropping fairly rapidly.

---

[27] These estimates assume the use of eight-row equipment; if six-row equipment were used the optimal size would drop to 1,325 and 716 acres, respectively, and the necessary investment to $726,910 and $329,626; Roy N. Van Arsdall and William A. Elder, *Economies of Size of Illinois Cash-Grain and Hog Farms,* Agricultural Experiment Station Bulletin 733 (Urbana: University of Illinois College of Agriculture, 1969), pp. 15, 20, 27, and 32. The change from six-row to eight-row equipment on the cash grain farm would justify the addition of 316 acres, almost precisely double an original 160-acre homestead!

[28] Although I know of no scholarly attempt to measure the attitudes of Americans toward land ownership, my own conversations with rural people have convinced me that many of them have a strong sentimental and emotional attachment to their land even when it does not produce any significant income; they would feel quite guilty about selling "the old family place."

[29] Although the author, regrettably, has never seen fit to publish his results, an important study of dispersed farm operating units in Minnesota is in Everett G. Smith, Jr., "Road Functions in a Changing Rural Environment," unpublished doctoral dissertation, University of Minnesota, 1962.

Two Myths

The rapidly rising cost of farm land, and the increase in part-owner farming, have pretty well destroyed a long-cherished myth that farm tenancy is somehow bad. Perhaps it was good to own your farm when land was cheap and farms were small, but tying up a quarter of a million dollars or more in land might not be the best possible use of working capital.[30] In fact, tenancy has always been accepted as a fact of farm life in some of our most productive and heavily capitalized farming areas; the Grand Prairie of east central Illinois, for example, traditionally has had the greatest yields, biggest machines, largest farms, and highest rates of tenancy in the Middle West. Today a young man cannot hope to put together a farm large enough to make efficient use of modern farm machinery unless he inherits it or rents land from his neighbors, and the stigma which some sociologists have tried to attach to farm tenancy has disappeared, especially if the tenant is working from a base of land which he owns.

The increasing size of farms, the rapidly rising cost of farm land, and problems of inheritance are also destroying the myth that corporation farming is wicked. Our sense of fair play dictates that a man's children should receive equal shares of his estate, but a man who has worked hard all his life putting together a reasonably-sized farm does not want to have it divided up again as soon as he is gone. The farm must be bequeathed as a unit, but it would be unfair to leave it all to one child and to leave the others nothing; it would be equally unfair to leave it all to one child and to expect him to pay the others for their shares, especially if he is already in his middle years and the farm is worth a quarter of a million dollars or more. The best solution is to leave the farm to a family corporation, which can pay a manager's salary to one child, and equal dividends to all. An almost unbelievable amount of arrant nonsense has been written about corporation farming; within a generation, I suspect, most family farms in the Middle West will have been forced to incorporate because of the pressures of inheritance.

Farm Population

One possible solution to the inheritance problem, of course, would be conscious limitation of family size; it would be just great, for example, to have one son and marry him off to your neighbor's only daughter, although marriages of convenience have not had as much appeal for Middle Western farm families as they have had for the royal houses of Europe. Nevertheless, the size of farm families in the Middle West does appear to be decreasing; comparison of census data with topographic maps indicates that the mean number of persons per rural household dropped from just under six persons in 1870 to three persons in 1970 (Figs. 12–15).[31] These figures seem to say that a decrease in the size of families should have halved the rural population between 1870 and 1970. The popular mind attributes any decline in the size of rural households (and attendant rural depopulation) to the outmigration of surplus young people, but perhaps limitation of family size might have become more important than is commonly suspected.

An index based on the assumption that the number of rural houses in a township has not changed during an entire century is patently an exceedingly crude one, yet the mean number of persons per rural household has had a narrowness of range and a consistency of change from area to area that really are rather impressive (Figs. 12–15). If the range in family size has been as narrow as these figures seem to indicate, and if the density of farm population is a function of family size and average size of farm, then variations in farm population density are largely the products of variations in farm size.[32] If we assume that the size of farms did not change very much between the time the land was alienated and 1935, we might very well conclude that the geography of land alienation is worthy of considerably more attention than

---

[30] Farmers in England learned a long time ago that owning the lease is far better than owning the land itself.

[31] In this sentence, and in the remainder of this section, I have used the term "rural" rather loosely to include all people and/or houses outside incorporated places, and I have implied, quite incorrectly, that it is synonymous with "farm."

[32] John Fraser Hart, "Some Components of Rural Population Distribution in Indiana in 1950," *Proceedings of the Indiana Academy of Science*, Vol. 71 (1961), pp. 210–18.

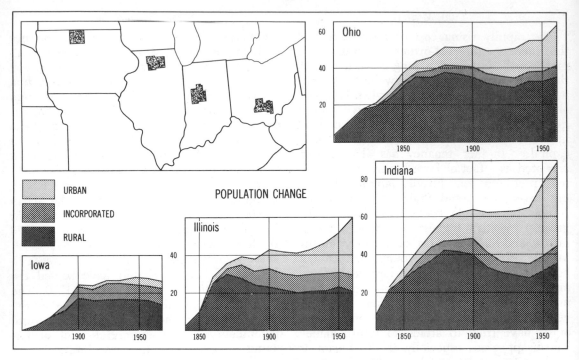

FIG. 18. Population change by categories of residence in four groups of nonmetropolitan counties. The Urban category includes all people in incorporated places of 2,500 persons or more, the Incorporated category includes all people in incorporated places of less than 2,500 persons, and the Rural category includes all people outside incorporated places. Reproduced from Hart, op. cit., footnote 5, by permission of the Louisiana State University Press.

it has received thus far, especially if we accept the assumption that the density of the farm population has any relationship to the size and spacing of central places.[33]

TOWNS AND CITIES

The growth of the population in most nonmetropolitan areas of the Middle West has conformed to a standard model which is illustrated by four scattered blocks of counties (Fig. 18).[34] The rural population "exploded" in the early years, reached its peak within the lifetimes of the first settlers, and has remained more or less stable ever since; any decline in the rural farm population has been fairly well counterbalanced by an increase in the rural nonfarm population.[35] The growth of popu-

lation in incorporated places has been a function of their size; the largest places have grown the most, and the smallest have grown the least.[36]

The incorporated places can be grouped into three rough generations according to their dates of incorporation, which are crudely correlated with their present population size. The third, and youngest, generation consists of small towns and villages which have been incorporated since about 1880. They came into being to serve a rural population which had already stabilized or even begun to decline, and most have not prospered; their

---

number of 2,500 persons, and its entire population has been transferred to the "urban" category by census fiat. Failure to make allowance for this fact can produce some fairly silly results; Wilbur Zelinsky, "Changes in the Geographic Patterns of Rural Population in the United States, 1790–1960," *Geographical Review*, Vol. 52 (1962), pp. 492–524.

[36] John Fraser Hart, Neil E. Salisbury, and Everett G. Smith, Jr., "The Dying Village and Some Notions about Urban Growth," *Economic Geography*, Vol. 44 (1968), pp. 343–49.

---

[33] Brian J. L. Berry, *Geography of Market Centers and Retail Distribution* (Englewood Cliffs, N. J.: Prentice-Hall, 1967), pp. 26–35.

[34] Hart, op. cit., footnote 5.

[35] The most dramatic change in the "rural" population at the county level customarily has occurred when an incorporated place has reached the magic

population has been stagnating slowly upward during the twentieth century, but relatively few have attained the magic population of 2,500 persons which is necessary to qualify them as urban places according to the census definition.[37] The incorporated places of the third generation are mainly rural service centers which fill the interstices in a network of older incorporated places of the second generation (which, in turn, are interstitial to the first generation).

The second generation urban places were incorporated within the first few decades of settlement. Most originated as rural service centers: railroad towns with stockyards and grain elevators; county seats and administrative centers with a modest range of professional services; power sites where dams could be constructed for flour and lumber mills ("Falls" and "Rapids" are common city name suffixes). The second generation places had an earlier start than the third generation, they initially served a growing and prospering rural population, and they had more time and greater opportunity to develop additional functions which were not so completely dependent upon the local agricultural economy. Today they range in size from small towns to middle-sized metropolises.

The urban places of the first generation, unlike those of the second and third, were coincident with or even antecedent to settlement. The town was the gateway to the frontier, the outfitting center and the jumping-off place. It was the intending settler's last contact with society and civilization, his final opportunity to buy the tools and equipment he would need before he plunged into the wilderness to carve out a new life for himself. A gateway, of course, leads both ways, and the town which had served as the outfitting center and the jumping-off place became the collecting and shipping center as soon as the land began to produce surpluses. The most successful gateway cities were located at critical transport nodes between the older settled areas and productive new hinterlands; large numbers of newcomers had to be able to reach them and move into their

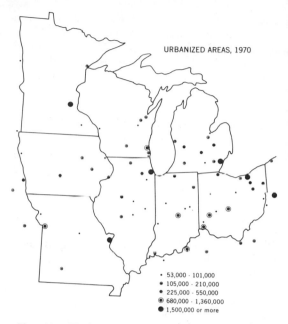

Fig. 19. Each urbanized area includes at least one city of 50,000 or more persons and the surrounding densely built-up area. The urbanized area is a more accurate representation of a city's size and population than the SMSA, which is defined in terms of entire counties and includes considerable acreages of non-urban land.

hinterlands without difficulty, and goods had to pass easily to and fro between the hinterland and the older settled areas.

The Middle West was settled during the Steam Packet/Iron Horse epoch of American history, when wagon roads, canals, and low-capacity regional railroad networks were handmaidens of the waterways.[38] The great gateway cities of the Middle West, which have grown to become the leading metropolises of 1970, were transportation centers on navigable waterways: Pittsburgh, Cincinnati, and Louisville on the Ohio River; St. Louis and St. Paul-Minneapolis on the Mississippi; Kansas City on the Missouri; and Cleveland, Detroit, Chicago, and Milwaukee on the Great Lakes (Fig. 19). The three second-sized urbanized areas of 1970 which were not on waterways were all on the National Road (Fig. 2); Columbus and Dayton were at the two principal river bridging points in Ohio,

[37] John Fraser Hart and Neil E. Salisbury, "Population Change in Middle Western Villages: A Statistical Approach," *Annals*, Association of American Geographers, Vol. 55 (1965), pp. 140–60.

[38] John R. Borchert, "American Metropolitan Evolution," *Geographical Review*, Vol. 57 (1967), pp. 301–32.

and Indianapolis was at the most important crossroads in Indiana, the intersection of the National Road with the Michigan Road, which connected the Ohio River with Lake Michigan.

Specialization

It was only a matter of time until the collecting and shipping centers also began to process the products of the prosperous agricultural areas they served. The initial processing activities reduced bulk to save shipping costs; hogs were butchered and salted down, wheat was ground into flour, and corn was made into whiskey. Cincinnati was "Porkopolis" and Chicago was "Hog Butcher to the World," Kansas City and Minneapolis-St. Paul became great flour milling and meat packing centers, but Louisville has never boasted very much about its distilleries (Fig. 19). Among the smaller centers, Decatur claims to be the "Soybean Capital of the World;" Cedar Rapids is the home of Quaker Oats; Corn Flakes, Post Toasties, and other breakfast delights are made in Battle Creek; and half a dozen or more cities are major meat packing centers.

A logical next step for the farm service center was the manufacture of agricultural equipment, first simple farm tools, and later more complex machines. Peoria is the home of Caterpillar Tractor, and Moline boasts that it is the "Farm Implement Capital of America;" in 1967 factories in Minnesota, Wisconsin, Iowa, and outstate Illinois (excluding Chicago) produced three-fifths of the nation's farm machinery.[39] The manufacture of farm machinery farther east in the earlier days had established a tradition and a know-how which were easily transferred to the manufacture of automobiles; factories in Michigan, Ohio, and Indiana produced four-fifths of the nation's motor vehicles and equipment in 1967.

The Illinois-Indiana line divides the urban/industrial Middle West into an eastern district which is dominated by Detroit and the manufacture of automobiles and their components, and a western district which is dominated by such agriculturally-related industries as food processing and the manufacture of farm machinery; Chicago, quite appropriately, straddles the boundary, and serves as the capital for the entire region (Fig. 19). The eastern edge of the Middle West, in northeastern Ohio, is part of the Northern Appalachian primary metal working district which focuses on Pittsburgh and Cleveland, and is intermediate between the Middle West and the Northeast.

The size and prosperity of the Middle Western states have fostered the growth of the cities which contain their state capitals and state universities. The two functions are combined in Minneapolis-St. Paul, Columbus, Lansing, Madison, and Lincoln; Indianapolis, Des Moines, and Springfield are state capitals; and Ann Arbor, Champaign-Urbana, Columbia, and Lafayette are state university towns (Fig. 19). The growth of such places to metropolitan size is ironical, because our forebears hoped to protect the weakest and most susceptible members of society (legislators and students) against the snares and temptations of the wicked and sinful city by locating the capital and the state university as far away from it as possible in a setting of rural purity. Jefferson City, Iowa City, and Bloomington have managed to retain their nonmetropolitan status, but many of their denizens seem to find this no special cause for jubilation.

THE FARM VOTE

Although agriculture dominates the lives of farm people, townspeople, and to a considerable extent, even city people in the Middle West, it is nonetheless paradoxical that the states to which political pundits regularly refer when they write about the farm vote include five of the twelve largest cities in the United States (Fig. 19). The whole idea of a farm vote, at least in presidential elections, appears to be the product of 1) a fairly close balance between metropolis and outstate in most of the Middle Western states, and 2) the willingness of appreciable numbers of farmers to defect from the Republican Party, or at least to refrain from supporting it, when they are unhappy about farm prices.

---

[39] The ubiquitous food processing industry was half again as important in these four states as in the nation as a whole, employing twelve percent of the production workers (as against eight percent in the nation) and accounting for sixteen percent of the value added by manufacturing (as against ten percent for the nation).

REPUBLICAN VOTE IN PRESIDENTIAL ELECTIONS, 1932 · 1968

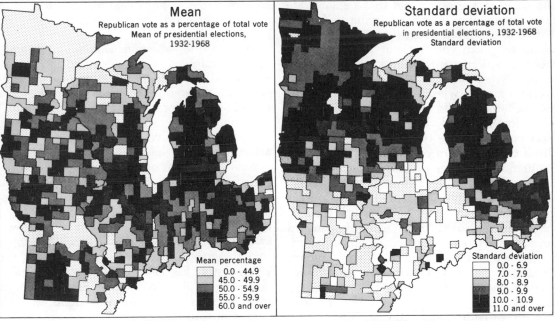

FIG. 20. The mean and standard deviation of the percentage of the total vote cast for the Republican candidate in ten presidential elections, 1932–1968, for each county in the eight Middle Western states. Ralph Sanders did all the computations on data extracted from Scammon, op. cit., footnote 40.

If fifty-five percent of the vote is a safe margin, most of the counties in the Middle West were safely Republican in the ten presidential elections between 1932 and 1968, and parts of southern Michigan, northern Illinois, and the western Ozarks were bastions of Republican strength (Fig. 20).[40] Far fewer counties were safely Democratic, yet these counties cast a high percentage of the total state vote. In six of the eight states more than a quarter of the total vote came from one or two metropolitan centers which, for the most part, have been strongly, solidly, and consistently Democratic (Table 2 and Fig. 20). A Democratic metropolis in each state was counterpoised against a rural Republican outstate vote. In order to carry the state in a presidential election, which might turn on no more than 50,000 votes, the Democrats had to

win away a fraction of the Republican vote outstate, or the Republicans had to break the Democratic stranglehold on the vote of metropolis.

How could this be done? Apparently most Americans were set in a firm political mold long before they were old enough to vote, and they do not break it often or easily. Even those who preen themselves on their political

TABLE 2.—PRESIDENTIAL ELECTIONS, 1932–1968

State	Vote in metropolis as a percentage of the total vote in the state[a]	Republican vote	
		Mean	Standard deviation
Illinois	52.1	48.8	6.16
Missouri	44.9	45.2	6.36
Michigan	35.9	48.8	9.43
Minnesota	35.6	45.1	8.32
Ohio	26.0	50.0	8.34
Wisconsin	25.5	47.3	10.00
Indiana	21.7	51.3	6.23
Iowa	8.4	51.5	8.27

[40] I am grateful to Ralph Sanders for computing the means and standard deviations for data which I had extracted from Richard G. Scammon, ed., *America at the Polls: A Handbook of American Presidential Election Statistics, 1920–1964* (Pittsburgh: University of Pittsburgh Press, 1965).

[a] Metropolis is Cook County, Illinois; Jackson and St. Louis counties and St. Louis City, Missouri; Hennepin and Ramsey counties, Minnesota; Wayne County, Michigan; Cuyahoga and Hamilton counties, Ohio; Milwaukee County, Wisconsin; Lake and Marion counties, Indiana; and Polk County, Iowa.

independence actually vote consistently for one party or the other, and they demonstrate their independence only by trying to find at least one candidate from the other party for whom they can vote without having to hold their noses. Perhaps the best-known exception to this generalization has been the Middle Western farmer, who is notorious for voting as his pocketbook tells him to vote, rather than as his forebears did. Mapping changes in the farm vote might be quite interesting, especially if these changes could be correlated with fluctuations in farm prices.

If farmers were less loyal politically than other voters, or were more willing to refrain from voting if they were dissatisfied, the fact should be revealed by a map of standard deviations from the mean vote in ten presidential elections (Fig. 20). High standard deviations in the Republican strongholds would have indicated a high degree of political volatility and unreliability, but the map fails to provide much support for such a hypothesis. Instead, it shows a volatility belt stretching from Minnesota across Wisconsin and Michigan into northeastern Ohio (the area settled mainly by Yankees, Yorkers, Germans, and Scandinavians), and a reliability region in Missouri, Illinois, and Indiana. The urban/metropolitan counties tend to be somewhat more stable than adjacent rural counties, but the map clearly raises more questions than it answers about the nature of Middle Westerners and the way in which they vote.

DISTINCTIVE TRAITS

What is a Middle Westerner? A congeries of traits seems to be more or less characteristic of the breed, although no single trait is unique, and none is distinctive. None of them is mandatory for residence in the area, and one need not be a native to hold any or all of them. Some, at least, might be considered standard American traits, which is not especially surprising, because the Middle West, after all, is the American heartland. These caveats and provisos notwithstanding, the identification of this congeries of traits helps one to understand the people of the region and why they do the things they do.

Most of the following adjectives are applicable in varying degree to most genuine Middle Westerners, as I perceive them:

Pecuniaristic:—A deep faith that all values can eventually be measured in terms of money: "the worth of a man is indicated by his income."

Materialistic:—Blatant worship of the almighty dollar, or even ostentation of income, is generally considered bad taste, but conspicuous consumption can serve the same purpose: an expensive house in the "right" neighborhood, wearing the latest fashions, status-oriented travel to places others cannot afford to visit, the most powerful and expensive speedboat or snowmobile.

Self-assured:—A value system based on money is unlikely to be questioned by a prosperous people, and the Middle West has been enormously successful in terms of its own system of values; "somebody must be doing something right." Critical re-evaluation of the value system has never really been necessary, and many Middle Westerners have seldom, if ever, been afflicted with self-doubts of their own righteousness.

Functionalists:—"If it works, I'll buy it, and not ask any questions; if it doesn't work, let's get rid of it and get something that does work."

Technologic:—Almost unbroken prosperity (especially in comparison with other parts of the nation) can easily be attributed to a predilection for the latest and most modern machines and techniques. New and better machines always have been invented in the past; why should the future be different?

Competent:—An almost childlike faith in perpetual progress through technology is coupled with enormous technological sophistication and competence, and a profound respect for hard work.

Simplistic:—"If I ask a guy why he does something, and if he gives me an answer that makes sense, I don't see any need to probe any deeper."

Up-to-the-minute:—A preoccupation with the present and a fascination with the latest fashion is accompanied by an impatience with, or even contempt for, the past: "a Middle Westerner is a guy who neither knows nor cares who his grandfather was nor where he came from."

Xenophobic:—A suspicion of anyone different is reflected in an isolationist stance in international affairs, in a deep distrust of all governmental activity on the domestic scene, and by strong social pressures on all non-conformists, whether Catholic, Slav, black, long-haired, or bearded.

EPILOGUE

Middle Western traits are of special interest to geographers, because the Middle West is the heartland of professional geography in the United States. A high percentage of American geographers were born, bred, and/or educated within this region; more than half of the nation's advanced degrees in geography between 1960 and 1965 were conferred within a 500-mile (800 km) radius of the Chicago Loop.[41]

Geography, for most Americans, is a subject that is taught in the elementary schools, and the numerical strength of the profession at the college level has been concentrated in teacher-training institutions. The subject has been scorned by the old-line liberal arts colleges of the East, but it has been received more warmly in the Middle Western state universities, which have had a stronger sense of total public service, including vocational training. Most of the geographers in the Middle Western state universities have abdicated the teaching of undergraduates to others, however, and they have preferred to concentrate their own efforts at the graduate level; a major component of the geography graduate programs in these universities has been the production of faculty members for teacher-training institutions, and a high proportion of the graduate students have been recruited from such institutions.

As a general rule, the old-line liberal arts colleges are highly selective, admit only the best students, and draw them from a large area, whereas teacher-training institutions attract students from the local area who have weaker high school records and poorer placement test scores. Graduates of teacher-training institutions tend to reflect the narrow, parochial, specialized, and often remedial nature of their programs. In other words, a

significant proportion of the professional geographers in the United States have been recruited from a group of students who had weaker credentials for college admission, and who have not been exposed to the breadth of interests, reading, and knowledge that ought to be part of a good liberal arts education.

Furthermore, many American geographers reflect their Middle Western provenance by their strong bias for explaining as much as possible in terms of economic values, and by their willingness to dismiss cultural, historical, and environmental variables as irrational, if not downright immoral. Little in the background or experience of a native Middle Westerner has prepared him for the shock of encountering a person who believes that anything could be more important than money. The region's pecuniary value system, and the social pressures of xenophobia, have forced its people into a single homogeneous economic mold, and have squeezed out their economic eccentricities, those differences that distinguish one culture group from another.

The native Middle Westerner also has a limited sense of history. The past, for him, is fit only to be torn down and replaced by something new and better just as quickly as possible. Such a rejection of the past, unfortunately, can lead to confusion of causes and effects when two variables are highly correlated in the present, and the role of causation may be assigned to either. A simplistic explanation based on the subsumptive hypothesis of economic causation will assign the role of cause to the variable which best fits current fashions in economic theory, whereas historical research can show quite clearly that such an explanation is untenable.

Finally, the native Middle Westerner tends to ignore the physical environment, or to take it for granted. The region is physically homogeneous, and it was settled at a time when man was flexing his technological muscles. He was making a wide variety of inventions with which to tame nature, and in the Middle West he found a natural environment that was easy to tame on a large scale. Land was cheap, labor was dear, and every effort was made to maximize production per man. Land was squandered by the standards of western Europe, where land is so dear that production

[41] John Fraser Hart, *Geographic Manpower: A Report on Manpower in American Geography*, Commission on College Geography, Publication No. 3 (Washington: Association of American Geographers, 1966), pp. 8–14.

per acre must be maximized, and labor is cheap enough to be used prodigally. The farmer in Europe adjusts his fields and his crops to every physical nuance of his land, and his fields are so small that a Middle Western farmer could hardly turn his tractor around in one of them. A farmer in the Middle West thinks in terms of large regular fields as entities, and he cannot afford the luxury of making allowances for variations within any particular field; in effect, he largely ignores the physical environment, and Middle Western geographers have followed his lead.

Many geographers in the United States reflect the Middle Western influence by their bias in favor of economic explanations and against explanations which are based on cultural, historical, and/or physical environmental factors. But given a land survey system which allowed any man to make a reasonable living if he was willing to work hard enough, was it inevitable that some form of economic determinism would develop in such a rich, inviting, and homogeneous physical environment as the Middle West? Two generations of American geographers have rejected, almost as an article of faith, the notion that the physical environment determines human destiny, but many Middle Western geographers, in their homogeneous environment, have gone one step farther and rejected the physical environment as a factor in human affairs.

ACKNOWLEDGMENTS

The author expresses his appreciation to Patricia Burwell, Sandra Haas, Arlette Lindbergh, Margaret Rasmussen, and Terry Martin for their helpfulness, their efficiency, and their unflagging cheerfulness.

THE DEMISE OF THE PIEDMONT COTTON REGION

MERLE C. PRUNTY AND CHARLES S. AIKEN

ABSTRACT. The cotton-producing complex which dominated the Piedmont region from the early nineteenth century to mid-twentieth century began to disintegrate during the 1950s. By 1967 only a few small production "islands," vestiges of the traditional region, remained. Rapid disintegration of the region was occasioned by the interplay of a complex set of forces, most of which operated negatively. Most of the region's farmers perceived small cotton acreage allotments as noneconomic. They turned to alternative activities rather than the pursuit of cotton culture under new land operating systems and a new cotton growing technology. Most of the growers and ginners of the region failed to make the technologic transformations necessary to continuation of a viable cotton production complex. Those few who did are responsible for the persistence of the vestigial production islands. KEY WORDS: *Allotments, Alternatives, Cotton, Disintegration, Gins, Multiple tenant, Technologic lag.*

REGIONALIZATIONS treating patterns of rural land use, particularly its agricultural components, are among the more common types of areal generalizations which the geographical profession has employed. In most instances agricultural regions have been identified to facilitate description, then analysis, of agricultural production and the spatial patterns or systems associated therewith. Derivative from these have been numerous studies of individual crops, or commodities, including the dispersals of economic plants into diverse areal settings. Only a few geographers have directed their efforts toward understanding the processes whereby particular areas of the earth become distinctive agricultural regions. Among these, Spencer and Horvath, in a provocative study, have analyzed the origins and evolutions of the American "Corn Belt," the Philippine coconut landscape, and the Malayan rubber region.[1]

If the processes which generate agricultural regionalizations are of geographical significance (and they are), then the processes underlying disintegrations of such regions also should command our attention. Analyses of the disintegration of extinct agricultural regions, such as those of ancient Mesopotamia and the tidewater rice plantation area in nineteenth century Georgia and South Carolina, are studies in historical geography. However, a few Anglo-American regions presently are decaying and the disintegration processes which they are undergoing may be observed through field investigation. One of these is the Piedmont cotton-growing region of the American Southeast.

Cotton, the distinctive "common denominator" and fulcrum to Piedmont land use systems from about 1800 until the middle 1950s, persists today only in a few small scattered "islands"—the rural communities which continue in its culture. The overwhelming preponderance of those broad interfluves and rolling hills of the Piedmont which produced the crop for decade after decade no longer support it at all.

Although there are factors which motivate abandonment of an agricultural commodity and cause disintegration of an agricultural region based upon it, counter forces tend to maintain production of the commodity even in the face of decline. Buchanan has reasoned that one of the major characteristics of an established agricultural region is a tendency to sustain itself as a result of capital investments, special skills, and ancillary institutions

Dr. Prunty is Professor of Geography at the University of Georgia in Athens and Dr. Aiken is Assistant Professor of Geography at the University of Tennessee in Knoxville.

[1] J. E. Spencer and R. J. Horvath, "How Does An Agricultural Region Originate?" *Annals,* Association of American Geographers, Vol. 53 (1963), pp. 74–92.

geared to its particular type of agriculture.[2] The institutionalized aspects of the agricultural region have received relatively little attention in geographical studies, especially if typically located off the farm. A premise developed herein is that an agricultural region may survive, and even prosper, when external forces work against production of its distinctive commodity if the strength of its internal, production-related, institutions is substantial; but that it does not survive if the institutions fail to retain technologic and economic viability in the face of stresses at the farmstead or operational level. In cotton-based agricultural regions, the cotton gin has been nodal to the nonfarm institutional structure. Thus this analysis focusses upon technologic and economic change, including the role of the gin, in the recent demise of the old Piedmont cotton region.

The emergence of the Piedmont as the first of the southern upland cotton specialty areas—and from it the whole cotton-growing complex that spread across the South into western and southern Texas—generally has been attributed to the "invention" of the cotton gin by Eli Whitney.[3] This widely-accepted view recently has been reexamined by Aiken, who placed preeminence upon international demand, "market for cotton, not the ease of preparation of cotton for market," as the underlying factor which stimulated cotton production in the upland South from 1800 onward.[4] Aiken also attempted to correct the idea that Whitney "invented" the cotton gin.[5] Roller type gins had been in use in cotton-growing areas for centuries before

Whitney produced an improved type of gin that was efficient when employed to separate seed from fiber of "upland," annual, "green seed" cotton. The Whitney gin (modified and improved with saw-teeth) became a key part of a rapidly emergent institutional complex as a new agricultural region appeared between 1800 and 1815 in response to European demand for cotton fiber. This region expanded rapidly and by 1840 occupied most of the area presently known as the Piedmont cotton region.

The cotton gin has been significant in the cotton industry because cotton is processed before it is moved from production areas to market.[6] Modern gins represent large capital investments. Customarily they are not single enterprises devoted solely to ginning but are parts of businesses which may also include cotton warehouses, fertilizer and farm equipment sales, seed cleaning and sales, herbicide and insecticide application and mechanical harvesting services on a "custom" basis, and farming activities per se. In addition, ginners frequently lend capital, in the form of fertilizer and seed, to farmers in the spring and regularly buy the farmers' cotton in the fall. Frequently ginners resell cotton to textile mills, or for export, after they have aggregated suitable volumes of the fiber in uniform lots. Thus gin plants are specialized fixed capital; knowledge of the methods of cotton production and of the art of ginning are accumulated skills; ginning and the businesses associated therewith are critical institutions ancillary to cotton culture. Employment of Buchanan's reasoning leads to the premise that the cotton gin not

---

[2] R. Ogilvie Buchanan, "Some Reflections on Agricultural Geography," Geography, Vol. 44 (1959), p. 12. Buchanan stressed that "the specialized area, like the specialized worker, will fight to the last ditch before accepting a change in specialization, and stability of character . . . is a natural, almost inevitable result."

[3] R. H. Brown, Historical Geography of the United States (New York: Harcourt, Brace and World, Inc., 1948), p. 36. It would be unfair to attribute to Brown alone the mistake of referring to Whitney's improved version of the gin as its invention, for many others have committed the same error.

[4] C. S. Aiken, "An Examination of the Role of the Eli Whitney Cotton Gin In The Origin Of The United States Cotton Regions," Proceedings, Association of American Geographers, Vol. 3 (1971), pp. 5–9.

[5] Aiken, op. cit., footnote 4, pp. 6–7.

[6] Until approximately 1940 the yield, by ginning, from 1450 pounds (660 kg) of in-seed cotton was approximately 500 pounds (230 kg) of fiber. During the decades since 1950, the seed/fiber ratio has declined somewhat, as a result of the efforts of plant breeders, to about 1250–1300 pounds (569–590 kg) of seed cotton per 500 pounds of ginned fiber. The traditional average gross weight of a bale of ginned fiber has been 500 pounds of which 478 pounds (220 kg) has been cotton fiber and 22 pounds (10 kg) has consisted of jute bagging and steel straps, called ties. The value of the fiber, per pound, has been roughly nine to ten times that of the cottonseed after ginning (though the prices of the two commodities fluctuate independently of one another). Obviously the locations of gins adjacent to cotton fields reflect classic bulk-reducing locational principles.

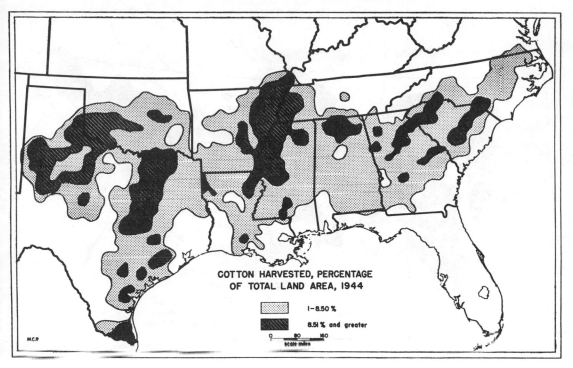

FIG. 1. Cotton harvested, 1944. (Reproduced from Prunty, op. cit., footnote 7, p. 205, by permission of *Economic Geography.*)

only contributed to the origin of the Piedmont cotton region but also has acted to maintain parts of a disintegrating region. In other parts the failure of the gin to retain viability, along with production technology, has been critical in the disappearance of cotton culture.

DISINTEGRATION OF THE REGION

Prunty's analysis of southeastern cotton distribution identified seven regions of high density production as of the 1944 crop year (Fig. 1).[7] The basis for this delimitation was a critical value (8.51 percent, or more, of land area devoted to cotton) which was developed from a cumulative frequency curve and employed as a regional boundary after a large number of spot field checks. When the same value was employed to identify the principal cotton growing areas of 1924, the regions identified for 1944 were nodal to 1924 cotton districts.[8]

The cotton acreage in the Southeast decreased from 18,397,300 acres (744,817 ha) in 1944 to 12,606,000 acres (510,364 ha) in 1964, a decline of 31.47 percent. For the Southeast as a whole, the decrease resulted mainly from reinstatement of crop acreage allotments, under Federal aegis, from 1950 onward. Cartographic analysis of the changes in the distribution between 1944 and 1964 revealed that the decline was far from uniform throughout the Southeast (Figs. 2 and 3).[9] The Inner Coastal Plain, the High Plains of southwestern Oklahoma and western Texas, and the south Texas coastal plains actually had increases in cotton acreage (Fig. 2). These, plus the Mississippi valley, were also the principal areas exhibiting production increases (Fig. 4). Although the Mississippi valley and northern Alabama had decreases, they amounted to less than the 31.47 percent average decline for the whole Southeast. The Black Prairies

---

[7] Merle Prunty, Jr., "Recent Quantitative Changes in the Cotton Regions of the Southeastern States," *Economic Geography*, Vol. 27 (1951), pp. 202–07.

[8] Prunty, op. cit., footnote 7, p. 206, Fig. 14.

[9] The outer limit of cotton culture includes all counties which had one percent, or more, of area devoted to production of the crop in 1944 and/or 1964 (Fig. 2).

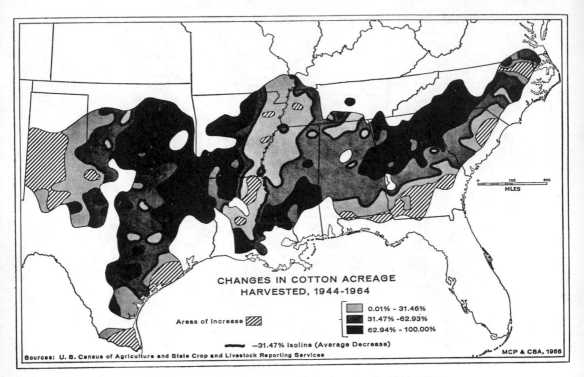

FIG. 2. Changes in cotton acreage harvested, 1944–1964.

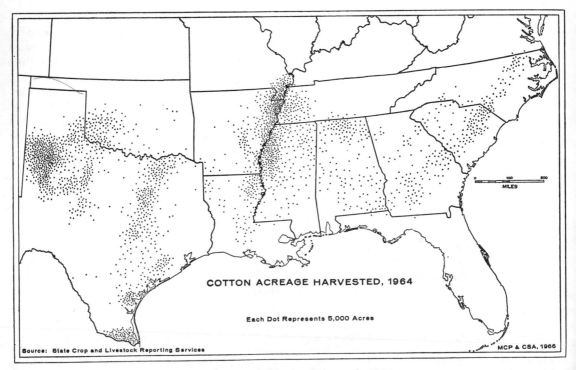

FIG. 3. Cotton acreage harvested, 1964.

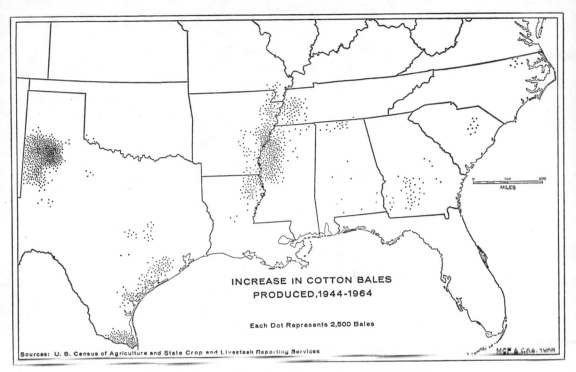

FIG. 4. Increase in cotton bales produced, 1944–1964.

of eastern Texas had losses well above the average but the Piedmont was the outstanding region of acreage declines. Its decreases were greater than 62.94 percent, more than twice the southeastern average. Abandonment of cotton was the principal factor which caused the extreme declines in the oldest of the major cotton regions. Conversely, acreage increases on the Inner Coastal Plain of the Carolinas, Georgia, and Alabama were made possible by the transfer of released cotton acreage allotments in Piedmont counties to the coastal plain counties in these states.[10]

---

[10] William A. Imperatore, *Effects of Federal Controls on the Basic Geographic Characteristics of Cotton Production in Georgia*, unpublished M.A. thesis, University of Georgia, 1963. The Agricultural Adjustment Act of 1938 apportioned the national allotted acreage of cotton to individual farms on the basis of their acreage devoted to cotton during the preceding three years. It required the grower to preserve the history of his allotment. The allotment could be employed only upon the farm to which it was attached; C. C. Cable, Jr., *A Chronology of Government Programs for American Upland Cotton*, Bulletin No. 587 (Fayetteville, Arkansas: University of Arkansas, Agricultural Experiment Station, 1957), p. 6. By 1961, Federal regulations permitted

The amount of cotton produced in 1964 was greater than in 1944, despite net acreage declines, because of increases in per acre yields (Figs. 4 and 5). Production in the Southeast in 1964 amounted to some 12,100,000 bales in contrast to 11,200,000 bales in 1944.

---

a farmer to retain rights to his allotment if he planted at least seventy-five percent of it only once in each three years. Thus released, or non-planted, acreages became available in numerous Piedmont counties (and elsewhere) and were transferred on a year-by-year basis to farmers of the Inner Coastal Plain who wanted to increase their production. Acreage increases in portions of Oklahoma and Texas occurred primarily because of similar releases in the eastern parts of those states. After 1963, the Federal legislation permitted outright sale of an allotment, hence its movement not only from its farm-of-origin to an adjacent one in the same county but also from county to county. Many Piedmont farmers responded by selling their interests in cotton allotments. Since 1964 it has been legal to rent, or lease, an allotment for cultivation on a farm other than that to which it is attached. The resultant complex arrangements whereby economically desirable production units are put together were analyzed by James S. Fisher, "Federal Crop Allotment Programs and Responses by Individual Farm Operators," *Southeastern Geographer*, Vol. 10, No. 1 (1970), pp. 47–58.

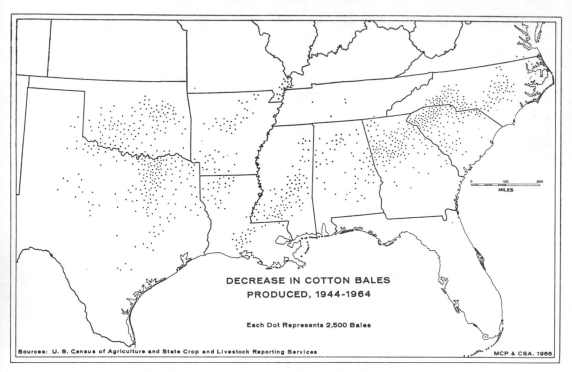

FIG. 5. Decrease in cotton bales produced, 1944–1964.

Areas which had experienced less than the average 1944–64 acreage decrease (31.47 percent), as well as those with acreage increases, provided the expansion in production (Figs. 2 and 4). Areas experiencing production decreases were those in which greater than average acreage declines occurred during the twenty-year interval; the declines in cotton acreage were too large to be offset by increases in yields. The Piedmont's production losses were prominent (Fig. 5).

By 1964, the southeastern cotton growing regions differed substantially from those identified by Prunty in 1951 (Fig. 1). We decided a comparable regional delimitation, based on 1964 data, was necessary in order to determine not only areal variations of the regions but also actual persistence—or absence of it—in the case of the Piedmont (Fig. 6). The major cotton regions in 1964 were delimited by reducing the critical isoline value of 8.51 percent (Fig. 1) by 31.5 percent, i.e., the proportion of the acreage decline in cotton harvested in the Southeast between 1944 and 1964. The resultant value, 5.83 percent, retained comparability with the 1944 delineation because the critical values employed for each

year bear the same proportionate relationship to the total areal distribution for the respective years. In 1944 the Southeast contained seven major cotton-growing regions; by 1964 there were only six. Continued acreage declines on the Piedmont resulted in its disintegration as a major cotton region (Fig. 6). So great were the declines that much of the Piedmont essentially had vanished from the "cotton habitat."[11]

THE STUDY AREA

At this stage a change in the scale of the investigation and a redefinition of the area under study was essential. Massive decline

[11] The value used to distinguish the 1964 cotton regions (5.82 percent of land area devoted to cotton acreage harvested) also was tested via a cumulative frequency curve whose composition indicated that this value was valid in differentiating relatively high density cotton production areas from those of relatively low density (Fig. 6). One percent of total land area devoted to cotton harvested was employed to identify the "cotton habitat," i.e., the approximate outer limits of cotton culture in the Southeast (Figs. 1 and 6). The shrinkage of the habitat since 1944 underscores the distinct regionalization which production of the crop has undergone since World War II. (Figures 1 and 6 were constructed from county data.)

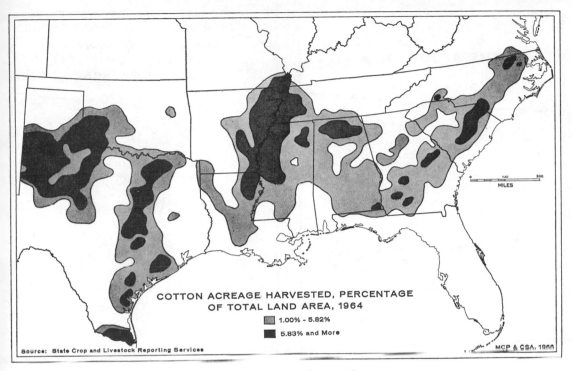

FIG. 6. Cotton acreage harvested, 1964.

in cotton acreage became a prime factor in defining the study area (Fig. 2). A county was included if it: 1) experienced at least a 62.94 percent decline in cotton acreage (twice the southeastern average) between 1944 and 1964; 2) had one or more percent of its area devoted to cotton in 1944; 3) had at least one active cotton gin in 1944; and 4) was contiguous to one or more counties which met the first three criteria. Three counties which met the last three conditions, but which had acreage declines of less than 62.94 percent, were surrounded by counties which satisfied all four conditions. Because their smaller decrease history made these counties important as cotton islands in a sea of decline, they were included in the study area (Fig. 7). All but four of the study area counties were either entirely or partly within the Piedmont physiographic province. These four counties were excluded in order to facilitate generalizations fitting the Piedmont alone. The area thus defined as the Piedmont cotton region of the twentieth century extends from south central North Carolina to eastern Alabama and includes eighty-eight counties.

THE COTTON ISLANDS

The cotton acreage remaining in the region in 1964 obviously was not evenly distributed; that condition persists. The Piedmont today has small scattered concentrations of cotton fields surrounded by large expanses of woodland (characteristically occupying sixty-five to seventy-five percent of land area), pasturage and forage crops, soybeans, and corn—but containing no cotton. Existence of these production islands presented three challenges: 1) identification of their locations; 2) explanation of the disintegration of the cotton complex in the areas surrounding them; and 3) counterpoint explanation of the survival of the complex within the islands.

Cleveland County, North Carolina, was obviously a high density cotton production island on the Piedmont in 1964 (Fig. 6). To identify other such islands the critical value of 5.83 percent was reduced by one-half and used to construct additional isolines (Fig. 8). Three other islands were identified by this procedure; the four comprise major concentrations of cot-

FIG. 7. The study area.

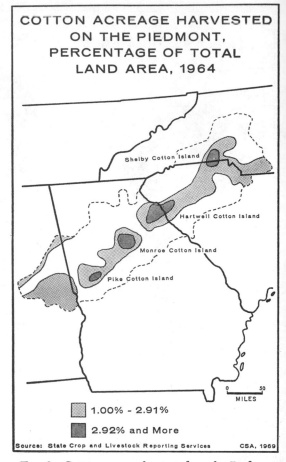

FIG. 8. Cotton acreage harvested on the Piedmont, 1964.

ton culture remaining on the Piedmont.[12] However, because of scale, the isoline procedure applied to county data did not reveal all concentrations of production, because county data hide substantial intracounty variations. Cartographic analysis at a larger scale became necessary.[13] Field observations in

---

[12] Names are attached to the four islands for convenience only (Fig. 8). Shelby, North Carolina, and Hartwell and Monroe, Georgia, are county-seat towns and small central market places. The Pike island takes its name from Pike County, Georgia.

[13] Partly because of logic and partly in response to queries raised in K. H. Stone, "Scale, Scale, Scale?," *Economic Geography*, Vol. 44 (1968), Guest Editorial, we have employed a micro-to-macro scale succession as an organizational and analytical medium in treating the region. We wish to thank Professor Stone for access to manuscript of his more comprehensive "A Geographer's Strength: The Multiple-Scale Approach," *Journal of Geography*, Vol. 71 (1972), in press.

1967 and 1968 produced a map of the distribution of individual cotton fields. When generalized by consolidating tracts of less than five acres, this procedure resulted in a map which revealed numerous small cotton islands not identified by the isoline procedure (Figs. 8 and 9).

It seemed trivial to attempt to devise a precise definition for a cotton island. If viewed at a small scale, each of the major cotton regions in the Southeast are cotton islands surrounded by areas devoted to land use systems dominated by other crops. The island concept is relative in a spatial context; an area that is a cotton island on the Piedmont might be almost a cotton desert in the alluvial Mississippi valley. In a historical context the Piedmont islands are simply vestiges of a once great cotton area; they are not permanent

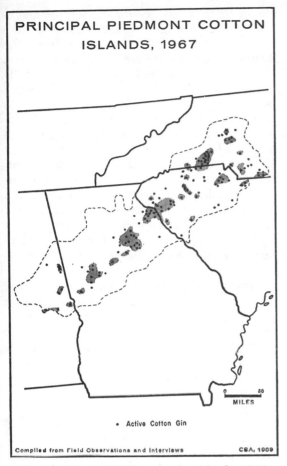

FIG. 9. Principal Piedmont cotton islands, 1967.

features but only surviving remnants of the older agricultural region.

Allotments and The Islands

Why has so much of the traditional cotton growing region disappeared? Clearly, the answer is not simply the impacts of Federal crop acreage allotment programs. Every other cotton growing region has survived the effects of proportionally equal reductions in allotted acreages; this micro-scale consideration does not indicate why the Piedmont region, alone, has disappeared. At intraregional or mid-scale it also is apparent that acreage allotment constrictions alone do not supply the answer, though they have been pervasive influences; some farmers on the Piedmont today have found it profitable to continue cotton production in the face of stringent acreage allotments

while most of the residents of erstwhile region did not.

At a still larger scale, size of the individual farm allotment has been viewed by some as critical to continuance of cotton production. Hart stated that "in the early 1960s . . . an allotment of 50 acres was considered the absolute minimum for profitable production making use of machinery, yet two-thirds of all cotton producers had allotments of less than 15 acres."[14] Since allotments have become more stringent since the early 1960s while fully mechanized production has become even more pervasive (more than ninety percent of the southeastern cotton crop was machine-harvested in 1970), the idea that a certain minimum size of allotment is essential to continuance of production is untenable.[15] Some operations that contain relatively small acreage allotments can and do produce quite efficiently. For example, Justus found that nineteen of forty-two southeastern Missouri farms had less than twenty-four acres (0.7 ha) in cotton in 1959 and that both the highest-cost and least-cost producers within the group grew less than twenty acres (8.1 ha); the least-cost producer grew his lint for slightly less than thirteen cents per pound.[16] Size of allotment per farm does not necessarily reflect the operational system within which the farm operator views the cotton allotment.

Various operational systems have been devised, largely since 1955, which permit the

---

[14] J. F. Hart, *The Southeastern United States* (Princeton, New Jersey: Van Nostrand, Inc., 1967), p. 25. Many other writers have made essentially the same observation.

[15] M. C. Prunty, "Some Contemporary Myths and Challenges in Southern Rural Land Utilization," *Southeastern Geographer*, Vol. 10, No. 2 (1970), p. 4–6.

[16] F. E. Justus, Jr., *Cotton Production Costs and Returns*, Bulletin No. 758 (Columbia, Mo.: University of Missouri Agricultural Experiment Station, 1960), pp. 1–19. In 1963 Prunty reviewed production cost studies conducted by agricultural experiment stations in California, Texas, Missouri, Louisiana, Alabama, Georgia, and North Carolina. These studies, including that of Justus, encompassed approximately 250 farm enterprises which had cotton allotments of as small as 9 acres (3.5 ha) to more than 100 acres (40 ha). Efficiency, as reflected in per-pound production cost, was not positively associated with allotment size. Production costs in 1970–71 were substantially higher than a decade earlier.

operator who wishes to grow cotton to aggregate sufficient allotted acreage to constitute a viable production unit. Though well known to most cotton growers, these systems have not been examined or recognized by geographers until quite recently; fortunately, at least some of them now are identified. The more important involve various forms of multiple tenancy. Fisher found instances in the central Georgia Piedmont in which neoplantation operators had become the tenants of many nearby small farmers; the neoplantation managements had optimized the size of the cotton area to which machinery and cash-wage labor force was applied by renting or leasing the allotments of their smaller neighbors who lacked the necessary capital for mechanized production.[17] Aiken has noted that many operators have obtained a scale of operations which parallels the plantations by aggregating allotments, under their management, through lease or rental of either allotments or whole farms.[18] The individual field units in such an operation may be scattered throughout an area within a radius of ten to twelve miles (15 to 20 km) of the operator's home farm; Aiken referred to such operations as "fragmented neoplantations." Multiple-unit operations at less than plantation scale, involving part-ownerships and/or multiple-tenancy, are another medium whereby allotments are aggregated into functionally viable units.[19]

Still other farmers operate small cotton allotments successfully by avoiding the purchase of expensive machinery, such as mechanical cotton harvesters. Usually these people "swap work" with neighbors who possess the machines or they pay for the services of neighboring machine and operator on a custom basis. Custom services available from the nearby cotton ginner are used extensively in most cotton regions and have been particularly important in the Piedmont. Many a small farmer depends upon the nearby ginner to apply herbicides at planting time and insecticides during the growing season, and to machine-harvest the crop during autumn. In short, those farmers who wish to produce cotton have developed several operational patterns which offset the stringencies of cotton acreage allotments. Thus, from an operational viewpoint the evidence does not support the idea that allotment size has been the primary factor in the regionwide demise of cotton culture.

However, when Hart's observation is viewed in the context of the initial decision-making process, at the individual farm level, a different set of consequences to small allotment size emerges.[20] The results obviously may differ drastically from those at the operational system level after the decision to use an allotment has been made. In 1961, approximately seventy percent of all cotton allotments in the Piedmont were of ten acres or less.[21] What choices were available to farmers with small allotments during the middle 1950s and early 1960s? Obviously a machinery inventory suitable for cotton production under modern techniques could not be supported by a ten acre allotment; a contemporary two-row cotton harvester alone retailed at that time for about $15,000. Thus a ten acre cotton farmer could not produce the crop mechanically, only on his farm, by himself. He could: 1) grow cotton in the traditional non-mechanized manner and hand-pick it—a high-cost, low-return, high-risk venture; 2) rent the allotment to a multiple tenant, provided entrepreneurs of this sort were operating in his neighborhood; 3) prior to 1964, release his acreage allotment at least one year out of three; 4) after 1963, sell the allotment outright; 5) after 1963, lease or rent the allotment for cultivation on another

---

[17] J. S. Fisher, *Modifications of Rural Land Occupance Systems: The Central Georgia Piedmont,* unpublished doctoral dissertation, University of Georgia, 1967, pp. 115–40. The beginnings of allotment leasing and renting by neoplantations are specifically noted in William T. Mealor, *The Plantation Occupance Complex in Dougherty, Lee, and Sumter Counties, Georgia,* unpublished M.A. thesis, University of Georgia, 1964, p. 33. Plantations which are tenants of small holders exhibit a near-reversal of the characteristic tenant-plantation relationship of pre-World War II years.

[18] C. S. Aiken, "The Fragmented Neoplantation: A New Type of Farm Operation in The Southeast," *Southeastern Geographer,* Vol. 11, No. 1 (1971), pp. 43–51.

[19] Fisher, op. cit., footnote 10, pp. 49–53.

[20] Hart, op. cit., footnote 14.

[21] Compiled from unpublished records of the Agricultural Stabilization and Conservation Service, U. S. Department of Agriculture, Washington, D. C., for the 1961 crop year.

landholding; 6) depend upon custom machine services, from a neighbor or nearby ginner, to produce the crop after he had planted and initially cultivated it; or 7) from 1955 onward, place his allotted acreage in a Federal crop acreage diversion program, the "Soil Bank," which paid him a rental crudely equivalent to the estimated net profit the allotment would produce under prevailing values and crop yields.[22] Even options 1), 2), 4), 5), and 6) might not be available to the small farmer if the ginners, and all their ancillary services, in his area had gone out of business; without a ginner the cotton farmer could not market his crop.

Alternative Enterprises

Among alternatives available to the Piedmont farmer were enterprises functionally unrelated to cotton farming. Numbers of farmers shifted to other specialisms and, in the process, essentially abandoned cotton cultivation years ago. Durand recently delineated significant concentrations of dairy farms in four Piedmont areas.[23] Lord has classed the Georgia Piedmont as the largest single poultry producing (primarily broilers, secondarily turkeys) area in the nation, and the North Carolina Piedmont as the fifth largest; the industry also is present in the Alabama Piedmont.[24] A small area at the southern edge of the region in Georgia specializes in peaches; in South Carolina, the Piedmont counties of Spartanburg, Edgefield, and Aiken are all large peach producers. Tobacco retains its traditional significance in the central North Carolina Piedmont though, like cotton, it has been plagued by acreage and poundage allotments during recent decades. All of these agricultural specialisms had their beginnings in the area several decades ago; their origins are not related to the recent disintegration of Piedmont cotton culture. Their growth, particularly that of the poultry industry, definitely has been associated with the decline in cotton cultivation during the 1950–1970 decades.

In Madison County, Georgia, a rural area in the sea of cotton decline between the Hartwell and Monroe islands, the number of farm operators did not change significantly between 1950 and 1960.[25] However, the acreage devoted to cotton—including unplanted allotments placed in the Soil Bank—had decreased about fifty percent to some 10,300 acres (4170 ha) by 1960. By 1951 sales of poultry products had become a greater revenue source than cotton and from 1955 onward generated more than twice the revenue of cotton. Tenancy declined by more than twenty percent. Almost half of the farm families obtained more income from nonfarm than from farm employment. More than thirty percent of the families received income from off-farm employment of two or more members. In 1955, the year before inauguration of the Soil Bank program, slightly more than thirty percent of Madison County consisted of idle cropland, some ninety percent of which had been placed in the Soil Bank by 1960. It is clear that Madison County farmers did not give cotton top billing when decision-making in the 1950s.

Areally dominant in the region, and normally second only to poultry in production of rural income, are the forests. The rapid urbanization and industrialization of the Piedmont has been associated with repeated decisions to plant the old family farm to trees. Some of those who have migrated to the cities have sold or leased their farms to timber and pulp-paper concerns; these firms have immediately

[22] The Conservation Reserve (Soil Bank) Act went into effect in 1956. Farmers could place up to thirty acres (12.1 ha) of allotted cropland in the Soil Bank with no diminution in payment levels; beyond thirty acres, the payment rate decreased. Farmers could place land in the Soil Bank for periods of three, five, or ten years. If trees were planted, ten-year contracts were mandatory. Rental payments were based on land values, prevailing land rents, and land productivity. W. C. McArthur, *The Conservation Reserve Program in Georgia: Its Effects in the Piedmont and Coastal Plain*, U. S. Department of Agriculture, Farm Economics Division (Washington, D. C.: Government Printing Office, 1961), pp. 1–2, indicates that about seventeen percent of the cropland of the Piedmont was in the Soil Bank by 1960. About seventy-eight percent of the Piedmont acreage placed in the Soil Bank consisted of whole farm units, which indicates that marginal small farmers were the principal participants. The Soil Bank program expired on January 1, 1971.

[23] L. Durand, Jr., "Dairying In The South," *Southeastern Geographer*, Vol. 10, No. 2 (1970), p. 30.

[24] J. D. Lord, "The Growth and Localization of the United States Broiler Chicken Industry," *Southeastern Geographer*, Vol. 11, No. 1 (1971), p. 38.

[25] M. C. Prunty, "Idle Rural Land Phenomena In Madison County, Georgia," *Southeastern Geographer*, Vol. 1, No. 1 (1961), pp. 39–49.

planted all non-forest land to trees and have razed existing structures in order to qualify their holdings as unimproved nonfarm land for tax purposes. Thus the decision to migrate generally has placed the land in a condition which has precluded its use for cotton culture for the foreseeable future.

Beef cattle production has become essentially ubiquitous to the Piedmont since World War II. Beef cattle rank second to poultry throughout the region as a source of income from livestock and poultry ranks first among all farm enterprises in gross value; indeed, the two frequently are produced on the same landholding. Although some cow herds are found on farms which produce cotton, more frequently they are components of general farm or livestock specialty operations sans cotton. Many of the relatively small farmers of the central and inner Piedmont buy stocker calves which they graze for a season and then resell; rural residents with urban employment are important within this group as are also semi-retired farmers. In general, the average size of cow herd increases from inner to outer Piedmont and the relatively large herd of 250–300 brood cows, devoted to production of feeder calves, is primarily an outer Piedmont phenomenon. Grain feeding of beef cattle to slaughter condition has been and is relatively rare.

The lures of alternative activities such as beef or poultry, or urban employment, clearly have not had the impacts on the cotton islands that they have had on other parts of the Piedmont. Why not? The answer may lie in adoption of a modern cotton production technology in the islands but not elsewhere.

The Plantation Heritage

One possible explanation for the survival of the cotton islands is that they are in areas with concentrations of relatively large landholdings. Presumably, if this were the case, the large holdings would possess cotton allotments of sufficient sizes to justify the machines necessary for production under modern techniques and, therefore, local concentrations of production would persist. However, the cotton islands then would be concentrated primarily in the outer or lower Piedmont, which con-

tained the preponderance of cotton plantations during the nineteenth and early twentieth centuries (Fig. 9). Clearly, the present cotton islands and most of the Piedmont's old plantations are not areally coincident. Landholdings of plantation size were, and are, distinctly less frequent north and west of the principal axis of the residual cotton islands.[26]

The cotton allotments in the cotton islands are not large; this fact, alone, discredits the notion of a plantation heritage. Walton and Morgan counties, Georgia, in the Monroe island, had 1967 allotments averaging seventeen (6.9 ha) and twenty-five (10.1 ha) acres respectively; Franklin and Hart counties, Georgia, in the Hartwell island, had allotments averaging only nine (3.6 ha) and ten (4.1 ha) acres respectively.[27] The Shelby island is dominated by small farms and small allotments; the Pike island contains a mixture of large and small landholdings.

The traditional cotton sharecropping system was associated primarily with landholdings of plantation size and, therefore, characterized cotton culture on the outer Piedmont as late as 1950. By 1961, however, the cotton sharecropper had almost disappeared from the Piedmont.[28] Scattered small communities of cotton sharecroppers exist south and southeast of the Hartwell island; they are uncommon within the islands themselves. Relatively elderly Negro farmers comprise most of the vestigial sharecroppers. Numerous small allotments that had been on sharecropper farm units prior to 1960 have reverted to the landholdings of which each sharecrop unit was a part and presently cannot be detected as separate production entities. Indeed, the erstwhile cotton plantations of the outer Piedmont, with few exceptions, have abandoned cotton cultivation altogether and have turned to other activities.

[26] The inner or upper Piedmont was dominated by small farm free holders during the nineteenth century and has retained the tradition of the small independent farmer to the present. Curiously, the cultural distinctions and presumed culture boundary between outer and inner Piedmont—though mentioned by many writers—have not been analyzed by a geographer.

[27] Georgia State Office, Agricultural Stabilization and Conservation Service, U. S. Department of Agriculture, *Annual Report 1967* (Athens, Georgia, 1968), pp. 31–34.

[28] Prunty, op. cit., footnote 15, p. 3.

The Boll Weevil

Nearly everyone who has written anything about cotton in the Southeast during the past fifty years has found some way to assign to the boll weevil invasion a fantastic ability to initiate changes in land use and crop combinations, socioeconomic structures, or both. For once, the little insect is not a culprit. The boll weevil had, essentially, little to do with disintegration of the cotton complex of the Piedmont, although it hit the western and southern parts of the Piedmont with disastrous results. Tallapoosa County, Alabama, for example, ginned 30,300 bales in 1914, the year prior to the arrival of the boll weevil, but only 11,900 bales in 1916 and only 7,800 in 1921; Wilkes County, Georgia, ginned 32,600 bales in 1914 but only 2,500 in 1922.[29] By 1921 the insect had spread across the entire region but the damage in the inner and northern portions, because of cooler average temperatures and more frequent and more severe winter freezes, was not nearly so great as elsewhere. In the North Carolina portion, boll weevil damage was minimal; acreage devoted to cotton expanded steadily until Federal acreage controls were installed in the 1930s (Fig. 10). Cleveland County, North Carolina, virtually doubled its acreage in cotton between 1919 and 1929.

Most communities had achieved a substantial recovery from the boll weevil invasion by the late 1920s, but the Piedmont never again achieved the density of cotton production that it possessed prior to the boll weevil era. In 1909, cotton planted in the region totalled some 3,900,000 acres (1,578,947 ha) but by 1939 (with allotments in effect) the acreage totalled 1,600,000 (647,773 ha). Some, but not all, of the decline in acreage resulted from the boll weevil's depredations, for acreage allotments were imposed before full recovery had occurred (Fig. 10). However, the Piedmont cotton region was fully viable through the World War II years and into the early 1950s. The boll weevil, though still present as

[29] U. S. Department of Commerce, Bureau of the Census, *Cotton Production and Distribution, Season of 1916–17* (Washington, D. C.: Government Printing Office, 1918), pp. 108 and 112; and idem, *Cotton Production in the United States, Crop of 1923* (Washington, D. C.: Government Printing Office, 1924), pp. 9 and 13.

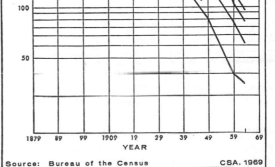

FIG. 10. Piedmont cotton acreages, 1879–1964.

in other cotton areas, was reasonably well controlled. The present cotton islands contain some areas that were hard hit by the weevil and some that were not. Conversely, the non-cotton Piedmont of today contains areas that the weevil ravaged and others that he affected only slightly. The pattern of his depredations is irrelevant to the present issue. Disintegration of the region commenced after adjustments to the boll weevil had been made; we cannot attribute the inception or the continuance of regional disintegration processes to the little immigrant from Mexico.

Interregional Competition

It is generally accepted that the costs of growing cotton have been somewhat higher on the Piedmont than in the other principal cotton regions. From this, Hart reasoned that there has been a relative regional weakness at the marketplace, i.e., that production declines have been associated with the region's inability to compete adequately for its share of the nation's cotton markets.[30] However, because of the manner in which Federal production controls have operated, interregional competition has not been significant. An allotment to grow cotton has amounted to a guaranteed share of the national output of the commodity and a price guarantee as well. When the volume produced has been greater than the market could absorb, the Commodity Credit Corporation has purchased and stored a sufficient amount of the crop to maintain its price at a level predetermined by the Secretary of Agriculture in accord with the Congressional stipulations in the various Agricultural Adjustment Acts. This system has, in effect, eliminated periods of depressed prices and crop surpluses at the farm market level—though large surpluses have developed several times in the holdings of the Commodity Credit Corporation. Thus the competition among regions that normally occurs on a free or open market has been, for all practical purposes, vitiated in the cotton trade since inception of the Agricultural Adjustment Acts some thirty-five years ago. During the 1940s, when price support and acreage allotment provisions were not in effect, the demand generated by World War II conditions was so great that interregional competition did not develop.

The pricing systems which have evolved under the Agricultural Adjustment Acts, in the case of cotton, are quite complex and are not at issue in this analysis. Consistent with grade and quality variations, they have been uniformly applied to the crop in all areas. Piedmont-produced cottons generally have occupied intermediate positions on the grade-and-quality scale of cotton market prices. Price levels have been too low to permit a

farmer who did not employ modern production techniques, including mechanization, to grow the crop at a reasonable profit regardless of the region in which he was situated. Conversely, those growers who have employed the best available technology have enjoyed reasonable profits—again, without regard to region. The fact that cotton production costs have been somewhat higher on the Piedmont, then, has not placed the efficient grower of that region in a marginal position; cotton, within the suite of available production alternatives, has been attractive. For the farmer who did not keep pace technologically, however, cotton growing became a marginal or submarginal venture by the middle 1950s, if not earlier. Most of the region's growers exhibited technologic lag by that date and, in consequence, examined alternative enterprises carefully.

Terrain and The Islands

Are certain terrain traits areally associated with the persistence of the cotton islands and, conversely, with the disappearance of cotton elsewhere? Can it be demonstrated that the islands have gentle topographic gradients and are therefore better suited to employment of tractors and mechanical harvesters in cotton growing? If terrain is a factor, the areas of current cotton cultivation should exhibit gently rolling to flat terrain, presumably on broad interfluves, suitable for machine cultivation in large field units. Surrounding non-cotton areas should be hilly or dissected with high local relief.

However, no common set of terrain traits typifies the principal islands. The Monroe island occupies broad, relatively flat, interfluves and contains many relatively large fields (Fig. 9). The Hartwell island and part of the Shelby island, conversely, are relatively severely dissected.[31] On the other hand, cotton culture has almost vanished from many areas of broad, gently rolling to undulating

[30] John Fraser Hart, "Loss and Abandonment of Cleared Farm Land In the Eastern United States," *Annals*, Association of American Geographers, Vol. 58 (1968), p. 430. The absence of interregional competition, because of Federal manipulations of the cotton price structure, was recognized in the theoretical locational model employed by Paul I. Mendell and Luther G. Tweeten, "The Location of Cotton Production in the United States Under Competitive Conditions: A Study of Crop Location and Comparative Advantage," *Geographical Analysis*, Vol. 3 (1971), p. 335–37.

[31] Terrain conditions representative of the Monroe and Hartwell, Georgia, areas, respectively, are illustrated by: *Watkinsville, Georgia, Quadrangle*, Scale 1:24,000 (Washington, D. C.: U. S. Department of Interior, Geological Survey, 1964); and *Royston, Georgia, Quadrangle*, Scale 1:24,000 (Washington, D. C.: U. S. Department of Interior, Geological Survey, 1959).

interfluves, particularly those southeast of the principal axis of the cultivation islands on the outer or lower Piedmont (Fig. 9).

Taken as a whole, the rolling terrain of the Piedmont has presented greater challenges to farm mechanization than has the terrain of more level cotton-growing regions and Piedmont cotton farmers were slower to mechanize than were those of other regions. Smaller farms, smaller cotton allotments, and smaller amounts of working capital probably contributed to this technologic lag. Perhaps even more significant to the retardation of mechanization than the actual terrain or other impediments was the manner in which Piedmont topography was perceived by many agricultural specialists and researchers. As a group, these agricultural leaders viewed the prospects for mechanization of Piedmont farms pessimistically and so advised the farming public. At the time of the introduction of tractors, one study assessing the methods of cotton production on the Piedmont noted:[32]

> There is a scarcity of large level fields and it is difficult to combine fields because of the irregular nature of the land, therefore tractor operated machinery to reduce labor costs scarcely seems practicable.

More than twenty years later, when tractors were essentially ubiquitous but mechanical cotton harvesters had been available only six or seven years, a study distributed by Alabama Polytechnic Institute (now Auburn University) advised landowners that:[33]

> . . . Mechanical equipment that is currently used in other cotton producing areas is not satisfactory for extensive use in the Piedmont Area of Alabama. This is particularly true of those machines required for chopping and hoeing, and for harvesting the crop . . . . In the face of increasing competition from cotton-producing areas that can adopt low-cost production practices, many farmers in the area [the Piedmont] may find it advisable to consider alternative enterprises in which they have better competitive opportunities.

[32] O. M. Johnson and H. A. Turner, *The Old Plantation Piedmont Cotton Belt* (Washington: U. S. Department of Agriculture, Bureau of Agricultural Economics, Division of Land Economics, 1930), p. 5.

[33] M. White, *Cotton Production Practices in the Piedmont Area of Alabama*, Circular 102 (Auburn, Ala.: Agricultural Experiment Station of the Alabama Polytechnic Institute, 1951), pp. 21–23. The views expressed in this publication paralleled those of many agricultural specialists in Georgia and North and South Carolina at that time.

Mechanization of Piedmont cotton production was by no means an insurmountable problem; indeed, in many areas it presented no more problems than it did on the inner coastal plains. The best evidence to support this view lies in the fact that, in 1967, at least eighty percent of the region's crop was machine-harvested.[34] By that time machine harvesting had been practiced successfully, in growing amounts, for almost fifteen years on the Piedmont. The farmers who grow cotton in the islands today made the transition to mechanized production methods rather easily during the decades following World War II. Terracing on some hillside fields was redesigned; broad-based terraces over which harvesters could lumber replaced narrow "bench" terraces of the horse-mule era. However, the prospect of adapting terrain to machines, and machines to terrain, probably was discouraging to some farmers and may have contributed to their failure to revolutionize their production technology. The transition was more difficult to make—indeed, apparently was never attempted by many—when assertions to the effect that machines could not be used on the Piedmont were issued by the various agricultural extension services.

Summary

We have rejected cotton acreage allotment declines *per se*, the plantation heritage of the outer Piedmont and the old sharecropping farming system, the boll weevil, interregional competition, and terrain conditions as non-central—in a causal sense—to disintegration of the Piedmont cotton region. The impact of small size of cotton allotment and alternative enterprises require further consideration. Migration of Piedmont farm people to cities after World War II was part of a nationwide phenomenon, hence neither regionally unique nor causal to disintegration. The Soil Bank arrived on the regional scene after disintegration had started; it was temporally coincident but not antecedent to much of the region's disintegration.

[34] U. S. Department of Agriculture, Consumer and Marketing Service, Cotton Division, *Weekly Cotton Market Review*, Vol. 49 (June 7, 1968), Appendix C, Table 22.

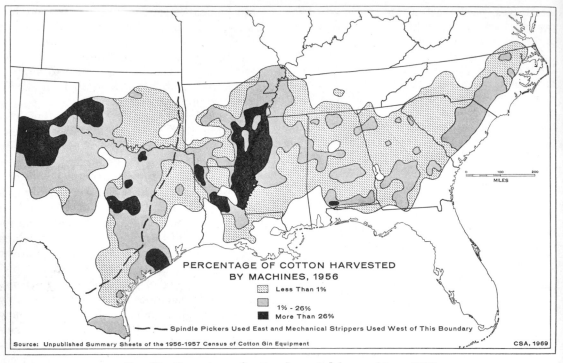

FIG. 11. Percentage of cotton harvested by machines, 1956.

THE REVOLUTION IN TECHNOLOGY

Technologic changes in cotton-growing clearly required scrutiny, but it was considerably less clear how innovations in technology could be examined. We decided to rely heavily upon interviews with the owners of the remaining active cotton gins in the region in order to establish the nature and role of technologic changes. These men know the production traits and histories of their customers better than anyone else. They know why some have failed, and others succeeded, in making the transition into modern cotton culture. They also know the plight, problems, and prospects of cotton gins and ancillary enterprises as do no others. The ginners of the Piedmont in 1967 thus became the principal focus of the investigation.

In 1945 there were 1,149 gin plants on the Piedmont.[35] By 1967 only 138 active gins were left (Fig. 9). Owners of ninety-eight of these were interviewed to obtain informa-

tion concerning their current customers, loss of other customers, the nature of farm and gin machinery associated with their enterprises, and the nature of other activities integrated with their ginning businesses.[36]

The New Production Technology

Modern techniques in cotton production center on the mechanical harvester.[37] Perfection of mechanical harvesters came after many decades of effort; the first patent for a spindle-type picker was issued in 1850 and the stripper

---

[35] U. S. Department of Commerce, Bureau of the Census, *Cotton Ginning Machinery and Equipment in the United States—1945* (Washington, D. C.: Government Printing Office, 1946), p. 7.

[36] Attempts to interview the other forty ginners failed for various reasons: deaths in their families; serious illnesses of a few men; some refused to be interviewed; a few could not be contacted or located. Several gin owners who had abandoned operations in recent years also were interviewed but were excluded from the study because the interviews produced no information not obtained from active ginners.

[37] We have relied heavily upon personal experience and observation in this section. Both of our immediate families own farms which have been engaged in cotton production for more than fifty years; the farms are operated through multiple tenant arrangements today. The family of the junior author also has been heavily committed to the cotton ginning business for four generations.

method was employed initially in 1871.[38] It was not until the late 1920s, however, that spindle pickers were perfected to a level where a farm implement company was ready to introduce trial machines.[39] Spindle pickers are employed in areas in the Southeast in which the machine is taken into the field two or more times, in order to harvest open bolls as soon as possible and to permit submature bolls to stay on the plant for maturation. Stripper harvesters, on the other hand, are employed to harvest the crop in a once-over operation after all bolls are open. These machines are effective on the High Plains of Texas and Oklahoma where the crop runs little risk of damage from rains in autumn after the bolls begin to open; harvesting customarily proceeds after the first frost. The spindle harvester is utilized almost exclusively east of the Black Prairies of Texas (Fig. 11). Only the spindle picker is used on the Piedmont.[40]

Farmer acceptance and initial utilization of the spindle picker was slow; there were only 107 of these machines in the whole country by 1946. As late as 1950 no more than eight percent of the national crop was machine harvested and by 1960 only about one-half of the crop was so harvested.[41] The spindle harvester operated in only a few areas in the Piedmont as late as 1955–56 (Fig. 11).

Several factors appear to have retarded acceptance of mechanical pickers. The machines are expensive but cost was only one factor. The intensive nature of traditional cotton production demanded large labor inputs for three operations: 1) seedbed preparation and planting; 2) thinning and weeding; and 3) harvesting. In areas dominated by large farms, such as the outer Piedmont, there was little incentive for management to seek a machine

which reduced labor for harvesting because a large labor force still was needed for the other two operations. The possible socioeconomic consequences of displacement of thousands of rural-farm residents also may have retarded adoption of the pickers.[42] Small-scale farming operations such as those of the inner Piedmont presented almost no market for the mechanical harvester.

Ginners (and others) are quite emphatic when noting that mechanization of planting (to eliminate spacing of plants by the hand-hoe) and evolvement of herbicides (to eliminate weeding by the hand-hoe and intertillage in general) did not develop coincidentally with the advent of the cotton picker. The technology of herbicides was developed in the early 1950s; herbicides were widely employed in other regions by the middle and late 1950s but Piedmont producers lagged in adopting them.[43] We estimate that the Piedmont lagged some six or seven years behind the Mississippi valley. By the early 1960s, those Piedmont farmers growing cotton had—for the most part, but not altogether—integrated both mechanical harvesting and the use of herbicides into their production systems. However, by that time regionwide disintegration of the cotton complex was well advanced.

---

[42] A number of sociologists (and others) thought that tractors and mechanical harvesters threatened unemployment in a time when unemployment was widespread, and issued warnings concerning the consequences of mechanization. An example is C. S. Johnson, E. R. Embree, and W. W. Alexander, *The Collapse of Cotton Tenancy* (Chapel Hill: The University of North Carolina Press, 1935), pp. 43–44. Rural out-migration appears to have proceeded faster than farm mechanization and until recently, forced landowners toward mechanization.

[43] Herbicides customarily are incorporated into the seedbed at the time of planting. Preemergence chemicals are designed to eliminate (or at least, retard) the germination of weeds and grasses until the cotton plants have emerged and have established themselves. Postemergence herbicides, commonly sprays, are applied relatively early in the cotton growth cycle to eradicate weeds and grasses which may have escaped the effects of pre-emergence applications. The number of postemergence applications is influenced by rainfall; an excessively rainy late spring or early summer reduces the effectiveness of the herbicides and may require two or even more postemergence applications. After the cotton plants fully shade the space between adjacent rows, herbicides normally are not employed because shading suppresses the growth of pest plants.

---

[38] H. P. Smith and others, *The Mechanical Harvesting of Cotton*, Bulletin 452 (College Station: Texas Agricultural Experiment Station, Agricultural and Mechanical College of Texas, 1932), pp. 5–6; and James H. Street, *The New Revolution in the Cotton Economy* (Chapel Hill: The University of North Carolina Press, 1957), pp. 107–12.

[39] Street, op. cit., footnote 38, pp. 112–29.

[40] The spindle picker also is used in the irrigated cotton-growing districts of the Southwest and California.

[41] U. S. Department of Agriculture, Consumer and Marketing Service, Cotton Division, Memphis, Tennessee, unpublished summaries of Cotton Harvested by Machines, by States, for 1950 and 1960.

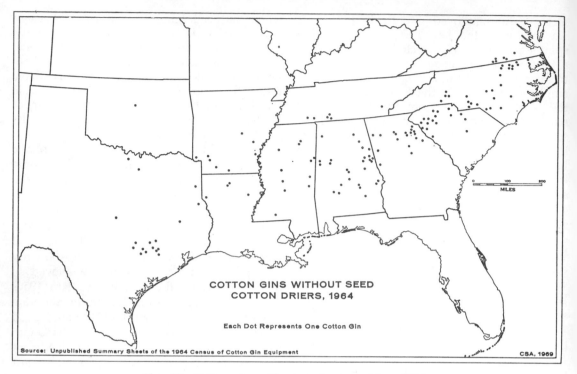

FIG. 12. Cotton gins without seed cotton driers, 1964.

Effects on Ginning Technology

Machine harvesting introduced three new problems into the cotton ginning operation. These were difficulties associated with damp machine-harvested cotton, compression of the harvesting season, and trash incorporated into the cotton by machine pickers.

Machine-picked cotton is higher in moisture content than hand-picked cotton in part because each picker spindle is constantly moistened to improve adherence of the fiber as harvesting proceeds. Moisture also comes from plant leaves and other trash that the picker gleans along with the cotton. The non-selective nature of the harvest with the machine also is partly responsible: moist parts of a field are harvested along with those that are dry for, once the machine is in a field, the tendency is to harvest the entire field.

Damp seed cotton deteriorates if it is not dried and ginned promptly and non-dried cotton tends to clog the ginning machinery. Ginners have had to install seed cotton driers, machines which were developed in the early 1930s in response to problems with damp hand-

picked cotton.[44] By 1945 only 3,093 of the 10,836 gins in the United States had these devices and they were less common in the Piedmont than in the other cotton regions.[45] As late as 1956, when drying machinery had been available for better than a quarter of a century, only some fifty-eight percent of Piedmont gins possessed this equipment whereas eighty-eight percent of the gins in all the other regions were drier-equipped.[46] By 1964 the Piedmont contained more gins without drying equipment, proportionately and

[44] F. L. Gerdes and C. A. Bennett, *Effect of Artificially Drying Seed Cotton Before Ginning on Certain Quality Elements of the Lint and Seed and on the Operation of the Gin Stand,* U. S. Department of Agriculture, Technical Bulletin 508 (Washington, D. C.: Government Printing Office, 1936), pp. 2–8.

[45] U. S. Department of Commerce, op. cit., footnote 35, passim.

[46] U. S. Department of Agriculture, Agricultural Marketing Service, Cotton Division, unpublished summary sheets of the 1956–57 Census of Cotton Gin Equipment. These unpublished summaries, along with those for the 1964 Census of Cotton Gin Equipment, are in the offices of the Cotton Division in Memphis, Tennessee.

in absolute numbers, than any erstwhile cotton-growing region (Fig. 12).

Another problem associated with machine-harvested cotton is the compression of the harvesting and ginning season. Hand-picking used to start in late summer as soon as the first few bolls were open and extended into late autumn or early winter. With machines it is necessary to await the ripening of most of the bolls; thereafter the whole picking operation is completed in a few weeks. The effects of the compressed season on ginning are illustrated by Bolivar County, Mississippi.[47] In 1944 when essentially the entire crop was hand-picked, eleven percent was harvested prior to September 16, sixty-four percent between September 16 and November 14, and twenty-five percent after November 14. During 1964, under machine-harvesting conditions for more than eighty percent of the crop, fourteen percent of the harvest was accomplished before September 16 and only three percent after November 14. Thus eighty-three percent was harvested between September 10 and November 14; more than half the crop was picked in one month, between mid-September and mid-October.

In all southeastern cotton growing areas except the Piedmont the compressed harvest season led to introduction of high-capacity ginning equipment. Ginners have not increased storage capacity, since growers strongly prefer to avoid the downgrading of fiber quality that generally results from storing moist machine-picked cotton. The grower wants his cotton ginned immediately. A typical 1945 gin plant could process one bale in about fifteen minutes. A comparable 1967 high-capacity plant could process a bale in three to eight minutes.[48] In 1967 we could find only one modern, high-capacity cotton gin on the entire Piedmont.[49] None of the others had undergone a full-fledged capacity transformation.

Trash is a third ginning problem associated with machine-picked cotton. Bits and pieces of boll hulls, leaves, and even small branches and stems are ingested by the picker. This trash must be removed before ginned cotton is suitable for use by a textile mill. The late 1940s saw the development of the lint cleaner, a machine that is installed between the gin stands and the press, which produces the finished, strapped bale.[50] The ginners of the Piedmont generally were slow to obtain and install lint cleaners. By 1964, the largest concentration of gins in the Southeast without lint cleaners was in the Piedmont (Fig. 13). In a general sense, the technological revolution which struck the ginning industry from 1945 onward involved gin capacity, moisture problems and cotton drying, and trash removal.[51] Most ginners in other cotton growing regions responded rapidly and adopted the necessary technologic improvements but those of the Piedmont, in general, did not.

Piedmont Ginners Today

By 1964 the average production per gin on the Piedmont was less than half the average for southeastern gins; in the four principal cotton islands, bales produced per gin ran from one half to virtually equal to (but not exceeding) the southeastern average.[52] Most

diameters. Ninety saw stands were available by the early 1950s. During the 1950s and 1960s manufacturers developed stands with a hundred or more saws and increased the saw diameters to sixteen or more inches.

[49] The plant is located in the Alabama Piedmont. Its management has done an excellent job of catering to the needs and interests of cotton growers in its vicinity.

[50] The lint cleaner removes small bits, called "pepper trash," that have escaped the cleaning devices (burr machines and impact cleaners) which extract larger pieces of trash before the in-seed cotton goes to the saws in the gin stand.

[51] We believe that several "revolutions" have occurred in ginning technology in the past. These may have been related to large-scale shifts in land utilization systems involving cotton in ways not identified heretofore.

[52] U. S. Department of Commerce, Bureau of the Census (1964), op. cit., footnote 47.

---

[47] U. S. Department of Commerce, Bureau of the Census, *Cotton Production in the United States, Crop of 1944* (Washington, D. C.: Government Printing Office, 1944), p. 29; and idem, *Cotton Production in the United States, Crop of 1964*, p. 31.

[48] A. L. Smith, *Continental Gin Company and Its Fifty-Two Years of Service* (Birmingham, Ala.: Birmingham Publishing Co., 1952), p. 99. Increases in the number of stands per plant meant more labor and greater unit operating costs, and were viewed as poor solutions to capacity problems. Most ginners resolved their problems by installing higher capacity units. In 1945 most gins had three or four seventy to eighty saw stands. The saws had twelve inch

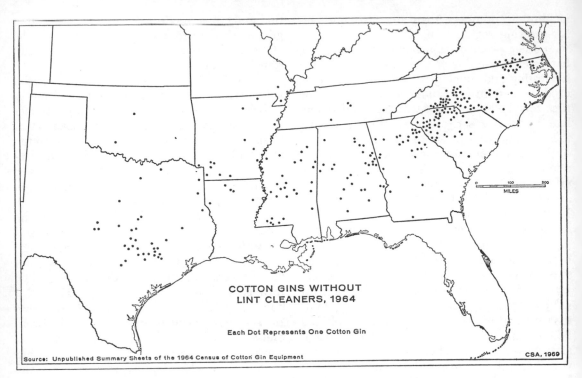

FIG. 13. Cotton gins without lint cleaners, 1964.

of the gins which were operating in 1944–45 had gone out of business and still more ceased operations between 1964 and 1967. What is the status of the remaining ginners?

In the past, the Piedmont has had two general types of gin operations. The custom gin served the public and survived by competing effectively in its trade area for the business of independent cotton growers. The farm gin was located on the farm—usually a large one—of its owner. The latter type supplemented the ginning of its own cotton by ginning the fiber of farmers in its immediate vicinity. Relative accessibility had been the primary consideration in a farmer's selection of a gin but with the advent of the new ginning machinery, such as driers and lint cleaners, farmers began bypassing outdated gins. Thus installation of modern auxiliary machines and other contemporary ginning equipment was the method used by the more successful Piedmont ginners to compete for volumes of fiber until fairly recently.

As cotton production continued to decline, location and conventional competition methods became progressively less effective. A gin-

ner might possess the latest in ginning machinery but this did not prevent nearby farmers from abandoning the crop. Some ginners developed promotional schemes designed to encourage farmers to continue production of cotton. Thirty-six of the ninety-eight gin owners interviewed worked actively to encourage planting of the crop (Table 1). Because their promotional efforts were distinctive and effective, we have classed these ginners as promotional and the others as nonpromotional. Gins that have been both farm and custom types in the past are in both groups.

Since some promotional schemes are also methods of competition, it is difficult to distinguish between the two. In its simplest form, promotion consists of nothing more than "talking up" the advantages of growing cotton. Generally, however, promotion is more complex and has more tangible characteristics. Many promotional ginners secure the best planting seed for their customers; they hold meetings with farmers to disseminate information about improved cotton varieties and the best of production techniques; they issue letters, to both growers and potential growers,

TABLE 1.—ACTIVITIES ASSOCIATED WITH PIEDMONT COTTON GINS, 1967
(N = 98)

Activity	Promotional gins (N = 36)		Nonpromotional gins (N = 62)	
	Number	Percentage of total	Number	Percentage of total
Farm-oriented:				
Cotton farming	32	89	44	71
Farm supply	31	67	39	63
Fertilizer sales	29	81	49	79
Cotton buying	26	72	39	63
Planting seed production	23	64	3	5
Seed processing	17	47	10	16
Cotton warehousing	15	42	10	16
Manufacture of fertilizers	6	17	4	7
Feed mixing	2	6	7	11
Farm implement sales	1	3	2	3
General:				
Coal sales	5	14	14	23
Grocery store	2	6	13	21
Ice manufacture	1	3	3	5
Hardware store	2	6	1	2
Sawmill	0	0	3	5
Cotton oil mill	1	3	4	7

Compiled from interviews.

which provide production and marketing facts, list their available services, and exude confidence in the coming growing season. Many of the promotional ginners provide custom farming services in the form of mechanical planters, herbicide and insecticide application equipment, and mechanical harvesters.

Promotional efforts achieve their climax in the "one-variety" cotton communities. Premium prices received from sale of the one-variety seed and the greater yields and prices obtained from the improved fiber variety (which when aggregated in large volume is quite appealing to textile mills) encourage the farmers to continue growing the crop. The ginner is central to the whole cotton effort in the one-variety cotton community. In order to obtain the cotton and seed which they promote, ginners tie farmers to their plants by supply and ginning contracts arranged each spring.

In attempting to maintain cotton production, ginners are not seeking merely to protect investments in gin plants. In most instances the cotton gin is a less important consideration than ancillary enterprises (Table 1). This is not a new situation but it is more critical today than twenty years ago because of recent losses in ginning volumes.[53] As a group, promotional gins are associated with ancillary activities to a greater degree than are nonpromotional gins; their association is proportionally greater where the ancillary enterprise is strongly farm-related. Seed and warehousing functions are more important to promotional than non-promotional gins. We did not attempt to obtain profit-loss statements from gin owners in regard to their various enterprises. However, many owners candidly noted that the gin enterprise itself was not a great money-maker but was functionally central to their ancillary enterprises—which definitely were profitable. Thus survival of some of the best and most active ginning operations of the Piedmont is not explainable primarily in terms of cotton fiber, but in terms of ancillary enterprises.

[53] R. F. Anderson, H. R. Smith, and Z. M. Looney, *An Evaluation of the Costs and Quality of Ginning in the Piedmont Area of Georgia, Seasons of 1950–51 and 1951–52*, Bulletin 280 (Experiment, Ga.: University of Georgia College of Agriculture Experiment Stations, 1953), pp. 29–30.

What of the ginners' customers? Approximately eighty percent of the cotton volume the ginners handled in 1967 came from multiple tenants, about ten percent from small independent farmers whose crops were machine-picked, and about ten percent from small holders who still hand-picked their crops. The latter group was dominated by relatively elderly Negroes. In many instances the ginners themselves are multiple tenants engaged in farming enterprises and are the overwhelming force in continuance of cotton cultivation in their islands. Some multiple tenants even had bought closed gins in the early and middle 1960s—at distress prices—and then modernized their equipment in order to insure their own viability as cotton growers (these were nonpromotional, farm-located gins).[54]

Cotton gins have been employed in location theory as examples of concentrating industries with small tributary areas.[55] Generally, the examples do not fit the present distributions of Piedmont gin customers, a condition that simply underscores the disarray of production areas occasioned by the disappearances of many former growers and ginners. Hauls of more than twenty miles (30 km) to a suitable gin are common. Multiple-tenant and ginner interlinks, and the promotional efforts of certain ginners, have produced situations in which a gin is quite active in an area producing almost no cotton and its customers bypass two or more gins to reach it. The interrelated interests of the multiple tenants and the more progressive ginners, especially the promotionally oriented ones, are respon-

---

[54] A new modern gin might cost $200,000–250,000; abandoned ginning equipment of rather recent vintage, which can be had at grossly depreciated prices nearly anywhere in the Piedmont today, is a source of replacement gin parts for other cotton regions. Active Piedmont ginners frequently buy closed gins to ensure adequate peak harvest capacity or to acquire a parts-repair inventory at little cost.

[55] August Losch, *The Economics of Location*, tr. by William H. Woglom (New York: John Wiley & Sons, 1967), pp. 11 and 365–67; E. M. Hoover, *The Location of Economic Activity* (New York: McGraw Hill Book Co., 1948) pp. 32, 86, and 221; and C. D. Covey and J. F. Hudson, *Cotton Gin Efficiency as Related to Size, Location and Cotton Production Density in Louisiana*, Bulletin 577 (Baton Rouge: Agricultural Experiment Station, Louisiana State University, 1963).

sible for the residual production in the cotton islands today.

At least 13 of the 138 contemporary gins are obsolete by any standard. Included among these are eight plants that we consider hobby operations. These are curious relics with a volume of operation too small for any possibility of profit or even of loss-leader value in attracting business to ancillary enterprises. Family or personal pride, or prestige, appears to be the motivating factor for continuance; it is not economic considerations. These gins and their customers are located outside of the principal cotton islands and play no real role in the islands' struggle for survival. The customers of these plants are small farmers who hand-pick their cotton. As a group, they are more than forty-five years of age and the hobby ginners also are older men. Both groups probably will disappear within a decade.

THE CAUSAL INTERFACE

The critical time for the survival of the Piedmont cotton region was the first half of the 1950s. Until that time the region was a viable cotton-growing complex. Progressively more stringent application of acreage allotments then placed the vast majority of the small farmers—who were growing the crop under the traditional system, including hand-harvesting—in a position wherein they viewed alternative land uses as more profitable than cotton culture, or cotton production as distinctly unprofitable, or both. Holders of small allotments were the backbone of the industry. A mechanized and relatively low-cost technology for growing the fiber was available. A few growers moved to it but most did not because they failed to perceive the new production technology as one of their alternatives. Equally important, most growers failed to comprehend the operational system of multiple-tenancy, through which small allotments could be profitable under the new production technology. Those that tried the multiple-tenant system were quite successful; the great majority of the Piedmont cotton growers of the 1950s avoided it and exhibited technologic lag to the point of redundancy.

Perhaps the Piedmont's small growers would have been foolish to move to the modern production technology at a time when the ginners

FIG. 14. Abandoned double-battery cotton gin near Winterville, Georgia.

of the region could not adequately process the machine-harvested product. The ginners, too, exhibited surprising technologic lag. Their failure to recognize the new production technology as essential to survival of cotton growing produces a fascinating speculation: had they equipped their gins to handle machine-produced cotton, and had they engaged in their 1967 level of promotional and grower-supporting activities, most of the regional cotton complex might have survived. As it was in the early 1950s, the grower who wanted to move to mechanized production had to search to find a ginner willing to equip himself to handle the machine-harvested fiber.

Thus an aggregation of technologic lags at grower and ginner levels, of lags in developing viable land operational systems by landowners, and of alternative opportunities for the small farmers, led to the disintegration of the Piedmont cotton complex. The Soil Bank and subsequent cropland retirement and allotment diversion programs of the Federal government hastened the disintegration process by increasing the number of options available to these farmers who had not made the transition into the modern production technology.

GOODBYE TO THE ISLANDS

The cotton islands on the Piedmont today attest to the entrepreneurial vigor and technologic adaptability of several hundred—apparently not more than 2,000—men. Most are cotton growers of the multiple-tenant type; the remainder are those few ginners who have modernized their plants. The two groups have formed an interlinkage that, for the present, is effective. The role of the individual, as he affects regional inertia, or regional persistence, has been inferred in this study. The persistence of certain farmers as cotton growers might be due to their possession of "skills peculiar to the particular form of agriculture practiced."[56] However, the contemporary Piedmont multi-tenant has survived by learning new skills associated with a new type of cotton production. Is this persistence or innovation? These farmers have demonstrated their nonconformity by producing cotton with machines

---

[56] Buchanan, op. cit., footnote 2, p. 12.

which they were told could not be used on the Piedmont. How significant is the adaptive individual to the maintenance of other regions?

No matter how important inertia or persistence may be, the present little islands of cotton culture on the Piedmont cannot maintain themselves indefinitely. Many of the Piedmont's remaining gins are close to obsolescence and even the more modern ones will need renovation in a few years. The ginners who now support and promote the crop and the farmers who now grow it will begin to retire in a few years. Who will replace them? Even now, neither cotton-growing nor ginning is a young man's game on the Piedmont.

Before these men retire or pass away, other forces may spell the end of the islands. Cotton culture is highly sensitive to Federal land resource programs and allotments and these have a history of many changes. As ginning technology continues to change, the shortage of adequate gins probably will contribute to disappearance of what remains of the Piedmont cotton region, as the absence of an adequate ginning technology retarded its origin some 175 years ago. Even though they are "fighting to the last ditch," we give the growers and the ginners no more than twenty years until their little islands of cotton culture are gone forever.

POPULATION CHANGE IN NORTHERN NEW ENGLAND

GEORGE K. LEWIS

ABSTRACT. A substantial increase in the population growth rate of northern New England is revealed by the 1970 Federal Census. Vermont, New Hampshire, and Maine have experienced relatively low population growth rates since the mid-1800s, or even undergone population losses. Population increases have been greatest in the Burlington, Vermont, area, in southern New Hampshire, and in south coastal Maine. Extensive construction of limited access highways, a surge in second home ownership, an increase in recreational facilities, and the establishment of new plants and offices in northern New England are related to current growth patterns. KEY WORDS: *Growth centers, New England, Population change.*

IN the years of national and regional assessment immediately after World War II, New England appeared to be a region in serious economic trouble. The war years had been prosperous ones for New England as a whole, temporarily halting the economic decline which had overtaken the region in the 1920s and 30s. The Council of Economic Advisers were among the first to survey New England's postwar economy, using the recession of 1948–49 as an indication of the seriousness of the situation. They wrote:[1]

New England is, of course, not without its economic disadvantages. It is deficient in many raw materials of modern industry. Its transportation costs, power costs, and taxes are higher than those costs in several other regions. Much of its plant and equipment is old and needs modernization. In some industries its labor costs are relatively high as the results of high wage rates, restrictions on work conditions, and somewhat higher costs of social legislation. Some of its economic disadvantages are the result of the failure of New Englanders to make the most of their assets. Others are the result of its early economic growth. Finally some of its disadvantages are the result of inaction or unwise action by various government authorities, both local and federal.

The CEA study was shortly followed by an even more detailed report on New England's

Dr. Lewis is Professor of Geography at Boston University in Boston, Massachusetts.

[1] *The New England Economy,* A Report to the President transmitting a study initiated by the Council of Economic Advisers and prepared by its Committee on the New England Economy (Washington, D. C., 1951).

economic problems, sponsored by the National Planning Association.[2]

It was soon apparent that only Connecticut would participate actively in the nation's postwar economic growth, oriented toward durable consumer goods, aircraft, and military hardware. Massachusetts' and Rhode Island's large industrial bases were weaker structurally, but still contained such vital sectors as electronics and electrical machinery. The rapid increase in demand for military hardware after 1950 reversed the temporary economic decline of Massachusetts and Rhode Island.

Maine, New Hampshire, and Vermont, on the other hand, continued to be areas of declining population growth and outmigration, of widespread land abandonment, and of severe local economic depression. The Federal Census of 1950 confirmed these trends and revealed that all three states were lagging in population growth behind the country as a whole, and to a lesser degree, behind the three southern New England states. With the exception of a few bright spots, the gloomy picture of the late 1940s continued on through the next decade, and the 1960 Census revealed an even greater lag between northern and southern New England. It is now apparent, however, that the points of regional growth evident in the 1950s have spread rapidly, and that new growth areas in northern New England have appeared. The impact of these developments on population

[2] *The Economic State of New England,* Report of the Committee of New England of the National Planning Association (New Haven, 1954).

trends in northern New England has been swift and dramatic. The region now has the fastest growing state in New England (New Hampshire) and the third fastest state (Vermont), both of which are increasing their population as fast or more rapidly than the country as a whole.

NORTHERN NEW ENGLAND AS A REGION

Northern New England is not a particularly meaningful region by any of the more traditional definitions. It possesses no homogeneous characteristics, be they climate, topography, the distribution of maple sugar houses, or the proportion of French Canadians. It has no regional capital, unless one suggests that Boston may, indeed, still play such a role on a modest scale. Perhaps its strongest regional element is the fact that southern New Englanders and non-New Englanders think it a place sufficiently different from home and rich in amenities to be worth a visit. Much state promotional literature has played on this theme with obvious success.

When Cohen proposed a realignment of New England's boundaries he, too, recognized the dualism of New England.[3] He felt, however, that the more urbanized and industrialized portions of southern New Hampshire and southwestern Maine should be included in one or the other of his two new "combination regions" in the south. The rest of New England, also divided into two subregions, was essentially the northern New England treated in this study. The separation of New England into northern and southern subregions was used by the Council of Economic Advisers in its 1951 study, referring to "the three Southern industrial states of New England."[4] The National Planning Association frequently subdivided New England into a northern and southern section.[5]

The rationale for the present use of such subregions lies in the historic pattern of population change within New England. Since the Census of 1850 the rate of population increase

of each of the three northern states slowed down with respect to the three southern states, and continued at a relatively reduced level until the Census of 1970. Northern New England became the region largely bypassed by the American Industrial Revolution, where farming held on the longest and the Yankee was still supposed to live in his New England village. It became an area sought out by tourists, campers, hunters, fishermen, and genealogists, to be followed in more recent years by skiers, land speculators, and snowmobilers.

The three northern states occupy seventy-eight percent of the total land area of New England, but in 1970 they had only eighteen percent of the population. This area includes vast tracts of wilderness, pockets of intensive agriculture, innumerable calendar-postcard villages, and a small number of cities. The largest of these, Manchester, New Hampshire, had only 87,754 residents, and the entire region supported only ten other cities over 20,000 in population.

HISTORY OF SETTLEMENT TO 1890

The northern area had its greatest share of New England's total population in 1790, when 685,558 persons lived in the three southern states, and the population of what is now Vermont, New Hampshire, and Maine was 323,850. These people were concentrated near the coast of Maine and New Hampshire, and along the principal river valleys in the interior (the lower Connecticut, the Merrimack, the Piscataquis and the Salmon Falls, the Androscoggin, the Kennebec, and the Penobscot).

Permanent settlement had just begun in the interior hill country, encouraged by the end of the French and Indian Wars and greatly stimulated after the American Revolution. Between 1790 and 1800 Vermont's population (already 85,425) increased by eighty percent, and in the following decade Maine's population grew from 96,540 to 151,719. Such interior settlement took place, however, at great human cost and for meagre rewards. It is not at all unlikely that, had the American Revolution taken place fifty years earlier, and an easy crossing of the Appalachian barrier been established by 1750, northern New England's settlement as we now see it might never have taken place.

---

[3] Saul B. Cohen, "New England's Boundaries: How Realistic Are They?", *The New Englander*, August, 1964, p. 8.

[4] *The New England Economy*, op. cit., footnote 1, p. 30.

[5] *The Economic State of New England*, op. cit., footnote 2.

For half a century, the establishment of new settlements and the expansion of existing ones was almost exclusively an agricultural phenomenon. Rural population growth rates in Maine ran at relatively high rates (1820–30 rate—33.5 percent) until the Census of 1840, but from then on the rate decreased rapidly (1840–50—9.0 percent; 1850–60—3.9 percent) until the rural population rate of the 1860–70 decade was minus 5.5 percent. New Hampshire's rural population growth rate dropped even earlier, and her rural population began to decline before 1860. The story in Vermont was much the same.

THE NEW ENGLAND VILLAGE

The New England village stereotype was virtually completed by 1860, the model followed by such reconstructions as Sturbridge Village in Massachusetts. Wright captured the image of such towns with his description:[6]

the road enters the elm-lined street of an old village. A graceful steeple is seen through the trees. Facing the grassy "common" stand a few new buildings, usually a business block, a high school built of brick, a marble bank, or a small public library. Otherwise the village seems outwardly much as it has seemed for a hundred years. White wooden dwellings, often exquisite in their proportions in the detailed work of their doorways and windows, stand apart from one another on shaded lawns.

The only village element missing from Wright's description and found almost ubiquitously in northern New England is the Civil War memorial. Cast in bronze or carved from granite, the typical monument is a young man, forage cap at a jaunty angle and rifle across his shoulder, stepping off to Chancellorsville or Antietam. These monuments might just as well have represented the departure of all youth from northern New England villages and hill farms, part of the greater migration underway throughout the region in the 1850s and 1860s. The mothers, fathers, and sisters were marching off, too, only into the factory towns in Massachusetts and toward the farmlands of Illinois.

The Civil War, the expansion of the factory system, and the opening of Western states combined to close the door on rural, agricul-

---

[6] John K. Wright, "Regions and Landscapes of New England," in *New England's Prospect 1933* (New York: American Geographical Society, 1933), p. 14.

TABLE 1.—RATES OF POPULATION INCREASE, NEW ENGLAND AND UNITED STATES, 1890–1970, AND PROPORTION OF NATIONAL POPULATION IN NEW ENGLAND

Decade	Percentage rate of population increase		Population of New England as a percentage of national total
	New England	United States	
1890–1900	19.0	20.7	7.3
1900–1910	17.2	21.0	7.1
1910–1920	12.9	15.0	7.0
1920–1930	10.3	16.2	6.6
1930–1940	3.3	7.3	6.4
1940–1950	10.4	14.5	6.2
1950–1960	12.8	18.5	5.9
1960–1970	12.7	14.2	5.8

Source: U. S. Census of Population, 1960, and individual state summaries for 1970.

tural expansion in northern New England. Scarcely a new farmhouse or barn, general store or church, was built in rural areas after 1870. It was now the turn of the small manufacturing town, already established at its riverside location, to grow Winooski, Vermont, on woolen cloth and Springfield on machine tools, Laconia, New Hampshire, on railroad cars and Lisbon on piano boxes, Biddeford, Maine, on cotton textiles and Rumford on paper.

Northern New England was reaching an equilibrium. Farms were numerous and prosperous, and land abandonment was slowing down, the small cities were reaching their population maxima as national competitive factors began to take effect. Between 1880 and 1890, northern New England grew only 43,000 in total population while the three southern states increased by nearly 650,000.

POPULATION GROWTH, 1890–1960

During most of the nineteenth century New England's rate of population increase lagged far behind that of the United States as a whole. Until the Census of 1880 the New England rate ran at about one-half of the national figure, and in four out of the first ten Census periods this region was the slowest growing in the country. By 1890, however, large-scale industrial expansion and urban growth in southern New England, accompanied by a slowing down of agricultural expansion in the Middle West and changes in national immigration patterns, raised New England's growth rate closer to the nation's (Table 1). In 1900 the two rates were sepa-

TABLE 2.—RATES OF POPULATION CHANGE

Decade	Maine	New Hampshire	Vermont	Massa-chusetts	Rhode Island	Connecticut	New England	United States
1900–1910	6.9	4.6	3.6	20.0*	26.6**	22.7**	17.2	21.0
1910–1920	3.5	2.9	–1.0	14.4*	11.4	23.9**	12.9	15.0
1920–1930	3.8	5.0	2.0	10.3*	13.7*	16.4**	10.3	16.2
1930–1940	6.2*	5.6*	–0.1	1.6	3.8*	6.4*	3.3	7.3
1940–1950	7.9	8.5	5.2	8.7	11.0*	17.4**	10.4	14.5
1950–1960	6.1	13.8*	3.2	9.8	8.5	26.3**	12.8	18.5
1960–1970	2.4	21.5**	14.0*	10.5	10.1	19.6**	12.7	14.2

* = Higher than New England mean rate.
** = Higher than United States mean rate.
Source: U. S. Census of Population, 1960, and individual state summaries for 1970.

rated by only 1.7 percent, but once again New England's comparative growth rate began to decrease, and by 1940 it was only half the national rate.

The immediate post-World War II years did not indicate any significant change in this downward trend. New England was running consistently well behind the country. The gap actually appeared to be widening in the 1950s as the national growth rate increased by 4.0 percent (to 18.5 percent) while New England's rate increased by only 2.4 percent. The 1960 Census reported six states gaining over forty percent in population during the previous decade, but none of them was in New England. Strong new growth points were clearly established in such states as Florida, Arizona, and California. The 1970 Census revealed, however, a significant decrease in the national growth rate which was not accompanied by a similar drop in New England's rate. The six northeastern states held their own, registering a decline of only one-tenth of one percent in their growth rate over ten years.

INTRAREGIONAL GROWTH RATES

The gross growth rate for New England masks important differences between individual states. The steady decline in New England's growth rate from 1890 to 1930 was by no means experienced by all six states. For the most part, the total New England rate was pulled down by steady, rural losses in Maine, New Hampshire, and Vermont. Vermont actually lost population during two census periods. The three southern states, on the other hand, tended to experience higher growth rates, often higher than the nation. Connecticut exceeded the national rate of

increase during the entire 1890–1930 span (Table 2). The separation into a northern cluster and a southern cluster shows clearly until 1930, and broke down only during the depression decade. The 1950 Census showed, in part, a return to the earlier pattern. Connecticut and Rhode Island were growing faster than New England as a whole, and Massachusetts had the highest growth rate of the remaining four states.

The 1960 Census revealed quite a different pattern. Connecticut increased its growth rate to 26.3 percent, well above the national figure, and ranked twelfth in the country. Massachusetts and Rhode Island were not sharing in these population gains. In northern New England New Hampshire was recording a growth figure of 13.8 percent, second only to Connecticut for the 1950s. By 1970 Vermont, whose growth rate of 3.2 percent in the 1950 decade was the lowest in New England, showed a sharp increase to 14.0 percent, and New Hampshire jumped another 7.7 percent to 21.5 percent, making it the most rapidly growing state in New England for the 1960s. For the first time since 1830 a northern New England state increased population at a rate higher than the country, and a second state came within two-tenths of one percent of exceeding the United States figure. Mean growth rates for the three most recent census periods show the new surge of growth in northern New England and the leveling-off of the high post-World War II growth rate in southern New England (Table 3).

ABSOLUTE INCREASES, 1940–1970

The percentage growth figures of the several states give an indication of the preferences of migrants within the United States.

TABLE 3.—RATES OF POPULATION CHANGE, NORTHERN AND SOUTHERN NEW ENGLAND, 1940–70

Decade	Northern New England	Southern New England
1940–50	7.5	11.1
1950–60	7.8	14.1
1960–70	10.6	13.2

Source: U. S. Census of Population, 1960, and individual state summaries for 1970.

Since birth and death rates vary only slightly among the fifty states, we must attribute those state growth rates in excess of the national figure to in-migrants from other states, and in some cases from other countries. States with relatively high growth rates appear to be more attractive places to live and work or to retire. Nevertheless, growth rates are rates, and reveal nothing of the number of persons involved. Alaska's thirty percent population increase from 1960 to 1970, for example, over twice the national figure, represented a gain of less than 70,000 persons, one-sixtieth the numerical increase in California, which gained only twenty-five percent in the same time period.

Over the past three census periods New England has added approximately 3,195,000 people to her 1940 population of 8,437,290 (Table 4). Of this total, only 475,000 new residents (fifteen percent) were recorded in the three northern states. It is during this latest decade, however, that northern New England has registered its largest proportional increase. Between 1960 and 1970, northern New England's population increased 207,992, or 18.5 percent of the New England total.

TABLE 4.—POPULATION INCREASES, NORTHERN NEW ENGLAND, 1940–70

	Northern New England	New England
1940 population	1,697,981	8,437,290
1940–50 increase	126,782	877,163
1950 population	1,824,763	9,314,453
1950–60 increase	141,304	1,194,914
1960 population	1,966,067	10,509,367
1960–70 increase	207,992	1,124,304
1970 population	2,174,059	11,841,663

Source: U. S. Census of Population, 1960, and individual state summaries for 1970.

TABLE 5.—ABSOLUTE POPULATION INCREASES AND RATES OF INCREASE, NORTHERN NEW ENGLAND, 1940–1970

	Maine	New Hampshire	Vermont
1940 population	847,226	491,524	359,231
1940–50 increase	66,548	41,718	18,516
Percentage increase	7.9	8.5	5.2
1950 population	913,774	533,242	377,747
1950–60 increase	55,491	73,679	12,134
Percentage increase	6.1	13.8	3.2
1960 population	969,265	606,921	389,881
1960–70 increase	22,783	130,760	54,449
Percentage increase	2.4	21.5	14.0
1970 population	992,048	737,681	444,330

Source: U. S. Census of Population, 1960, and individual state summaries for 1970.

During that same period, southern New England's population increase actually dropped 70,000, in contrast to the large increase she had experienced between 1950 and 1960.

In northern New England the numerical increases have shifted among the several states, with Maine recording the largest increase between 1940 and 1950, and New Hampshire the largest between 1950 and 1960 and 1960 and 1970 (Table 5). In both of these census intervals New Hampshire's increase exceeded those of the other two northern states combined. By 1970, Vermont has taken over second place in numerical growth, adding nearly 55,000 new residents in ten years (Fig. 1).

POPULATION GROWTH, 1960–70

The areas of greatest population growth in northern New England between 1960 and 1970 were in a broad arc extending from Grand Isle County, Vermont (at the northern end of Lake Champlain) southward along the Green Mountains into southern Vermont and New Hampshire and thence northeastwards along the Atlantic coastline to Hancock County, Maine (Fig. 2). Within this band are three concentrations: one in Chittenden County, Vermont, focusing on Burlington; a second in southeastern New Hampshire, focusing on Boston; and a third in south-central Maine, focusing on the Portland-Augusta axis, but also looking southward toward Boston.

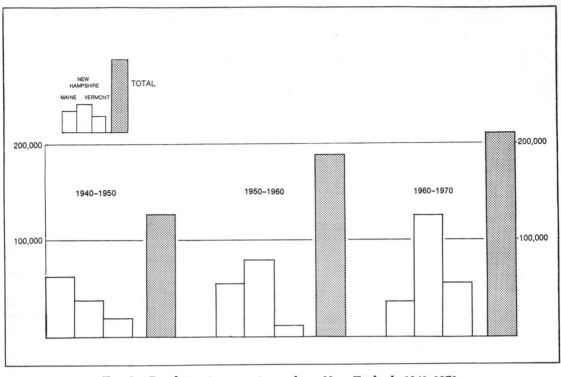

FIG. 1. Population increases in northern New England, 1940–1970.

The three major concentrations are tied together by two discontinuous bands of rapidly growing cities and towns. The first extends from the Stowe-Mt. Mansfield area in Lamoille County, just east of Burlington, to the Snow Valley-Stratton ski area in southern Vermont. Several small cities serve as foci in this area: Bennington, Brattleboro, Rutland, and Barre-Montpelier. The second band extends from Cheshire County, New Hampshire, to York County, Maine. This is a hilly area interrupted by clusters of low mountains and numerous ponds and lakes.

It is to this irregular, U-shaped, growth region that virtually all of northern New England's present population increase has been directed, both from within the region and from outside. It would appear from the 1970 Census that the earlier evidences of scattered and localized population growth of the 1950s have become well-established, and that further population increases can be expected not only within the current growth region, but also northward in currently stagnant or declining cities and towns.

FACTORS IN POPULATION GROWTH

The reversal of northern New England's long downward trend of population growth (Table 1) can be traced, directly or indirectly, to the proximity of Boston and New York, and to the urbanized areas surrounding or lying between these cities.

Accessibility

Accessibility to northern New England has been radically improved since the 1950s, not only with the virtual completion of the regional Interstate Highway program, but also with the construction of such limited access highways as the Taconic Parkway, and with the upgrading of major state roads to high-speed use throughout the area. It was not until the 1960s that the Interstate Highway System effectively penetrated northern New England, and that all the adjoining sections in Massachusetts, Connecticut, Rhode Island, and New York were completed (Fig. 3). Travel times have been reduced in some instances as much as 50 percent. The auto-

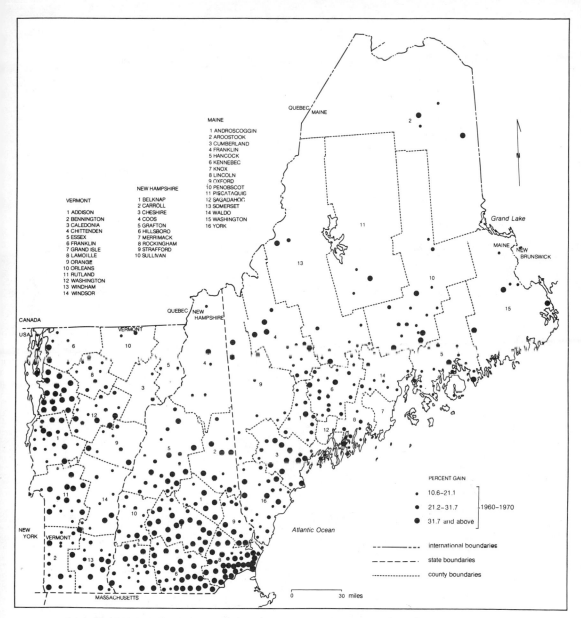

Fig. 2. Cities and towns in northern New England that experienced population increases of 10.6 percent or more between 1960 and 1970.

mobile travel time from Boston to Burlington, Vermont, has been reduced from seven and a half (1950) to four hours (1970) with the completion of Interstate 89. The center of the White Mountains skiing complex is four to four and one-half hours from Boston; Portland, Maine, is only two hours and twenty minutes from Boston; and Concord, New Hampshire, an hour and three-quarters.

Travel times to much of Vermont, New Hampshire, and southern Maine from the New York City area range from three and one-half to six hours.

Second Homes

The population concentrations of southern New England and the New York metropolitan area have been the major source of second-

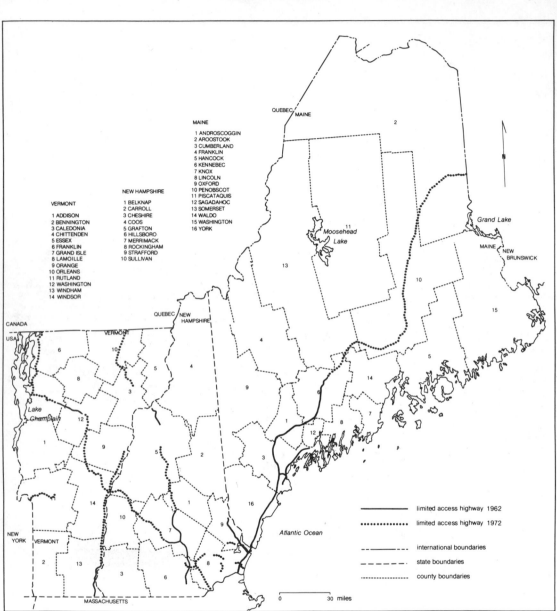

FIG. 3. Development of limited access highways in northern New England, 1962–1972.

home buyers or builders in northern New England (Fig. 4). Although these second-home owners are not recorded in state or federal censuses, they stimulate the growth of local service activities and the creation of substantial numbers of new jobs. These jobs, in turn, are filled by local folk moving in from isolated rural towns and by in-migrants from adjacent states. These services and jobs might appear to be highly seasonal, but the whole

nature of second-home living in northern New England has changed from a typical summer stay of limited duration to frequent weekend use throughout the year, including extensive stays in winter. Furthermore, owners who cannot use facilities throughout the year themselves find tenants easy to obtain.

The local supermarket, druggist, filling station, sporting goods store, carpenter, and plumber all benefit. The planned highway

FIG. 4. Madonna Village condominia in Jeffersonville, Vermont. (Stanmar, Inc.)

shopping center, which local real estate developers feared might never come to northern New England, is now represented by at least one and sometimes two or three new complexes on the outskirts of every large city or town in the region.

Recreation Jobs

The recreation-tourist industry has, in addition, created its own new job market. The building of motels, ski developments, and marinas has provided a large number of jobs, and traditional slack periods associated with such industries are continuously contracting in length. Moreover, the northern New England local labor force has long been accustomed to seasonal income, such as cutting pulp in the forest, driving school buses, digging potatoes, and canning fish.

Manufacturing

Manufacturing expansion has also contributed to regional growth. The 1930s seemed to signal the slow but steady disappearance of factories from northern New England, from Winooski, Vermont, to Bucksport, Maine. Plant buildings were old, machinery obsolescent, power expensive, and markets increasingly distant. The catastrophic collapse of one-industry cities like Manchester, New Hampshire, and Sanford, Maine, came to represent nationally the decline of manufacturing in New England. Local attempts at attracting new industries and renting empty mill buildings brought some relief, but this was often offset by the low wage scales such industries brought with them. Leather tanneries from Massachusetts, fleeing high-cost union labor, were notorious in this respect.

FIG. 5. International Business Machines Corporation complex in Essex Junction, Vermont. Mount Mansfield in right rear. (IBM Corporation)

The new manufacturing era for northern New England is best exemplified by the establishment of a branch plant of the International Business Machines Corporation in Essex Junction, Vermont, during the 1950s (Fig. 5). The rapid growth of Chittenden County, Vermont, can be attributed in part to this single move. Single manufacturing facilities have moved into other small northern New England communities (Middlebury, Vermont; Jaffrey, New Hampshire), and industrial parks have been successfully established on the outskirts of larger cities (Nashua, New Hampshire; Biddeford-Saco, Maine). Sanders Associates, a fast-growing electronics company, got its start in an abandoned factory in Nashua, New Hampshire, established plants in other states and foreign countries as it expanded, and finally built its corporate headquarters directly on the New Hampshire side of the New Hampshire-Massachusetts boundary.

Educational Expansion

Population growth has also been stimulated by the revitalization of the three state higher educational systems, not only at the university level, but also at the former state teachers colleges. Rapid expansion of enrollment and construction of physical plant has occurred on a large scale at virtually every public institution, and on a smaller scale at regional private colleges. Durham, New Hampshire, site of the University of New Hampshire, grew 61.1 percent between 1960 and 1970. The state teachers college towns of Castleton, Vermont, Plymouth, New Hampshire, and Gorham, Maine, grew 49.2 percent, 31.6 percent, and 35.9 percent, respectively, in that same period.

FIG. 6. This type of abandoned farmhouse, once commonplace in rural northern New England, has been eagerly sought after for its restoration possibilities and low cost; this one is in Gaza (Sanbornton), New Hampshire. (Photo: Stephen T. Whitney)

The extraordinary population gains of the greater Burlington, Vermont, area reflect the coincidence of educational expansion and industrial growth, reinforced in this case by a concentration of medical, legal, and financial facilities and services in Burlington. A population increase of over 22,000 occurred in Burlington and its immediate hinterland between 1960 and 1970.

Massachusetts Overspill

The small towns of southern New Hampshire are becoming bedroom suburbs of Boston. Like their counterparts in Montgomery County, Maryland, and Fairfield County, Connecticut, Hillsborough and Rockingham counties in New Hampshire offer lower cost living and access to open space and scenic amenities within a reasonable distance of work and shopping. Industrial plants along the western and northern stretches of Massachusetts Route 128, Boston's first major circumferential highway, are only twenty to thirty minutes from Pelham, New Hampshire (1960–70 population increase—107.6 percent), and jobs in the Merrimack Valley cities of Lowell, Lawrence, and Haverhill are even closer to New Hampshire boundary towns like Atkinson (1960–70 population increase—125.3 percent).

This overspill is not new; it could be identified clearly after the 1960 Census.[7] The completion of Interstate 93 and new construction of Massachusetts Route 3 have accelerated southern New Hampshire's growth, and extended the area involved well beyond Manchester and Concord into Cheshire, Merrimack, and Strafford counties. Many of these same smaller New Hampshire towns also serve a more immediate residential suburb

[7] R. C. Estall, *New England, A Study in Industrial Adjustment* (New York: Praeger, 1966), p. 241.

TABLE 6.—CITIES AND TOWNS EXPERIENCING POPU-
LATION LOSSES, 1940–1970, NORTHERN
NEW ENGLAND

State	Total Number of Cities and Towns	1940–50	1950–60	1960–70
Maine	495	217	264	214
New Hampshire	255	85	81	20
Vermont	248	116	143	59
Total	998	418	488	293

Source: U. S. Census of Population, *Number of Inhabitants,*
Maine, New Hampshire, and Vermont, 1950, 1960, 1970.

TABLE 7.—POPULATION LOSSES IN VERMONT, 1940–50,
BY SIZE OF COMMUNITY

Size of Community, 1940	Number Losing Population, 1940–50
0–100	7
101–500	39
501–1000	42
1001–5000	27
over 5000	1

Source: U. S. Census of Population. *Vermont Number of Inhabitants,* PC (1). 47A.

function for the larger cities of southern New Hampshire, of which Nashua is the most vigorous. Hudson, New Hampshire, which lies across the Merrimack River from Nashua, experienced an eighty-one percent increase in population during the 1960s. The monotony of modern American tract housing, almost unknown in northern New England before 1955, now stretches across many a former New Hampshire pasture.

Retirement

A number of northern New England communities became summer colonies for the wealthy of Boston, New York, and Philadelphia well over a century ago. It was not surprising, therefore, that some of these same areas later attracted retired folk, first perhaps for the summer, and then on a year-round basis. Farm and village abandonment created a relatively low-cost stock of reasonable housing so that persons of more modest means were also able to buy "a place in the country" to retire to (Fig. 6). College and private preparatory school towns like Bennington, Vermont, Hanover and Exeter, New Hampshire, and Brunswick, Maine, provided additional amenities and cultural activity for retired individuals.

The Maine coast, from York County on the south well into Hancock County on the north, has been steadily attracting retired persons to such villages as Wiscasset, Damariscotta, and Castine. The construction of the Maine and New Hampshire Turnpikes and Interstate 95 has put the entire Maine coastline within a reasonable excursion to Portland to shop, and a not impossible trip to Boston to hear the Symphony.

AREAS OF POPULATION LOSS

Not all of northern New England is sharing in recent population growth. Many small cities and towns are relatively stagnant or are actually losing population. Such communities are by no means unique to the Northeast; nearly every state in the union has one or more areas which are currently experiencing population loss. Substantial population loss began relatively early in northern New England, however, and the long decline in population was well under way in many towns by the Civil War.[8] An examination of those cities and towns which are experiencing actual population loss helps in visualizing the population dynamics of northern New England (Table 6).

By 1950, population losses were so widespread in Vermont, New Hampshire, and Maine that a population equilibrium boundary could be delineated not far north of the Massachusetts border (Fig. 7). The Champlain Valley of Vermont, the lower Connecticut Valley, southern New Hampshire, and coastal and interior southern Maine were the only areas of population increase. In contrast, only a small number of communities in the three southern states lost population between 1940 and 1950. Forty-two percent of all municipalities in northern New England had losses in population between 1940 and 1950. Vermont had the highest proportion (forty-eight percent), and Maine the largest number (217).

Losses were primarily in the smaller villages (Table 7). Bloomfield, Vermont, whose popu-

---

[8] Hirsch lumps all population peaks for U. S. counties prior to 1890 in one category, but northern New England nonetheless stands out clearly on his map; F. A. Hirsch, "Population Peaks of U. S. Counties," *The Professional Geographer,* Vol. 17 (1970), p. 90.

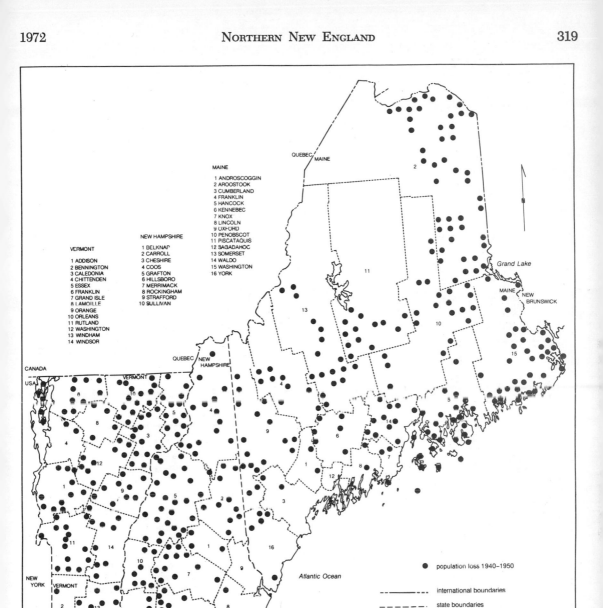

MAINE

1 ANDROSCOGGIN
2 AROOSTOOK
3 CUMBERLAND
4 FRANKLIN
5 HANCOCK
6 KENNEBEC
7 KNOX
8 LINCOLN
9 OXFORD
10 PENOBSCOT
11 PISCATAQUIS
12 SAGADAHOC
13 SOMERSET
14 WALDO
15 WASHINGTON
16 YORK

NEW HAMPSHIRE

1 BELKNAP
2 CARROLL
3 CHESHIRE
4 COOS
5 GRAFTON
6 HILLSBORO
7 MERRIMACK
8 ROCKINGHAM
9 STRAFFORD
10 SULLIVAN

VERMONT

1 ADDISON
2 BENNINGTON
3 CALEDONIA
4 CHITTENDEN
5 ESSEX
6 FRANKLIN
7 GRAND ISLE
8 LAMOILLE
9 ORANGE
10 ORLEANS
11 RUTLAND
12 WASHINGTON
13 WINDHAM
14 WINDSOR

●   population loss 1940–1950

– – – – – –   international boundaries

– – – – – ·   state boundaries

·················   county boundaries

0   30 miles

Fig. 7. Cities and towns in northern New England that experienced population losses between 1940 and 1950.

lation had peaked in the nineteenth century, is a typical case, showing a decline in the 1940s from 326 to 291. Losses were also recorded in a number of small manufacturing cities, particularly those dominated by a single factory complex. Lisbon, New Hampshire, a small mill town in Grafton County, dropped from 2,103 in 1940 to 2,009 in 1950. A few settlements dependent upon mineral exploita-

tion, forest industries, or commercial fishing also experienced population losses. The closing of canneries in Eastport, Maine, resulted in a population decline from 5,161 in 1940 to 4,589 in 1950. Over sixty percent of the losses took place in the smaller rural towns, primarily communities whose 1940 population was less than 1,000.

The 1960 Census showed a sizable increase

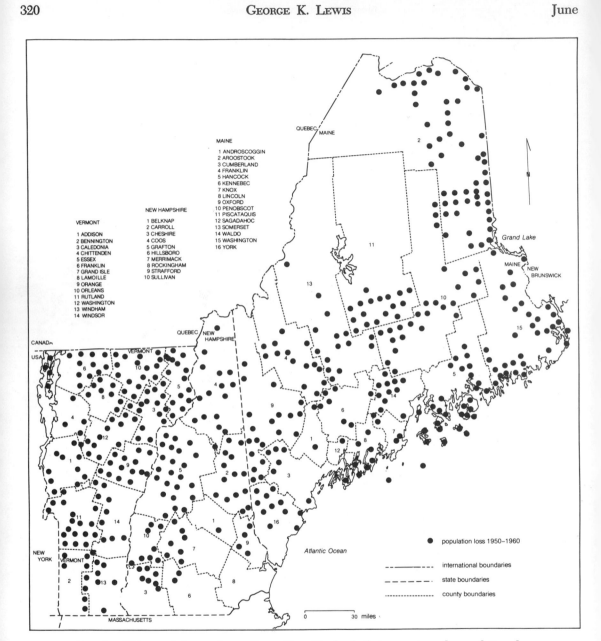

FIG. 8. Cities and towns in northern New England that experienced population losses between 1950 and 1960.

in areas of population loss (Fig. 8). Nearly fifty percent of all cities and towns in northern New England were now experiencing population losses, and the isolated pockets of population growth of 1950 had either contracted (the Champlain area around Burlington, Vermont) or disappeared (the Bangor, Maine, area on the lower Penobscot River). Fifty-three percent of cities and towns in

Maine and fifty-seven percent in Vermont recorded losses during the 1950s. Again, the drain was concentrated in the small rural towns. A few large manufacturing cities, having experienced temporary increases through military contracts for World War II and the Korean War, now joined the slump. Biddeford, Maine, a textile town, dropped from 20,836 to 19,255 between 1950 and 1960.

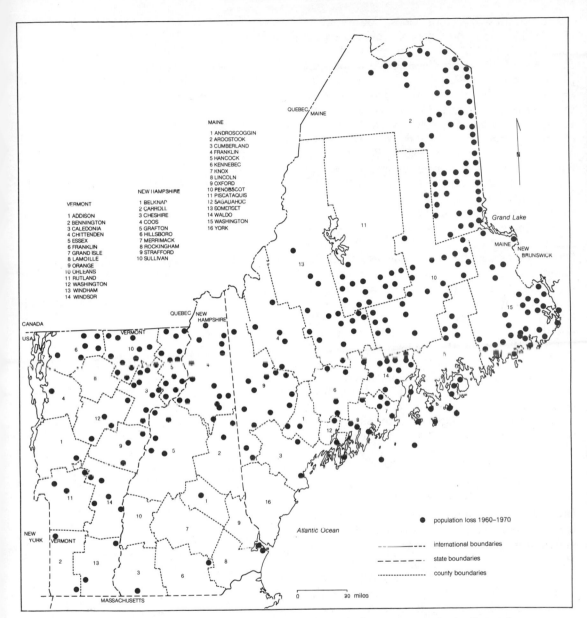

Fig. 9. Cities and towns in northern New England that experienced population losses between 1960 and 1970.

The regional turn of events revealed by the 1970 Census is dramatically mirrored in the number and distribution of cities and towns in northern New England whose population growth trends were reversed (Fig. 9). The total number of communities experiencing population losses dropped from 488 in 1960 to 293 in 1970 (Table 6). The proportion of "loss" communities dropped from fifty-seven percent to twenty-four percent in Vermont and from thirty-two percent to eight percent in New Hampshire. The proportion remained relatively high only in Maine, which dropped from fifty-three to forty-three percent.

A scattering of losses remained in central and southern Vermont and New Hampshire, but the dense concentration of towns losing population was now restricted to Orleans and

Essex counties, Vermont, Coos County, New Hampshire, and portions of four adjacent counties. Eight of the ten political subdivisions of Lamoille County, Vermont, lost population in the 1950–60 decade, but no city or town in the county recorded a loss in the following decade. Carroll County, New Hampshire, went from losses in fifteen of eighteen communities in 1960 to losses in just one in 1970. In southern Maine, York County, with twelve losses of twenty-eight cities and towns in 1960, dropped to zero in 1970. A new population equilibrium line extended roughly from Newport, Vermont, to Brunswick, Maine. An increasing number of the losses south of this line during the 1960s were larger cities, including Manchester, Portsmouth, and Laconia, New Hampshire; St. Johnsbury, Vermont; and Portland, Bangor, Auburn, and Waterville in Maine. Ten of twenty-six incorporated places of 10,000 population or more in northern New England lost population in the 1960s. This "central city" type of population loss was accompanied in almost all ten cases by concomitant suburban population increases. Elsewhere, however, the losses recorded by the 1970 Census in northern New England were part of the continuing drain of the back country.

WHAT PRICE AMENITIES?

None of the principal factors involved in northern New England's growth pattern (accessibility, disposable income, increased leisure time, the desire for second homes, and population increases in the American Megalopolis) shows any signs of diminishing as we move toward the 1980 Census. It is therefore not out of order to speculate on the impact of continued high growth rates for New Hampshire and Vermont, and to suggest that Maine's population increase rate may well rise to similar levels in the nineteenseventies.

The most obvious response is that northern New England will change, as it already has in certain areas, to a very considerable extent. Such changes, welcome to some and hateful to others, could become self-defeating. The amenity base, on which part of the current population growth rests, is a fragile thing, and people are the greatest threat to the basic elements of amenity—quiet, solitude, beauty, orderliness, green trees, and blue water. Each new permanent resident, as well as each transient visitor, puts an additional burden upon the amenity base.

Highway congestion, long ski lift lines, crowded shops, honky-tonk commercial highway strips, transistor radios, mobile home villages, sleazy subdivisions—in short, all the things one hoped one had left back in Boston or Bridgeport, Newark or Cleveland, are appearing in northern New England in greater and greater numbers.

To a region long accustomed to a relatively low standard of living, to multiple jobs to make ends meet, to land selling for five dollars an acre, any growth is "good." Attempts to introduce zoning into northern New England cities and towns encounter enormous resistance. Landowners see a threat to the opportunity "to cash in on the old farm" at last, and local merchants see potential business in jeopardy. After starving all those years, who can now deny them their windfall? After all, the retired folk and the summer folk and the winter folk and the fall foliage folk and the hunters don't have to make a living there.

There are a few encouraging signs that state and local governments are not unaware of these dangers. Vermont's billboard law, although not without continued resistance, is still in effect, and the Vermont legislature has enacted what amounts to a state subdivision control law. Thousands of square miles of northern New England are still undeveloped. The wise application of a wide variety of land development policies, from wilderness to high-density condominia, could insure the coming thousands of new residents and visitors of a landscape that could represent the best of contemporary America.

SMALL TOWN IN PENNSYLVANIA*

PEIRCE F. LEWIS

ABSTRACT. Americans have always shown strong affinity for small towns. Some, as exemplified by Bellefonte, Pennsylvania, developed into places of very real importance in the cultural and economic life of the United States in the past, but have found it increasingly difficult to compete effectively in a world of heavy industry and quaternary economics. Changes in American taste and technology suggest that small towns might again play a meaningful role in contemporary society. Three generations of economic and demographic difficulties have caused physical and psychological damage which sharply limits Bellefonte's ability to play such a role. KEY WORDS: *Bellefonte, Cultural urban geography, Landscape of America, Pennsylvania, Small town, Technological change, Town.*

"Almost nobody likes where they're from any more . . ."—Unidentified California Chamber of Commerce official[1]

AMERICANS have seldom been entirely happy where they lived. The very act of migration to the United States (for whites anyway) signalled that however else immigrants differed, they joined together in the hope that their new homes would be preferable to the old. The whole history of westward migration was continued testament to Americans' chronic geographical dissatisfactions, and contemporary census figures still reflect the ceaseless American search for a better place to live.

Throughout our history, however, domestic Nirvana has proved elusive. Yeoman farmers may have been chosen by God—as Jefferson suggested—but they did not choose to remain farmers any longer than they could help. Zion was a town, or even better a city, and if it was not the City of God, it at least gave hope for a better life than the distinctly unromantic drudgery of the average dirt farm. But the city too has gone sour in the United States, a fact which is proved anew each time the Census counts the migration from central cities to the suburbs, or the quickening flow of Puerto Ricans returning home, or disillusioned Negroes heading South again.

The immediate reasons for our urban dissatisfactions are obvious enough—the unremitting accumulation of machine-made filth, the bitterness of racial fears and angers, and the chronic prospect of political and financial bankruptcy. One senses, however, that the disenchantment with American cities has profounder reasons than garbage and race riots—that in a very basic way Americans dislike big cities not because they are cities, but because they are *big*. Although Americans have lived in towns for a long time, most of them have not lived in big towns for very long. Throughout most of our history, especially during the long early period when our national attitudes and personality were taking form, a good share of the country and a good share of the country's leadership lived in that nebulous but unmistakable class of urban phenomena which we call "small towns."

This essay concerns American small towns, and treats them at two separate levels. On the first and general level, it considers American small towns as a group and assays their importance in reality and in myth. At the second level, the essay seeks understanding

* The Pennsylvania State University's Central Fund for Research helped pay for photographic and archival material for this study. I am also grateful to John O'Connor of State College, who generously let me take pictures of the old prints in the Tavern Restaurant's superb collection. The staff of the Penn State Room of the Penn State University Library, and of the Centre County Library and Historical Society in Bellefonte also helped me enormously by making available all kinds of fugitive material that I could never have found myself. Above all, I can never adequately pay my debt to dozens of Bellefontonians, ex-Bellefontonians, and adopted Bellefontonians, friends and unwitting co-conspirators in framing this study.

Dr. Lewis is Professor of Geography at Pennsylvania State University in University Park.

[1] Quoted by Joseph Morgenstern in *Newsweek*, July 5, 1971.

of small towns through an examination of one particular community, Bellefonte, Pennsylvania, a town which is not atypical of its class. At both levels, the essay argues that American small towns are very special kinds of places which in combination form a region of the United States as distinctive and important as New England, the South, or the Midwest—and that like those seminal regions, small towns have played a special and central role in the evolution of our national life. It will argue that to discard or ignore our small towns—as many Americans have long been willing to do—is likely to prove neither wise nor profitable in the long run.

SMALL TOWNS IN AMERICA

"How closely the development of our cities and towns reflect our people and our history!"— Christopher Tunnard and Henry Hope Reed[2]

To many Americans, a study of small towns in the last third of the twentieth century must seem at best an exercise in antiquarianism, at worst a waste of time and a romantic hoax. Everyone knows, after all, that small towns have been dying for a long time, and that optimistic statements to the contrary will not postpone their demise.[3] Why not pronounce the requiem and be done with it?

A closer look at the facts, however, suggests that obituaries may be premature. Small towns may be sick, but they are far from dead; indeed, many appear healthy when compared with parts of Manhattan Island. From a purely quantitative standpoint, moreover, small towns are with us in sizeable numbers and a not inconsiderable population inhabits them.

Precise estimates are difficult, of course, simply because the quality of small-town-ness is hard to pin down—though usually easy to recognize when one is in its presence. Although definitions are slippery, the Census

TABLE 1.—PLACES LOCATED OUTSIDE URBANIZED AREAS IN THE UNITED STATES, 1960 AND 1950

Size of population of place in 1960	Number of places	Approximate population in millions	Percentage of national population
10,000–24,999	610	9.2	5.2
5,000– 9,999	995	6.9	3.9
2,500– 4,999	1,806	6.3	3.5
1,000– 2,499	4,151	6.5	3.6
Total	7,562	29.0	16.2
Change, 1950–1960	+ 295	+ 2.3	− 1.5

Source: *U. S. Census of Population, 1960.*

statistics are at least suggestive (Table 1). If one counts all places "located outside urbanized areas" with a population from one thousand to twenty-five thousand people, one finds a total of 7,562 places, with a population in the neighborhood of 29 million. This number is only slightly less than the 31.5 million which Wattenberg and Scammon estimated as the population living in the whole Eastern Megalopolis.[4]

Even these numbers, however, do not begin to measure the importance of small towns in American life, for they are quite out of proportion to their numbers or population. Almost all our twentieth century presidents, for example, were small town boys, and the Senate—typically a rather bucolic body—has more than its share. The House of Representatives, not to mention a good many statehouses, is overinfluenced by small town people, many of whom are elected by constituencies which are demographically stable and fairly homogeneous—a condition which tends toward large and dependable pluralities, seniority, committee chairmanships, and power.

The American Romance with Small Towns

But the importance of small towns is more than political. From early times, Americans have conducted a passionate love affair with their small towns—and· when, more recently, some Americans fell out of love, their hatred has been just as passionate. In most American mythology, however, small towns have occupied something of the same place as Paris has to the French, or the green countryside to the English: they are central to the American experience.

[2] Christopher Tunnard and H. H. Reed, *American Skyline: The Growth and Form of Our Cities and Towns* (Boston: Houghton Mifflin, 1953), quotation from Mentor edition (1956), p. 15.

[3] Not everybody agrees with this view. See, for example, J. F. Hart and N. E. Salisbury, "Population Change in Middle Western Villages: A Statistical Approach," *Annals*, Association of American Geographers, Vol. 55 (1965), 140–60 where it is shown that a good many Midwestern villages are growing, even though they are losing central-place functions.

[4] B. J. Wattenberg and R. M. Scammon, *This U. S. A.* (New York: Pocket Books, 1967), p. 102.

For a people who adopted so many English environmental tastes, it may seem strange that Americans rarely took to the rural countryside with British enthusiasm.[5] Some Americans have wished they had, among them Washington Irving who asseverated that "the fondness for rural life among the higher classes of the English has had a great and salutary effect upon the national character."[6] The untamed vastness of American territory, however, seldom lent itself to manicuring in the British fashion, and for a good share of our history, towns served the same function they did in medieval Europe—havens against recalcitrant and often hostile country and opportunities for economic betterment. Richard Hofstadter has pointed out that the American farmer was from earliest times a commercial animal, very much at home in the economic environment of a town, and little given to romancing over bucolic virtues.[7] And although Turnerian doctrine holds that the frontier was conquered by yeomen farmers, as often as not the frontier was urban—with towns planted sometimes before the first furrow was turned. Many of the towns were imaginary, and never got beyond the steel-engraved fictions of nineteenth century promotional literature.[8] This fact considerably warmed Charles Dickens' already overheated anti-Americanism and provoked a description of hapless Cairo, Illinois, which suggests that a few American small towns (at least) managed to conceal their charms from foreign visitors if not from their native promoters:[9]

> "At length . . . we arrived at a spot . . . more desolate than any we had yet beheld . . . a breeding-place of fever, ague, and death . . . a dismal swamp . . . a hotbed of disease, an ugly sepulchre, a grave uncheered by any gleam of promise; a place without one single quality in earth or air or water to commend it: such is this dismal Cairo."

One dimly begins to perceive that Dickens did not share the American dream. Frontier settlement without a town at the forefront was simply unthinkable to most Americans, and a little swampwater was unlikely to dampen the national hope.

Rarely, however, has the American romance with small towns extended to big cities, and it is clear that Americans see their small towns as something quite different—and more virtuous—than large cities.[10] (Like the British, we have found it easier to fall in love with European cities—Paris, Rome, Vienna—than with our own.) Nowhere is our preoccupation with small towns more striking than in the realm of literature; indeed, American authors have seemed almost bewitched by small towns and the imagery of small towns.

Although this essay is not the place for an extended literary review, small towns are essential—not incidental—to American literary expression.[11] I am not referring to standard boosterism—although that can be found in various times in various places. Savor, for example, Timothy Dwight's 1794 effusion on Greenfield, Connecticut:[12]

> "Fair Verna! loveliest village of the west;
> Of very joy, and every charm possess'd,
> How pleas'd amid thy varied walks I rove,
> Sweet cheerful walks of innocence, and love,
> And o'er thy smiling prospects cast my eyes,

---

[5] Two brilliant essays by David Lowenthal and Hugh Prince, and a third by Lowenthal, outline the nature of British and American environment and environmental tastes; they are among the high points of recent geographical writings; "The English Landscape," "English Landscape Tastes," and "The American Scene," *Geographical Review*, Vol. 54 (1964), pp. 309–46, Vol. 55 (1965), pp. 186–222, and Vol. 58 (1968), pp. 61–88. Elsewhere, I have noted the persistent American bias for English architectural forms, Peirce Lewis, "The Geography of Old Houses," *Earth and Mineral Sciences*, Vol. 39 (1970), pp. 33–37.

[6] "Rural Life in England" from *The Sketch Book*, Vol. II (New York: G. P. Putnam, 1860), p. 84.

[7] Richard Hofstadter, *The Age of Reform* (New York: Knopf, 1965), chapter 1, "The Agrarian Myth and Commercial Realities," pp. 43 ff., "In a very real and profound sense . . . the United States failed to develop (except in some localities, chiefly in the East) a distinctly rural culture."

[8] See, for example, Chapter 13, "Cities for Sale: Land Speculation in American Planning," in John Reps' brilliant and opulent *The Making of Urban America: A History of City Planning in the United States* (Princeton: Princeton University Press, 1965).

[9] Charles Dickens, *American Notes* (London: 1842), Chapter XII.

[10] When Lincoln Steffens, Ida Tarbell, and *McClure's* discovered the shame of our cities in the early 1900s, Americans were outraged but not disappointed. Cities, after all, were expected to be corrupt. Jefferson had said so, and Boss Tweed confirmed it.

[11] The point is made convincingly and at length in the definitive work on the subject, I. M. Herron, *The Small Town in American Literature* (New York: Pageant Books, 1959), which has an exhaustive and useful bibliography.

[12] Quoted in Herron, op. cit., footnote 11, p. 38.

And see the seats of peace, and pleasure, rise,
And hear the voice of Industry resound,
And marks the smile of Competence, around!
Hail, happy village!"

(One must conclude that age does not necessarily improve a literary product, although it may help ripen it.)

Small towns have never entirely emerged from this mauve miasma, which grew progressively thicker during the nineteenth and early twentieth centuries, when tan-cheeked barefoot boys romped in droves under spreading chestnut trees, and the saccharine doggerel of Edgar Guest arrived on the doorstep, wrapped in the four-color cheerfulness of Norman Rockwell's *Saturday Evening Post* covers. Currently, even the sober Megalopolitan Establishment is not immune to the small town romance; the *New York Times,* which weekly assures Nature of its editorial approval, recently eulogized the September asters which "mask the village dump."[13] Somehow it is hard to imagine the *Times* endorsing asters which mask the Jersey City Sanitary Landfill. The romance simply is not there.[14]

Overlooking the vitriol and the saccharine, however, an impressive roster of serious American novelists have set their major books in small towns—where the towns are more than mere backdrops, but loom as large as any of the individual human characters. This preoccupation with small towns by major and minor authors is largely independent of time or region, although the dark shadows of the human spirit tend to be chronically gloomier south of the Mason-and-Dixon Line than elsewhere.

Consider only a few of the authors and the divergent regions they represent. Hawthorne's *Scarlet Letter* is unthinkable outside that grim New England town, just as the Southerners, Faulkner and Thomas Wolfe, are hard to imagine without Jefferson and Altamont. Mark Twain's Mississippi River hamlets, Steinbeck's Monterey, John O'Hara's depraved Pennsylvania towns, Sherwood Anderson's Winesburg, and Sinclair Lewis' Gopher Prairie

all form part of a literary tradition that is peculiarly small-town, peculiarly American, and absolutely central to our national psyche. Lewis was doubtless sincere when he called Main Street "dullness made God," but American literature without Main Street is simply inconceivable.[15] The same cannot be said for either the city or the country.

Non-fiction too—both scholarly and popular—reflects the American preoccupation with the small town experience. The literature is very large, especially in sociology, but much of it displays an unconcealed and quite unscholarly dismay at the prospect that small towns in the United States are demoralized and disappearing—a view almost unanimously held by students of the subject.[16] Plainly, a good many Americans—artists, scholars, and popular writers alike—think small towns are important and make no bones about it.

In the final analysis, however, small towns have been important in American life not merely because our literati thought so, but because people at large thought so too. Indeed, some evidence suggests that we are still a profoundly small town people—although we have become urban, we have not necessarily become urbane. Three recent public-opinion polls make the point.[17] The first, a Gallup Poll taken in 1966 (before the rash of 1967 race-riots exacerbated anti-urban feelings),

---

[13] *The New York Times,* Sunday, September 12, 1971, Section 4, p. 16.
[14] There must be a special seductiveness to small-town garbage disposal. Wallace Stegener has a pleasant chapter on the town dump in *Wolf Willow* (New York: Compass Books, 1955), a charming evocation of his boyhood in a small Saskatchewan town of forty years ago.

[15] Apparently inconceivable even to unreconstructed urbanoids; see, for example, Peter Schrag's puzzled and bemused "Is Main Street Still There?," *Saturday Review,* January 17, 1970, pp. 21 ff.
[16] An ambitious bibliography of scholarly works on the subject is Suzanne M. Smith, *An Annotated Bibliography of Small Town Research* (Madison, Wisconsin: University of Wisconsin Department of Rural Sociology, 1970). A sampling of titles makes a recurring litany, increasingly plaintive with the passage of time:

"The Doom of the Small Town" (1895)
"Declining Villages of America" (1923)
"A Town That Has Gone Downhill" (1927)
"Villages are Dying—and Who Cares?" (1931)
"Is the Small Town Doomed?" (1944)
"The Passing of the American Village" (1952)
"Can Our Small Towns Survive?" (1960)
"Is Main Street Still There?" (1970)

[17] All three polls are cited in R. P. Devine, "Citizen Attitudes toward their Cities," in Edward Henry, ed., *Micro-City* (Collegeville, Minn.: St. John's University Center for the Study of Local Government, 1970), p. 42.

asked people in four categories of places where they would prefer to live if they had free choice. The second, a Gallup Poll of 1970, simply asked people where they would live if they had a choice. And the third, confined to the state of Minnesota, merely reported whether or not Minnesotans were satisfied living where they were.

Several conclusions emerge from these three polls. First, people are generally biased in favor of the kinds of places where they presently live or perhaps grew up—not a surprising discovery—but there is a strong nationwide predilection toward small and rural places. Second—and this is hardly a revelation either—our big cities are neither beloved nor much admired. (The city dwellers who thought they would prefer small town living, according to Gallup in 1966, numbered some twenty-two million people.) It would appear that a good many Americans think that their country is put together wrong, and that if they had their way, the patterns of a half-century or more ago would suit them better. Comparisons with earlier public opinion surveys suggest that this feeling has grown in recent years, not diminished.[18]

Much of this sentiment may represent simply the lavender-scented nostalgia which surrounds the dimly remembered past. Our memories tend to be selective, so that a contemporary apartment dweller in Brooklyn or Chicago is reminded daily that he may be assaulted when he steps into the street or subway—by air pollution, inflation, or the business end of a blackjack—but conveniently forgets that in a small town of the nineteenth century one might wade in manure to cross the street, ran the danger of contracting dysentery from the municipal water supply, and had his every move watched and criticized by the town's self-appointed arbiters of public morals.[19]

But there is more than nostalgia here, perhaps. The town gossip may still lurk behind her organdy curtains, but the manure and B. coli are gone, and cable television brings the opera even to Gopher Prairie. What remains is a belief that small towns are built at a scale which permits the inhabitants to exercise meaningful control over their local environment if they choose to do so—that community relations are more stable and more neighborly in a small town than in a city—that the cost of urban living may be too high if it is bought with physical danger and hatred.

Few reflective Americans would take the extreme Jeffersonian position that cities are necessarily vicious, but that is scarcely the point. By turning our farms into factories-in-fields, our cities into armed camps, and our small towns into demoralized shells of their former selves, there is little alternative but the suburbs—hardly the New Jerusalem for whites, and mainly inaccessible to blacks. What the polls may be suggesting, perhaps, is that a nation which can create a marvelous technology ought to possess the resources and the cunning to halt the degeneration of its small towns, and hopefully be able to restore at least some of them to their former dignity and importance.

But what is the genuine probability of retrieving our small towns—or any significant number of them? It has been thirty years now since Lewis Mumford asked "will life continue to ebb out of the villages and country towns and regional centers? Will urban life come to mean the further concentration of power in a few metropolises whose ramifying suburban dormitories will finally swallow the rural hinterland?"[20] Although Mumford presumably did not mean his questions to be rhetorical, they appear so now. The villages and towns have indeed ebbed, and the city-cum-suburb continues to eat up the countryside. But can the process be retarded, and does it matter anyway?

---

[18] An extremely detailed public opinion poll concerning residential preference was taken by the Roper organization in 1948, and badly needs updating. Cited in E. S. Lee, et al., *An Introduction to Urban Decentralization Research* (Oak Ridge, Tennessee: Oak Ridge National Laboratory; distributed by the National Technical Information Service, U. S. Department of Commerce, 1971), p. 34, the poll published an elaborate series of cross-tabulations of socioeconomic status and preferred city size. About forty percent of the total sample preferred "small town" or "small city" living; people of high education and high income were slightly less favorable to small towns than others.

[19] Nineteenth century streets constituted "a sort of equine latrine," to quote J. C. Furnas, *The Americans, A Social History of the United States 1587–1914* (New York: Putnam's, 1969), p. 457.

[20] Lewis Mumford, *The Culture of Cities* (New York: Harcourt Brace, 1938).

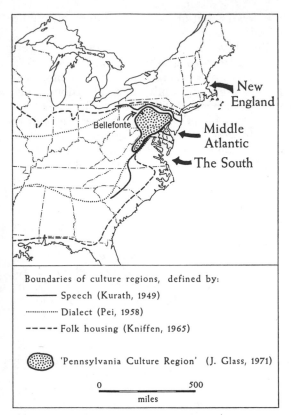

Boundaries of culture regions, defined by:

——— Speech (Kurath, 1949)

·············· Dialect (Pei, 1958)

----- Folk housing (Kniffen, 1965)

'Pennsylvania Culture Region' (J. Glass, 1971)

0   500

miles

FIG. 1. Bellefonte in the context of eastern American culture regions and the funnel-shaped distribution of Middle Atlantic culture. It is tempting to think of the Pennsylvania culture region as a sieve at the neck of the funnel, filtering and flavoring Middle Atlantic culture before it spread westward across the mid-continent. (Sources: Kurath, Pei, and Kniffen, op. cit., footnote 24, and Glass, op. cit., footnote 23.) Kniffen's southern boundary marks the edge of the Middle Atlantic area only from Philadelphia to mid-Virginia; beyond that, his line divides two parts of the South.

The answers will not come through wishful thinking, but neither are they likely to emerge from treating towns as digits in an economic hierarchy. Cities and towns are more than economic machines (although a good many urban geographers seem unaware of the fact). They are creatures of very particular cultures and very particular histories (both history and culture subsume economics, of course), and the judgment of their value must be made in social—not merely financial terms. What it boils down to, perhaps, is that we need to look at some real towns—where people love and worship and squabble and stink—and try to understand where these individual places fit

into the regional fabric of the United States in this final third of the twentieth century.[21]

BELLEFONTE, A TOWN IN PARTICULAR

There is no "typical" American small town, any more than there is a typical American city, typical region, or typical human being. Towns, districts, and people all own peculiarities and eccentricities that, by their very deviation from ordinary norms, lend flavor and interest to their personalities. Conversely, to be sure, no place is utterly unique, and it is usually the mixture of communality with individuality which makes places (and people) interesting and worthy of notice. The subject of this essay, Bellefonte, Pennsylvania, is eccentric enough—but not too eccentric—to suggest what an American small town has been and perhaps can be.

The main reason I chose Bellefonte is admittedly a personal one: I know the town fairly well. I have lived near it for nearly fifteen years, although never actually *in* it—thereby perhaps retaining some tattered shreds of objectivity about the place. I have visited it repeatedly, have talked with hundreds of its citizens in innumerable situations, and have read quite indigestible volumes of writing about it.[22] Gradually, over the years

[21] Urban geographers, for the most part, have not been very comfortable asking social, much less axiological questions about cities and towns. Mostly, they have been content to act as if towns were economic machines, thus flying in the face of facts, common sense, and a large sociological literature. *Middletown* and *Yankee City* both contain considerable excellent social geography, but professional geographers apparently did not read them. Recent work, mainly in black ghettos, suggests that refreshing changes may be afoot, however. See, for example, R. L. Morrill, "The Negro Ghetto: Problems and Alternatives," *The Geographical Review*, Vol. 55 (1965), pp. 339–61. But the real *tours de force* are William Bunge's *Fitzgerald: Geography of a Revolution* (Cambridge, Mass.: Schenkman, 1971) and *The Geography of the Children of Detroit*, Discussion Paper No. 3 (Detroit: The Detroit Geographical Expedition and Institute, 1971). In both books, Bunge's extraordinary group demonstrates that urban geographers can indeed talk to real people, deal with real social phenomena, and look with their eyes at real places and try to understand what they see.

[22] The history of Bellefonte, Centre County, and the Commonwealth of Pennsylvania have been worked over fairly assiduously. This essay draws on most of the main sources, but is so liberally larded with my own personal interpretations that disentangling them with individual footnotes would be a point-

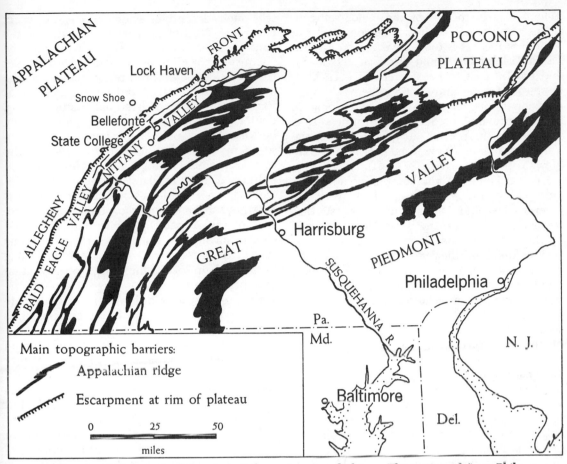

FIG. 2. Bellefonte, in the context of the eastern Appalachians. The main road from Philadelphia and Harrisburg went by way of the Susquehanna Valley to Lock Haven, thence to Bellefonte via Bald Eagle Valley. Until recently, the direct route from Harrisburg across the ridges was forbidding. (Sources: U. S. Geological Survey and Army Map Service topographic maps.)

I have developed an exasperated fondness for the town, like one's feelings for a once vigor-

less game. Major sources for Bellefonte and Centre County: J. B. Linn's *History of Centre and Clinton Counties, Pennsylvania* (Philadelphia, L. H. Everett, 1883); J. T. Mitchell's *Centre County History from the County's Beginnings to 1915* (no publisher, no date cited); and "Bellefonte, Pennsylvania, a Rendez-vous with History", a pamphlet published about 1965 by the Bellefonte Area Jaycees, Chamber of Commerce, and County Historical Society, and based on the work of Hugh Manchester. I have also relied heavily on the clipping file of the Penn State Room of the Pennsylvania State University Library. For Pennsylvania, the standard histories are W. F. Dunaway's *A History of Pennsylvania* (New York: Prentice-Hall, 1935) and S. K. Steven's *Pennsylvania, Birthplace of a Nation* (New York: Random House, 1964), the latter an example of what state histories might be, but seldom are.

ous and dignified great-uncle who in his dotage has begun to forget things, drink too much, and chase after girls.

Less subjectively, however, Bellefonte is not an inappropriate object for study, both on temporal and spatial grounds. In age, the town is old enough to be interesting, yet not so old that it has become preciously antique. About as old as the Constitution, Bellefonte spans our entire National experience and has participated actively in much of it.

Regionally, Bellefonte is harder to pigeonhole. Located in almost the exact center of Pennsylvania on the border between the Appalachian Plateau and the Folded Appalachians, Bellefonte neither acts nor looks like part of Appalachia (Figs. 1 and 2). Nor does it

belong clearly to any of the major self-conscious traditional cultural regions of the
United States. It is too far west to be Eastern
(a Philadelphian would sneer at the idea),
and too far east to be Western or even Midwestern. It is certainly not Southern, although
occasional bits of word-usage and domestic
architecture hint at Southern affinities. It is
clearly Northern, but completely lacks the
Yankee flavor of New England and upstate
New York.

Central Pennsylvania, however, is not just a
cultural hybrid. Recent seminal work by
Joseph Glass and others indeed suggests that
Pennsylvania's claim to being the "keystone"
of the United States is more than fustian—
that colonial southeastern Pennsylvania may
be the very headwaters of America's cultural
mainstream.[23] Of the three main currents of
west-trending American culture—New England, the Middle Atlantic, and the South—the
second was confined to the narrowest section
of the Atlantic coast, little more than the
hinterland of the city of Philadelphia.
Linguistic and architectural evidence, however, suggest that this tiny coastal foothold
was the narrow end of a funnel-shaped stream
of migration, which eventually spread the
cultural influence of the Middle Colonies
(more accurately, southeastern Pennsylvania)
in a 500-mile swath westward (Fig. 1).[24] We

still lack definitive evidence on the exact
nature of Pennsylvania influence west of the
Appalachians, but it now seems likely that the
"Pennsylvania Culture Region" may have set
the tone for cultural life in much of the
central United States. (Indeed, it may be that
Pennsylvania has not been much studied as a
distinctive American culture region, simply
because it resembles mainstream America in
so many ways that it hardly seems worthy
of study—quite unlike the highly flavored
cultures of New England, the South, the Midwest, or even California.) Andrew Jackson is
supposed to have remarked that America begins at the Appalachians. If that cultivated
frontiersman was right—and there is some
evidence that he was—then Bellefonte may
be located precisely where that transmutation
first began to occur on a large scale—on the
very threshold of middle America. Bellefonte
may not be in a "typical" region, but it is
certainly in a crucial one (Fig. 1).

For my purposes, however, Bellefonte's
main claim to interest is that its history
typifies the experience of myriad American
small towns that clawed their way to suprem-
acy over a local region, enjoyed a brief but
glittering moment of glory, and then—inca-
pable of coping with exigencies of the twentieth
century—began a long and catastrophic de-
scent into economic and social depression
where they remain to this day. Indeed, Bellefonte's history is almost a caricature of the
"typical" small-town experience, for its period
of grandeur was grander than most, and the
depths to which it has sunk have been cor-
respondingly more ignominious.

Vital (and Mortal) Statistics

A first look at Bellefonte's unexciting
census returns, however, would suggest no
such dismal conclusions, for the numbers
seem very ordinary and undramatic.[25] In 1970,
about 6,000 people lived inside the corporate
boundaries, with another two or three

[23] J. W. Glass, "The Pennsylvania Culture Region:
A Geographical Interpretation of Barns and Farm-
houses," unpublished doctoral dissertation, Pennsylvania State University, 1971. See also R. R. Pillsbury,
"The Urban Street Patterns of Pennsylvania Before
1815: A Study in Cultural Geography", unpublished
doctoral dissertation, Pennsylvania State University,
1968; John Florin, "The Advance of Frontier Settlement in Pennsylvania, 1638–1850: A Geographic
Interpretation", unpublished masters thesis, Pennsylvania State University, 1966; and E. R. Marsh,
"Geographical Isolation and Social Conservatism in
Pennsylvania Small Towns," unpublished doctoral
dissertation, Pennsylvania State University, 1971.

[24] The pattern was apparently mapped first by
Hans Kurath and a large research group working on
colloquial word use in *A Word Geography of the
Eastern United States* (Ann Arbor: University of
Michigan Press, 1949; paperback 1967), and later
by Kurath and Raven McDavid in *The Pronunciation
of English in the Atlantic States* (Ann Arbor, University of Michigan Press, 1962). Fred Kniffen
picked up the same pattern in folk architecture; his
map is published in "Folk Housing: Key to Diffusion," *Annals,* Association of American Geographers,
Vol. 55 (1965), 549–77; Henry Glassie treats the

pattern as a flow of ideas in *Pattern in the Material
Folk Culture of the Eastern United States* (Philadelphia: University of Pennsylvania Press, 1968).
Mario Pei has a similar map in *Language for Everybody* (New York: Pocket Books, 1958), p. 53, based
on dialectical differences.

[25] 1970 Census data were not available when this
essay was written, save for basic population enumer-
ations. Remaining figures are from the 1960 Census.

thousand living within a mile or so of the borough (town) limits.[26] Names in the telephone directory are mainly British or German, with about four percent Italian and a small number of Slavs. The town is overwhelmingly white, and the bulk of people were born either in Bellefonte or in Centre County, of which the town is county seat. In 1960, twenty-seven percent of the workforce was in manufacturing (almost exactly the national average), the unemployment rate of 4.3 percent was somewhat lower than the national average, and median family income almost exactly matched Pennsylvania's, in turn slightly above the national figure.

Like wrong turns on the electrocardiogram of an apparently healthy person, however, Bellefonte's statistics show several signs that something is amiss—and seriously so.

1) Although the town's population grew by about six percent between 1960 and 1970, it would have grown by twelve percent if its population were immobile · and reproducing normally (Fig. 3).[27] The deficit of six percent represents probable net outmigration for the decade. In slightly different terms, Bellefonte probably suffered a net loss of one out of sixteen people during the decade.

Now an occasional loss of population is no cause for despair, but two other items suggest that the loss is both chronic and debilitating.

---

[26] Throughout this essay, population figures for Bellefonte include the incorporated borough *plus* Spring Township, which surrounds Bellefonte completely. Although the combined total includes more farmers than I would like, Bellefonte has repeatedly annexed parts of Spring Township, and this is the only possible way to obtain comparable statistics for the same area from decade to decade.

[27] Net migration estimates for Bellefonte are based on two credible but unprovable assumptions: that natural increase in Bellefonte has not differed significantly from Pennsylvania's natural increase, and that the increase was about the same during the 1960s as the 1950s. The first assumption is necessary because the county hospital is located in Bellefonte and grossly inflates both birth and death data for the town. The second is necessary because 1970 data on natural increase were unavailable when this was written. From 1870 to 1950, natural increase data for Pennsylvania came from H. T. Eldridge and D. S. Thomas, *Population Redistribution and Economic Growth, U. S. — 1870–1950* (Philadelphia: American Philosophical Society, 1964), Vol. 3, Table A 1.6, p. 246. The 1960 natural increase datum is from the U. S. Census.

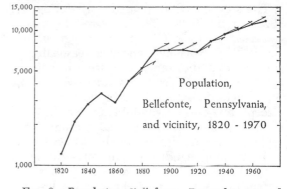

FIG. 3. Population, Bellefonte, Pennsylvania, and vicinity, 1820–1970. Heavy line represents combined population of Bellefonte borough and Spring Township which completely surrounds Bellefonte. Short barbed lines from 1870 to 1960 show how population would have grown each decade, had change resulted only from natural increase. The difference in slope between the heavy line and the barbed line presumably results from net migration into or out of Bellefonte. Where Bellefonte's line is steeper than the barbed line, there was probably net in-migration to town; where the barbed line is steeper, net migration was outward from town. Size of angle between the two lines represents magnitude of migration. Greatest migrational losses apparently occurred between 1890 and 1920.

2) With a sex-ratio of 91.5 (cf. the United States at 97.1), the population is unusually female-dominant, and this dominance is especially strong in the age group between 15 and 30 years old. Bellefonte's population loss, it must be concluded, comes from its young men—who are leaving town as soon as they have a chance.

3) Most disconcerting of all, these losses have been going on more or less continually since the 1890s (Fig. 3). Indeed, if Bellefonte had grown by natural increase alone— with no migration either inward or outward —the population would be about half again larger than it is today. In slightly different terms, for every two people in Bellefonte today, another one has left town permanently at some time over the last eighty years. To compound the injury, there is good reason to believe that a disproportionate number of emigrants came from the population group that Bellefonte could least afford to lose—the young males on the threshold of their productive lives who normally furnish a community with a wellspring of energy and ideas,

The slow bleeding paused only during the 1920s and 1930s. These were depression decades, however (the 1920s in agriculture, the 1930s universally), and it is reasonable to suppose that the immigrants were essentially refugees, not optimistic newcomers who sought out Bellefonte in hopes of a bright new future. Except for those two dubious decades, the demographic hemorrhage has continued for eighty years. In effect, nobody in town—save a diminishing handful of ancients—can even remember when the town was prosperous and optimistic. As a result, Bellefonte has lost not only population, but has lost its memory of hope. Small wonder that young people rage against the town, impatient for graduation and emancipation, and small wonder that older people—many of them—have gone beyond pessimism to a state of numbed resignation.

Clearly it was not always that way. One can look at past population statistics and find people crowding into Bellefonte; one can read the town's history to learn that three governors of Pennsylvania were Bellefonte natives, and four other governors lived in the town; one can count the writers, inventors, and artists who lived and worked there; one can walk through the streets of the town and look at its buildings, tangible monuments to high morale, intelligence, and pride, and a sorry contrast with the works of recent years.[28] All the evidence points to the ineluctable conclusion that Bellefonte's past glories are more than the bombastic conceits of local historians. Bellefonte—and other Bellefonte's all over America—were places of substance and significance. It is common practice now in the United States to prove one's urban *machismo* by scoffing at small towns as seats of hapless provincialism. The person who in 1890 so sneered at Bellefonte would simply have labeled himself as an ignoramus and a fool.

What happened? What circumstances of time and place raised Bellefonte to its former eminence, and what forces cast it down?

---

[28] The native Pennsylvania governors were Andrew Curtin (1861–1867), James A. Beaver (1887–1891), and Daniel H. Hastings (1895–1899). Governors William Bigler (1852–1858) and William Packer (1858–1861) lived in Bellefonte for a time; John Bigler was Governor of California from 1852 to 1856, and Robert J. Walker was Territorial Governor of Kansas in 1857.

Historic Crises and Geographic Change

Bellefonte's present condition—like that of any human community—is the product of all its past conditions. It can be likened to a single frame taken from a motion picture film, senseless out of context, but comprehensible if seen as part of a coherent sequence. Like a film, and like most human history, however, Bellefonte's chronology tends to be highly episodic. Periods of long stability are separated by fast-moving events which—to continue the cinematic metaphor—change not only the cast of characters but the stage-set as well.

This is merely another way of stating the obvious: that major historic changes are interlocked with major geographic changes, so that the history of a place can be seen as a sequence of geographic milieux, each coloring and controlling an episode like the scenery of a play, but changing rapidly to accommodate the next group of actors who move to center stage. Unlike a stage-set, however, local geographic scenery cannot be shunted quickly into the wings when an episode is over, and Bellefonte's present landscape is a rich but untidy pastiche of scenery and more than a few actors left over from earlier episodes. In Bellefonte, as elsewhere, latecomers are likely to find the contemporary stage-set baffling without some knowledge of what preceded it.

In Bellefonte's case, it helps make sense of present conditions to divide the town's past into four historic-geographic episodes. The beginning of each episode was marked by crisis—one at the town's beginnings in the 1790s—a second just before the Civil War—a third at the turn of the twentieth century—and the last about the time of World War II. Each crisis was shocking and disruptive because it represented a shattering departure from previous conditions, and partly because the changes were initiated by events far away and largely beyond the control and even the comprehension of local people. At the base lay those elemental changes in nineteenth century technology and social organization which turned the whole Western world on end—and Bellefonte with it; Henry Bessemer's new process for making steel in far-off Sheffield—Justin Morrill's Land Grant Act, shoved through Congress while the Southerners were away—a new canal around the St. Mary's Rapids in the wilds of upper Michigan —Andrew Carnegie's machinations in the corporate board rooms of Pittsburgh—a new law in 1945 to buy veterans a free college education when they returned from the wars.

In retrospect it is easy enough to spot these periods of crisis. They appear as abrupt flexures on the graph of Bellefonte's population growth (Fig. 3). One can see them in the town's architecture, where the style and function of buildings may change within the length of a block (or even in the middle of a building itself), reflecting the town's changing *Weltanschauung*—and the ability to pay for it. Newspaper clippings and local histories do not tell of the crises, however, for townspeople only dimly understood the forces which were moving them, and even if they somehow sensed them, often were unwilling to voice their fears. For as time has gone on, Bellefonte's ability to adapt to change has atrophied, just as the causes of change have grown more complex, the inertia of change less controllable, and the seats of power located farther and farther from the town. The story of Bellefonte's decreasing understanding and control of its own destinies, perhaps, is an unwitting microcosm of the recent history of man on earth.

The Crisis of Birth: 1795 and After

"By Heavens, Thompson, I have discovered an empire!"—Capt. James Potter, British Provincial Army, overlooking the Nittany Valley, 1764[29]

For every town like Bellefonte, uncounted numbers died in birth. Any large-scale American topographic map is spattered with ghostly names, the only remnant of myriad urban dreams. That Bellefonte was one of a select company of villages that did survive and ultimately prosper resulted from a combination of basic physical advantages, huge quantities of good fortune, and a significant but unmeasured volume of mendacity and low cunning. But cunning and luck are unreliable things, and Bellefonte's long-run success sprang from a natural setting of more than usual virtue.

The key to the town's success, as was almost always the case in the United States, was its control of routes leading to a valuable hinterland. Bellefonte's market area was—and still is—the ridgegirt Nittany Valley which, except for the Great Valley of southeastern Pennsylvania, is the largest of the fabled limestone lowlands of the northern Appalachians (Fig. 2). Even before the Revolution, land-hungry pioneers had begun to filter in from the fat but crowded Piedmont farmlands between Philadelphia and Harrisburg, but recalcitrant Indians (with English help) had made things too hot for settlers, who discreetly retired to safer climes for the duration of the war. With the Peace of Paris in 1783, however, settlers swarmed northwestward, quickly snapping up those small patches of fertile soil that the formidable Endless Mountains had to offer. One of the choicest areas, it was quickly learned, was the Nittany Valley.

Then, as now, the problem was how to get there. The direct route northwest from Harrisburg required travelers to cross the widest section of Pennsylvania's Ridge-and-Valley, a misty lovely region, but so tedious to reach that hundreds of square miles still remain roadless (Fig. 2).[30] It was longer but much easier to head up the Susquehanna from Harrisburg, first through a series of now-famous watergaps, and thence north to the great hook where the river turns abruptly west and finally southwest, a path which essentially circumvented the main ridges and brought the traveler into Bald Eagle Valley. Thence, the way into Nittany Valley was absurdly easy, through any of several watergaps in Bald Eagle Mountain, the ridge which encloses the Nittany Valley on the northwest. Thus, by the time the traveler had reached his goal—truly the end of the line—he had followed a path which looked on a map like a huge question-mark, so that he was entering the Valley not from the southeast—apparently the logical origin—but from the northwest (Figs. 2 and 4). The route was circuitous but the goal was worth it; the Nittany Valley contained the best land between the Great Valley and central Ohio.

[29] Quoted in Paul Dubbs, *Where to Go and What to See in Centre County* (State College, Pa.: The Centre Daily Times, 1961), p. 19.

[30] Lester E. Klimm, "The Empty Areas of the Northeastern United States," *Geographical Review*, Vol. 44 (1954), pp. 325–45 and map.

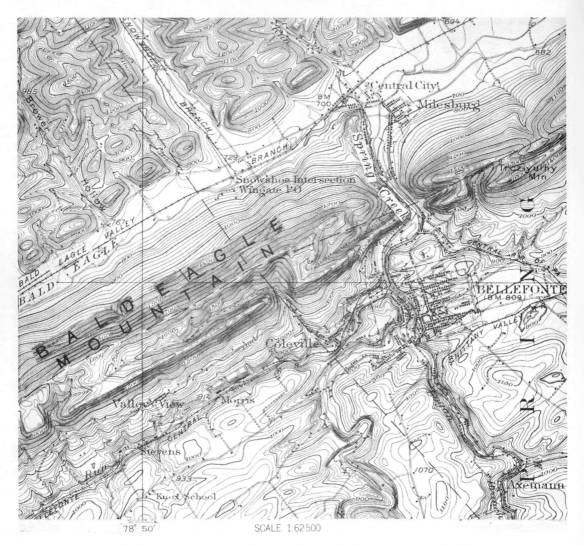

FIG. 4. Bellefonte and vicinity. (Source: U. S. Geological Survey "Bellefonte Quad-rangle," 1908, 1:62,500.) Main access to Bellefonte was originally from the northeast by Bald Eagle Valley to Milesburg, thence via the Spring Creek watergap into town. Rolling country in the south-southeastern part of the map is the Nittany Valley, mainly fertile farm-land. North-northwest of Bald Eagle Valley are the rough foothills of the Allegheny Plateau.

Bellefonte's founders chose to put their town on Spring Creek at the neck of the largest watergap into the Nittany Valley (Figs. 4 and 5). Like most places on the American frontier, the town was plotted and planned before there had been any significant rural settlement; here, as elsewhere, it was an urban frontier. There were no geographic rule-books to tell the planners where to place their town or lay out their streets; then as now they simply used the conventional wisdom of the day. For street plan, they used William Penn's Philadelphia grid-pattern, well enough suited to the nearly level Coastal Plain, but here imposed with grim consistency on the Appalachian hills (Fig. 6). The result is some picturesque urban scenery, and precipitous grades on many of the town's streets (Fig. 7).

It is puzzling, however, to read how the town's location was chosen. At first glance, the location is so obvious that one assumes the town fathers knew what they were doing all along; all traffic entering or leaving the Nittany Valley by way of the Spring Creek

FIG. 5. Aerial photo of Bellefonte, taken over Milesburg, looking approximately south through the Spring Creek watergap. (Cf. Fig. 4 for orientation.) Dark line in right foreground is a railroad; light line to left is Milesburg-Bellefonte highway. Wooded hills in the foreground are the shoulders of Bald Eagle Mountain, with Bellefonte sprawling across the southeastern entrance to the watergap. Beyond town is the rich farmland of Nittany Valley, Bellefonte's hinterland. In the southeastern distance are the parallel ridges of the Folded Appalachians, barring easy access from Harrisburg and the Pennsylvania Piedmont.

watergap must pass through Bellefonte or very near by (Figs. 4 and 5). But one reads the early records in vain hope of finding reference to this dazzling insight. Instead, the founders put their town here because of a large limestone spring, the "Belle Fonte," which was to become the town's water supply and main symbolic totem. Then too, there were deposits of iron ore close by—like the spring, associated with a major cluster of Appalachian thrust faults. Locationally, however, all the evidence suggests that the founders had simply blundered into a good thing.

It was not long, however, before they discovered what they were onto, and here the tale of geographic inevitability takes one of those unpredictable turns that makes locational scientists cross their fingers and say learned things about random error. Central

Pennsylvania was growing, and the huge counties which had been carved from Penn's original grants were proving excessively large for travel conditions of the day. The legislature, newly moved to Harrisburg, was receptive to the demand for new and smaller counties in the West, and as the nineteenth century opened, it had been decided to set up a new county with its seat somewhere in the upper valley of Bald Eagle Creek. Shipping on this uncertain waterway was never reliable, and no sane person would have considered taking a boat upstream from Milesburg, a village which lay three miles downstream from Bellefonte at the outer opening of the watergap and had sensibly been put at the head of what was optimistically termed "navigation" on Bald Eagle Creek (Fig. 4). Geographic science and sober good sense dic-

FIG. 6. The core of Bellefonte, c. 1870. (Source: B. Nichols, *Atlas of Centre County, Pennsylvania*, Philadelphia: A. Pomeroy and Co., 1874.) Basic patterns already well established. The grid street pattern, ignoring topography, came from Philadelphia; the "diamond" market-square in front of the Court House is also characteristically of Pennsylvanian provenience. Eighteenth century European pattern of row houses in the old town between Howard and Bishop Streets; open space is entirely behind the houses. Larger lots and setbacks in post-Civil War areas west of Spring Creek and in northeastern sector. Incipient class division, with small workers' houses west of Spring Creek and along south margin; larger houses of wealthier neighborhoods to the northeast. Industrial area, railroads, and abandoned canal concentrated in Spring Creek Valley. Main business district, then as now, between Court House and railroad.

tated that the seat of the new Centre County should be put at Milesburg, but Bellefonte's city fathers had other ideas. In early 1800, according to the story, they caused a boat to be hauled shrieking up the rocky bed of Spring Creek from Milesburg to Bellefonte, and then rushed the news to Harrisburg that the "first boat of the season" had reached Bellefonte, naturally neglecting to mention that it was also the last.[31]

Whether impressed by a town with commercial connections or merely stunned by a place capable of such derring-do, the Pennsyl-

vania legislature promptly confirmed Bellefonte as seat of Centre County, thereby guaranteeing the town's future, and condemning Milesburg to oblivion. It scarcely matters whether the story is true or not, and some have rudely suggested that it is not. The story is simply too characteristic to be untrue. When settlement patterns are fluid, minor random events commonly play inordinately important parts in setting the course of long-run geographic patterns. It was true then, and it is still true today.

So it was with Bellefonte. When it became county seat in 1800, it had a handful of houses, a grist mill, and a forge. After that

[31] This story is in Linn, op. cit., footnote 22.

FIG. 7. Grid patterns make no compromise with topography. View is north toward Bald Eagle Mountain in distance; Court House tower is at left in middle distance. Houses are quintessential middle-income mid-nineteenth century Pennsylvania Georgian; porches are typical Pennsylvanian American, a concession to climate and wider streets.

fateful year, however, things began to change rapidly. By 1805, an academy had been chartered, in 1806 the town was incorporated as a borough (Pennsylvania's quaint way of designating towns), and by 1810 it had a population of 303. In command of county government and in command of the watergap, Bellefonte was altogether the most important place for miles around.

Because it was, trade and tradesmen gravitated to the growing village. Aside from farm goods and lawyers—the standard stock-in-trade of American county seats—Bellefonte had another resource at its disposal, for iron had been found in the Nittany Valley. It was patchy stuff, occurring in lenses which seldom extended more than a few hundred yards in any direction. The concentration of metal was high, however, and this combination of smallness and richness exactly suited the technology which Pennsylvania pioneers could bring to bear. By 1820, some forty furnaces were recorded in the main producing areas of central Pennsylvania, each with a handful of workmen who dug iron and a little lime in summer, chopped wood for charcoal in winter, and hoped that their crude cast ingots would fetch enough to keep them alive.[32]

Whether or not it supported the workmen and their families is hard to say, but iron supported the town—and grandly. The wealthiest iron men lived in town (leaving the ironmasters to look after the works), where they put up houses in the latest Georgian style. As in Philadelphia, a city that Bellefonte hoped to emulate, the houses were fine substantial things—stone to begin with, later brick, and still later of wood—full two stories high with symmetrical end chimneys, ridgepoles parallel to the street, and windows and doors properly

---

[32] My main source of information on Bellefonte's iron manufacturing is personal communications from Harold V. Johnson.

BELFONT CENTRE CO

FIG. 8. Belfont (sic) in 1847. (Source: lithograph by T. Sinclair, Philadelphia, courtesy of the Tavern Restaurant, State College, Pennsylvania.) Typical of this genre of "panoramic views," this old print contains a good deal of artistic license; building in the far distance at right seems to be the Court House. The general impression is accurate, however: at mid-century, the form and location of buildings in Pennsylvania towns is still semi-European and Georgian; the layout is extremely conservative compared, say, to New York state towns of the same period.

and evenly spaced in the best Georgian-English fashion (Fig. 8). Quite unlike the radical and obviously deviant New England villagers, Bellefontonians clung to the proper European tradition and put their houses close to each other and the street. Open space was a kind of afterthought, left out of sight behind the houses (Fig. 6).

There was good reason for this, or at least the Pennsylvanians thought so. New Englanders might believe that a town was the City of God and leave room for churches and schools (and even a green) in their new Zions. No such nonsense in Pennsylvania: there was plenty of room for churches and schools outside the business district, and parks were simply silly; what was all that countryside for, anyway? A proper town was for trade, and the town center was a commercial, not a social or religious place, an idea which Pennsylvanians built into their town plans and sent west to conquer a continent.[33]

Within a few years—perhaps as early as 1830—the Nittany Valley had filled with as many farmers as it could comfortably accommodate, and if Bellefonte had stayed a simple farm center, its population might well have leveled off. The iron trade kept growing, however, partly because of America's insatiable appetite for metal things, partly because substantial competition from western mines

[33] Midwestern downtowns are almost entirely commercial, whether settled by New Englanders or Middle Colonists. West of a Pittsburgh-Buffalo line, it is a rare town that has a New England green for a core. Ohio's Western Reserve contains the most important exceptions.

and manufacturers was still years in the future, but mainly because Bellefonte's iron men reasoned that their industry could not survive without cheap access to the growing national market. And that, quite simply, meant improved roads.

The first one in 1822 was built overland, a turnpike southeast toward Harrisburg as directly as any road across the grain of the Appalachians could be built. By absolute standards, it was probably a terrible road, but as good as most others of its time. Water transportation was theoretically easier, although Pennsylvania streams were so wide and shallow that they were useless for boats of any reasonable size. But the Erie Canal's stunning success was not lost on the Pennsylvanians, who straightway set about building a statewide canal system to compete with the Yorkers.[34] In 1834, Bellefonte men got a charter for the Bald Eagle and Spring Creek Navigation Company, designed to run a canal from the Susquehanna at Lock Haven along Bald Eagle Creek and then through the Spring Creek watergap to Bellefonte (Fig. 9). Bellefonte was cunningly designated as the upstream terminal of the system, and thus the place to which everybody in the Nittany Valley would have to come if they were to take advantage of this new and cheap transportation. The canal took fourteen years to finish, but in 1848, Bellefonte joined the world, for better or for worse.

Meantime, things had been going very well, and the town looked it. With the iron works now consolidated on a firmer financial basis, the old courthouse assumed new elegance with a fine new Ionic porch. Numerous substantial Georgian houses were built—the grandest at the corner of Spring and Bishop Streets, the residence of Henry Brockerhoff, one of the new wave of German immigrants who had struck it rich in America and built their houses to prove their substance and their attachment to their newly adopted home (Fig. 10). Ostentatious he may have been, but it was the quiet ostentation of a man who was proud to live where he lived and was not

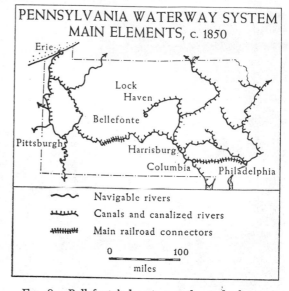

FIG. 9. Bellefonte's location at the end of a main canal spur briefly made the town the trade center for much of central Pennsylvania's most productive country. (Sources: Dunaway, op. cit., footnote 22, p. 679; and R. E. and Marion Murphy, *Pennsylvania: A Regional Geography*, Harrisburg: The Pennsylvania Book Service, 1937, p. 120.)

afraid to show it. In its own modest way, Bellefonte was the architectural equal of most Pennsylvania towns, which in the early nineteenth century was saying a good deal. The town's finest houses today still date to this period, a tangible but diminishing monument to an age of prosperity and permanence.

The halcyon days were not to last, however, and the 1850s saw a series of disasters that left Bellefonte nearly prostrate, and faced the town with a challenge that it very nearly failed to meet. The basic problem, as usual, was a change in economic geography, dictated partly by local conditions, but also by changes in the world at large. First of all, the iron furnaces were running out of fuel. A good-sized furnace—which employed perhaps fifty men—consumed an acre of hardwood forest per day.[35] With a hundred furnaces running in a four-county area, only the remotest woods had escaped the woodsman's axe. In addition, many of the smaller furnaces were not very well run, and could survive only if prices were so inflated that even the grossest inefficiencies

---

[34] By 1840, Pennsylvania had an incredible 1,000 miles of canals in operation, S. E. Morison and H. S. Commager, *The Growth of the American Republic* (New York: Oxford University Press, 1962), Vol. 1, p. 499.

[35] Furnas, op. cit., footnote 19, p. 33.

RESIDENCE OF THE LATE HENRY BROCKERHOFF,
COR. OF SPRING AND BISHOP STS.,

FIG. 10. Henry Brockerhoff's great Georgian mansion, built 1838, destroyed by the Atlantic Refining Company, 1958, to make room for a gas station. Figure 14 is a view from the same place in 1970. (Source: Linn, op. cit., footnote 22.)

might be overlooked. Until cheap transportation was available a local ironmaker pretty well had things his own way, but by the late 1840s British ironmakers had lowered world prices substantially. This new competition spelled bankruptcy for dozens of inefficient furnaces and foundries, and Bellefonte lacked the diversity of industry to soak up unemployment. For those who were thrown out of work, the only recourse was to leave town, which they did in droves. Things were made worse in the summer of 1853, when Bellefonte was smitten by a plague of "bleeding flux" (the symptoms sound like cholera) and during the dreadful month of July, ten bodies a day were buried in the town cemetery—this from a population of 1,200 people. (There is no record of those interred less formally, or in family plots.) For the first time in its history, the Bellefonte community lost population, perhaps as much as a third of its total num-

bers (Fig. 3).[36] It was a crisis of the first order.

The Crisis of Victorian Technology

"Don't forget to speak scornfully of the Victorian Age. There will be time for meekness when you try to better it."—J. M. Barrie[37]

It is easy enough to attribute Bellefonte's woes to cholera epidemics and the depletion of charcoal. In fact, the town was facing a crisis shared by the United States as a whole —a crisis provoked by economies of scale which had been developed in England during the previous few decades, and which now for the first time were filtering into the United States. Bellefontonians did not know it (no-

[36] The outskirts of town in Spring Township lost more people than Bellefonte, probably because forges and furnaces were mainly located there.

[37] Quoted by John Maass in *The Gingerbread Age* (New York: Bramhall House, 1957), p. 2.

body did), but it was the forefront of the Industrial Revolution, and the whole human geography of the United States was changing. What Bellefonte did realize, however, was that she had to operate on a wholly different scale, and in a different competitive market than she had previously done.

Part of the problem had been solved already. Although the economic depression of the 1850s had cruel effects in Bellefonte, it had squeezed out inefficient operators and forced new efficiencies on those who survived. At the same time, coal had been discovered on the Allegheny Plateau near Snow Shoe, some twenty miles northwest of Bellefonte (Fig. 2). It was difficult to ship out, however, since the eastern edge of the Plateau is the formidable Allegheny Front, an escarpment nearly 1,500 feet high and dissected into a wilderness of knobs and narrow winding valleys nearly twenty miles across. To bring the coal from Snow Shoe to Bellefonte required more ambitious transportation than pack horses. The Bellefonte iron men moved quickly to provide that transportation, and in 1859 the Bellefonte and Snow Shoe Railroad brought its first locomotive into town.

Suddenly, things began to happen very quickly. In part the rapid changes were tributes to the energy and perspicacity of Bellefonte's iron men, who recognized the challenge and knew how to meet it. But it was also a portent that things were speeding up everywhere. In another three decades the town would be left behind in a swirl of history and changing geography, but in the meantime the stage was set for its greatest moment.

The economic events are simple enough to describe, for they are laid against the familiar and dramatic background of the Civil War. In 1861, the price of pig iron, F.O.B. Philadelphia, sank to $20.25 per long ton, the lowest price since the beginning of the century; three years later, as Grant battered the defenses of Richmond, the price was $59.25.[38] Only the year before, when American feudalism died with Pickett's men on Cemetery Ridge, Bellefonte joined the new industrial world by sending a railroad spur

to the main Philadelphia-Pittsburgh line. Bellefonte's newly fueled and newly economical iron industry was ready to provide munitions for the Union armies in their last days— at the newly attractive price, of course.

The new prosperity quite naturally encouraged growth in existing industries, but other enterprises expanded and diversified as well. Nor did prosperity end with Appomattox. A machine shop and foundry (1864) was followed by a glass works (1867), a manufacturer of railroad cars (1873), a large planing mill (1879), a nail works (1881), and in 1883, *mirabile dictu*, the Edison Electrical Illuminating Company, financed by the inventor himself, and only his second such venture in the entire United States.

Economics, however, do not take the full measure of what was happening in Bellefonte. In our myopic twentieth century way, it is often difficult to understand that small towns a century ago were not in the backwater of civilization, but represented some of the best that the United States had to offer. Bellefonte's best was demonstrated in several ways. For its size, the town was a rather considerable publisher of books, journals, tracts, and newspapers. Her leading men were esteemed throughout Pennsylvania, and sometimes on the national scene as well. It was, for example, a Bellefonte man, Andrew Curtin, who served as Governor of Pennsylvania during and after the Civil War, who helped galvanize the state behind Lincoln during the grim days after Fort Sumter and the defeats at Bull Run. Bellefonte was proud of Curtin, to be sure, but not surprised. Bellefonte men, after all, were supposed to be men of stature.

Reading the local histories and walking through the streets of what remains of Civil War Bellefonte, one cannot help but be struck by the confidence of the place, the calm certainty that Bellefonte was important and would remain so. The buildings show it as well as the balance sheets (Fig. 11). In the commercial district—now firmly ensconced along the two blocks of High Street between the Court House and the new railroad station —many of the old Georgian buildings were pulled down to make room for new Gothic and Italianate structures, with the two eras often standing proudly but somewhat incongruously next to each other. Two new hotels

---

[38] These and other data on iron prices come from *Historical Statistics of the United States, Colonial Times to 1957* (Washington: Bureau of the Census, 1960), Table M-208, pp. 365–66.

FIG. 11. Bellefonte at its zenith of wealth and influence. The view is eastward across Spring Creek with Bald Eagle Mountain at the left. The double row of trees across the creek in the center marks High Street, ending at the Court House. At the left, the affluent north side of town is punctuated by spires of Protestant churches; new Victorian mansions appear on the outermost fringes. Spring Creek valley is the industrial axis, grain mills at the left, part of the iron works to the right. The high quality of this lithograph reflects Bellefonte's affluence in the last third of the nineteenth century. (Source: Thomas Hunter lithograph, Philadelphia, 1878, courtesy of the Tavern Restaurant, State College, Pennsylvania, and the Penn State Room, The Pennsylvania State University Library.)

opened to accommodate the increasing flow of visitors—both aggressively *au courant* in architectural style (Fig. 12). With expanding population (it doubled between 1860 and 1890), new houses were built, and old houses were expanded and remodeled. Victorian remodeling often left a house with two Georgian stories and a third bedecked with carpenter-Gothic furbelows, looking like an aging dowager trying to recapture her flaming youth with a hennaed wig. Elsewhere downtown, new "business blocks" were erected in the series of increasingly eclectic styles that marked American commercial architecture during the golden years of Queen Victoria. Domestic architecture flowered too, especially on the north side which had become the town's first elite neighborhood, and the housing fashions of New York and Newport arrived almost simultaneously in Bellefonte, all

soundly and permanently executed by men who obviously loved the town and meant to stay there. On the south side of town, gradually relegated to workers and shop clerks, houses displayed a decorous and necessary simplicity—with smaller yards and often only tentative departures from the old Georgian forms (Fig. 7). Everywhere, Bellefonte iron was cast into railings, brackets, fences, and that metal menagerie of lawn animals so beloved of Victorian landscape architects.

Altogether, it was Bellefonte's hour of greatness. In later years it would become vogueish to call the town "smug," and for detractors from neighboring places to sneer at the town's history as the conceits of a senile ancient to whom we must listen, but about whom we snicker behind his back. It is an easy sneer, but based on ignorance. Before the century was out, Bellefonte would

FIG. 12. The Brockerhoff Hotel, built 1866, closed 1959, from the Court House steps. The main building is conservative Italianate, typical of the post-Civil War period. The roof, apparently changed into a Nürnberg-eclectic style about 1890, suggests that Bellefonte knew how to keep up with the times.

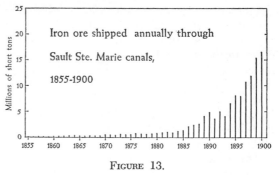

FIGURE 13.

produce two more governors of Pennsylvania and send two more of its sons to be governors of other states. Others were United States senators, still others served in the national cabinet. And many of them, like Andrew Curtin, continued to call Bellefonte their home, long after they had achieved national prominence. Few of America's metropolises can claim such a per capita spawning of leadership. Indeed, if New York City had produced statesmen at the rate of Bellefonte, it would have become necessary to create several dozen new states to accommodate the surplus of governors and senators.

The Crisis of Twentieth Century Technology

"I was born into a world that ceased to exist almost as soon as I came into it. In the first twelve years of my life, rural America was swept away as though it had been a picture on a blackboard that had suddenly been erased."—Edmund G. Love[39]

Then, suddenly, it was all over. A town built on agricultural processing and small iron plants was abruptly confronted with the manufacturing and marketing technology of the twentieth century. Unlike the crisis of the 1850s, the malady could not be cured by building a new railroad line, or by tightening belts until the panic was over. There simply was no place in this new world for small producers of expensive pig iron, just as there was

no place for small meat-packing towns on the prairies or textile towns in New England.

Paradoxically, Bellefonte's doom was spelled even before her moment of glory had begun. Mesabi iron was discovered in 1844, the Sault Ste. Marie locks opened Lake Superior to deepwater navigation in 1855, and the Bessemer process was perfected by 1856. This combination should have ruined the Bellefonte iron industry before the Civil War, but corporate organization was lacking to bring western iron to market at competitive prices. As a result, the town lived and prospered on borrowed time, although it is doubtful if the town fathers would have behaved any differently, even if they had known it. Success is sweet, even though one knows it is temporary.

Bellefonte's *coup de grace* was administered in the 1880s by the partnership of Henry Clay Frick's coke holdings with Andrew Carnegie's iron—a combination which would produce the United States Steel Corporation before the new century was a year old. The explosion of trans-Appalachian iron and steel production is reflected most generally in the record of iron ore traffic through the Soo Canals (Fig. 13), the demand for ore skyrocketing as the huge new mills rolled into production. 1884 was the first million-ton year, but two years later, traffic had doubled. By 1890, nine million tons passed through the canals, and over sixteen million tons in 1900.

The profits from pig iron reacted accordingly. Until 1883, the price had rarely fallen below $22 a ton, more often floating in the neighborhood of $30 or $40. From 1888 to the beginning of World War I, the price rarely rose above $22. Pittsburgh could afford to sell iron at that price, but not Bellefonte.

[39] E. G. Love, *The Situation in Flushing* (New York: Harper and Row, 1965), p. 1.

The effect in Bellefonte was shattering—
and ultimately fatal to the industry which
supported her. Indeed, the town's population
curve in the last half of the nineteenth century
looks like the Soo Canal traffic turned upside
down. In 1890 the community's population
was 7,136. Ten years later, it had increased
by precisely one person. Thirty years later—
in 1920—the total stood lower than it had in
1890 (Fig. 3).

The migration statistics ring like a dismal
knell. In the 1890s, the town of about seven
thousand people lost 900 of its citizens
through net outmigration. In the 1900s, the
loss was another 870. In the 1910s, 880. Over
the course of a generation, net outmigration
amounted to about 2,600 people.

These events, of course, were not unique to
Bellefonte. Alter the dates, the population
statistics, and the names of products, and one
has the history of hundreds of other villages
and towns across the country—all of them
unable to achieve the economies of scale of a
Pittsburgh, a Chicago, a Minneapolis, or any
of a host of lesser places. Bellefonte's experience is merely more dramatic than most others'
—partly because her successes had been so
great, and her fall from grace so sudden and
so catastrophic.

Not surprisingly, it took many years for
Bellefontonians to comprehend the magnitude
of the disaster.[40] Prosperity, after all, had
become habitual, and it was not easy to
absorb the idea that depression in Bellefonte's iron industry was not just a temporary
setback, not simply another of the financial
panics which periodically plagued nineteenth
century America. Nor was it entirely un-
reasonable to retain a measure of optimism.
It was not until 1915, for example, that the
last of the iron furnaces finally succumbed,
and even then new hope was encouraged by
the founding of two small metal plants, an
engineering company, and a brass works
which located in old factory buildings in the

valley of Spring Creek. And the economic
distress would have been much worse except
for the increasing production of limestone
from quarries north of town. Because their
activity increased in proportion to the output
of the Pittsburgh mills (the very cause of the
town's decline!), they provided a certain
ironic relief at the time of the town's direst
need. Simultaneously, the quarries and mines
also provided Bellefonte with its first variation from its almost purely Anglo-German
population by enticing a small but significant
number of Italian immigrants to the hard and
dirty work. (The lime crushers also began
polluting the air with lime dust, and have
been doing so ever since.)

Then too, the 1920s saw a small increase in
population that promised hope to some that
possibly the worst was over. A handful of
new buildings was put up—the inevitable
movie theater and the equally inevitable rows
of California bungalows along the edge of
town. But the respite was only momentary,
and eventually there came a time when the
full realization of disaster must have been
understood by everybody in town.

Old-timers in Bellefonte disagree exactly
when that realization occurred. Some suggest
that it came with the Depression, although the
Depression's force was doubtless blunted by
the knowledge that everybody else in the
country was in the same boat, and that rural
areas were generally better off than the big
cities. Others believe that the full impact
came after World War II. But there is no
disagreement with the general proposition
that a generation and a half of economic woe
had overlain the town with an almost palpable
blanket of gloom.

Spirit is an intangible thing, and because
it is hard to measure, many geographers and
would-be social scientists have been loath to
talk about it. But one must talk about it—
• the *genius loci* of the town—if one is to understand what happened to Bellefonte and other
small towns throughout America during the
first half of the twentieth century. For just
as surely as the town lost money and people,
it also lost a good deal of its spirit and its
pride. In some people the loss provoked a
feeling of resignation to the cruelty of an
inevitable fate; thus, when the once-distin-
guished Bellefonte Academy closed its doors

---

[40] This reaction was not unique to Bellefonte. Love,
op. cit., footnote 39, says about his home town of
Flushing, Michigan, just before 1920, "The technological revolution that had been creeping into the
large cities for some time flooded through the
country. It came so suddenly and the changes were
so thorough that most people didn't realize that the
old way of life had gone."

in bankruptcy in 1934, there was no serious effort to save the institution—once a source of joy and pride. Sometimes, fear prompted acts of desperation; the town launched on an orgy of demolition which left much of Bellefonte's best architecture in ruins, not to clear the way for some fine new ornament to the town (as Bellefontonians had demolished buildings in the decades after the Civil War), but to make room for literally anything to produce a little income. Above all, however, there was a growing feeling that Bellefonte was not merely beyond saving, but probably not worth it anyway. The combination of fear, resignation, and cynicism left the town in poor condition to meet new crises. Unfortunately for Bellefonte, another agonizing challenge was yet to come.

The Crisis of the Affluent Society

"What do the kids in Mason City want to do? What do the kids in Iowa want to do? They want to get out. I'd get out, go to California if I could."[41]

Until World War II, Bellefonte could at least take consolation in the fact that the source of her woes was far enough away to be impersonal, hard to identify, and certainly impossible to control. Now, with the end of the war, the town was faced with a new threat —maddeningly visible only twelve miles away. The tiny neighboring borough of State College, the seat of Pennsylvania State College, became a Mecca for thousands of returning veterans, newly returned from the wars to collect on the government's promise of free higher education through the G.I. Bill of Rights. Within a decade of the war's end, State College had exploded into a kind of boom town prosperity, and the town threatened to become the central-place for all of mid-Pennsylvania. To Bellefonte—still deeply rooted in nineteenth century ways—her upstart neighbor represented everything that was abrasive and confusing and dangerous about the new ways of the twentieth century.

To a considerable extent, Bellefonte's visceral suspicions were richly justified. In general terms, State College signaled the arrival of a new world, where academic pursuits were no longer the monopoly of the privileged

classes, but were becoming as important economically as the manufacture of heavy machinery. If Bellefonte had difficulty coping with the mass production technology of the early 1900s, she was totally unequipped to meet the challenge of a world of quaternary economics—where a man would make a good living designing electronic circuitry, but could not find employment pouring cast iron—where a college education would become prerequisite for elementary clerical jobs.

The contrast between Bellefonte and State College is peculiarly striking, moreover, because the latter is perhaps the largest purely "college town" in the United States, and represents an unusually pure form of quaternary enterprise. Thus, from the point of view of many Bellefontonians, State College's sudden success was acutely galling, for the new town was obviously growing rich, yet apparently doing nothing very useful. To make matters worse, many Bellefontonians could remember when State College was little more than a gaunt Gothic building in a cow pasture, when sows took their ease in the muddy main street of the village, and when State Collegians came diffidently to the county seat to do their shopping. Postwar State Collegians, by contrast, were brash newcomers who neither knew nor cared of Bellefonte's previous glories, and who made it tactlessly plain that they thought the county seat a backwater and its inhabitants hayseeds. If there were ever an urban generation-gap, it had arrived here in the decade after 1945.

Postwar events combined to make the comparison more and more invidious. The Cold War stimulated government investment in military research, and the college (soon to be renamed The Pennsylvania State University) hatched a brood of new, shiny, and prosperous research firms, many founded by ingenious and industrious professors of chemistry or engineering. Hordes of veterans and their families demanded instant housing, and the town and campus took on an air of fevered modernity as high-rise dormitories and Cape Cod Ramblers spread untidily across bucolic fields where the Agricultural School's experimental heifers had recently grazed. By 1950, the Census counted over 17,000 people in State College, almost double the size of the Bellefonte community.

---

[41] Schrag, op. cit., footnote 15, p. 21.

The impact on Bellefonte was mixed. On the one hand, increasing numbers of Belle-fontonians began commuting the twelve miles to new jobs in State College, thus relieving part of Bellefonte's unemployment problem and probably helping to stanch the flow of young people leaving town. On the other hand, the new quaternary town struck a crippling blow at Bellefonte's sagging self-esteem, for although there were plenty of new jobs at the University, many Bellefontonians could qualify only for menial positions—janitors, grounds keepers, and the like. Very few qualified for well-paid prestigious posi-tions in the academic ranks. In the sup-posedly classless society of postwar America, there was no doubt where Bellefonte stood.

Still worse—because it was a visible process—Bellefonte's shops and services began mi-grating to State College, first a trickle, then in a steady stream. To be sure, Bellefonte's retail establishment had never really re-covered from the collapse of the iron industry, and the occasional closing of an old store sur-prised nobody; it was simply something that "just happened," regrettable but unavoidable. One after another, however, Bellefonte stores established branches in State College, and when the shopkeeper compared receipts from his two outlets, Bellefonte often became the branch, or was closed completely. Important service facilities began doing the same thing. Thus, the county's daily newspaper moved its main office and printing plant to State Col-lege. The mayor of Bellefonte, a contractor, resigned his office so that he could move to State College. Even more exasperating, official agencies and utilities began to move out, re-locating where they could serve a larger, more affluent population. Nobody was surprised when the Internal Revenue Service opened a State College office, but it was high irony when the unemployment compensation office did it. The State Police moved to a post along the highway halfway to State College. Public utilities moved too, the regional offices of Western Union and the new telephone build-ing. Even Bellefonte's lawyers found it more profitable to operate in State College, where growth had spawned a booming business in land speculation and attendant real estate litigation. Other professionals, too, found the academic environment of the college town

more to their liking than the stifling anti-intellectualism of Bellefonte, and droves of them moved. Even the county judge lives in State College and commutes the twelve miles to the court house. Bellefontonians remark sourly that "State College'll steal the Court House next if we don't look out."

Reaction and Demolition

"I can't stand this . . . I'm going to leave . . ."—
Bellefonte municipal official, 1970[42]

When Bellefontonians denounce State Col-lege, it is more than mere venting of spleen against an abrasive *nouveau riche* neighbor; rather, the cynical embittered remarks are fairly accurate reflections of how deeply Bellefonte resents its maltreatment at the hands of the twentieth century. Anger, how-ever, is only one of several reactions. Many people have grown resigned to the situation, summarizing their feelings in the old tired question, "Well, what can you do about it?"

Many have done something about it by leaving town, often for permanent residence in State College. The *émigrés* include a con-siderable number of vigorous competent peo-ple, and it is hard to avoid the conclusion that Bellefonte would be better armed against the slings and arrows of the twentieth century if at least some of these people would return home. When I mentioned this possibility to a talented young artist, born in Bellefonte and now making an excellent living in State Col-lege, he spoke angrily of the inflexibility and mean-minded provinciality of his home town. "They laughed at me in Bellefonte," he says bitterly. "I'd never go back."

Others, however, have tried to improve Bellefonte by changing its physical character. In the absence of any clear idea of what the town might become, well-meaning citizens have tried to make the town look as much like State College as possible, presumably hoping that if Bellefonte put on the plastic and alumi-num trappings of a modern city, that it would somehow become one. At best, these efforts have failed to produce the desired results. At worst, the physical "improvements" have se-

---

[42] Quoted in the *Pennsylvania Mirror,* November 16, 1970, pp. 1 and 7. The official was in process of walking out of a characteristically acrimonious meet-ing of the Borough Council.

riously damaged the town's pleasant small-town atmosphere—one of its few remaining assets.

As in countless other American towns, serious damage has been inflicted by highway building, and two recent examples are particularly dismal. Bishop Street was an important old road leading out into the Nittany Valley— a street with no very illustrious architecture, but still pleasant because of its line of trees on both sides. The State Highway Department was persuaded to widen and repave the street, with the result that the trees have been cut, traffic moves faster and more noisily, and the undistinguished houses stand cruelly exposed to view. Howard Street, with some fine Georgian buildings, was similarly "improved" so that the trees are gone, asphalt laps against domestic doorsteps, and heavy truck traffic from a nearby interstate highway uses the street as a shortcut to (of all places) State College. What had previously been pleasant residential streets have become truck highways, bringing no measurable improvement of the town's economy, and certainly not of its environmental quality. Many Bellefontonians are pleased, however, since the state paid the bill for new pavement—not the town.

The damage has been even worse downtown, where bulldozers have been busily engaged in the wrecking operations that Americans continue to call "urban renewal," with no touch of irony. Like all American towns, of course, Bellefonte has been tearing buildings down for a long time, usually to replace them with other buildings. Significantly, however, pre-1900 replacements were often costly affairs, generally built in the best style of the day, and obviously built to last by people who held the town in high affection. Without exception, however, buildings of the last two decades have been banal in design and of shoddy construction. Lest this remark be misconstrued as an attack on contemporary architecture, let me hasten to note that I have no such intention. It is simply a fact that when *fin de siècle* Bellefontonians built neo-Romanesque buildings, they built good neo-Romanesque, and the town has more than its share of reasonably distinguished Richardsonian buildings. It is fair to say that there is not a single example of

FIG. 14. The Brockerhoff mansion stood here. The large Georgian building beyond the gas station is the Brockerhoff "Block." It too has been torn down (1971) to make room for a Colonel Sanders Kentucky Fried Chicken outlet.

distinguished post-1920 architecture anywhere in the business district—nowhere even a bad imitation of Yamasaki or Pei, much less Sullivan or Wright. It is a sad fact—but nonetheless a fact—that the disintegration of Bellefonte's self-esteem is unwittingly memorialized in the disintegration of its residential and business districts over the last seventy years.

The continual loss of excellent buildings is reflective of the town's malaise, and the way in which buildings were lost is equally revealing. Business, government, and even religion have cooperated in some of the most hurtful demolitions. Architecturally, the most grievous loss was the premeditated wrecking of Henry Brockerhoff's great Georgian mansion in 1958. The building and its surrounding formal gardens, good enough to be registered with HABS (the Historic American Buildings Survey), were willed to the Catholic Church as a nunnery, but the Church sold them to the Atlantic Refining Company, which tore down the house, poured asphalt over the gardens, and built a gas station replete with revolving plastic sign on the site of the wreckage (Fig. 14).

Physically, Bellefonte has suffered grievously from this and uncounted earlier demolitions. Indeed, it is surprising that the town retains as much good architecture as it does; it is a tribute to what the town once was, for only a very great treasure could survive such dedicated plundering. It is no surprise, however, that these successive demolitions have

neither strengthened the town's spirit, nor
have they stemmed the stream of outmigration
from Bellefonte. The 1970 Census suggests
that net outmigration continues at a higher
rate than at any time since World War I. At
the same time, it is difficult to find anyone in
Bellefonte who is willing to assert any real
confidence in the town's future.

THE FUTURE OF AMERICAN SMALL TOWNS

"Are we worth saving? And if so, why?"[43]

Over the last half century, journalists and
scholars alike have repeatedly asked the
question, "Will (or can) the small town survive?" Presumably, it is not a question of
whether small towns will survive physically;
although many of our smaller hamlets have
literally disappeared, nobody really believes
that small towns as a class are going to evaporate—any more than New York is going to
evaporate, despite its myriad urban woes.
Rather, the proper question is: are small
towns so isolated from the national mainstream that their residents are effectively
exiled to some kind of cultural Siberia? Has
the small town so declined in importance that
it no longer need be considered in framing
serious questions about the United States and
its culture?

Plenty of ready-made answers are available,
mainly from folk who had prejudged the issue
long ago. Small town aficionados, for example, smile bravely and assert that small
towns are far from dead—that indeed they
are the hope of the land. On the other side,
Sinclair Lewis and the *New Yorker* ("not for
the old lady in Dubuque") declared them
irrelevant long ago. Any serious diagnosis of
small town prospects, however, demands a
more dispassionate appraisal of their potential
function in the economic and cultural life of
contemporary America.

Economically, of course, the small towns of
America are often in bad shape, simply because many of them like Bellefonte arose and
flourished in an economic environment which
ceased to exist before the turn of the century.
As transportation and communications grew
swifter and cheaper, the iron laws of eco-

nomics, 1890 vintage, decreed that we had too
many towns, spaced too closely together.
Today, a good many nineteenth century towns
seem plainly obsolete. Many Bellefonte
émigrés would endorse this view.

But the 1890 geographic rules no longer
govern the American economy. Although
Bellefonte obviously cannot compete with
Pittsburgh or even State College, it is entirely
possible that in the last third of the twentieth
century she need not try. Two things have
changed and both suggest that a new environment is developing in America which may
accommodate more than a few apparently
obsolete Bellefontes.

First of all, American residential tastes are
changing rapidly and drastically. The most
powerful migratory streams of the twentieth
century—to the city and to the sun—have
lost much of their momentum; the glamorous
city has lost much of its glamour, and the
bloom has faded even from the Californian
rose.[44] In a nation where bestsellers declare
that society and technology are moving too
fast for human beings to retain their mental
and physical health, the deliberate pace and
antique patina of small towns—only recently
the object of derision—seem to make them
increasingly attractive as places to live.[45] The
1966 Gallup Poll, for example, estimated that
about twenty-two million urban Americans
would rather live in small towns. Willie Mor-
ris, the small town boy who went from Yazoo
City, Mississippi, to New York to become
Editor-in-chief of *Harper's,* quoted a school-
teacher from his home town who suggested
what might be the most important reason—
that people who are overwhelmed by the
impersonal size of a big city feel that small
towns provide an individual with at least
some chance to control his personal destiny:[46]

"You can live in a small town and be sorry for
yourself that the world passes you by—and suddenly you realize that the world isn't passing you
by at all—that it's all here. We've got a lot of
friends in big cities, and they seem to be beating
their heads against the wall all the time. That's
not so true here. One individual can affect a small

---

[43] The title of a moving essay by Elmer Davis in
But We Were Born Free (New York: Garden City
Books, 1954).

[44] "Many Californians Leave as Glamour Wanes,"
New York Times (Sunday, Sept. 12, 1971, pp. 1, 66).
[45] The bestseller cited is Alvin Tottler, *Future
Shock* (New York: Random House, 1970).
[46] *Yazoo: Integration in a Deep-Southern Town*
(New York: Harpers Magazine, 1971), p. 54.

town. At least, you can decide what you believe and stand for it. I can remember a lot of failure. It's not too bad to try and fail. When I don't try, it bothers me deeply."

One can argue, of course, that for most Americans a wish to live in a small town amounts to Tom Sawyerish romanticizing, a kind of pipe-dream which cannot come true simply because small towns do not have the economic base to support more people. But that too may be changing, as improved telecommunications allow industry—especially quaternary enterprises—to become more and more footloose. In a day when the New York Stock Exchange talks seriously of abandoning Wall Street for the bosky hills of northern New Jersey, amenities have become a hugely significant element in the formulas of economic location. In this new arithmetic, a town may find more economic value in green trees, pure air, and a good architect than in capturing the new facilities of a gray-iron foundry or hosiery factory. A town like Bellefonte, which retains a good deal of its small town charm (despite assaults by Colonel Sanders and his Kentucky-fried legions), may find that its obituary notices have been printed prematurely. And when a new interstate highway is built past Bellefonte's door, so that one can drive to half-a-dozen large cities in the span of a morning or afternoon, the town's doom seems less than certainly sealed.

Although it may be tempting to predict a bright future for Bellefonte and its fellow American small towns, euphoria is dampened by a realistic examination of the town's present condition. Bellefonte's physical resources are real enough—handsome commercial and residential districts, a plentiful supply of good water, a nearby university and transcontinental highway, and some of the best hunting and fishing country in eastern United States within a half hour drive of downtown—to mention a few. Bellefonte's main limitations, however, are intangible— mental outlook, social temperament, psychological atmosphere—hard to measure and impossible to touch, but which taken in combination leave small reason for optimism about the town.

At the root of all the problems, many Belle-

fontonians are deeply demoralized. In conversation after depressing conversation with residents of all age groups—with businessmen, factory workers, teenage students, municipal officials, housewives, professional men and women, janitors, student and faculty observers from the nearby university—conversations which have taken place under all sorts of conditions and spread over a period of thirteen years, I have rarely met a person who thought that Bellefonte's future was bright. As one perceptive high school teacher summed it up: "Practically everybody who lives here is very critical of the town." And resignation begets resignation. A student at Bellefonte High School remarked to me, "Nobody feels responsible for Bellefonte . . . Nobody cares." Although such statements may be overdrawn, they are not unrepresentative.

The source of demoralization is easy to identify. Three generations of economic trouble, three generations of almost constant outmigration, three generations of watching Bellefonte's children leave town upon reaching adulthood, three generations of being told incessantly that Bellefonte was a tired worthless place—all these have carried the town beyond the threshold of pain to a state of pessimism and resignation which often approaches despair.

It would be useful if some scholar would map the geography of despair. The pessimism which overlies the town like a soggy blanket stifles real improvement in Bellefonte's condition more certainly than any tangible thing, and this situation surely is not confined to one small Pennsylvania town. Out of pessimism has come a kind of grim conservatism that has little necessarily to do with political attitudes.[47] It reflects the fear shared by passengers in a sinking lifeboat that any movement,

[47] Nonetheless, small towns and small cities appear to be politically more conservative than either rural areas or big cities. Photiadis, working in Minnesota, found businessmen in towns between 5,000 and 15,000 most conservative of all urban places he studied. Haer, in Washington state, found greatest conservatism in towns between 25,000 and 100,000. J. Photiadis, "Community Size and Aspects of the Authoritarian Personality among Businessmen," *Rural Sociology*, Vol. 32 (1969), pp. 70–77, and J. L. Haer, "Conservatism-Radicalism in the Rural-Urban Continuum," *Rural Sociology*, Vol. 17 (1952), pp. 343–47.

any change threatens survival itself. This reluctance to entertain new ideas, of course, discourages departures from established patterns of thought and behavior—those very departures which might provide a basis for responsible optimism about the town's future. The fear of change, for example, has certainly discouraged efforts to suppress the emission of choking gray dust from nearby lime crushers, for fear that jobs would be lost—this despite the fact that many houses remain unpainted because the owners have despaired of trying to keep them clean under daily deposits of grime. The same fear has paralyzed action to prevent further demolition of Bellefonte's distinguished old buildings; demolition is the way things have always been done, and alternative behavior is thought to be risky.

Paradoxically, there is almost equal fear of stability. There is, after all, very little in the American national experience to prepare a community to accept a condition of slow growth, or perhaps no growth at all—nothing, in short, which prepares it to grow old gracefully. Several years ago, a Bellefonte businessman voiced a national article of faith when he said matter-of-factly, "If you don't grow, you die." Torn between the desire to grow and the inability to do so, the town grows increasingly frustrated, bitter, and panic-stricken.

Proposals for innovation are met not merely with fear but often with incredulity. Large numbers of Bellefontonians have never traveled much beyond the confines of central Pennsylvania, and they simply do not possess the range of experience which would enable them to compare Bellefonte with some remembered image from afar. Television comes in, to be sure, but the images are somehow unreal. Architectural restoration, for example, is rejected out of hand by many Bellefontonians on grounds that "it won't work." When told that it has indeed worked in places as diverse as Alexandria, Virginia, and Marshall, Michigan, and brought a good deal of economic prosperity in the bargain, natives tend to display stolid disbelief or merely reply, "Well, it probably wouldn't work here." Meantime, the distinguished old buildings continue to come down, and with each new demolition Bellefonte's physical and psychological options grow narrower and narrower.

It is scarcely surprising that impetus for change has come less powerfully from local sources than from outsiders, newcomers to town, or local boys who have returned to town after long periods in distant places. The old Penn Belle Hotel, for example, is gradually being restored to a measure of its former grandeur by an Italian quarry worker's son who has worked in Philadelphia, has spent about ten years outside Bellefonte, and believes profoundly that he has an obligation to contribute his experience and intelligence to the town's betterment. Across High Street from the hotel, the shabby old Bush Arcade was bought and its flamboyant eclectic facade restored by a State College realtor, who expects to make a tidy profit from renting shops downstairs and refurbished apartments on the upper floors. And little by little, a few influential Bellefontonians are coming to believe that the town does not need to disembowel itself in order to survive in the last third of the twentieth century, and that Bellefonte can survive and even prosper on its own terms—not those of 1890 Pittsburgh or 1945 State College. It is too early to know whether these beliefs will be justified.[48]

It is not too early to suggest, however, that America would profit handsomely if the health of her small towns took a turn for the better. At the most elemental level, it is hard to justify the abandonment of the homes of thirty million Americans. Just as significant, perhaps, small towns are important tangible reminders of who we Americans are and where we came from—not in the form of sanitized "historic" restorations, but as genuine organic members of the American landscape. The mindless gutting of Bellefonte, Pennsylvania, and a host of other small towns represents a deliberate obliteration of cultural memory. a vice which George Orwell has correctly warned us that no free country can readily afford. Above all, our small towns may yet provide us with a place to live, environmentally attractive, and controllable by those who inhabit them. If we cannot find room for such places in the evolving geography of the United States, the whole nation will be the poorer for it.

Footnote 48 is found in the Addendum on page 374.

Bellefonte iron

AMERICA'S CHANGING METROPOLITAN REGIONS

JOHN R. BORCHERT

ABSTRACT. America's metropolitan areas continue to serve distinct functional-nodal regions. For each region the metropolis is the single most important center of economic organization and culture diffusion. But the classic model of metropolis and region is changing. Business and migration linkages appear to be more national than regional. The regional metropolis is decentralizing and dispersing. The resource-based economy of the region has ceased to support most of the economic growth of the metropolis; meanwhile the metropolis lends increasing economic support to the surrounding region. The existing political-geographic framework is not suited to these changes. National policies are likely to be directed increasingly to management and organizational reforms which recognize both the nature and the inertia of the evolving urban-regional system, and aim to make it work better. KEY WORDS: *Decentralization of metropolis, Intergovernmental fiscal transfers, Metropolis, Metropolitan functions, Metropolitan region, Population change, Urban growth policy.*

FOR many Americans, crossing the threshold of a big city continues to excite the emotions and the intellect. The intensity of activity grows; a skyscraper skyline appears in the distance; or a vast pattern of lights spreads across the night landscape. Passing trucks bear the names of distant but obviously connected places; planes converge on a major airport; impressive signs mark the home sites of firms whose names, products, or services are familiar across an extensive territory. It is easy to get the feeling that here is the heart of an empire.

Those are the conditions which define the word "metropolis." The quest to understand the dimensions and functions implicit in that landscape has motivated numerous, substantial studies of metropolitan centers and their regions.[1]

Yet, as this is written, a persuasive voice from a national television network fills the

Dr. Borchert is Professor of Geography at the University of Minnesota in Minneapolis.

[1] Basic works include Robert E. Dickinson, *City Region and Regionalism* (New York: Oxford University Press, 1947), and Otis Dudley Duncan, et al., *Metropolis and Region* (Baltimore: Johns Hopkins University Press, for Resources for the Future, 1960). Sequels include Dickinson's *City and Region* (London: Routledge and Kegan Paul, 1964), and Beverly Duncan and Stanley Lieberson, *Metropolis and Region in Transition* (Beverly Hills: Sage Publications, 1970).

room with statements from important Americans who say that the cities are finished, that the nation is on a disaster course if people continue moving to fewer and larger places.

If the metropolis is the heart of a regional system, and overgrowth is leading to a debacle at the metropolitan center, the surrounding metropolitan region must be either victim or accomplice in the process. Will the metropolis and its region continue to be necessary parts of the framework for both understanding and operating America? Or are they going the way of the passenger train?

AMERICA'S MAJOR METROPOLITAN CENTERS

The measures of a metropolis are many.[2] The three selected here are population size, as a measure of potential crowds; retail sales, as a measure of market concentration; and total deposits in local banks and savings and loan associations, as a measure of the availability of capital to build and finance new and creative activities (Fig. 1). Crowds, markets, and investment capital are taken as the essentials of a metropolis. They assure the numbers of people to raise the probability of interaction and innovation, the buying power to attract high-order goods and services, and the financial capacity and local interest likely

[2] See Jerome P. Pickard, *Metropolitanization of the United States* (Washington: Urban Land Institute, 1959).

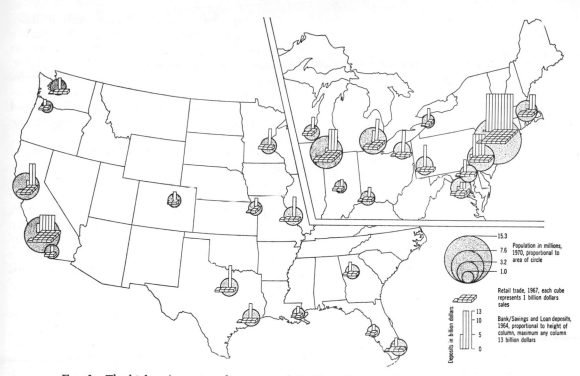

Population in millions, 1970, proportional to area of circle

Retail trade, 1967, each cube represents 1 billion dollars sales

Bank/Savings and Loan deposits, 1964, proportional to height of column, maximum any column 13 billion dollars

Deposits in billion dollars

FIG. 1. The high-order metropolitan areas of the United States. Source: *Statistical Abstract of the United States, 1970.*

to build speculatively to promote or attract new activities at that place.

Twenty-eight metropolitan areas in the United States have distinctively high rank correlations between these three measures of metropolitanism (Fig. 1). These twenty-eight fall into three size groups (Fig. 2). The first-order center is New York, America's national metropolis and "world city," with more than fifteen million people.[3] Seven second-order centers range from 2.8 to 9.6 million in population. Five have challenged New York's dominance over a large area at some time in the nation's westward expansion—Boston and Philadelphia, Chicago, Los Angeles and San Francisco. The other two are the greatest specialized centers of government and industry, respectively: Washington and Detroit. The remaining twenty third-order centers range in size from 1.0 to 2.4 million and reflect unique regional resources which gave them a major comparative economic ad-

vantage at some stage of the nation's development thus far.[4]

A Historical Legacy

The sizes and locations of these twenty-eight centers are, in a sense, a legacy. The great ports of the northeast Atlantic seaboard were built at critical natural harbor locations facing western Europe in the Wagon-Sail epoch (Fig. 3). Locational criteria for Washington were decided in the same epoch. The great ports of the North, on the Great Lakes and the western rivers, grew at places of critical importance in the age of the Iron Horse and Steam Packet. Together those cities comprise the major nodes within the "core" region of the United States—the Manufactur-

[4] Size orders and subsequent references to specific epochs in the development of the American transportation system and industrial technology are based on J. R. Borchert, "American Metropolitan Evolution," *Geographical Review*, Vol. 57 (1967), pp. 301–32. For an excellent summary of "Urbanization and Regional Economic Development," see chapter 1 in David Ward, *Cities and Immigrants* (New York: Oxford University Press, 1971).

[3] Peter Hall, *The World Cities* (New York: McGraw Hill Book Company, 1966 and 1971).

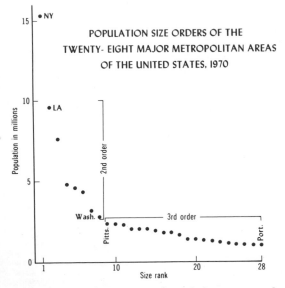

FIG. 2.   Population size orders of the twenty-eight major metropolitan areas of the United States, 1970. Data from *U. S. Census of Population, 1970*. (New York and Chicago are defined as census Standard Consolidated Areas; San Francisco includes San Francisco-Oakland and San Jose SMSAs; Los Angeles includes Los Angeles-Long Beach, San Bernardino-Riverside-Ontario, and Anaheim-Garden Grove-Santa Ana SMSAs; Ann Arbor SMSA is included with Detroit; Kenosha and Racine SMSAs are included with Milwaukee; Boston is SEA not SMSA; other combinations include Miami and Fort Lauderdale-Hollywood, Dallas and Fort Worth, Seattle and Tacoma.)

ing Belt and Corn Belt, or the Megalopolis-Midwest corridor (Table 1).

Boston, New York, Philadelphia, and Baltimore on the Atlantic; Pittsburgh, Cincinnati, St. Louis, St. Paul-Minneapolis, and Kansas City on the western rivers; and Buffalo, Cleveland, Detroit, Chicago, and Milwaukee on the Great Lakes reflect locational decisions made when, first, wagon roads and, later, canals or pioneer regional rail nets supplemented the main coastwise and inland waterways. The emergence of New Orleans and San Francisco as major cities belongs to the same epoch.

Atlanta, Denver, and Dallas-Fort Worth, in the interior, and Houston, Seattle-Tacoma, and Portland, on the coasts, reflect the opening of new inland resource regions and multiple rail routes across the West and South in the Steel Rail epoch. The addition of San Diego to the metropolitan scene during the same era suggests the distinctive strategic geography of the nation's navy when America emerged as a world power and proprietor of the Panama Canal.

Among newcomers to the list of major metropolitan centers, Miami and Tampa-St. Petersburg reflect the importance of amenity in the Auto-Air age. Phoenix will soon join the roster of major centers for the same reason. Meanwhile, decentralization of metropolitan growth within the northeastern "core" region is bringing former lesser centers into the family of high-order cities. Indianapolis is the first; Columbus and Rochester will soon follow.

The names of these twenty-eight big urban areas are familiar to all Americans. Most of them have embodied the symbols of traditional urban America for four generations or more. Those symbols have included centralized economic and political power; societal

TABLE 1.—MAJOR EVENTS IN METROPOLITAN EVOLUTION

Section of the United States	Epoch				
	Wagon/Sail	Iron Horse/ Steam Packet	Steel Rail	Auto/Air/ Amenity	Total
	Attained Metropolitan Threshold				
Megalopolis/Midwest "Core"	9	7	0	0	16
West/South "Periphery"	0	3	8	1	12
Total	9	10	8	1	28
	Attained High Order				
Megalopolis/Midwest "Core"	6	6	3	1	16
West/South "Periphery"	0	2	3	7	12
Total	6	8	6	8	28

Source: Compiled from Figure 3 for the twenty-eight major metropolitan centers of the United States. Development shifted from the core to the periphery during the Steel Rail epoch, and centers in the periphery attained high order during the Auto/Air/Amenity epoch.

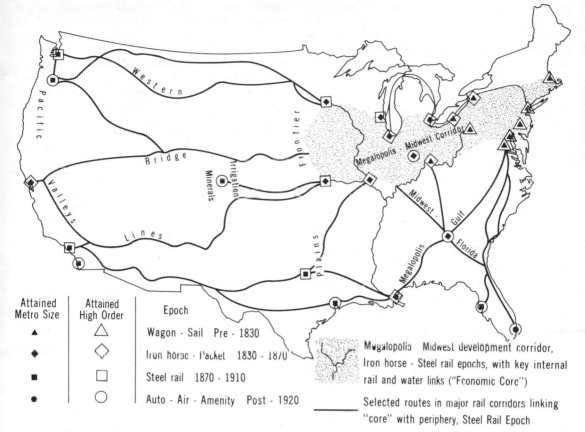

FIG. 3. The historical emergence of America's high-order metropolitan areas. Dates of epochs: Wagon-Sail—before 1830; Iron Horse-Steam Packet—1830–1870; Steel Rail—1870–1920; Auto-Air-Amenity—since 1920. Source: Borchert, op. cit., footnote 4.

innovation and disorganization; institutional prestige; monumental architecture (especially office skyscrapers); and high-order professional services, entertainment, and goods in response to large potential markets. The recent additions to the group are symbols of more recent dimensions of American urbanism—low density subdivision, growth by assimilation of rural areas and small towns into a suddenly expanded metropolitan circulation system, large immigration to regions of climatic amenity, and investment in relatively accessible but less-exploited parts of the traditional Manufacturing Belt.

As both household terms and products of historical national evolution, these metropolitan areas are integral parts of our culture. Their existence and character constrain public responses to opinion polls, "objective" evaluations of potential commercial or office lo-

cations, and most other conceptions of what is or is not "optimum" in the nation's settlement and economy.[5]

THE METROPOLIS IN ITS REGION

The rest of the nation fills the spaces between these major metropolitan centers. In those spaces are the smaller cities and the

[5] "All optima depend on past experiences . . . can only be defined in terms of given initial conditions. There exists no optimum optimorum that is independent of the past;" Edwin von Boventer, "Urban Hierarchies and Spatial Organization," *Ekistics*, Vol. 32 (1971), pp. 329–36, reference on p. 329. An example is the effect of the historically evolved location of the American Manufacturing Region on the determination of the optimum market location for manufacturing; Chauncy Harris, "The Market as Factor in the Localization of Industry in the United States," *Annals*, Association of American Geographers, Vol. 44 (1954), pp. 315–48.

small towns and farm settlements—the
services and firms with lower population
thresholds or less need for propinquity. The
rest of the nation must look to these high
order centers for whatever services are distinctive to them.

A combination of doctrine and documenta-
tion tells us that each major metropolis is the
capital of a surrounding region, carved from
the slab of intermetropolitan space. To varying degrees, individuals and institutions located in the major center penetrate and
organize the surrounding territory. They
generate flows of goods, services, and information which focus upon the metropolis; and
the flow patterns on the map describe a nodal
region.[6]

The metropolis is the capital of its nodal
region by virtue of two roles. First, it is the
dominant center for organizing the economy
of the region: production, distribution,
finance, and business services. Hence, it provides the dominant business link with the rest
of the United States and the world through
its high-order financial, professional, and
cultural establishments. Second, it makes the
region more cosmopolitan. It is the prime
importer of culture and technology diffusing
outward from the world's principal centers
of innovation toward the recesses of the
American hinterland.[7] And it further diffuses
these innovations along the transportation and
communications network that links the metropolis with its nodal region.

Organizer of the Regional Economy

One possible measure of the extent of the
region in which a metropolis dominates the

---

[6] For a careful and rigorous description of the
spatial and functional characteristics of the full range
of size orders, but especially those of lower order,
see Brian J. L. Berry, *Geography of Market Centers
and Retail Distribution* (Englewood Cliffs: Prentice-
Hall, 1967). An early and succinct statement of
functional relationship between metropolis and metropolitan region was formulated by N. S. B. Gras in
An Introduction to Economic History (New York:
Harper and Brothers, 1922).

[7] Diffusion of selected technological innovations
from higher- to lower-order urban centers is described
in Brian J. L. Berry and Elaine Neils, "Location, Size,
and Shape of Cities as Influenced by Environmental
Factors," Chapter 8 in Harvey S. Perloff, ed., *The
Quality of the Urban Environment* (Baltimore: The
Johns Hopkins University Press, for Resources for the
Future, 1969).

organization of the regional economy is the
extent of dominance of correspondent banking
links.[8] Banks in a city of any given size order
carry accounts in other, "correspondent" banks
located in higher order metropolitan centers.

In virtually every city, the correspondent
banking links with one high-order center are
more numerous than those with any other
center of the same order. For example, Sioux
Falls, South Dakota, banks have accounts in
correspondent banks in several higher-order
centers across the United States, but the
number of accounts with banks in Minneapolis-St. Paul greatly exceeds the number
in any other city. Hence the Twin Cities
dominate the correspondent banking of Sioux
Falls. But the Twin Cities are a third-order
center, and Sioux Falls also has correspondent
banking ties with centers of still higher order.
Chicago is its dominant second-order metropolis, and it has numerous links to the nation's
first-order center at New York. In this same
way, every lower order city in the country
may be assigned to a dominant second and
third-order center. The larger centers tend to
dominate clusters of surrounding smaller
places; and the clusters suggest a nation-wide
complex of nodal regions.

These correspondent bank accounts reflect
relatively large and frequent transfers of
funds. They represent linkages between distributors and retailers, between shippers and
suppliers, between parent and branch plants,
between processors and sources of raw materials. In this variety of ways, to the extent
that it dominates banking linkages, the metropolis is evidently the organizing center for
the economy of the region.

New York is the national financial metropolis by the correspondent banking measure,
as it is according to all other measures. The
entire nation is its territory. In no other place
do the banks have correspondent ties with
virtually all cities of all size orders throughout
the country.

The seven second-order centers vary greatly
in their regional financial penetration and

---

[8] Data for this section are taken from *Rand Mc-
Nally International Bankers Directory* (Chicago:
Rand McNally and Company, 1967). Duncan, et al.,
op. cit., footnote 1, and Duncan and Lieberson, op.
cit., footnote 1, made extensive use, respectively, of
interregional financial flow data and intermetropolitan correspondent banking linkages in their analyses
of metropolitan-regional relationships.

strength (Fig. 4). Although Philadelphia and Washington interrupt locally from Pennsylvania to Virginia, New York is the dominant second-order center for virtually all of the South. New York, Chicago, and San Francisco dominate correspondent banking over most of the area of the United States at the second-order level.

Regional penetration by third-order centers also varies widely (Fig. 5). The spacing of centers is the most important variable accounting for the extent of their regions, but other variables are also significant. Regional Federal Reserve banks help to extend the dominance of Atlanta, Dallas, and Minneapolis-St. Paul. In contrast, other centers have weak and short regional ties if their growth is both recent and unrelated to major development of wholesaling and rail transportation. To be sure, the spacing of the centers is in part a function of the population density and intensity of development of the intervening hinterlands, and thus the spacing in part simply reflects the character of the metropolitan regions rather than explaining their size. But the location—and spacing—of these major cities is also a product of the economy and technology at the critical time of their growth. Hence, both the size of the hinterlands and the character of their development are in part legacies from earlier eras. Development of major regional wholesaling and rail transportation centers and federal reserve center designation are also legacies from earlier times.

Thus the location and extent of the regions of metropolitan economic dominance, like the centers, are unique products of the nation's historical evolution.

"Cosmopolitanizer"

The dominant migration field is one possible indicator of the extent of the region for which each metropolis is the center of culture diffusion, because the migration field is also an information field.[9] People migrate from the hinterland to the metropolitan center because they have information about it as a place to live and work. They get the information through regional television and radio stations or networks, metropolitan newspapers, and trips to the metropolis for business, recreation, or to visit relatives who have already migrated. In fact, a single trip commonly combines two or more of these purposes.

The migration-information field is an important reflection of the fact that many individuals and institutions in the metropolis do indeed reach the hinterland with a great variety of information. It also reflects the fact that the center is dynamic, or is viewed that way. It is a place where innovation and growth are creating opportunity, attracting labor and entrepreneurs. It is one of the major centers of action in the national economy and brings the frontiers of the national economy within relatively easy reach of the people of its region.

The dominant fields of migration and banking for many of the principal metropolitan centers have strong similarities (Figs. 5 and 7). This probably indicates that personal information fields are strongly influenced by regional business and recreation ties which are also reflected in the financial linkages. On the other hand, there are some outstanding discrepancies between the two patterns, notably the contrasts between banking and migration fields for Los Angeles, San Francisco, Chicago, New York (Figs. 4 and 6), and to a lesser extent, Miami (Figs. 5 and 7). The discrepancies reflect two of the most powerful forces of change in post-World War II America—the migration of whites from the North and West to California and Florida and the migration of blacks from the South to major cities of the North. These discrepancies further suggest that regional migration ties are less constrained by historical legacies than are the regional ties of finance and commerce.

Nevertheless, the major metropolitan centers of the nation do have regions in which they appear to dominate the organization of the economy and the process of culture diffusion. These centers vary greatly in the strength and extent of their regional financial and migration fields. The variation appears to reflect both legacies from the historical-economic geography of the nation and powerful current social and political forces. By superimposing the regions upon maps of mining, forestry, agricultural, and industrial

---

[9] For extensive references, see Richard L. Morrill, *The Spatial Organization of Society* (Belmont, California: Wadsworth, 1970), pp. 222–23 and 236–37.

CORRESPONDENT BANKING LINKAGES TO SECOND ORDER METROPOLITAN CENTERS

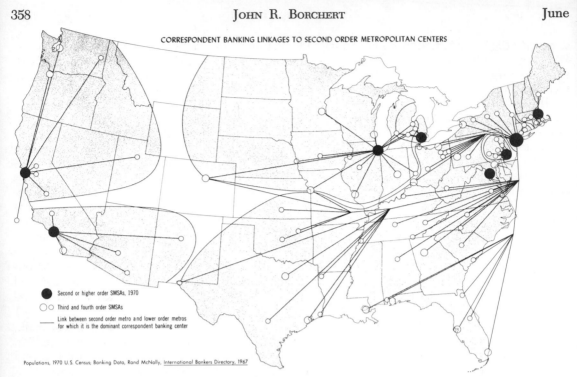

FIG. 4. Dominant correspondent banking linkages to second order metropolitan centers from third and fourth order centers, 1967. New York is defined as the dominant second-order center for a given lower order metropolitan area if it has more than twice as many correspondent banking links as any other second order center. This assumes that half of that metropolitan area's links to New York result from New York's first-order function.

CORRESPONDENT BANKING LINKAGES TO THIRD ORDER METROPOLITAN CENTERS

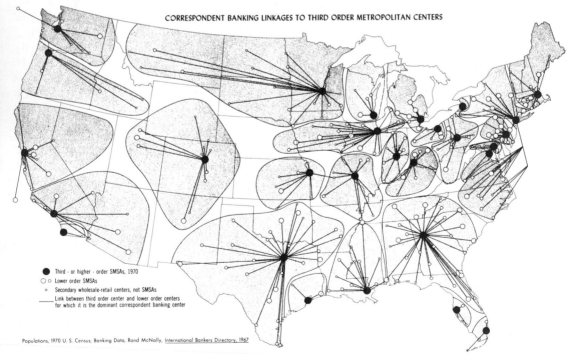

FIG. 5. Dominant correspondent banking linkages to third order metropolitan centers from lower order centers, 1967. New York is defined as the dominant third order center for a given lower order metropolitan area if it has at least four times as many correspondent banking links as any other third order center. Second order metropolitan areas are defined as dominant third order centers if they have more than twice as many correspondent banking links as any other third order metropolitan area.

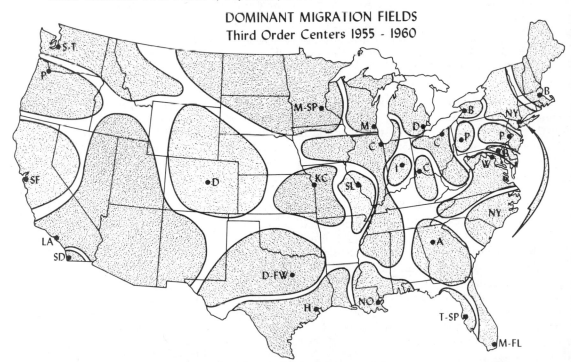

DOMINANT MIGRATION FIELDS
Second Order Centers 1955 - 1960

Numbers are migrants to center
per 10,000 state population

Fig. 6. Dominant migration fields of second-order metropolitan centers, 1955–60. Based on number of migrants per ten thousand 1960 residents from each state to each of the second order centers. In the eastern half of the country, although the eastern regional centers were dominant, their flows only slightly exceeded those to Los Angeles or Miami in numerous states. Data from *U. S. Census of Population, 1960.*

DOMINANT MIGRATION FIELDS
Third Order Centers 1955 - 1960

Fig. 7. Dominant migration fields of third-order metropolitan centers; counties are assigned to the high order SMSA which attracted the largest number of their out-migrants, 1955–1960. Based on a map in Russell B. Adams, "Migration Geography: A Methodological Inquiry and U. S. Case Study," unpublished doctoral dissertation, University of Minnesota, 1968.

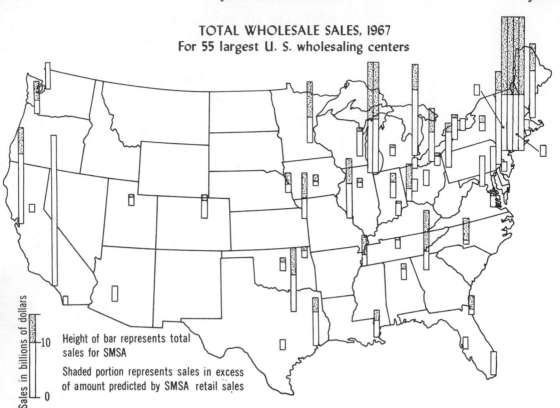

TOTAL WHOLESALE SALES, 1967
For 55 largest U. S. wholesaling centers

Sales in billions of dollars

—10   Height of bar represents total sales for SMSA

Shaded portion represents sales in excess of amount predicted by SMSA retail sales

0

FIG. 8. Wholesale sales volumes, total and potential "export surplus," for all Standard Metropolitan Statistical Areas whose total sales were at least as high as those of the lowest-ranking third-order center in 1967. "Potential export surplus" is the total wholesale sales minus the SMSA retail sales multiplied by the national ratio of wholesale to retail sales. In other words, it is the local volume of wholesale sales in excess of estimated locally generated wholesale buying power, or an estimate of the ability of a given center to penetrate regional or national markets. Data from *U. S. Census of Business, 1967.*

production and upon maps of personal income, education, and housing, one can infer much about both the regional organization of the economy and the population characteristics and functions of most of the major metropolitan centers.

DISPERSAL OF FUNCTIONS

Alongside the clear evidence of metropolitan regionalism in the United States there is equally clear evidence of some multiple discordant sets of metropolitan regions. There is also abundant evidence of non-regionalism —a single, scrambled national market in which any place can, and often does, relate directly to any other place without benefit of propinquity or hierarchy.[10]

---

[10] The importance of this is recognized in Duncan, et al., op. cit., footnote 1, pp. 5 and 37–38.

The pattern of major wholesaling centers illustrates the complexity of metropolitan-regional organization of the economy. The correspondent banking linkages of individual low-order centers with all other metropolitan areas, not simply with their dominant center, illustrate the scrambled national pattern of organization. The same pattern is illustrated by the migration flows from selected states to all high-order metropolitan areas, not only to the dominant regional center.

Major Wholesaling Centers

One measure of wholesaling is the total volume of wholesale sales for the metropolitan area for 1967, year of the most recent business census (Fig. 8). This includes all types of merchant wholesaling, brokerage, and factory distribution centers. Another measure is an estimate of "surplus" wholesale sales, the

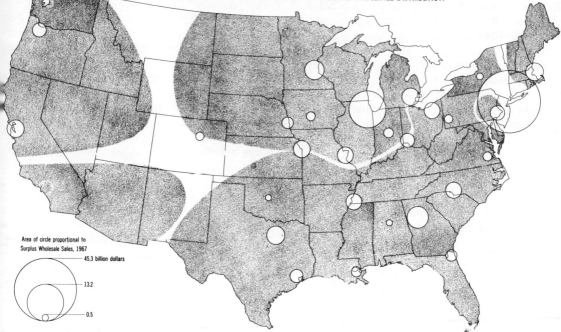

THE TWENTY-EIGHT LARGEST U.S. CENTERS OF EXTERNAL WHOLESALE DISTRIBUTION

Area of circle proportional to
Surplus Wholesale Sales, 1967

45.3 billion dollars

13.2

0.5

FIG. 9. The twenty-eight largest centers of potential external wholesale distribution. (See caption of Figure 8 for explanation.) These centers are not identical with the twenty-eight major centers of finance-population-retail buying power. The second order correspondent banking regions are shown on the map because the strength of New York, Chicago, and San Francisco appears to be roughly proportional to the aggregate strength of lower order centers in their respective second-order banking regions. The patterns suggest that, in addition to performing high-order distribution functions to the nation, New York carries out second-level functions for the East and South; Chicago performs similar second-level functions for the Midwest, and San Francisco for the West.

volume of total wholesale sales in excess of "estimated local requirements" (Fig. 9). The local "requirement" is simply the local retail sales volume multiplied by the ratio of wholesale sales to retail sales in 1967 for the nation as a whole. In other words, it is an estimate of the amount of wholesale trade generated by the local retail trade. Thus "surplus" wholesale sales is a measure of the center's ability to penetrate an outlying territory, either as a distributor of goods imported from the rest of the nation or as a collector of commodities for wholesale distribution to national or world markets.

Wholesaling strength is much less correlated with population, retail sales, and finance than the latter three are correlated with one another. Many lower-order metropolitan areas have larger wholesale sales than San Diego or Tampa-St. Petersburg. Memphis and Char-

lotte rank high among the much more populous third-order centers. The discrepancies are most striking when one compares potential export surplus sales. Nine lower-order centers appear in the nation's top twenty-eight (Fig. 9). In addition to Memphis and Charlotte, three other lower-order southern cities—Jacksonville, Richmond, and Birmingham—are important distributors. Omaha, Des Moines, and Oklahoma City join the high-order centers on the Plains Frontier as important distributors to the West or assembly points in the flow of commodities from the agricultural interior to the East.

There probably are three reasons for the discrepancy between regional wholesaling importance and other measures of metropolitan size and functional importance:

1) Some centers are very large, specialized commodity markets—for example, Memphis

in cotton, Portland in lumber, or the Corn Belt and Plains Frontier cities in agricultural produce. But two other factors are clearly more important.

2) The major classes of wholesale goods (groceries, hardware, auto parts, machinery, drugs) apparently have a range which is less than the distance between high order centers in most parts of the country. Hence there may be simply a need for more major wholesale distribution centers than major population centers of one million or more.

3) There is also apparently significant locational inertia in the wholesaling business.[11] Richmond continues to dominate Virginia, notwithstanding the greater growth and size of the Norfolk complex; Jacksonville continues to be the prime distributor to Florida; Charlotte continues as a major competitor of Atlanta, despite Atlanta's much greater recent growth and present size; Syracuse persists as the major regional distribution center for western and northern New York. Although these patterns can be traced back at least to the rail era, their viability is maintained today by the comparatively low threshold and range of the critical commodities, and also by strategic locations between megalopolis and one or more outlying high-order centers.

Thus the pattern is both a legacy from the past and an expression of adaptation of old centers to new locational circumstances. It is a reminder of an axiom in the evolution of the nation's settlement pattern. As the urban system evolves, older centers may well take over established regional service functions and successfully specialize in them, yet the same centers may, simultaneously, slip behind others in overall size and importance within the urban system. Thus the pattern of metropolis and region becomes increasingly kaleidoscopic as time passes.

Banking and Migration Linkages

In addition to its correspondent banking links with its dominant regional metropolis, each lower-order center also has financial ties with other places of the same or higher order

---

[11] For a detailed scholarly interpretation of the historical development of American wholesaling, see James E. Vance, Jr., *The Merchant's World: The Geography of Wholesaling* (Englewood Cliffs: Prentice-Hall, 1970).

in other parts of the country. These links with other centers, in the aggregate, greatly exceed those with the regional metropolis. For a sample of thirty-one low-order metropolitan areas across the country, correspondent banking links to their third-order regional centers account for less than two-fifths of all links to all higher-order centers.

These non-regional ties reflect the links between parent and branch plants, raw material producers and processors, migrants and home relatives or businesses, specialized distributors and major industrial plants (Fig. 10). Thus, the map shows ties between aircraft production centers at Wichita and Seattle; between cities in all of the oil fields and Dallas or Tulsa; between major soybean processing centers and markets at Decatur, Memphis, and Minneapolis. Ties with New York and either San Francisco or Los Angeles are almost ubiquitous, for they provide links, in turn, with virtually every other place in the country.

It appears that cities in the eastern part of the Manufacturing Belt, compared with places of similar size in the rest of the country, have more limited national connections. The maps suggest that the economic organization of the Northeast—focused strongly on New York—is more parochial and more hierarchical than that of other regions.

Migration flow patterns show a similar dispersal (Fig. 11). Except for Florida and California, 1955–60, migration from each state to its dominant regional metropolitan center was greatly exceeded by the total migration to all other high-order centers. This was especially notable in the Northeast, where most major centers are relatively slow-growing, but it occurred even in Georgia, notwithstanding the great attraction of Atlanta and the comparatively local nature of much Southern white migration.

The importance of the national "scramble" pattern of migration reflects the strength of national information fields, which are related to national patterns of recreational travel, business and educational ties, and communication networks of all kinds. The pervasive drawing power of California and Florida centers is probably most significant for the degree to which it reflects the increasing importance of life style compared with other variables in the decision to migrate.

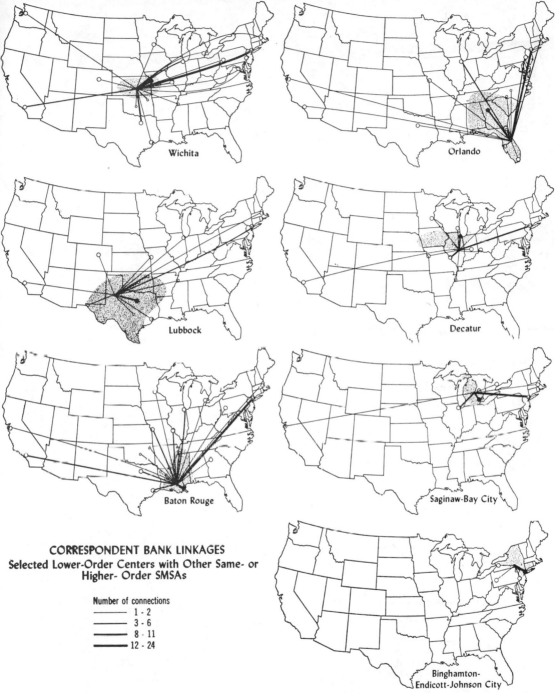

FIG. 10. Correspondent banking ties with the dominant third-order regional center compared with connections to all other same- or higher-order centers throughout the United States, for seven selected lower-order SMSAs, 1967. Source: *Rand McNally*, op. cit., footnote 8.

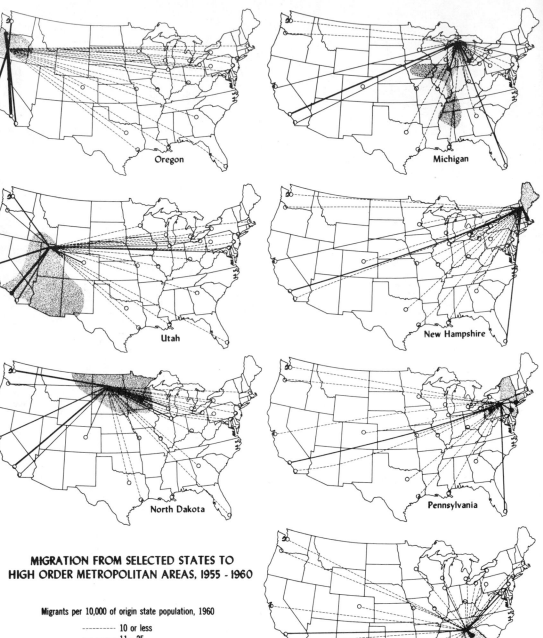

**MIGRATION FROM SELECTED STATES TO
HIGH ORDER METROPOLITAN AREAS, 1955 - 1960**

Migrants per 10,000 of origin state population, 1960

- -----   10 or less
- ———   11 - 25
- ———   26 - 50
- ———   51 - 100
- ———   101 - 150
- ———   More than 150

FIG. 11. Migration from each of seven selected states to its dominant regional metropolis and to all other high order centers in the United States, 1955–60. Source: *U. S. Census of Population, 1960.*

Thus migration networks, like correspondent banking networks, are more national than regional. It appears that the major metropolitan centers are less important as regional capitals than they are as major components in the national system of markets and supplies of labor, entrepreneurship, and capital. A large city can play those national roles today without necessarily being a regional capital. The overriding importance of diverse, non-hierarchical national linkages has perhaps always been a characteristic of regional social and economic systems. But the importance is probably increasing with the ever-growing flexibility of communications and transportation and ever-rising share of services in the nation's business.

CHANGING FLOW OF ECONOMIC SUPPORT

A considerable body of tradition tells us that the great cities are supported economically by the resources of their hinterlands. They stand at the top of a hierarchy which builds upward from the basic wealth and primary production from the land. Although this is obviously true in terms of essential material goods and a portion of the metropolitan economy, it can no longer be true in terms of new growth of jobs and consequent new growth of individual buying power. Employment in agriculture and mining have been declining for two decades or more. Manufacturing employment is growing substantially slower than metropolitan population and at less than half the rate of growth of total employment.

The relatively rapid growth of metropolitan jobs, population, and income cannot be explained by increasing services to the hinterland. Rather one must look to the growth of inter-metropolitan flows of trade and investment capital and the greatly increased multiplier on so-called basic employment due to the growth of services. In short, the metropolitan areas have depended for their new growth upon themselves and one another.[12] Although the resource-based economy of the region has ceased to support most of

the new growth of the metropolis, the metropolis has lent increasing economic support to the surrounding region. This has come in two ways: through expansion of the urban field and inter-governmental revenue transfers.

Expanded Circulation Systems

Expansion of each urban circulation system is a result of post-World War II highway improvements and the accompanying increase in the speed and convenience of both automobile travel and trucking. Friedmann and Miller used the term "urban field" to describe the phenomenon.[13] The effects on the settlement and circulation patterns are well-known. Commuters live as far as fifty or sixty miles from the traditional downtown districts, and multipurpose automobile trips crisscross metropolitan areas between a multiplicity of residential, employment, service, and recreational locations. Branch plants and corporate headquarters dot the map all across this same broad field, bringing new jobs and socioeconomic ties to former farm trade centers. A second ring of commuting is initiated by these branch plants and offices. Where high-amenity sites are present, part-time recreational and retired residents add further to the economic impact of the metropolis on the region.

A study of Minneapolis-St. Paul shows that the urban field, defined by a given level of accessibility, has increased from less than one thousand square miles to more than fifteen thousand square miles in forty years. The metropolis now has a circulation framework so extensive that it would not be fully built up, even at recent rapid growth rates and low suburban densities, within the next six centuries or more. Berry's work showed similar development of the commuter field around every metropolitan center in the United States more than ten years ago.[14]

[12] The declining importance of "the historic hamlet-village-town-city hierarchical agglomerative system . . . as a grid on which the economy can be hung" is discussed in Robert McNee, *A Primer on Economic Geography* (New York: Random House, 1971), p. 35.

[13] John Friedmann and John R. Miller, "The Urban Field," *Journal of the American Institute of Planners*, Vol. 31 (1965), pp. 312–19.

[14] Brian J. L. Berry, *Metropolitan Area Definition: A Re-evaluation of Concept and Statistical Practice*, Working Paper No. 28 (Washington: U. S. Bureau of the Census, 1968). This work is discussed under the heading, "Patterns of Urbanization and Urban Influence in 1960," in Brian J. L. Berry and Frank E. Horton, *Geographic Perspectives on Urban Systems* (Englewood Cliffs, N. J.: Prentice-Hall, 1970), pp. 36–53.

The trend continued through the 1960s (Fig. 12). The counties which experienced a net in-migration fall mainly into three groups: the urban fields of the high-order metropolitan areas, except for Pittsburgh and Buffalo; about two-thirds of the low-order metropolitan areas; and a few key non-metropolitan areas on the average American's mental map of the good life: parts of the coast and lake district in peninsular Florida; the southern Ozarks and Ouachitas; the Blue Ridge and northern Appalachians; the Colorado, Idaho, and Montana Rockies, with notable concentrations around Aspen, Jackson Hole, and Flathead Lake; and the highly publicized parts of the southwestern deserts, Sierras and Cascades, and Pacific shores. The other areas of net in-migration large enough to be reflected in county data are mainly non-metropolitan growth centers within agricultural regions of generally declining population.

Absolute increases were small in the remote amenity regions, however, and in the isolated non-metropolitan growth centers. Most of the net in-migration, in absolute terms, occurred in the urban fields of the metropolitan areas. Meanwhile, the central cities, and in many cases the central counties, of the major metropolitan areas registered net out-migration or net decline of population, for the urban rebuilding process at this time is resulting in lower densities than those which prevailed when the core city areas were previously developed, in the railroad era.

Intergovernmental Transfer Payments

In 1967, year of the most recent census of governments, state and federal governments paid a total of 20.1 billion dollars in aids to local governments. The money was used mainly to help pay the costs of education, welfare, and roads and streets at the local level. Well over ninety percent of the aid funds were raised by state taxes and paid by state governments. Of the total aid payments, 8.2 billion dollars, or about forty-one percent, went to local governments within the twenty-eight high-order metropolitan areas.[15]

Since the money to pay for these aids came from state general revenue, it was raised mainly through taxes on income, sales, or property. The twenty-eight high-order metropolitan areas generate approximately fifty percent of the nation's personal income, forty-five percent of the retail sales, and forty-five percent of the assessed property value. Thus, they account for forty-seven percent of the combined income, sales, and property tax base; and they probably account for at least as large a share of the revenue pools from which state aids are paid. On the other hand, these metropolitan areas contain only forty-two percent of the nation's population. Their relatively high per-capita wealth, of course, is generated in part by organizing important components of both the national and regional economies, and in part by high-order services provided for a large territory. Because they are major generators of wealth, they are also major sources of support for the welfare and income redistribution functions of state government.

The aids, or intergovernmental transfers, are distributed mainly on the basis of population. Intergovernmental transfer payments to local units averaged $99 per capita within the high-order metropolitan areas, $102 per capita in non-metropolitan areas. Per-capita payments were about equal regardless of metropolitan or rural setting.

In short, the high-order centers probably generated about forty-seven percent of the aid money on the basis of their wealth, and about forty-one percent of the money was returned to them on the basis of their population. Thus, about six percent of the intergovernmental transfers, or approximately 1.2 billion dollars, represents a shift from major metropolitan areas to outlying non-metropolitan regions. Most of this shift is accomplished through state government programs. These are aggregate numbers, of course, and there is undoubtedly some variation among metropolitan areas and states. Nevertheless, it

---

[15] National aggregate data on transfer payments to all local governments and to those in non-metropolitan areas are taken from the *Statistical Abstract of the United States, 1971* (Washington: U. S. Government Printing Office, 1971), p. 414. Data on payments to high-order centers are taken from *U. S. Census of Governments,* Volume 5, "Local Government Finances in Individual SMSAs and their Component Counties," (Washington: U. S. Government Printing Office, 1968), pp. 234–346. Populations for 1967 were interpolated from data in the *Statistical Abstract of the United States.*

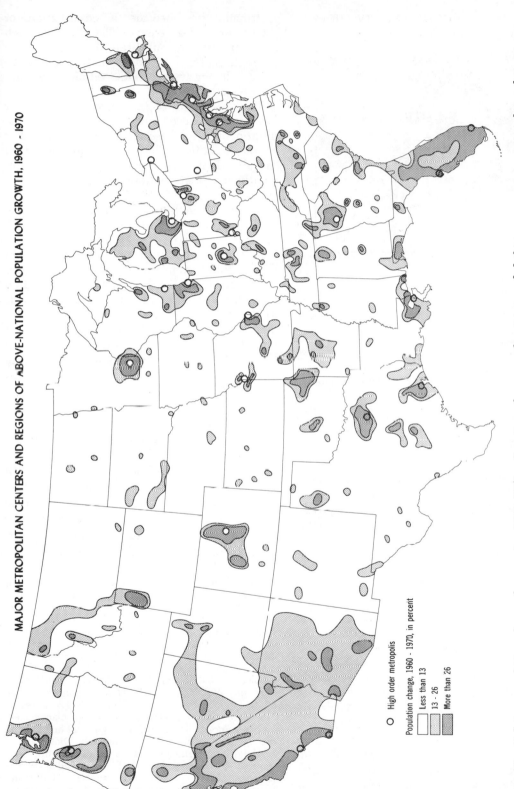

MAJOR METROPOLITAN CENTERS AND REGIONS OF ABOVE-NATIONAL POPULATION GROWTH, 1960 - 1970

○ High order metropolis

Population change, 1960 - 1970, in percent

Less than 13
13 - 26
More than 26

FIG. 12. Relative population change by county, 1960–1970. Counties whose growth rates exceeded thirteen percent experienced population increase faster than the nation as a whole and generally had net in-migration. The map illustrates the focus of most net immigration upon the outer reaches of the metropolitan fields and several well-known but more isolated amenity areas. It also reflects the emphasis on amenity regions and low density commuter zones in the modern growth of metropolitan areas and their regions. Source: *U. S. Census of Population, 1970.*

PERCENT OF LOCAL GOVERNMENT REVENUE FROM
STATE - FEDERAL TRANSFER PAYMENTS

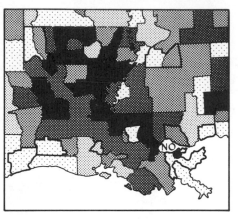

- 40
- 50
- 60
- 70

FIG. 13. Transfer payments from higher levels of government as a percentage of all local government revenues, by county, for portions of the multi-state hinterland of New Orleans, illustrating the impact of state boundaries upon redistribution of urban income to rural areas. Data from *U. S. Census of Governments, 1962.*

appears that the high-order metropolitan areas today are giving increasing economic support to their regions through intergovernmental transfer payments as well as through basic income dispersed into widened urban fields through long-distance commuting, branch plants, offices, and vacation homes.

Accompanying Problems

The increased flow of economic and social energy into the hinterland has produced two significant problems. First, the expansion of metropolitan circulation systems, with accompanying decentralization, has weakened the historic regional center—the monumental downtown of the central city. With the growth of multiple outlying centers of trade, services, offices, and manufacturing, these outlying centers attain market thresholds and scale economies comparable to the larger, independent low-order metropolitan areas. Consequently, for many purposes, the giant

metropolis has become a conurbation of several low-order centers. The ability of such a conurbation to substitute functionally for a single-centered regional metropolis is already demonstrated both empirically and theoretically.[16]

The weakening of the regional city center has also been accompanied by dispersal of the metropolitan tax base among a large number of municipalities. This, in turn, has produced the abundantly documented problems of uncoordinated metropolitan services and facilities, and inability to obtain tax revenue in the parts of the metropolis with ability to pay, and to apply it in those parts where it is most needed.[17]

A second significant problem stems from the restraint imposed by state boundaries upon income redistribution through taxation of metropolitan wealth to support state aids to local governments in low-income, nonmetropolitan regions. Metropolitan wealth, in almost every case, continues to be generated in significant part by managing the economy of a multi-state region, yet state aid programs stop at state lines.

In the New Orleans region, both the relative and absolute levels of intergovernmental transfers to rural counties decline sharply across state boundaries from Louisiana into either Arkansas or Mississippi (Fig. 13). In thirty-six of forty cases of counties abutting across the state line, local government income from transfer payments is higher on the Louisiana side. The pattern of interstate differences is complicated, however, by the

[16] Boventer, op. cit., footnote 5, compared the Ruhr agglomeration with Paris, observed that "it is difficult to argue that one or the other situation is better" with respect to regional and national economic and cultural development, and went on to develop a theoretical basis for suitability of those two, and intermediate, forms of metropolitan growth.

[17] The initial comprehensive description of the problem probably was Robert C. Wood, *1400 Governments*, Vol. 9, New York Metropolitan Region Study (Cambridge: Harvard University Press, 1961). For a succinct analysis of the fiscal management problems posed by political fragmentation of both the metropolis and the region, see Dick Netzer, "Federal, State, and Local Finance in a Metropolitan Context," in Harvey S. Perloff and Lowdon Wingo, Jr., eds. *Issues in Urban Economics* (Baltimore: Johns Hopkins University Press, for Resources for the Future, 1968).

effect of urbanization. Both Louisiana and Mississippi make relatively low transfer payments to higher income urban areas. In both states the actual per-capita transfer payments are twenty to fifty percent lower to principal urban counties than to low-income rural counties.[18] However, Mississippi holds payments to non-metropolitan places such as Vicksburg, Natchez, or Greenville to levels which Louisiana applies to New Orleans, Shreveport, or Baton Rouge. In other words, although Mississippi is in the New Orleans metropolitan region, its local governments do not share in revenue transfers based upon the wealth of the regional metropolis because the state boundary stops the flow. Hence an urban-to-rural revenue shift must be based on much smaller urban areas in Mississippi than in Louisiana.

In the Minneapolis-St. Paul region, actual transfer payments per capita are fifty to sixty percent less in the central counties of the metropolitan area than they are in rural counties of central and northern Minnesota, ten to forty percent less than those in rural western Minnesota (Fig. 14). The most striking change appears at the western boundary of the state. Rural North and South Dakota counties receive per capita aid payments forty to sixty percent below those in neighboring counties in Minnesota. This is partly due to differences in state policies. The Dakotas use state taxes less, local taxes more, to support local services. But the difference is mainly an expression of the fact that there are no large metropolitan centers in the Dakotas which create, on the one hand, substantial inequities in local tax base and, on the other, an opportunity for redistribution of a large amount of metropolitan revenue through a system of state aids. Thus the difference in state policies may well be simply another expression of the difference in metropolitan structure. In any case, local governments in the Dakotas do not share revenue transfers based upon the wealth of the regional metropolis because, again, the state boundary stops the flow.[19]

PERCENT OF LOCAL GOVERNMENT REVENUE FROM STATE - FEDERAL TRANSFER PAYMENTS

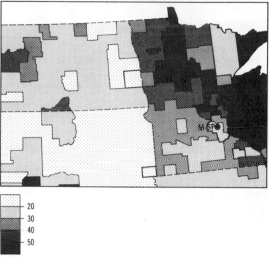

- 20
- 30
- 40
- 50

Fig. 14. Transfer payments from higher levels of government as a percentage of all local government revenues, by county, for portions of the multi-state hinterland of Minneapolis-St. Paul. Data from *U. S. Census of Governments, 1962.*

In summary, the regional metropolis has taken a new form on the land with the availability of automobiles and highways. The metropolis also has a new functional relationship to the regional economy with the growth of the welfare state. The contemporary political-geographic framework is not suited to either of these changes.

THE FUTURE PATTERN

Metropolis and region have evolved their present patterns through successive epochs of American history, and they are continuing to evolve. How they got to be as they are is clear at least in broad outline. In the next phase they will probably continue to be shaped in large part by legacies from the past, by the attraction of amenity sites and lo-

[18] Derived from figures in the *County and City Data Book, 1967* (Washington: U. S. Bureau of the Census, 1967), Table 2.
[19] The significant drop in the state share of local government revenue between Minnesota and Wis-

consin is mainly the result of different tax structures (Fig. 14). Wisconsin collects a larger share of revenue at the state level and redistributes more to local governments; Minnesota collects a larger share at the local level. Within Wisconsin, one finds a pattern of metropolitan-to-rural transfer very similar to that in Minnesota. Absolute payments per capita to Milwaukee County were fifty to sixty percent below those to rural counties in northwestern Wisconsin.

cations, and by forthcoming federal government policies and actions.

Inertia of the Existing Structure

Four-fifths of the national population increase during the past decade took place within standard metropolitan areas, and virtually all of the increase occurred within metropolitan commuter fields.[20] The high-order metropolitan areas increased much faster than the nation as a whole and reversed, at least temporarily, the gradual long-term decline in their share of the national population. The rapid aggregate growth of high-order centers includes the comparatively slow growth of the older great cities in the Northeast and the very high growth rates of most Western and Southern high-order centers.

Notwithstanding a plethora of serious problems, great cohesion and persistence remain in the present pattern of major American metropolitan areas. Existing metropolitan areas and their regions are a set of powerful, interlocking institutions—business firms, governments, public service organizations, kinship groups, operating within their buildings, circulation networks, territories, and social webs. Few individuals or groups can break away at any one time without having to face an unknown world with no apparent market for the skills and rituals they have learned within the existing context. This is surely an important reason why, despite very large migrations and attenuation of each urban field, established large cities have continued to provide the framework for virtually all of the nation's population growth.

Attenuation of the urban field has provided a means to utilize amenity sites and reduce densities without in any sense abandoning the established metropolitan areas. Both reduction of density and decentralization of the railroad era cities are likely to continue, with accompanying expansion—increasingly planned and clustered—into the countryside. Berry foresees a clear end to the need for the traditional metropolis with increasing substitution of electronic communications for much of the personal contact and travel now considered necessary, yet Pickard anticipates

that "the lion's share of new communities would occur in urban regions or near the greatest metropolitan areas."[21] In short, the conservatism of the gross national pattern of population is quite consistent with the observed painful but exciting metamorphosis of the older parts of the great cities.

The Pull of Amenity

Although numbers are not large relative to the national urban population, very fast relative growth rates appear in many counties with high natural amenity (Fig. 12). Expanded commuter fields—themselves in part an expression of a quest for more open space—surround all of the major metropolitan centers and show very fast growth rates around all except Buffalo and Pittsburgh. Beyond that, in every major metropolitan field where the opportunity presents itself, the belt of rapid growth frays outward indefinitely in the direction of neighboring hills, lakes, reservoirs, or mountain forests. Notable areas of rapid residential expansion also appear in remote natural amenity areas in the Ozarks, Ouachitas, and Rockies. In several cases these include the locations of planned new towns, although those account for a comparatively small part of the activity.

The more remote fast-growth amenity regions are being populated in part by the greatly increased numbers of footloose young adults, with minimal needs and commitments, who reflect that particular stage in the life cycle of the post-World War II wave of new population. But a much greater component of the new settlers in these regions consists of more traditional households who are either financially independent of a specific place and type of work, or are aware of the greatly increased variety of potential residential sites and conditions created by the expansion of the metropolitan circulation system. Those latter two groups embrace a very wide range of ages, incomes, and occupations. Their migration pattern is not new. It can be documented clearly for the 1950s in the 1960

---

[20] See map titled, *Population Change, 1960–70* (Washington: U. S. Bureau of the Census, 1971) for coverage of all counties.

[21] Brian J. L. Berry, "The Geography of the United States in the Year 2000," *Ekistics*, Vol. 29 (1970), pp. 339–51; and Jerome P. Pickard, "Is Dispersal the Answer to Urban Overgrowth?," *Urban Land*, Vol. 29 (1970), pp. 3–11, quotation from p. 8.

census, but it accelerated significantly in the 1960s.[22]

The gravitational fields of metropolitan areas and high-amenity areas are by far the most important factors explaining the population change map not only of the past decade but of the past half century. National or world events and movements have altered the rate and composition of change within this framework, but hardly the direction.

The National Policy Enigma

However, there is now, somewhat as there was during the 1930s, concern that the United States should have a National Growth (or Settlement) Policy.[23] Some have questioned whether there should, can, or will be such a policy; and discussions thus far have not fully clarified the meaning or purpose of such a policy. If policies do emerge which have an impact on the settlement pattern, they are most likely to be in two broad classes: social policies and development policies.

Likely social policies that would affect the map fall into two classes. There could be policies which, if implemented, would tend to make people, on the average, less tied to a given locale than they are now—policies which would increase mobility, hence increase differential growth among cities and among regions, and increase the pull of population into amenity areas. One example would be

simply a policy to encourage continued increase in diversity of service jobs; another would be to increase the amount and coverage of income guarantees; yet another would be to increase the strength and coverage of retirement programs. Any of these tends to increase, for the average individual at some stage of his life, the range of choice of residential locations.

On the other hand, those policies could have side effects which would tie people, on the average, more strongly to existing locations. For example, if such policies result in the development of large bureaucracies, their offices may well be tied to historic urban and suburban locations in response to public and political pressure to utilize existing infrastructure and maintain established communities and governmental units.

In either case, this group of policies is likely to be not only social but also fiscal. Their implementation probably will utilize increased transfer payments from federal to state and local governments, and they would reduce the present inhibition which state boundaries impose upon redistribution of income within metropolitan regions.

Development policies which are most discussed focus on either new towns or growth centers. Either case calls for funneling investment into selected urban places to which it is now going relatively slowly or not at all. The principal devices which have been suggested are direct subsidies or indirect tax concessions for new potential employers, although strategic mineral or agriculture support programs might be manipulated to produce similar results.

Unlike social policies, which would affect the welfare of virtually the entire population, these development policies stem from more localized motives. They aim either to arrest the movement from the heartland and save basic rural values, or to slow down urban overgrowth and reduce urban problems which result from crowding into slums many people who are unprepared for urban life and have moved to places where they do not wish to be.

These development policies have been criticized for both their methods and their motivations. It is unlikely that the legislative process will result in deliberate long-range commitment of national resources to the de-

[22] For example, Illinois and California accounted for major migration into the southern Ozarks and Ouachitas in the 1950s; California, Texas, Colorado, and Nebraska, to the Jackson Hole country; California, Oregon, Washington, North Dakota, Minnesota, and other Midwest states, to the Flathead Lake area. Source: *U. S. Census of Population, 1960,* "Mobility for States and Economic Areas."

[23] National Goals Research Staff, *Toward Balanced Growth: Quantity with Quality* (Washington: U. S. Government Printing Office, 1970); and *Urban and Rural America: Policies for Future Growth* (Washington: Advisory Commission on Intergovernmental Relations, 1969). For extensive reviews and critiques of the earlier of these reports, see the entire April issue of *Growth and Change*, Vol. 2 (1971), especially John Friedmann, "The Feasibility of a National Settlement Policy," pp. 18–21. For a comprehensive review and critique of components of recent specific federal legislation which, taken together, begin to suggest an urban growth policy, see Norman Beckman, "Development of National Urban Growth Policy," *Journal of the American Institute of Planners*, Vol. 37 (1971), pp. 146–61.

velopment of one region at the expense of others. Furthermore, the nation's farm programs have aided agriculture directly and small town business indirectly in the heartland for four decades, yet the drift away has accelerated. By improving both education and income, the farm programs have improved the mobility and adaptability of individuals who have chosen not to remain in farming. In rural areas of the nation where the farm programs have been most effective a slowdown of out-migration probably would not reduce the flow of problem populations to the cities. For several generations national lore told us that rural-to-urban migration, from the great commercial family farm regions, was the life blood, not the bane, of the big cities. Problems arose only with major migration of those two large rural populations which had not been significantly touched by the federal farm programs—the blacks from the rural South and the whites from rural Appalachia.

Thus, growth center and new town policies probably will have to be made internally more consistent and tied to more general national goals before they are translated into actions which will significantly affect the map. The more development policies are generalized, rather than place-specific, and the more social policies are committed to increasing the range of choice for individuals, the more likely it becomes that the geographic results will reflect the same kinds of choices which are already reflected in maps of past and current change. Existing metropolitan fields and perceived amenity areas will continue to exert a powerful attraction because they are powerful within American institutions, politics, or culture.

Meanwhile, numerous small growth centers and a small number of planned new towns outside the existing metropolitan areas will surely continue to appear.[24] A few may

eventually reach low-order metropolitan status. Among those which do, some will be growth centers in the agricultural regions. Some planned new towns will coalesce from the existing networks of small towns and rash of new leisure and retirement developments in the southern and southwestern mountains. Others will probably emerge in locations where the federal government has extensive land holdings, including high-amenity sites, which are relatively little known or off the popular routes of travel and migration. Examples would be certain reservoirs and neighboring varied terrain on the Great Plains, Colorado Plateau, and South Atlantic or Gulf Coastal Plains.

Perhaps the most important set of development policies will be the emerging array of laws and regulations controlling environmental quality. These already tend to be generalized; that is, they apply to activities of individuals and institutions wherever they may be. Insofar as they add to production costs, these environmental policies are likely to add to the advantage of locating near major markets to reduce distribution costs, or of locating in the highest-yielding raw material areas to hold down assembly costs. In either case, the locational result is to reinforce existing patterns.

Within the metropolitan zones of new growth and the emerging amenity-oriented population regions, environmental policies are likely to encourage greater clustering of development of residential, commercial, and industrial areas. This would follow if new regulations cannot be met without benefit of the scale economies achieved by community waste management systems. These policies are also likely to result in more clustered and zoned patterns of heavy industry with high nuisance levels. But regulations, in themselves, are unlikely to create new and sharply changed patterns of locational advantage.

Thus, environmental policies, like the major emerging social policies, seem more likely to make the familiar system work better, less likely to produce revolutionary changes in the national pattern of metropolitan centers and regions.

[24] Pickard, op. cit., footnote 21; the same issue of *Urban Land* has a list of "Large Developments and New Communities" compiled by the U. S. Department of Housing and Urban Development, January, 1969. All of the projects are located within the urban fields of metropolitan areas (mostly high-order) or (relatively few) within more remote high-amenity areas (Fig. 12). The projects have an aggregate projected population of about 3.5 million and an average density of 2.4 dwelling units per gross acre.

CONCLUSION

Metropolitan regions and their metropolitan centers are the products of long and continuing evolution. They are pre-conditions for public policies at least as much as they are expressions of those policies.

The metropolis, the region, and the relationships between them were unstable throughout the period of Westward expansion and development. They are again unstable in the era of automotive transportation and the welfare state. Regional centers are decentralizing. The circulation system in which the metropolis and region are embedded is more national than regional. And the metropolis has become a source of economic support for a large part of its region, complementing the historic reverse relationship.

The forces which have shaped—and continue to shape—the observed metropolitan and regional patterns are powerful and fundamental. On the one hand, current proposals often give too little weight to those forces in suggesting either sweeping new changes in the nation's urban structure or a return to the patterns of the rail era. On the other hand, static political boundaries and related institutions interfere with rational financing and organization of public services for metropolitan areas and regions as they now exist. Revised boundaries based upon metropolitan economic regions would pose many of the same problems because most of the wealth of the metropolis is generated in the national market, and rational redistribution probably will be operated eventually at the national level.

The great cities and their regions clearly will continue to be major components of the American urban system in the foreseeable future. They will also continue to evolve. Energies are likely to be directed increasingly to management and organizational reforms which recognize the nature of the evolving system and aim to make it work better.

Addendum

Footnote 48 for "Small Town in Pennsylvania," by Peirce F. Lewis:

Two recent events suggest that at least a few Bellefontonians are trying to reverse the evil trends of the past. The first event was announced in the Pennsylvania Mirror of September 4, 1971--a Community Career Conference for College-trained Centre County Native Sons and Daughters, sponsored by the Chamber of Commerce, and designed to "familiarize young, college-trained natives of Centre County with Centre County employers and vice versa." The second event, announced just as this essay was going to press, was a Chamber of Commerce campaign, aimed at revitalizing downtown business by improving the aesthetic qualities of the main commercial district. A small committee of businessmen, with the help of a local architect, is trying to convince merchants to remove overhanging plastic signs and kindred visual blemishes, and make a variety of cosmetic improvements to downtown storefronts. Despite its modest goals, the campaign created a mild sensation in the local press. For the first time in the memory of most people, Bellefontonians were acting in concert to improve the downtown's appearance rather than simply tearing down more buildings; the first time in a long while that responsible townspeople had displayed any genuine optimism about Bellefonte's future. It is much too early to predict whether these events are straws in the wind or only momentary aberrations.